Jacket—Shibaura Engineering Works in 1896

Endpapers—Shibaura Engineering Works in 1896

> *Upper left—Foundry workers (see page 27)*
> *Upper right—Lathe shop workers; supervisor is wearing hat*
> *Lower right—Carpenters in wood pattern shop*
> *Lower left—Work in electric generator shop*
> *Center—Boilermakers at work*

All pictures are from Shibaura seisakujo 65 nen shi *(65-year history of the Shibaura Engineering Works) and are reproduced courtesy of the Toshiba Corporation.*

Subseries on the History of
Japanese Business and Industry

*The Evolution of
Labor Relations in Japan
Heavy Industry, 1853–1955*

HARVARD EAST ASIAN MONOGRAPHS

117

Subseries on the History of
Japanese Business and Industry

Japan's rise from the destruction and bitter defeat of World War II to its present eminence in world business and industry is perhaps the most striking development in recent world history. This did not occur in a vacuum. It was linked organically to at least a century of prior growth and transformation. To illuminate this growth a new kind of scholarship on Japan is needed: historical study *in the context of a company or industry* of the interrelations among entrepreneurs, managers, engineers, workers, stockholders, bankers, and bureaucrats, and of the institutions and policies they created. Only in such a context can the contribution of particular factors be weighed and understood. It is to promote and encourage such scholarship that this subseries is established, supported by the Japan Institute and published by the Council on East Asian Studies at Harvard.

Albert M. Craig
Cambridge, Massachusetts

THE EVOLUTION OF
LABOR RELATIONS IN JAPAN
Heavy Industry, 1853–1955

ANDREW GORDON

Published by COUNCIL ON EAST ASIAN STUDIES, HARVARD UNIVERSITY, and distributed by HARVARD UNIVERSITY PRESS, Cambridge (Massachusetts) and London   1988

The Council on East Asian Studies at Harvard University publishes a monograph series and, through the Fairbank Center for East Asian Research and the Edwin O. Reischauer Institute of Japanese Studies, administers research projects designed to further scholarly understanding of China, Japan, Korea, Vietnam, Inner Asia, and adjacent areas. Publication of this volume has been assisted by a grant from the Shell Companies Foundation.

Library of Congress Cataloging in Publication Data

Gordon, Andrew, 1952–
    The evolution of labor relations in Japan.

    (Harvard East Asian monographs ; 117)
    Bibliography: p. 487
    Includes index.
    1. Industrial relations—Japan—History—19th century.
2. Industrial relations—Japan—History—20th century.
3. Labor policy—Japan—History—20th century. I. Title.
II. Series.
HD8726.G67 1985   331'.0952   85-3747
ISBN 0-674-27131-9 (Harvard Univ. Pr.)

For Naomi and Melvin Gordon

Acknowledgments

The advice and support of numerous individuals and institutions made this book possible and helped improve it. It is a pleasure to acknowledge this assistance. Professor Albert Craig has enjoyed the dubious privilege of reading versions of this work produced over an eight-year period: seminar paper, doctoral dissertation, and book manuscript. At each stage, his thoughtful criticism sharpened the argument and shaped my approach in important ways. As I began to revise and extend the dissertation, which ended its coverage at 1945, I discovered that Professor Thomas C. Smith was also engaged in the study of Japanese labor history. Through correspondence and discussion, I have learned much from his insights, cautions, and suggestions. Professor Edwin O. Reischauer also provided helpful advice at the seminar-paper and dissertation stages of this research. Professors Donald Shively, Sheldon Garon, Gary Allinson, and Sharon Minichiello read and commented on parts of this work at various stages, and I have profited from their criticism.

I was extremely fortunate to receive assistance from many individuals in Japan. Professors Hyōdō Tsutomu and Nimura Kazuo deserve special thanks. Their own writings on labor history suggested problems and approaches that I have explored in this book. My debt to them in this regard is acknowledged in the footnotes, but I wish to note briefly two important areas in which I have built upon their insights. Professor Hyōdō introduced the notion of a nineteenth-century era of "indirect control" in his seminal work on the history of Japanese labor relations, and I have elaborated upon this concept as I applied it to the particular cases that I studied. Professor Nimura's conviction that different traditions of craft organization in Japan and the West help explain the divergent courses of their union movements led me to explore this possibility. In addition, these two men were generous beyond all expectation with their time, knowledge, and advice during my stays in Tokyo of 1978–1980 and 1983. They introduced me to materials, read my very rough drafts in English, and discussed my work patiently and critically. Professor Komatsu Ryūji kindly lent me prewar labor-union magazines he discovered in the course of his own research, and Professor Utsumi Takashi was a steady friend and critic who helped me locate and read documents, contact company officials, and conduct interviews.

The men listed in the bibliography under "Interview" shared their varied experiences as personnel managers, workers, labor-movement activists, and bureaucrats with frankness and enthusiasm. In addition, Kanai Tatsuo and Kaneko Yoshio allowed me to use several rare documents in their possession. The personnel offices of Ishikawajima Harima International, Nippon Kōkan, Mitsubishi Heavy Industries, and Tōshiba Electronics went to great lengths to arrange several of these interviews. Sumitomo Heavy Machine Industries and the Mitsubishi Heavy Industries Yokohama Factory generously granted access to company documents.

Librarians and archivists at the following institutions made their collections available and led me to important documents: The Ohara Institute for Social Research, the editorial office and archive for the *Kanagawa ken shi* [History of Kanagawa Prefecture], the Kawasaki City Hall Records Office (bunshō-ka), the Tokyo University Economics Library, and the Harvard-Yenching Library. Miki Uchida, as research assistant, gathered and analyzed materials in several of these libraries and companies in Tokyo, and at the Harvard-Yenching Library. This was particularly important for the chapters on postwar labor relations.

Several organizations provided the financial support that allowed me to do research and writing over a several-year period: the National Defense Foreign Language Fellowship (as it was then called), the Japan Foundation, the Social Science Research Council, the Fulbright-Hays Dissertation Fellowship, and the Japan Institute of Harvard University. Of course, I alone am responsible for the views expressed here.

Florence Trefethen has exceeded her reputation as a superb editor. Nancy Koch was an extremely patient and competent typist, working on the dissertation and parts of the manuscript. My wife, Yoshie, helped me decipher handwritten documents. Of more importance, she has tolerated my occasional periods of obsession with this work and helped make rewarding the years spent on its completion.

Contents

Tables

Appendix Tables

Figures

The Evolution of
Labor Relations in Japan
Heavy Industry, 1853–1955

Introduction

Large factories first came to Japan in the second half of the nineteenth century. In each enterprise, a handful of owners or managers sought to control the activity of hundreds of wage earners. More or less self-consciously over the course of a century, laborers and their employers dealt with each other as adversaries with different objectives; in shipyards, factories, and steel mills, managers and working men in Japan created and several times reshaped the new social relationship of the industrial revolution. The timing of industrial growth, the actions of government bureaucrats, strategic business choices, and, perhaps most important but least understood, the attitudes and activities of the workers themselves, all combined to push this labor relationship in a distinctive direction. The result was something observers by the late 1950s started to call the Japanese employment system. In this book I shall describe the century-long process by which it emerged.

The publication by James Abegglen of *The Japanese Factory* in 1958 marked the start of a literary tradition in the social sciences now decades old and still vigorous. The timing of Abegglen's book and the start of this tradition of writing on contemporary Japanese labor and management is no accident. He would not have written anything like *The Japanese Factory* had he gone to Japan a decade or more earlier, for not until the early 1950s did Japanese employment patterns come to resemble those since described by sociologists, economists, and anthropologists observing and even participating in Japanese factory life. In this literature, the large Japanese factory emerges as home to a unique set of social and economic arrangements which have almost achieved the status of a proper noun, the "Japanese Employment System."[1]

Any brief description of the system risks oversimplifying a complex social and economic interaction, ignoring coercive aspects of life in a big firm, and exaggerating the permanence of "permanent employment," the influence of seniority by itself in setting pay levels, or the subservience of company unions. But this risk is worth taking. Even with appropriate qualifications, the Japanese labor relationship remains quite distinctive. We may set forth at the outset the following defining characteristics of the Japanese factory since the 1950s.

At the heart of the matter is a simple proposition: Blue-collar men in large firms enjoy a status in the enterprise more like that of a salaried employee than a wage worker, as conceived in the United States or most of Western Europe. These men are treated, and view themselves, as full members of the enterprise. This status is manifest in several aspects of factory life.[2]

First, since the 1950s, men defined as "regular" workers have enjoyed considerable job security, and the pursuit of a career in a single firm is a fairly common choice among blue-collar men. A layoff at big factories is rare and is carried out with difficulty even in recession. Managers can and do cut back, but they usually feel compelled to use a variety of more or less subtle tactics to avoid actually firing the regular workers. These job practices are often termed "permanent employment" (*shūshin koyō*), but the "permanent" label is misleading. It inaccurately suggests that most workers actually spend their careers with a single employer. In fact, mobility has always been present among skilled factory workers. The key feature of jobs in the factory is rather the ability of regular men to remain if they so choose.

Of equal importance is the system of so-called seniority wages and promotions (*nenkō joretsu*). The wage is paid as a monthly salary. It has come to reflect seniority and *other company-specific factors* to a significant degree. Pay is primarily contingent on a man's seniority, rank, and reputation or evaluation in the firm, with little explicit relation to job content or skill level. A wage level is not transferable to another firm in the same industry. The major portion of a worker's income, his base wage, rises regularly with each year on the job. The size of the average yearly pay raise and the range of discretion allowed management in rewarding the more skilled, diligent, or cooperative workers is set through bargaining with the union. A company also gives out promotions more or less regularly to workers who meet fairly minimal requirements. These practices impart a basic security about rising future status and income to workers who stay with the company, and they reinforce the long-term employment tendency.

Extensive non-wage benefits, termed company welfare in this book, form a third pillar of this Japanese employment structure. Typical examples of company generosity are health insurance, heavily subsidized housing or housing loans, inexpensive goods provided at company stores, and a wide range of company-sponsored leisure activities. The security afforded by such programs further encourages a person to stay with a firm and helps build a positive attitude toward the employer.

Finally, unions organized at the company level are the significant units of action and identification. This has not guaranteed weakness, cooperation, or docility in the past, but, beginning around 1950, hard-boiled policies of union-busting produced company unions noteworthy for weak ties to other company unions in the same industry and a strong sense of allegiance to the firm. Since then, most such unions have been willing consistently to moderate short-run demands to insure long-run company stability and future gains for the members. This behavior can be effective when union members expect to or indeed do remain for many years with a single employer, so the several aspects of the labor relationship reinforce each other.[3]

This structure of labor relations is a set of practices concerning the place of a worker in the company: his job-security, wages, non-wage benefits, and union organization. It evolved through the often troubled interaction of workers, managers, and bureaucrats. The following chapters will describe a process of conflict and compromise in the goals, interests, and activities of these three groups, never monolithic entities to be sure, which produced this Japanese pattern. We shall find that so-called "traditional" practices, seniority wages and "permanent employment" especially, were absent at the start and took root only as Japan became objectively more "modern" (industrial, urban, literate). As commonly defined, *traditional* and *modern* are not useful terms in which to frame this study.

Several important studies in the 1960s and 1970s have already discredited the simplistic view of Japanese employment practices as "traditional." Before these works appeared, scholars tended to explain the post-World War II Japanese employment system as the result of a carrying over of feudal, patriarchal, or agrarian values into the modern world. The rural hinterland produced the diligent daughters and second sons who formed the industrial work force.[4] Whether Abegglen applauded the system or some Japanese scholars condemned it, they saw it as a passing phenomenon. As Japan proceeded further along the path toward modernity and rationality, the "leftover" traditional practices of lifetime employment and seniority wages would, or ought to, give way to a labor relationship closer to some sort of Western model.[5] More recent works have made a valuable contribution in criticizing this perspective. While not in complete agreement among themselves, they have described the contemporary Japanese labor relationship as a rational response to modern problems of industrial organization, likely to persist rather than to converge with any Western model. In so doing, they have cleared up much historical confusion. In Dore's picture, for example, of innovative managers making rational choices, we can even see individuals acting to shape the historical evolution of social institutions. The debate is no longer about whether Japan is a unique case where traditional remnants persist in modern society.

This study of labor in Japan builds on these insights, but it will differ in two respects worth noting at the outset. First, it begins with historical concern. While a few Western scholars have looked explicitly and with some care at the history of the Japanese employment system, the writing of history was seldom the primary goal. The post-World War II literature on the Japanese factory has been written almost exclusively by sociologists, anthropologists, and economists. They understandably have shown only passing interest in the historical roots of contemporary practice. We acknowledge that the writing of sociology or economics is no sin, and much of this work is excellent; but this particular social-science literature has turned to the past only after explaining the present and offering predictions concerning future convergence or divergence.[6] As a result of thus driving the cart before the horse, an implicit, linear view of history emerged before serious historical study began, especially in the large body of work concerned with the issue of convergence. If Japan is slowly converging with the West, it must have been even more different or "traditional" decades ago and then gradually become less so. If it is not converging, the past is expected to reveal traditional roots of Japan's stubborn divergence. In either case, the initial preoccupation with the present and future has obstructed our view of the past. In fact, we shall find that Japanese labor relations resembled those of the West more at the outset, in the nineteenth century, than today.

Second, in this book issues of power and conflict occupy center stage. They have rarely done so in earlier studies of the Japanese employment system, which have, as a result, overlooked the contribution made by the Japanese worker. The very use of the term *Japanese Employment System* is both symptom and cause of this omission. Japanese scholars do not speak of the history of the Japanese employment system, but discuss the history of Japanese labor relations (*rōshi kankei shi*).[7] In this case, their language is more precise than ours, for it raises the problem of power and conflict by forcing us to think in terms of a relationship between workers and managers. To speak of the history of an employment system, in contrast, invites a one-sided view of the system as a management creation. Even the best of the Western-language studies have yet to see the history of labor relations as a dialectic process involving the interaction of workers, managers, and bureaucrats, all taking initiatives at some point and responding to events at others. They have assumed that workers before World War II were organized too weakly to have influenced management policy, and they credited management with an almost "exclusive monopoly on tradition" which enabled it to legitimate the practice of permanent employment by consciously remolding tradition. The chief question is often "Why did Japanese industrialists make certain kinds of choices?" A favorable labor response is assumed. When workers do enter the picture, they are portrayed either as an abstraction, the labor market, or as the "docile and diligent" products of a "comprehensive campaign of social engineering."[8] Only managers have been credited with the ability to innovate, to take initiative, and to shape practices found in Japanese industry. Workers are the willing objects of management policy, ready to accept the system imposed from above. Bureaucrats are hardly discussed.[9]

The innovations of managers will remain part of the story told here, but the values and activities of workers and bureaucrats will take on equal importance. Japanese workers were assertive participants in the factory. Their ideas and actions must be brought to life. Even early in this century, they possessed sufficient organization and autonomy to help shape the labor relationship, and their activity limited the choices available to management. Just as British workers manipulated the traditional notion of the "rights of a free-born Englishman," we shall find that Japanese workers manipulated values in their cultural tradition in pursuit of their own interests.

The Japanese labor relationship moved through several distinct stages between the 1850s and 1950s. The years from the opening of Japan to the West in 1853 through the failure of the early union movement in 1900 constitute a frontier era in Japanese factory life. In the nineteenth century, managers with little experience to guide them were unable to intervene effectively in the work place. Their control over labor was indirect.

The first significant change in this unsettled relationship came around the turn of the century, as economic and technolocial advances generated pressure for more effective organization of work. Managers articulated a coherent ideology of labor control, best characterized as paternalism, and they adopted important policies of more direct intervention, in part to give this philosophy greater substance; but, between 1917 and 1921, their efforts faced a serious challenge. The labor movement made a new start around the time of the Russo-Japanese War and grew tremendously after World War I. Skilled workers who took concerted actions to defend their interests against employers at times repudiated the paternal ideology and structure of control directly, although their demand for more systematic, favorable treatment within the existing hierarchy of the firm was probably more significant in the long run. A distinct working-class organizational style and set of attitudes is apparent in the activities and demands of workers in these early decades of labor-movement history; we shall discern a pattern of labor-management interaction leading to some wage and job policies now associated in particular with the Japanese factory. On balance, however, the arrangement of factory life at the end of these two eras of trial, error, and improvisation did not appear to many contemporary Japanese to be significantly different from that emerging or in place in Europe or America. Some managers spoke of "unique Japanese customs" in the workplace, to be sure, but, in the face of disputes and union organizing, these claims rang hollow to most workers, as well as to political, intellectual, bureaucratic, and a few management observers.

Responding to new economic problems as well as to the labor movement, factory managers changed their tack somewhat during the interwar years, from our perspective a period lasting until 1939. By the eve of World War II, the managerial and bureaucratic elite could speak with some justification of a distinctive Japanese pattern of labor management, but we must take care to distinguish rhetoric from reality, and distinguish the interwar system from that of later decades. Wage policies favoring senior men, programs for worker training, and promises of career security for a few all took on greater significance in these years; but attention to the process by which these practices emerged will clarify major limits in their application and reveal that tension and

insecurity remained dominant elements in the labor relationship.

Extensive intervention by the government bureaucracy marked
the years from 1939 to 1945. The state attempted to impose its
version of a proper labor relationship upon workers and managers
alike. The labor problem had concerned bureaucrats since at least
the 1890s, and they had promoted various labor policies earlier in
the twentieth century; but not until the demands of war and economic mobilization greatly increased government control over all
areas of civilian life did the bureaucracy become a decisive actor in
the labor relationship.[10] Legal and newly powerful labor unions
then brought fundamental change to the structure of labor relations in the first postwar decade, although they built on the past.
The union desire for consistent treatment by managers echoed
themes raised by earlier generations of workers and by some bureaucrats during the war. In the decade after 1945, the package
identified by the late 1950s as the Japanese employment system
took shape. Despite the scope of change, continuities bridge the
gap between the "imperial" and "democratic" versions of factory
organization. In fact, the more radical changes won by labor just
after the war did not stand up against a subsequent management
and government regrouping, so that continuities with previous
decades seem greater in 1955 than in 1947.

Several heavy industrial enterprises in the Keihin region, stretching southwest along the coast from Tokyo, will provide most of
the material for this study. Of course, one industrial sector cannot
perfectly represent the entire economy, and no group of companies
can recapitulate the full experience of all workers and managers
in an industry. The story of labor in the textile mills and the many
small enterprises so numerous in both modern and traditional
industry is not told here.[11] These stories are important. Light
industry was a source of some practices considered part of a Japanese system of labor relations. The small-scale sector, which employed over two-thirds of Japanese industrial labor before World
War II, was a source of diversity as well as pressure which affected
practices in the large factories.[12] Yet, the very young, mainly

female textile workers generally spent only a few years in the factory. They rarely became lifelong industrial workers. Heavy industrial firms, in contrast, dealt with workers more committed to factory labor, and the importance of this sector derives in large measure from the appearance of Japan's first career industrial wage laborers in shipyards, arsenals, machine factories, and steel mills. The institutions that evolved out of their interactions with managers set trends for Japanese industry as a whole.

Within heavy industry, the companies studied here occupy a somewhat special position. The very biggest of the big, the zaibatsu giants in shipbuilding and metal processing run by Mitsubishi, Sumitomo, or Mitsui, are not at the center of this work.[13] Japanese historians have covered labor relations in these zaibatsu giants rather thoroughly, and the choice of cases here in part reflects a desire to look at a slightly different stratum of the large-scale sector of the economy, the major companies employing thousands in the early 1900s, but not the three or four giants employing tens of thousands. Because research on the largest firms is readily accessible, comparisons to them are not difficult and will be found throughout the book. Despite a more rapid turn to direct control in the very biggest firms, and a faster response to labor unions in the 1920s, the similarity in lines of conflict and in outcome suggests that a similar labor relationship prevailed throughout Japan in large factories employing mainly males.

Government enterprises, especially arsenals and also the Yahata Ironworks, form another center of heavy industrial activity discussed only in passing. However, as references to the arsenals or the Yahata mill should indicate, conditions in these factories were usually comparable to those at the factories studied here. Mining is another sector outside the scope of this work, and it was an important souce of capital and technical innovation for heavy industry. The history of labor in the mines is fascinating but rather different from that of factory workers. It warrants a thorough separate treatment.

Five companies figure most prominently in this book. In the early years of industrialization, a few key enterprises were launched close to each other in the heart of Tokyo. These included the Ishi-kawajima Shipyard and the Shibaura Engineering Works. Com-munities of workers grew up around these companies, and smaller factories tended to cluster in the area. The labor movement of the nineteenth century was active in these communities. As heavy industry expanded in the late nineteenth and early twentieth cen-turies, major new enterprises were founded in the area running from Tokyo southwest along the coast to Yokohama and beyond, and older companies located new plants along this belt as well. Among these were the Yokohama and Uraga Dock Companies, founded in 1893 and 1896, respectively, and the iron and steel tube manufacturer Nippon Kōkan (NKK), founded in 1912.

Three of these firms were involved in shipbuilding or ship repair. This apparent imbalance in our focus stems from one methodo-logical and one historical factor. Important documents for heavy industry in the Keihin area survive in greatest number at ship-building concerns. Fortunately, the emphasis on shipbuilding can be justified historically as well. Heavy industry in Japan emerged from a handful of government enterprises launched in the baku-matsu era which continued in public or private hands after the Restoration. Among these, shipbuilding and ship-repair facilities played the major role. Tokugawa bakufu operations, such as the Yokosuka Shipyard or Nagasaki Iron Works (later Shipyard), and domain efforts, such as Mito's Ishikawajima Shipyard, were among those that made the transition to Meiji. Japanese heavy industry built upon a foundation laid by these yards. An analysis from 1930 explains that the shipbuilding industry received great atten-tion from the new Meiji Government, which inherited or bought various bakufu or han shipbuilding or armament operations. "These factories [Yokusuka, Nagasaki, Ishikawajima, Hyōgo] were ship-building enterprises in name, but they did not merely build ships." They manufactured the engines and machines required by these ships, and they produced more general machinery. By 1930, shipbuilders had continued and broadened this practice. They were involved in car and truck manufacturing and iron and steel production. The 1930 report concludes, "Thus shipbuilding has provided the foundation for Japan's machine industry. This is very likely because machine production was at a very primitive stage in early Meiji, and the only enterprises of relatively large scale, with capacity to undertake such efforts, were those in shipbuilding."[14]

The three shipbuilders studied here followed this pattern. The Ishikawajima Yard, especially, recapitulates much of the history of Japanese heavy industry as well as that of the working-class movement. The Mito domain founded it in 1854 in response to a bakufu directive, constructing the facility in Edo (later Tokyo) on the island of Ishikawajima in the mouth of the Sumida River which flowed through the heart of the city. The Mito daimyō himself, Tokugawa Nariaki, oversaw construction of the first vessel in 1856. The new Meiji Government inherited the shipyard with the Restoration in 1868 and used it for a time as an arsenal. In 1876, the government decided to concentrate its armament operations elsewhere and closed the operation, removing most of the machinery. A 31-year-old entrepreneur, Hirano Tomiji, immediately saw an opportunity to realize his ambition of founding a privately owned shipyard. Hirano rented the land, constructed a factory, and began operating the Ishikawajima Hirano Shipyard. The name of the enterprise changed several times in the following decades, to Ishikawajima Shipyard in 1889, to Tokyo Ishikawajima Shipyard in 1893, and finally to Ishikawajima Heavy Industries in June 1945. Difficulties in the early years were overcome with capital backing from Shibusawa Eiichi, among others, and over the years several major subsidiary ventures spun off from the shipyard, including an auto manufacturer, a turbine-engine company, and an aircraft manufacturer. In 1960, the company merged with Harima Shipyard to become Ishikawajima Harima Heavy Industries (IHI), one of the largest heavy industrial conglomerates in Japan.[15]

The Shibaura Engineering Works was the first private engineering enterprise in Japan. Its long, well-documented history makes it a case in some ways parallel to Ishikawajima. Tanaka Hisashige started an electric machine shop in central Tokyo in 1875 and began to make telegraphic equipment for the Ministry of Industry (Kōbushō). In 1878, the government bought most of Tanaka's equipment and hired away most of his employees, forcing the company to close for a while. Upon reopening, Tanaka shifted to the manufacture of more general machinery as well as telegraphic equipment. Business expanded with naval orders for ship machinery, and in 1882 the company moved to a new site in Shiba ward just a short distance from Ishikawajima and changed its name to Shibaura Engineering Works. Over the following decades, the two companies collaborated on several ventures, including the turbine manufacturer just noted, and many workers moved freely between the two factories.

After a difficult period in the 1890s, Shibaura emerged as the leading engineering firm in the nation, part of the Mitsui zaibatsu, and in 1925 it had opened a major new plant at Tsurumi, also in the Keihin industrial belt. The company proudly advertised the Tsurumi operation as the "model factory of Asia." Shibaura merged with another Mitsui affiliate, Tokyo Electric, a manufacturer of bulbs and electrical appliances, in 1939, and the new corporation, Tōshiba, came to rank next to Hitachi as Japan's major electronics firm.[16]

Three other companies enter the story between the turn of the century and World War I. The Yokohama Dock Company was founded as a ship-repair facility in 1893 and began operations in 1897, taking over ship-repair docks used by Mitsubishi's Nihon Yūsen Kaisha (NYK) shipping line. Some of the capital for the venture came from local Yokohama merchants, but Mitsubishi support was also crucial. Not only NYK capital but a steady flow of repair orders from NYK ships helped the Dock Company, nicknamed Yokosen by workers and local residents, expand. By the boom of World War I, it was the largest employer in Yokohama, with over 5,000 workers, and it began ship manufacture in 1917. Over the years, it expanded its operations to include production of steel frames, boilers, steam engines, and other machines for land use. In 1935, Mitsubishi Heavy Industries absorbed Yokosen, renaming it the Mitsubishi Heavy Industries Yokohama Factory.[17]

The Uraga Dock Company began in similar circumstances, although its history in later years was checkered. In 1896, a group of Tokyo capitalists joined to finance the enterprise during the boom in shipping and shipbuilding that followed the Sino-Japanese War. Operations began in 1900 at the dockyard, located in Uraga harbor well down the Miura peninsula from Yokohama on a site used as a dock by the bakufu decades earlier. As had Yokosen, the Uraga Dock started as a repair facility and later began shipbuilding, in 1911. It developed an extensive machine division as well. Throughout its prewar and wartime history, close ties to the Navy resulted in many military contracts. In 1961, Sumitomo Heavy Industries bought the company and still runs the facility as its Uraga Factory.[18]

Nippon Kōkan (NKK) was a major Japanese iron and steel producer, specializing in steel pipes from soon after its founding until the present. NKK offers insight into a third branch of heavy industry which demanded slightly different skills and produced a somewhat different labor relationship. Two university classmates founded NKK in 1912. Imaizumi Kiichirō provided expertise as a former technician from the Yahata Ironworks, and Shiraishi Genjirō was instrumental in raising capital, in large part from his father-in-law and zaibatsu founder, Asano Sōichirō. The two were determined to found a privately owned iron and steel mill, and NKK was one of Japan's first successful mills not run by the government. They chose a site along the coast in Kawasaki, right in the center of the Keihin industrial belt, and operations commenced in 1913. The company expanded rapidly and employed several thousand workers by the end of World War I. It became the region's major steelmaker and prospered greatly in the 1930s and war years, absorbing several smaller shipyards and steel mills along the adjacent coastline by 1945.[19]

The activities of these five enterprises span the century from the bakumatsu years through the present, ranging over the spectrum of heavy industrial endeavor. Located in a single region, the companies cooperated in joint ventures, concurrent management by some of the same executives, and the exchange of information on labor-union activists. Their workers also formed a single community. Movement among the companies was common, especially before the 1920s. Labor unions often attempted to unite workers from more than one of these factories, and they occasionally succeeded. From the activities and ideas of these workers, and the policies of their managers, we may reconstruct a history of the Japanese factory.

Part One
Workers and Managers in the Industrial Revolution

ONE

Organizing Industrial Workers

Japan was still a nation of farmers at the end of the nineteenth century. Over three-fourths of the population earned the major portion of its livelihood by working the land or the sea. Within a small but growing industrial sector, light industry dominated, so that, by 1900, shipyards, arsenals, or machine shops employed no more than 25,000, or 6 percent, of the nation's roughly 450,000 factory workers.[1] Heavy industry at this time occupied only a tiny niche in Japanese society. Yet, a history of labor relations in twentieth-century Japan must begin with a search for social origins reaching well back into the preindustrial past. A distinct working-class society as well as important managerial practices were already in place by the decade spanning the start of the twentieth century, and these patterns of behavior cast shadows well into the new century.

NEW WORKERS, OLD CUSTOMS

The first generation of industrial labor in Japan was a hybrid creation. European advisors in government-run shipyards, arsenals, or railroad yards trained the first native industrial wage laborers, but, while the Japanese learned skills in some measure alien, they behaved much like fellow artisans in indigenous crafts. The advent of Western industry did not bring an immediate, sharp social discontinuity.

The creation of a labor force began in haphazard fashion, reminiscent of the mythic efforts of the English hero of *Shōgun* to build a Western ship 250 years earlier. When a Russian schooner sank off the coast of the Izu peninsula in 1855, the bakufu permitted its crew to employ Japanese artisans and build a new ship. Russian officers with some knowledge of wood and metal work taught Japanese ship carpenters and blacksmiths in the area around the port of Heda how to make Russian-style tools and construct a new ship. This knowledge was not wasted, for, when Mito han officials built the Ishikawajima Shipyard in Edo in response to a bakufu directive, they dispatched their own han carpenters and smiths to work on the project, and they also brought in one Russian overseer and several of the Japanese trained by the Russians at Heda. These workers continued to learn Western shipbuilding techniques and built a total of 10 wooden ships, 4 at Ishikawajima and 6 more at Heda. Other men of artisan background, who helped design and construct the machinery used in ships made at Ishikawajima, were trained by the Dutch at the bakufu's Nagasaki Ironworks. The bakufu strategy was similar at the Yokosuka Naval Shipyard, founded in 1864. Officials reccruited local metal and wood artisans as well as farmers for on-the-job training by French instructors. The Japanese passed on the skills they learned to their fellow workers, as noted in the official history of the Yokosuka yard: "When A learned a skill he taught B. When B learned it he taught C."[2]

In this fashion, foreign technicians trained a mobile pool of workers which gradually spread throughout the country. The Nagasaki and Osaka Ironworks, the Yokosuka Naval Shipyard, and Ishikawajima were the most important training sites. Yokosuka employed as many as 43 French instructors at a time over a 13-year period ending in 1877, and they trained several thousand workers.[3] These men took their skills to other newer and smaller factories and emerged as leaders of working-class society; they "all went on in later years to become central figures in private factories."[4]

Managers who lost their men were unhappy. In 1867, one French technician at Yokosuka, Francois L. Verney, lamented that workers finally trained with great difficulty in Western skills left for jobs elsewhere, leaving behind only inexperienced workers, thus obstructing operations. Verney was forced to wonder where in the world he could recruit workers already skilled in relevant crafts.[5] But, for Japanese industry as a whole, this was welcome and inevitable. An observer looking back in 1910 commented that most of the ironworkers at various factories were trained at the arsenals. "There is hardly any worker today of 50 years of age or so who has not worked at an arsenal or naval yard, and hardly any worker in a machine or metal factory who was not thus trained." He noted, in addition, that most of the entrepreneurs running independent metal shops in the city had "polished their skills" at the naval or army arsenals. Ishikawajima and Shibaura, on the other hand, were privately owned factories that contributed to the training of workers. He claimed that "about 90 percent or more of the roughly 200 owners of small factories or machine shops scattered around Shiba ward today learned their trade at one or the other of the above private or public enterprises. Almost all the factories in the city are run by former workers of Koishikawa Army Arsenal, Akabane Naval Arsenal, Shibaura, or Ishikawajima."[6]

Despite the novelty of foreign technicians, brick factories, steam engines, and lathes, the skills demanded by modern heavy industry overlapped with indigenous craft skills in wood and metal work. The native artisans were retrained before they could build rifles, engines, or Western-style ships, but Western industry of the mid-to-late nineteenth century was not so advanced as to make the indigenous experience irrelevant. The majority of workers in the large factories of the nineteenth century practiced skills with indigenous roots, and a good number of them were retrained artisans[7] (Table 1). This continuity in personnel and in craft was of truly critical importance. It resulted in the spread of the social practices of preindustrial artisan society to workers in heavy industry.

The most important social relationships in the indigenous

Table 1 Occupational Breakdown of Meiji Workers, By Number and (Percent)

| Factory & Dates | Entirely New Trades | | | Trades Putting Indigenous Skills to Use | | | | |
| | | | | Metal Trades | | | | |
	Lathe Worker	Finisher, Assembler	Sub-Total	Casting	Forging	Boiler-making	Other	Sub-Total
Yokosuka Naval Arsenal 10/1878	210 (17.2)		210 (17.2)	54 (4.4)	130 (10.6)	180 (14.7)	—	364 (29.7)
Nagasaki Shipyard 1884	53 (7.7)	110 (16.1)	163 (23.8)	53 (7.7)	49 (7.2)	176 (25.7)	22 (3.2)	300 (43.8)
Osaka Iron Works 10/1897	36 (6.8)	84 (15.9)	120 (22.7)	42 (7.9)	43 (8.1)	218 (41.2)	9 (1.7)	312 (58.9)
Tokyo Arsenal 7/1896	606 (12.4)	968 (19.9)	1,574 (32.3)	—	214 (4.4)	—	235 (4.8)	449 (9.2)
Japan Railway Company Ōmiya Factory 1901	110 (9.4)	220 (18.8)	330 (28.2)	52 (4.4)	161 (13.8)	187 (16.0)	—	400 (34.2)

Trades Putting Indigenous Skills To Use

Factory & Dates	Wood Pattern	Carpenter, Ship Carpenter	Sawyer	Painter	Rigging, Sails, etc.	Other	Sub-Total	Total
			Wood Trades					
Yokosuka Naval Arsenal 10/1878	21 (1.7)	310 (25.3)	23 (1.9)	71 (5.8)	225 (18.4)	—	650 (53.1)	1,224
Nagasaki Shipyard 1884	53 (7.7)	168 (24.6)	—	—	1 (.1)	—	222 (32.4)	685
Osaka Iron Works 10/1897	13 (2.5)	64 (12.1)	11 (2.1)	7 (1.3)	2 (.4)	—	97 (18.4)	529
Tokyo Arsenal 7/1896	—	108 (2.2)	—	—	—	2,735 (56.3)	2,834 (58.5)	4,866
Japan Railway Company Ōmiya Factory 1901	303 (25.9)		35 (3.0)	100 (8.7)	—	—	438 (37.6)	1,168

Source: Yamamoto, Nihon rōdō shijō no kōzō, pp. 20–21

artisan tradition, in Japan as well as Europe, were those between master, journeyman, and apprentice.[8] Customary practice in the urban craft guilds of Tokugawa Japan dictated a 10-year apprenticeship, but demand for workers in an expanding economy reduced this to 6 or 7 years by the latter decades of Tokugawa rule. Apprentices were bound by custom and oral contract to stay the full term, and other masters were theoretically warned not to hire runaway apprentices. Once an apprentice became a journeyman licensed by the guild of a particular city, he was free to stay with his master or move to the employ of another, although journeymen were expected to serve the master an additional 6 months or 1 year before moving on. Eventually the fortunate journeyman inherited a master's position or received backing which allowed him to set up on his own.[9]

Movement of journeymen from master to master was, thus, an accepted practice among the licensed urban artisans. A special relationship continued between a journeyman and his original master, who had a customary right to "recall" his former apprentice in times of labor shortage; but mobility was the norm. The footloose traveler (*watari shokkō*) of the Meiji period, who moved with alacrity between factories and shipyards, and the journeymen who dreamed of one day owning their own shops were following time-honored customs.

A second feature of artisan society which influenced industrial labor was the absence of inter-urban guild networks. The importance of this negative factor emerges clearly when one considers the impact exerted by such networks where they did exist in Europe. Tokugawa craftsmen organized guilds separately in each city or town. Masters and journeymen formed separate associations within a guild responsible for regulating entry into the trade and setting wages. In Tokyo, the masons and sawyers maintained these groups until at least 1889, when labor leader Katayama Sen described them. He counted 1,200 to 1,300 mason journeymen and about 300 masters in Tokyo that year and found a similar ratio among the sawyers. Masters and journeymen in both trades met periodically to negotiate wage rates.[10] Yet, Meiji machinists did not reproduce the journeyman organizations of the Tokyo masons or sawyers. Neither they nor any group of masters or journeymen in modern industry regulated entry into the trade or set wages through negotiations. The urban guilds available as models had not been supple enough to cope with the changed economic conditions of the late Tokugawa period, let alone the needs of the new industrial workers. Guild artisans had supplied the needs of samurai customers in castle towns, but they had proved unable to move beyond the cities to capture the growing market in the countryside of the late Tokugawa Japan.[11] Instead, as the economy grew, unlicensed artisans serving the rural market increased in number. As urban craftsmen did not transform or expand their organizations to include these workers, they lost control over entry to the craft. Apprentices were able to break contracts and obtain employment elsewhere as journeymen without fear of retribution, the masters raided each other for apprentices. A 1793 law complained that apprentices in the cabinetmakers' guild abandoned their masters to seek work at other shops in the same trade. As apprenticeship became an increasingly uncertain commitment, masters devoted less energy to training and came to view apprentices as a source of cheap labor. Abuse of apprenticeship led to a further increase in the number of unlicensed artisans, depressing the value of journeyman labor. The distinction between licensed journeymen traveling to polish their skills with several masters, and less skilled, unlicensed wage laborers also moving in search of work was blurred.[12]

Journeymen in indigenous trades would clearly have gained by creating regional or national networks linking together the urban guilds, uniting both rural and urban laborers, and reasserting a measure of control over the conditions of their trade. Had they done so by the middle of the nineteenth century, the influence of Tokugawa crafts on industrial work would likely have resembled the impact of English craft tradition upon early trade unions there. In England, economic growth dating back to the 1400s had upset the local balance of masters, journeymen, and apprentices.

By the eve of the Industrial Revolution, urban English craftsmen had for several centuries been dealing with the problem of an expanding economy, competition from unlicensed rural craftsmen, and exploitation of apprentice labor. Elaborate "tramping networks" linking craftsmen in a trade throughout the country had evolved as one response to this problem. Unemployed journeymen tramped from town to town, and, at each stop, the local trade society either found the newcomer work or gave him a few pennies to help him along to the next "tramp station," thus preventing excessive competition for scarce jobs in any given locale. Hostility between "fair" urban journeymen and "foul" rural outsiders in the fifteenth and sixteenth centuries was very gradually replaced by a spirit of comradeship and mutual aid by the eighteenth century. The workers of early industrial England, whose skills were linked to those of preindustrial craftsmen more intimately than in Japan, built labor organizations out of craft networks that had evolved over centuries in response to preindustrial economic growth.[13]

Japanese artisans had not built such broad, inclusive craft networks when Western industry came to Japan. Industrial workers in almost all trades, old and new, were influenced by traditions of craft organization far different from those that had developed in Europe. Traveling journeymen were common in both Japan and Europe, but the English and European journeymen had developed means to control their numbers and distribute jobs before the Industrial Revolution.[14] In Japan they had not. Journeymen in traditional crafts, licensed or not, traveled from workshop to workshop with no way to control their numbers or movement so as to increase chances of success. The artisans competed with one another and with apprentices as they sought to accumulate the skill, capital, and backing needed to become masters. This unregulated lifestyle of apprentices and journeymen was reproduced by workers trained in new industrial establishments.

The Nagasaki area, site of a major Western-style ironworks sponsored by the bakufu, and home to a community of traditional artisans as well, offers a microcosmic picture of this cross-fertilization between factory and artisan organization. Counterparts to the Tokugawa apprentices, journeymen, and masters quickly emerged in the new Nagasaki Ironworks. Journeymen artisans moved freely between the Ironworks, later taken over by Mitsubishi as its Nagasaki Shipyard, and local shops engaged in traditional manufacture. Most of the laborers at the Ironworks came from artisan backgrounds, some from Tokyo but many from the local area. Those of local origin were seldom members of the urban guilds. They were usually unlicensed village artisans from the Nagasaki environs. They moved freely, in spite of nominal bakufu regulations, in entering or leaving the works, seeking work at small metal shops in town, or trying to set up on their own. In 1884, 76 percent of the 685 Nagasaki Shipyard workers practiced trades relying mainly on indigenous skills (Table 1). For several decades, traditional artisans brought not only their skills, but their unregulated mobility and their aspirations into this modern factory. They set the tone of worker behavior in heavy industry with frequent job changes, movement from small shop to large factory and back, disregard for ineffective craft restrictions, and the desire for independence.[15] By the turn of the century, similar communities had grown up surrounding the factories of Tokyo and Osaka. The senior workers had been trained by foreign technicians, but they absorbed and recreated preindustrial Japanese practices. The factories built in these decades faced the formidable task of breaking these men in to the pace of industrial production; union organizers had difficulty promoting a labor movement in such communities.

MEIJI WORKING-CLASS SOCIETY

Japan today is a society of remarkable social homogeneity; the lifestyle of the urban and suburban middle class is a powerful model dominating the national culture. To explain this homogeneity as a legacy of "traditional" society is unwise, for Japan of the late Tokugawa period was far more heterogeneous. Legal and social barriers unmistakably marked off the boundaries between samurai and peasant, rural dweller and urbanite. At the turn of the century, over three decades into the modern, Meiji period, the nation was remarkable for heterogeneity of a different type. The behavior and attitudes of industrial laborers in shipyards and factories distinguished them clearly from other more affluent and better educated urban dwellers as well as from villagers, rich or poor.

Industrial laborers were part of a larger category, the working poor, whose members included artisans in traditional trades, unskilled outdoor laborers, and rickshaw pullers. While demand for their skills and the relative steadiness of their employment put factory workers among the less miserable of this group, they were still part of "lower-class society," in the contemporary phrase. They by no means defined a labor aristocracy through their lifestyles or attitudes. Unsteady incomes and harsh conditions of work set them far apart from respectable, educated folk.

An average skilled worker who put in 10 hours a day plus overtime could expect to take home between 30 and 60 sen each day at the turn of the century (100 sen=1 yen). Yokoyama Gennosuke, pioneering observer of Japan's lower classes, considered the case of a relatively well paid worker with a family of four in 1899, who earned 50 sen a day, 26 days each month, for a total of 13 yen. He added up the cost of basic foods (rice, vegetables, and fish), cooking oil, fuel, and rent, threw in a little more than 1 yen for one seemingly inelastic necessity, drinking money, and found that the family had just 60 sen left for such other foods as miso and soy sauce, not to mention clothes. Yokoyama estimated that 60 to 70 percent of Tokyo's machinists could hardly support their families, and he painted a grim picture of a life marked by incessant domestic quarrels and indifference to the education of children. Other surveys tell a similar story.[16] Even the better-paid worker was barely able to afford food, clothing, and cramped, dirty shelter.

Work in the factory offered little relief from troubles at home. A reporter from the *Mainichi shimbun,* a paper interested in labor problems, paid a visit to the Shibaura Engineering Works in September 1895. The working day ran from 6:00 a.m. to 4:30 p.m. A deafening roar of hammers and a foul odor of smoke assaulted the earnest but sensitive reporter when he entered the factory. Several hours later, he was dizzy and could not hear: "Many of the workers are stationed quite close to the fire, swinging large hammers and blackened [with soot] or reddened [with heat]." He concluded matter-of-factly that, even if the hours were relatively short, the work was harder than that faced by most people! One needed skill and strength to last for even an hour.[17]

More than poverty and blackened faces set these men apart from their betters and marked off a gap between them and their managers. Japanese workers of this era were neither keen on taking orders nor enthusiastically committed to their jobs, and persuading them to submit to the discipline of factory labor was no easy task; it was far from accomplished by the turn of the century. The decided lack of diligence observed among the Japanese workers of this era is especially worth noting because standard explanations for the "successful modernization" of the Japanese economy point to diligent labor as a factor.[18] Also, Tokugawa economic historians have surmised that the spread of rural industry in the late Tokugawa years created a pool of day laborers ready to join the modern industrial work force.[19] Many observations of worker behavior in the Meiji years contradict these generalizations.

A Dutch advisor at the Nagasaki Ironworks, D. de Graeff van Polsbroek, expressed frustration over the lack of discipline among workers in an 1864 memorandum addressed to bakufu officials. He requested that factory gates be closed to prevent the free coming and going of workers, called for punishment of those who loafed on the job, and demanded that a Japanese doctor be called in to check on whether those absent were indeed ill, as they claimed. Another Dutch advisor, Kattendyke, complained that workers lacked patience and prudence and were unreceptive to rules or discipline.[20] Polsbroek also asked for the dispatch of workers from the Tokyo area, reputed to be more reliable, but the following rule, instituted at the Yokosuka Naval Yard near Tokyo in 1872, suggests that the big-city workers did not always live up to their reputation for diligence and that the Dutch complaints from

Nagasaki were generally applicable elsewhere. The rule specified severe punishment for "workers who, having registered in the morning, slip out of the factory and take advantage of the crush at the gates at lunchtime to slip back in and sign off."[21]

A lax attitude toward hours, rules, and holidays continued into the new century. A reporter noted in 1897 that the work day at a major Osaka shipyard ran from dawn to dusk, but that "usually some finish work in the morning and go home, others come to work in the early afternoon, and they all seem free to work and play as they please."[22] In the nineteenth century, managers seem to have tailored their policies to fit such behavior. Workers commonly took the day off on the day after payday, and many companies, including the Shibaura Engineering Works, accepted this as unavoidable. They simply placed payday on the day before the two monthly holidays. While this regular day off came only twice a month, workers jealously guarded the many customary festival holidays which served to break up the factory routine. At the Nagasaki Ironworks in bakumatsu years, these holidays added up to nearly three months off per year, including days lost to the weather.[23] In 1905, workers at the tightly supervised Koishikawa Army Arsenal in Tokyo refused to work on April 17. They called an unofficial holiday and turned the arsenal grounds into a festival site. Yokoyama claims they were reviving an older holiday which had been ignored in recent years.[24]

Workers were notoriously poor savers. A popular Tokugawa saying had it that the Edo-ite "never slept overnight on his money," and observers described factory men around 1900 in similar terms. In the words of an experienced technician (*gishi*) in 1902:

> The will or desire to save is shockingly low among metalworkers. In many cases they take the day off after payday. Further, the wives of the workers, anxious as to whether their husbands will really bring home the money on payday, gather in a group around the factory gate, demanding that their husbands turn over the wages [before they drink them away].[25]

The fears of the women huddled outside the gate were real enough. A good bit of drinking and brawling, and occasional trips to the brothels of Tokyo or Osaka, accompanied poor work-place discipline and low savings. A worker interviewed in 1902 for the first major government survey of labor, *Shokkō jijō*, claimed that he and his friends spent their money on gambling and women, went into debt, and then borrowed at high interest. Katayama Sen, usually one to stress the high moral standards of workers out of a desire to improve their public image, acknowledged that a difficulty facing the creation of a moderate labor union was that workers were short-tempered and ready to strike at the drop of a hat, and a contributor to the labor journal *Rōdō sekai* in 1897 described the typical worker of the nineteenth century as a hard-drinking, fighting, gambling type with no care for saving or for the future. [26]

Poverty, drinking, gambling, spendthrift ways, and limited horizons—this is one cluster of traits found among nineteenth century workers in Japan. Yet, another wholly different list of characteristics could be compiled as well: a strong desire for independence and advancement; a spirit of cameraderie and community; and a stubborn insistence that society accord respect to the working man.

A machinist described the desire for independence and advancement in 1910 when he noted that there were hardly any master workers over 50 years old to be found at Shibaura, Ishikawajima, or the arsenals. "The skilled and experienced among them, perhaps 80 to 90 percent, are either running their own factories or have saved some capital and have turned to some agricultural or commercial venture." [27]

Many of these workers failed in short order; it appears that desire for independence usually outran the ability to achieve it. Perhaps typical was the ill-fated attempt of one "An Rui Sei" (a pseudonym), inveterate traveler of the very early twentieth century, finally to leave the ranks of the "lunch-pail" (*bentō mochi*) laborer and found a bicycle-making operation. We never discover where he found the cash to start up, but, as he tells the tale in the Yūaikai journal some years later, the business soon failed when a customer with a history of bad debts back in distant Niigata could not pay for a major order. "An Rui" had already bought the parts and built the bicycles, and now he could neither pay nor stall his own creditors.[28] On the other hand, there is the occasional rags-to-riches saga offering hope to others like "An Rui." Ikegai Shōtarō was a lathe worker at Shibaura who left in the 1890s to set up shop on his own, with one hand-cranked machine, two apprentices, and his brother as the only adult "employee." At the time of World War I, he employed several hundred at the Ikegai Ironworks, and, by the 1980s, the firm had 2,000 employees and planned to invest in a factory in New York state.

Skilled workers also wanted respect from those in the mainstream of society. This spirit informed the activities of the Ironworkers Union, and, after this union failed, efforts to gain respect continued. The *Ni roku shimpō*, another paper interested in the plight of workers, sponsored a Workers' Festival, in essence a May Day without political overtones, on April 1, 1901. Speakers called for greater respect for workers and their contribution to society. The paper concluded that "the workers showed their true worth at this meeting," although a few roughnecks without tickets caused trouble by destroying property and later heading for the red-light district, Yoshiwara. Such people, the paper lamented, blemished the effect of a large, peaceful gathering and gave workers a bad name.[29] They also testify to the variety of behavior found among workers.

Along with hopes for independence and respect went efforts to help fellow workers. According to Katayama Sen, if a worker quit or was fired, others would try to help find him a job somewhere. "If he goes to another area there will be a worker willing to help him get a job at his factory, or, if not, put him up while trying to help him find work someplace."[30] A community spirit also surfaced within the work place in the form of customary practices of mutual aid, as described in 1899:

> Even in places where there are no unions, the workers carry out mutual aid. If a worker gets sick, the others at the factory get together and raise some money to take care of him. . . . They pass around a collection register, and everyone offers what he can. Especially at the arsenal,

which employs 6,000 workers, there are occasionally severe injuries or deaths, and in these cases the register is passed immediately. The usual practice is to contribute one hour's pay, but in especially severe or pitiful cases people give a half or a full day's pay. In the case of one old worker who fell and burned to death, over 500 yen were collected.[31]

Evidence of spontaneous mutual aid is not surprising. Work in these factories was indeed dangerous. The *Mainichi* estimated in 1899 that the average working life of an adult male lasted only from age 22 to age 40.[32] A mutual-aid fund was an important selling point for the Ironworkers Union of 1897 through 1900. Workers felt the need for such assistance, and some companies also responded by establishing mutual-aid societies. However, passing the register after the fact of an illness or injury was quite different from voluntarily contributing before the fact to a union aid fund or a company aid society. Ishikawajima set up a mutual-aid group in 1893, but the response was unenthusiastic. By 1902, only 80 of 623 workers were members.[33] The Ironworkers Union also encountered difficulty in collecting contributions to its fund. Workers likely to leave a company any month were not anxious to contribute to a company aid society, and a man who soon hoped to set up on his own and join the ranks of the small capitalists would not be anxious to support a union aid society.

How do we assess the apparently split personality of the Meiji worker, spendthrift in one account, determined to set up on his own in another, one day concerned above all with self-improvement and respectability, and the next likely to gamble and brawl in his spare time? Part of the problem is a matter of perspective. What managers saw as poor discipline—taking the day off after payday or windfall wages, or simply skipping work on a rainy day—can also be seen as the attempt by workers to maintain control over their lives; the social customs of an earlier day offered flexibility and a slower work pace. Frequent holidays are not necessarily a reliable sign of irresponsibility.

But perspective can not explain the full variety of worker behavior. Just as few Edo-ites exemplified at once all the characteristics ascribed to Edo urban culture, ranging from a stern merchant ethic to frivolous townsmen leisure habits, individual workers did not recapitulate all the traits present in the society as a whole. Some men probably modified their style with age, changing from a footloose traveler type to a sedentary worker. And finally, of course, individuals varied. Given the unsystematic quality of the evidence available, it is perilous, if tempting, to relate the varied types of workers to the varied backgrounds of the men in the Meiji factories. Certainly, the backgrounds were diverse and potentially influential: city or country born, literate or illiterate, factory trainee or Edo apprentice, are just a few axes of variation.

One distinction in particular was recognized as significant at the time. A wide range of observers, including some workers, suggest that a distinction in type of skill and training between men in trades new to Japan and those following indigenous crafts corresponded in a rough sort of way to the division of workers into men of more or less responsible ways.

Takayama Jiroichi entered the Ishikawajima yard as a boilermaker's apprentice in 1902. Boilermaking was a craft whose content derived in large measure from Edo-era foundry work, and Takayama graphically portrayed the distinctive boilermaker lifestyle. He first described the custom of the send-off subscription list. Ideally a form of *oyakata* welfare provided to charges going elsewhere to look for work, in this era the boilermakers abused the system:

> If I ran out of money, I would go to another factory. When I asked, "Who's the oyakata?" I would be told "so and so" and then, in today's terms, I'd threaten him. "I have to go to such and such a place, so give me traveling money." He would give me 3 or 4 yen and say, "Make this the end of it."

> The boilermakers of those days were by far the lowest. A joke of the time went like this: "Mother, mother, a boilermaker just went into the toilet!" "Don't worry about him. Even a boilermaker won't eat shit, so leave him alone." Even a coolie would run away when he saw a boilermaker.

Takayama also reported that some boilermakers followed the custom of the traditional gangster's greeting when meeting a new oyakata. This was a formalized litany in which the newcomer recited his birthplace, occupation, training, trainer, and work history (*jingi o kiru*).[34]

Indigenous skills such as boilermaking emphasized brawn and some know-how acquired with experience. The practitioners were reported to be a rough and tumble lot. Newer machine skills, by contrast, lathe or electrical work, required more school learning, systematic vocational training, and they made fewer physical demands. One labor manager at Mitsubishi's Kobe Shipyard in about 1914 summed up this distinction:

> Workers such as platers, blacksmiths, and boilermakers have violent personalities and rough behavior. Their ideas are not logical but simple and straightforward (*tanjun*). On the other hand, fitters, electricians, and other such workers are relatively clever, less violent, but more argumentative. The workers who talk back or argue logically with the attendance supervisor or inspector are usually of this type.[35]

In this managerial view, both types had their drawbacks. Workers may have been a varied crew, but they struck managers in almost all cases as unruly and unreliable.

Discipline was just one part of the problem from the management perspective. High mobility was another. Men in heavy industry moved frequently between factories or from large factories to small shops and back. Turnover in the textile industry was even greater, but the "mobility" of textile workers, usually teenage girls committed for only a short time to factory work, often took the form of escape from a heavily guarded dormitory. The travelers in heavy industry moved on their own terms, as was noted in 1902:

> Especially in times of prosperity when workers are in short supply, there are many who, on the basis of a trifling difference in wages, will readily switch to another factory ... or who constantly move from one large factory to another.[36]

For a similar statistical view of these mobile workers, consider the tenure distribution of the work force at the Ishikawajima Shipyard and Shibaura Engineering Works, in 1902 two of Tokyo's oldest (27 and 25 years) and largest private factories (Table 2). Over four-fifths of the work force had been on their present job for 5 years or less. The surveyors also remarked that, within a year, about half the workers shifted from one of these factories to the other.[37] On the other hand, the presence of even a minority of relatively long-term men is worth noting. Not all of the 15 to 20 percent with 6 years or more on the job could have been oyakata or foremen. This relatively sedentary minority, very likely including aspirants to higher rank within the firm, coexisted with the more numerous travelers. Indeed, it probably included graduates of the "traveler school" who at length had settled down at a single job.

Ishii Kumazō, in later years the head of the Uraga Dock Company's Kōaikai Union, was a typical young traveler just after the turn of the century. From 1901 until 1917, between the ages of 13 and 29, he changed jobs 8 times. Ishii began after elementary school at the Yokosuka Naval Shipyard as a trainee and stayed 4 years. Finally sure of his skill, he took a friend's advice and left for Osaka and the Sumitomo Casting Company, where he stayed another 2 years. His wages rose to double his pay at Yokosuka, but he tired of the factory and returned to try his luck at Uraga in about 1907. He soon left for Tokyo, spent 2 years in a small metal shop, and then moved to one of the arsenals. In 1910 or 1911 he returned to Uraga for a 2-year stint, spent 3 or 4 years in far southern Japan at a shipyard in Shimonoseki, and then returned to the Keihin area, working for a time at Yokosuka before entering Uraga for a third time in 1917. He remained until at least 1931.[38]

Mobility was similar among apprentices or trainees. Yokoyama remarked in 1898 that, although most Tokyo and Osaka metal or glass factories set the term for trainees at 5 or 6 years, very few trainees in fact completed their terms. "One hears that at a place such as Shibaura, where the company 'saves' over 20 yen on behalf of the worker out of his wages, to be returned on completion of his term, many trainees still run away from their contracts part

Table 2 Length of Continuous Employment at Shibaura and Ishikawajima, 1902

		Tenure						
		0–6 mos.	*7 mos.–1 yr.*	*2 yrs.*	*3 yrs.*	*4–5 yrs.*	*6 yrs.+*	*Total*
Shibaura	No.	113	64	64	66	74	77	458
	%	24.7	14	14	14.4	16.2	16.8	100
Ishikawajima	No.	79	63	120	148	99	114	623
	%	12.7	10.1	19.3	23.8	15.9	18.3	100

Source: Shokkō jijō, II, 11 (Shinkigensha edition)

way through, [losing the 20 yen]." He estimated that, in general, only about one-third of the trainees at such factories completed their terms.[39]

Some firms took steps beyond withholding of apprentice pay to retain skilled workers. They offered long-term contracts to a few, select skilled men, and groups of owners formed anti-poaching associations whose members agreed not to raid one another for talent. Also, the Yokosuka Naval Yard created a hierarchical pay scale in part to encourage workers to stay and rise within the company. These policies were ineffective. One worker wrote in 1898 that, although owners have been employing various means to keep labor in place and entice workers elsewhere to come to their factory, "in fact they are still troubled with spontaneous job-switching as well as poaching."[40]

Inducements to stay failed in part because most workers did not move from job to job merely in search of higher wages. Mobility was a central part of the "proper" worker career. The custom of "traveling" predated the high demand for skilled labor of the late nineteenth century. An anonymous machinist in 1898 provides an apt summary of this attitude to work and job-switching:

> A worker is someone who enters society with his skills and who travels far and wide with them. Who could possibly credit with a spirit of advancement those workers who cling to a single place and put up with all sorts of abuse? . . . Past and present, whatever the occupation, a worker is someone who travels broadly, enters factories here and there, accumulates greater skills and, overcoming adversity, finally becomes a worker deserving of the name.[41]

Standing between the traveler and the technical supervisor or manager frustrated at his mobility was the senior member of working-class society of the late nineteenth century, called by the traditional term for master, *oyakata*. The oyakata were a varied lot. Some owned small machine shops or shipyards, some were independent labor bosses who would contract the services of their charges to various large companies, some were labor bosses providing men exclusively for a particular large factory, and some were just powerful foremen, unable to intervene between company and worker to the extent of setting work contracts but able, nonetheless, to exercise much independent authority over hiring and wage decisions.[42] Oyakata of all types were important. They exercised some control over wage payment to the workers, either through distribution of contract fees or by setting the rate at which the company was to pay each worker. They served to some extent as employers, either hiring their own apprentices and subordinate laborers or making hiring decisions on behalf of the company. They had some responsibility for the training of apprentices or new workers. The oyakata all occupied positions of more or less independence between the company and the rest of the workers.

Ozawa Benzō of the Ishikawajima Shipyard and Aida Kichigorō of a Hakodate yard, two activists in the Meiji labor movement, were described as typical oyakata in the 1902 *Shokkō jijō* survey. They were independent operators, but they maintained a relationship with a particular company. They trained their own apprentices, whom they lodged and fed at their homes and led to work in a group. They set apprentice wages and paid them out of a lump sum received from the company, keeping a portion for themselves. In other cases, oyakata in the direct employ of a company were given no clear responsibility for apprentice training, and, with nothing to gain from the trainees, they were unenthusiastic teachers.[43]

By the early 1900s, oyakata more closely associated with a particular company gradually increased in number, while the fully independent labor boss lost ground. Yokoyama Gennosuke reports that, while the independent oyakata had been quite strong in Tokyo in around 1895, in 1905 he was part of a vanishing breed.[44] Yet, the status of oyakata and their relationship to the enterprise was never uniform; their decline was slow. The government Factory Report of 1904 stated that oyakata were still active in major shipyards and other large machine factories.[45] Even in the early twentieth century, managers could not ignore these men, for they possessed the skill, experience, and judgment necessary to organize the work process and actually get the job done. Technical supervisors just above them in rank had replaced the foreign advisors of earlier decades but lacked their qualifications. A sharp gap in status and in competence separated school-educated but ineffective technicians and the oyakata trained on the job, leading the director of the Shibaura Engineering Works to complain in 1903 that "there are very few technicians rich in skill and experience. Those so-called technicians are such in name only, and the real responsibility is in fact given over to the workers."[46] To cross cultures and borrow a more memorable phrase from Big Bill Haywood of the American I.W.W., also circa 1900, "The manager's brains are under the workman's cap."[47]

Working-class society at the turn of the century stymied managers who hoped to exercise "real responsibility." Mobile workers unreceptive to discipline were separated from their supervisors by their low social status and lack of commitment to the company. One management response was to surrender direct control over workers to the oyakata. At the same time, innovations in wage policy aimed at the travelers planted seeds of a more enduring, distinctive Japanese wage structure that would take root and grow in subsequent decades.

MEIJI LABOR RELATIONS
THE DILEMMA OF INDIRECT CONTROL

Indirect control over labor was an improvised, stopgap response of Meiji industrial managers. The technical supervisors criticized at Shibaura as "irresponsible" stood at the lower end of the management hierarchy, but they could not deal effectively with the workers beneath them. Several schools founded in the nineteenth century produced a steady flow of these technicians, who replaced foreign instructors sent home in the 1880s. Training institutes connected with the Yokosuka Naval Shipyard and the Tokyo Workers School, established in 1881, were among the most prominent.[48] The graduates hired by public and private factories had little practical understanding of the work process and a strong sense of social distance from the uneducated workers. They were aloof, stern, unpopular figures. The work-place air on occasion crackled with tension between workers and supervisors, as at this machine factory described in the *Shokkō jijō* survey of 1902:

> Y was a former head technical supervisor. He was quite distinguished [*erai*] and often scolded or reprimanded us. Once he called together all the foremen and told us that he had worked before in a textile factory and had almost been killed several times. "If any of you guys get upset and pull something like organizing a union, there'll be no forgiving you. If you bear any grudge and want to kill me, go ahead." At these words there was silence.[49]

If his knowledge and experience had been convincing, working men would likely have accepted the right of such a man to swagger. In fact, technicians lacked the competence to legitimize their authority. Another worker in 1902 complained that "there are many technicians these days who are unable to do their jobs as well as an oyakata." According to this man, even if an oyakata is not present during the actual work period, he can tell from the result whether the apprentice has been lazy, careless, or incompetent. The worker is afraid that, if he is found out, he will be let go by the oyakata, "so unlike cases where company technicians oversee the workers, there is no fooling around."[50] And a skilled machinist echoed this chorus in 1910:

> Today's so-called technicians have a grounding in theory but almost no knowledge of practical operations in the factory, which are in fact carried out entirely by the workers . . . but the technicians are unhappy with this, and the two sides don't get along well.[51]

Managers at least through the turn of the century had little choice but to adopt a strategy of indirect labor supervision and abdicate control of the work place to experienced oyakata. They lacked the experience or ability to control labor directly. A technician at the Mitsubishi Nagasaki Shipyard made the point emphatically:

> First, the company had no experience with construction work. Also it was difficult for the company to make direct contact with the workers. These were the primary reasons. In order to make up for the first of these defects the company had to rely on people with the necessary

technical expertise, and in the second place had to seek people with the strength to control the unruly workers. They were in the difficult position of looking for people who combined both these qualities. To put it simply, the company had to turn over management of the factory to the oyakata.[52]

The companies that adopted the indirect management strategy would procure orders for machinery, ships, or ship repair and then offer the job or part of it to various oyakata or foremen, usually through competitive bidding. The successful bidder would take responsibility for the job and pay his workers out of the price agreed upon, keeping the rest as profit. Members of the work group expected the successful bidder to share part of his profit as drinking money.[53] Even in 1865, a supervisor at the Nagasaki Ironworks recommended adopting an indirect management policy in a prescient memorandum. The only way to motivate lazy workers, he felt, was to take management authority away from bakufu officials, turn it over to supervisors with commercial motives, and appeal to the worker's instinct for profit by adopting a job-contracting system. In the rather primitive scheme he recommended, to no avail, the work group would contract for an entire job, buy the necessary materials, and keep the remainder of the job fee as its pay.[54] This plan was merely a bit ahead of its time. The indirect forms of labor management that developed in the following decades were quite similar.

One of the best descriptions of indirect management in action is left to us by Takayama Jiroichi, the Ishikawajima boilermaker:

> The shipyard did not hire me directly. Actually, at that time the person you would today [1961] call supervising foreman, who was then called *tōmoku,* held all the authority regarding hiring and firing. When seeking work we went to the *tōmoku* and asked, "Can you use me?" and he would answer, "All right, come tomorrow!" or "No, come back in a month," and the decision would be made right there. . . . Ishikawajima did not give out pay directly either. The *tōmoku* passed out wages at the entrance to each shop.[55]

The company did intervene formally between worker and *tō-moku* to some extent. It set a scale of day wages for regular workers ranging from 25 sen to 1.25 yen a day. It also took 1 day's pay per month from each apprentice and placed this in a "savings account" to be returned after completion of the term, and took a 3-yen "security deposit" from new apprentices. Taka-yama, as an apprentice, received periodic 2-sen-per-day raises from the company during the 7-year apprenticeship, which he never completed. He left Ishikawajima for the first time in 1904, forfeiting savings and deposit. In practice, such intervention was quite limited. "The Ishikawajima factory does not pay a bit of attention to worker education," according to a worker in 1898. An Ishika-wajima oyakata such as Ozawa Benzō, mentioned above, lodged, fed, and trained his own apprentices, all nominally employed by the company.[56]

Ishikawajima was typical. The Shibaura Engineering Works also relied on indirect control of labor. The company history of 1940 relates, "As with other factories, since the company was founded we have paid wages on a job contract basis." Shibaura managers were not happy with this. "It led to the evil of the oyakata boss keeping a percentage of those wages he was supposed to pay to the workers under his control."[57]

Managers controlled work indirectly out of necessity, but in time they resolved to create a more systematic, direct mode of labor supervision. A few enterprises began this effort in the nineteenth century. Some established a scale of day wages and ranks which implied that the company and not the oyakata evaluated workers and set pay. Some tried to by-pass the oyakata and sign selected men to long-term contracts on an individual basis. Others contracted with individuals for a given job, again circumventing the oyakata. These practices were reported to be on the rise by 1902. Some companies offered semiannual bonuses equivalent to one month's wage to workers with good records. Another strategy for controlling these men more directly was to impose fines and other punishments for tardiness, gambling, or smoking on the job, taking responsibility for discipline away from the oyakata. Finally, firms adopted forced savings plans, deducting from wages to keep individual workers "hostage."[58]

Continued high mobility in the Meiji years suggests these initiatives seldom drew workers into a closer relationship with the company. They placed only partial limits on the power of the oyakata, who were still the ones to decide who was slotted where in the wage scale, who was given how great a pay raise, who was signed to a long-term contract, or who was rewarded with a bonus or punished with a fine. Despite efforts to change the indirect style and despite some limits placed on oyakata authority, the indirect management strategy remained the most common approach in heavy industry in the nineteenth century.

At the Yokosuka Naval Yard, managers made a more determined effort to establish a direct mode of labor control. In the 1870s, the foremen and lower-level supervisors who trained new men and supervised shop-floor operations had themselves started out as lowly workers. Some were retrained artisans; the Russians at Heda harbor had trained at least one Yokosuka foreman in the 1850s. Others were individuals of commoner origin, recruited by Yokosuka and trained on the job by French instructors.[59] Actual control of the work process lay in worker hands. Staff technicians were few and controlled operations only indirectly.

This system was not working to the satisfaction of Yokosuka managers, who complained to the Naval Ministry in 1882 that the one or two technical supervisors per workshop could not adequately keep track of the attendance or diligence of the men or prevent the waste of materials. According to management, the problem lay in the vaguely defined responsibilities of these few lower level technicians (*kōshu*). These men were for the most part graduates of the Yokosuka Training School who were supposed to control the regular workers but could not do so. The yard therefore instituted reforms in 1882, creating work groups of from 7 to 15 workers and placing at the head of each group, as foreman (*gochō*), one of these technicians not of worker origin. They received caps as symbols of their new status directly above the workers. Yet, Yokosuka abandoned this attempt to assert more direct control of the work group several years later. Reforms in the work system in 1889 and 1890 specified that the foreman *be chosen from among the workers* in each work group; the yard returned control of the work process to the workers and their own leaders.[60]

The failure of the Yokosuka reforms highlights the impermeability of Meiji working-class society. The additional failure of wage policies designed to temper the wanderlust of the skilled traveler draws this same feature into sharper focus.

The income of workers in the nineteenth century derived from a combination of day wages and payment by the job or the piece. Such "payments by result" took a number of forms. The Halsey and Rowan premium systems were developed in the United States in the 1890s, and companies in Japan were using them before the decade had ended. One attraction was the possibility for supervisors to gain greater control over the work process by setting standard times or rates for particular jobs, but these early efforts at job, incentive, or piece-rate systems were primitive and unstable. Unit prices changed often, and in practice the oyakata themselves often set the rates.[61] Even so, managers persisted in the use of such wages. Whether control was direct or indirect, they felt the need for incentive pay stimuli. Yokoyama claimed that "almost all metal factories use job-contract wages to prevent loafing and increase productivity."[62] Use of a wide range of incentive wage schemes was one significant innovation of the nineteenth century that remained part of management strategy for decades. The managerial image of the lazy, uncooperative worker died hard.

The fixed day wage was the other major component of a worker's income. In the face of the fluid labor market, firms naturally set the day-wage portion on the basis of the experience and skill each man brought to the job. Work rules at Shibaura in 1893 specified that "an applicant's wages will be set according to his ability, as judged in a one-week testing period."[63] In addition to recruiting experienced men in this fashion, most companies encouraged aspirations to rise in rank and pay within the enterprise by constructing wage ladders of more or less complexity. Government enterprises such as the Yokosuka Naval Shipyard used the most elaborate wage scales. In 1873, Yokosuka instituted a hierarchy of

21 ranks, each with a corresponding day wage, ranging from 10 sen for the lowest trainee to 50 sen for the top supervisor.[64]

In adopting this wage scale, Yokosuka managers recognized that the lack of opportunity for advancement was an important cause of turnover and the loss of skilled workers. A wage ladder would encourage a worker to stick with the Yard and gradually climb in rank and pay. These were the arguments offered by the French supervisor, Verney, in recommending a similar policy in 1867; such thinking led to the 1873 pay scales.[65] Private companies did not generally use such elaborate wage hierarchies in the nineteenth century, but for similar reasons most began to offer yearly or semiannual pay raises to some of the workers. Managers hoped thereby to induce valued workers to stay with a firm.[66]

These pay scales, especially the complex ladder used at Yokosuka, were major innovations of the late nineteenth century. On the one hand, they represented a response to the labor market, since they sought to attract skilled workers. Pay at hiring rewarded the skill brought to the job. As at Shibaura, a worker sought by Yokosuka performed several tasks during a short evaluation period and was then slotted into the elaborate pay hierarchy at a level reflecting his ability.[67] No evidence suggests that in this era he was penalized as a mid-career entrant.

Wage scales of this period also sought to strengthen the *organization* of the firm, by keeping workers at Yokosuka or elsewhere in a direct relationship not mediated by oyakata. In this respect they enjoyed little success. A memorandum of 1875 at Yokosuka, two years after the new wage system was adopted, reports that the yard continued to face the problem of turnover among skilled workers, and, by the turn of the century, workers at the naval yards, arsenals, and private firms were still traveling, to the dismay of management; offers of promotion up a ladder of rank and pay did not induce them to stay.[68] Many companies stipulated pay raises at regular intervals in their work rules, but practice did not in fact go by the book. Yokoyama describes a variety of factories where only a portion of the work force won a raise in any given year or half-year, where inferior workers able to curry favor with the foremen gained arbitrary raises, and where in bad times firms cut pay or suspended increases for all workers to reduce costs and trim the work force by driving men away. To the extent that it came at all, promotion up a ladder of rank and wage levels was an unreliable reward for a minority of skilled workers.[69] In 1902, the *Shokkō jijō* research team interviewed two metalworkers living close by Ishikawajima and Shibaura and perhaps employed by one or the other. The younger of the two, age 34, had been with his company for 7 years. His day wage was 60 sen. His older friend, age 53, was only receiving 50 sen each day from the same company, despite 15 or 16 years on the job.[70] Skill determined a man's day wage at entry, and, unless favoritism or bad times intervened, it was the major influence upon subsequent pay raises. For young travelers like Ishii Kumazō or Takayama Jiroichi, pay increased through a career of job-switching. Skills acquired with experience were recognized with better offers from new employers as well as pay hikes at a single firm.

Nonetheless, this practice of increasing the day wage at theoretically regular intervals was the most distinctive innovation introduced into the labor relationship by nineteenth-century managers in Japan. The day wage was only part of total income, and raises were inconsistent rewards for a minority of skilled men. Yet, by the end of World War II, the regular "seniority wage increase" was nearly universal in heavy industry and other sectors of the economy, and, by the 1980s, Western observers were acclaiming it as one key to Japanese managerial success in building attachment to the firm. The first application of this idea in a factory setting came at a few government and private enterprises in the early decades of Japanese industrialization.

The regular raise was a response to day-to-day problems of slowing turnover and eliciting consistent, diligent service from the traveling worker. It was a rational step in the particular situation facing managers in the Meiji era.[71] The scarcity of skilled industrial workers in a society undergoing a sort of forced, relatively late industrialization led many Japanese managers early on to view the high rates of turnover as a major cost. In taking steps to reduce it, they apparently looked for clues to the more prestigious government bureaucratic organizations (or possibly their own white-collar divisions) where hierarchies of rank and pay were already in place. But to identify the *origins* of this practice in the strategy to slow turnover is barely to begin our story. Managers extended the regular pay raise and the possibility of rising in the firm downward to workers, in very gradual, piecemeal fashion. What were the factors that, over a period of 60 years, brought about the expansion and elaboration of the limited regular raise of the nineteenth century? While their concern does not appear at a similarly early stage of industrialization, managers in the United States and Europe at times viewed turnover as a problem, especially during and after World War I in the United States. But their strategies to secure labor did not produce similar extended wage ladders and regular promotions with little connection to job content or skill level. Part of the task of this book is to show how, in Japan, pressures exerted by workers and government bureaucrats interacted with management strategy to prevent Meiji wage policies from fading into obscurity as a curious relic of the early industrial era.

Managers of Japan's early heavy industrial enterprises had few indigenous precedents to guide them in developing a strategy of labor management. As a community of footloose workers unfamiliar with and unreceptive to strict discipline emerged, managers and technicians responded as best they could. They managed their factories indirectly, and they paid wages rewarding the traveler's skill but designed to keep hold of experienced workers. This was never a stable structure of control. Yokosuka tried to change to more indirect management. The Shibaura criticism of the "evil" of this system reflected a common management perspective. By the turn of the century, companies increasingly imposed their own wage structures on the oyakata; the indirect control structure was beginning to crumble. Yokoyama observed that one rarely found independent oyakata by 1905.[72] The vulnerability of the oyakata, trained on the job and unable to keep up with the introduction of more sophisticated technology from abroad which began in the 1890s, made possible the effort of the early 1900s to replace the oyakata with foremen integrated into a company control structure.

THE LABOR MOVEMENT AND THE WORKING CLASS

Mobile travelers exasperated the first union organizers in Japan as well as managers. The Meiji union movement reached its short-lived peak between 1897 and 1900, when a few social reformers enjoyed some success in building a union movement among skilled working men in Tokyo, Yokohama, and points north. They failed to sustain a lasting union, despite early, enthusiastic support in 1897, for some of the same reasons managers could not impose control directly on laborers. High mobility and petty bourgeois aspirations meant fluctuating membership rolls, unsteady payment of dues, and ineffective mutual aid. By 1899, even before the Peace Police Law placed a major legal barrier in front of union activities, active membership in the most successful group, the Ironworkers Union, had already dwindled from its height of 3,000 in 1898 to about 1,000. By late 1900, the union had all but dissolved. It would be 12 years before another labor organization of greater lasting import emerged.

Despite its institutional failure, the Meiji labor movement revealed patterns of organizational behavior and worker consciousness that would persist for decades, in some respects to this day, exerting continued impact upon the labor movement and labor relations.

An incipient Japanese working-class consciousness can be discerned in the demands raised in several nineteenth-century labor disputes, some involving the Ironworkers Union, and similar attitudes would characterize the labor movement in later decades. In separate actions in 1898 and 1899, locomotive engineers and machinists at the Japan Railway Company (JRC) pressed, with mixed success, for improved status within the enterprise, greater respect, and an end to what they called "discriminatory" treatment. Locomotive engineers, in 1898, demanded and gained rank equivalent to that of office staff and new job titles with positive connotations to replace existing titles which connoted low status and disrespect. From 1899 to early 1900, JRC machinists also demanded (and were denied) new titles as well as better treatment (*taigū*), the latter defined as the treatment already accorded the engineers. They specifically sought more rapid promotions, the semiannual pay raises and bonuses offered to white-collar officials and technicians, and reform of the confiscatory company savings plan.[73] These demands of the 1890s would be echoed by more politically aware workers of later decades, who inherited the concern of the railway workers for respect and status while they added the concern for the rights of labor. The desire or demand for "human treatment" and better terms of membership continued to be part of Japanese worker consciousness in the twentieth century.

The persistent call by Meiji-era workers for respect and treatment on a par with white-collar employees reflected an acute sense of an extremely low, if not in fact deteriorating, place in society. Nineteenth-century workers were neither respected nor well treated, despite the dismantling of the rigid Tokugawa class structure which had sanctioned discrimination by status. Almost all subjects of the Meiji Emperor were commoners in the 1890s; former samurai, peasants, artisans, and merchants were nominally social equals, but one senses that the skilled worker had fallen a notch since the Restoration. In Tokugawa Japan, the artisan ranked nominally above the merchant, at least, but, by the late nineteenth century, the new merchants of a vigorous capitalist society were popular heroes and models even for the children of former samurai.[74] By 1900, the new order of supposed equality was several decades old, yet many workers felt they were in fact part of a despised underclass. The samurai and artisans of Tokugawa cities had been separated by a legal status barrier; the educated, salaried bureaucrats, white-collar employees, or technicians, and the skilled wage laborers of Meiji industrial society were separated by a gap in social status equally forbidding. The workers were people left behind with little education and less hope for advancement. In the new era of self help and the self-made man, this was especially galling. The attitudes of JRC engineers and machinists, and insistent worker calls for respect from the mainstream of society, were early responses to a contradiction between the nominal leveling of old status distinctions and the persistence of semi-outcast status for many workers.[75]

Of equal importance, a Japanese mode of working-class organization can be discerned in the structure and goals of the nineteenth-century unions. Workers of later periods would organize themselves by workshop, factory, and company, not by craft, just as the iron-workers had done. This recurrent pattern first appeared in the 1890s. The Ironworkers Union called itself a craft union, but close analysis of its composition reveals that it was in fact an amorphous industrial union of workers in metal and engineering trades organized on the basis of workshop or factory units.[76]

Meiji workers organized factory unions by default. Because artisan society of the Tokugawa era offered them a declining tradition of craft organization limited to urban guilds, there was no other sensible place to begin. In sharp contrast to workers in England, other parts of Europe, and America, the Meiji workers had little access to a preindustrial tradition of inter-urban, regional, or national craft organization, formal or informal. This very different point of departure led to a very different labor history. In England and the United States, early unions built broad horizontal networks of mutual support and mutual aid. These unions were organized by craft and marked by a fairly inclusive sense of membership. All millwrights or masons were brothers in the craft. Trade unions naturally emerged from a well-developed tradition of craft organization.[77]

In Japan, this style of craft union was exceptional. Even in the case of ship carpenters, who built effective craft unions in both Yokohama and Tokyo in the 1890s, contacts between the carpenters in these two nearby cities were limited and informal in the 1890s. The future did not bring the spread of this type of craft union to other trades in heavy industry. Neither oyakata nor travelers ever asserted control over skill acquisition or entry to the trade; their predecessors had not done so and they, too, hardly made the effort. Had the oyakata in the Ironworkers Union been interested in maintaining horizontal craft links, they could have created institutional ties among several unions composed of workers in a single craft. They did not. Organization by craft was never a possibility. For Meiji labor activists, the founding of workshop or factory locals was a natural and sensible strategy. The workshop and the factory were the daily meeting places for workers where organizing activity, as well as work, took place.

While Japan's nineteenth-century labor movement failed, working-class society of the turn of the century remained an entity more or less unto itself, resistant to the efforts of company managers to intervene in the workplace. This society, marked by customs derived from the preindustrial past, posed a challenge to managers and union organizers alike. Managers had difficulty controlling men uncomfortable with factory discipline who believed advancement in skill or pay required frequent job-switching. Unions were unable to gain consistent support from men who viewed factory labor as a temporary phase in their careers and did not see themselves as lifelong wage earners or "brothers" in a trade.

Looking to the future from 1900, one would have predicted the reemergence of a strong union movement and the evolution of a Japanese species of class consciousness before predicting the advent of workers who closely identified with their employers. If not conscious of themselves as a class, most workers of this era unhappily placed themselves in the category of the working poor (*kasō shakai*). Very few felt themselves to be members of a particular company, and workers had not generally accepted the discipline of factory labor.[78] The following decades would witness a struggle between managers intent upon drawing workers, especially the oyakata, more tightly under company control and workers trying to raise their social status and build a labor movement upon the basis of workshop or factory organization.

TWO

Paternalism and Direct Management

MOTIVES FOR CHANGE

Indirect management was inefficient. Change in the technology of industrial production and corresponding specialization in the work process made this clear first to the largest and richest firms as early as the late 1890s. Beginning around the turn of the century, those most sensitive to the possibility that ineffective labor management drained profits undertook to devise a new structure of more direct control of work. Some of the middle-sized enterprises in the Keihin area, on the other hand, lagged over a decade behind in both the import of new capital equipment and changes in labor management.[1]

In the 1890s and early 1900s, equipment in even the leading firms was often primitive, with electric-powered machinery in short supply or not available. Managers relied on the manual skills of versatile, unspecialized artisans, either wood or metal workers, usually under control of oyakata masters. At the Kawasaki Shipyard in Kōbe in 1893, the separate shipbuilding and boilermaking sections shared two inadequate punching and shearing machines.[2] Manual skills demanding long experience were important even in new trades such as lathe work or machine finishing, one reason managers could still slide by relying on the unsystematic on-the-job training offered by oyakata masters. Takayama Jiroichi described work at Ishikawajima around 1902:

> I entered as an apprentice in the boiler section. . . . Things weren't so finely divided with a crane section, a shipbuilding section. Shipbuilding in those days could include anything. . . . We did planing, riveting, and drilling. Artisans of those days had to do everything. If they couldn't, they wouldn't be hired. . . . There was no speciality called riveter. Everyone was a shipworker (*zōsenkō*).

He notes that shipworkers also did marking and shaping of the metal and caulking. Asked whether markers did only marking, he replied:

> No. They used blueprints for big objects, but if it was small you made it yourself. A beam or a frame would be marked according to a pattern, but you marked a small object youself, and cut, bent, and planed it yourself. . . . We did riveting by hand, not pneumatic hammer. We drove the rivets with a meter-long hammer. We really had to lift it. . . . Half bent over the bottom of the ship, three of us would take turns driving the rivets. Before the rivet cooled down, we would rush to take turns pounding it. Also, there was someone who pushed down the metal sheet from the backside, called the *ateban*. We used a coal furnace to heat the rivets. It took four or five people to do the job.[3]

Even at Shibaura, considered the leading engineering firm in Japan, a place where the new, relatively cerebral trade of the machinist dominated, manual skills were important. The company history reported that "even a product finished on a tooling machine would not be sufficiently rounded or sufficiently squared, and would have to be entirely refinished by the hands of an experienced, skilled finishing worker (*shiagekō*).[4]

Just before the turn of the century, operations began to change in the large government enterprises and a few of the leading private companies, which introduced pneumatic hammers, overhead moving cranes, and some electric welding equipment. Increased specialization came with machines demanding specific new skills. The jack-of-all-trades shipworker or boilermaker gave way to the riveter, the driller, the layout man, and the puncher. The naval shipyards at Yokosuka and Kure and the Yahata Ironworks led the way among government enterprises, while the Kawasaki and Mitsubishi shipyards were leading innovators in the private sector.[5]

At Yokosuka an increase of 40 to 50 new machines a year in 1905 and 1906 brought with it greater specialization. The shipbuilding section was divided into 11 different shops in 1907, where previously there had been 4. The dock section expanded from 4 to 10 shops. The Kure Naval Yard broke down the category of shipbuilder into riveter, caulker, driller, and woodworker. Kawasaki greatly expanded its machine facilities. In 1893, there had been 2 punching and shearing machines for the entire yard; in 1903, there were 7 larger such machines for the exclusive use of the shipbuilding section, plus several other large electric or hydraulic machines. Due to similar advances, in 1904 the Mitsubishi Nagasaki Shipyard divided the previous catch-all category of ship assembly work into 6 specific categories: plater, anglesmith, caulker, furnace plater, driller, and riveter. Mechanization and specialization generally came first to the Kansai area where the largest shipyards were found, but eventually the considerable movement of workers among all these enterprises helped diffuse new skills.[6]

Pneumatic machinery and electric welding equipment did not reach Ishikawajima until World War I. Both had been used first at the Kawasaki yard in Kōbe and at Mitsubishi's Nagasaki yard, and, by virtue of a stint working in Kōbe, Takayama Jiroichi, now back at Ishikawajima, was familiar with the use of these machines.[7] With the advent of the pneumatic hammer, Ishikawajima differentiated riveters and caulkers for the first time, and divided occupations within the shipbuilding, forging, and installing sections into narrower categories. By 1917, workers specialized as riveters, caulkers, drillers, fitters, or plate shapers in all these shops.[8]

Such change in technology and the organization of work led managers to orchestrate workshop activity directly. Once they installed expensive machinery and set small work groups of from 5 to 15 individuals to work on narrowly defined tasks, smooth coordination of activities within and among work groups and workshops took on far greater importance than before; but managers, attempting to superintend an increasingly complex work process with greater efficiency, faced major challenges. The success of most work depended on the skill and judgment of foremen and workers with considerable experience, on cooperation among small work groups, and on teamwork within these units. Coordination and direct control of the activities of a wide range of such groups was no simple matter, for managers still had to defer to the judgment of experienced group leaders.[9]

NEW DEPARTURES: SHIBAURA AND ELSEWHERE

Policies of direct control usually began with efforts to limit oyakata power by drawing these men into the company as privileged foremen who would control their subordinates but follow management directions. The oyakata was to trade his freedom for the security and status offered by the company, not an unattractive proposition in an era when many were already losing the wherewithal to maintain their independence. Of course, even as foremen, these shop-floor coordinators retained authority and discretion; the effort to turn them into loyal company men was not simple or always successful. Managers also took some steps to extend their authority over the large body of regular workers. Policy toward them sought above all to encourage efficiency and stricter discipline, and in some cases to persuade the traveler to stay put. Enticements included retirement or severance pay, wages partially pegged to tenure, bonuses for attendance or long service, company-run mutual-aid societies, savings plans, and other welfare programs.[10]

Training programs were also part of the attempt to draw skilled workers into a more direct and dependent relationship with a firm. At the very largest enterprises, the Mitsubishi Nagasaki Shipyard and the Yahata Ironworks, company-sponsored education meant the creation of a company school. For the rest of even the larger heavy industrial firms, the dispatch of selected workers to local vocational training schools offered an affordable alternative. These programs sought to cultivate a core group of committed workers, potential foremen, and shop-floor leaders. Education programs broader in scope, encompassing regular workers, did not begin until World War I at the earliest.

The articulation of a paternal ideology in this era was another step designed in part to encourage dependence on the firm, although businessmen directed their praise of paternalism (*onjōshugi*) as much at the government as at the workers. Bureaucrats lobbying in favor of a factory law beginning in the 1890s provoked leading capitalists and company managers to extoll time and again the beauty of old Japanese customs of loyalty and benevolence, their importance to modern industry, and to stress the destruction such a law would wreak on them. Industry leaders refined and polished these well-worn arguments, seemingly oblivious to the actual shopfloor situation. They used them to cool the ardor of bureaucrats eager to impose legal reforms or to silence workers demanding higher wages.

The history of labor and labor management at Shibaura Engineering Works offers a comprehensive, if worm's-eye, view of these major changes. Direct control, company education, and paternalism were all part of Shibaura's reform of labor management of the early 1900s. In 1887, the company had been one of Japan's largest private firms, with 680 workers manufacturing steam engines and boilers for use on land and sea, but within six years Shibaura was on the verge of failure. It could not compete with both more advanced foreign manufacturers of generators and transformers and less expensive domestic electric and engineering firms which emerged in the 1890s to compete effectively at home for the first time. Adding to Shibaura's woes, the Navy, a major source of orders, developed its own machine-engineering capacity at Yokosuka. In 1893, the original owner of the Works, Tanaka Hisashige, sold a debt-ridden enterprise of only 135 employees to the Mitsui Bank. This sale marked a turning point for both Shibaura and Mitsui. It was the first zaibatsu move into the electric heavy industrial sector of the economy, and Mitsui financed significant expansion and reorganization of Shibaura. By 1898, the Engineering Works employed 750 workers and 96 staff employees.[11]

Mitsui quickly fired many of Tanaka's executives and technicians and brought in over a dozen of its own professional managers, but it took seven years for the Mitsui team even to make a dent in the Shibaura problem. Shibaura lost money steadily throughout the 1890s as two young Mitsui stars tried and failed to turn the fortunes of the enterprise around. In 1896, Ono Yūjirō correctly identified a confused array of products and inefficient production as the major problems, but he could do nothing to change this. As the company continued to lose money, there was some talk of closing it.[12] In 1897, control of the works shifted to Wakayama Genkichi, originally a naval technician and a young protégé of Masuda Takashi, himself the star young manager of the Mitsui enterprises in the mid-Meiji years. Wakayama recognized an insufficient machine capacity as part of Shibaura's problem in 1898. A sharp rise in production only increased overtime and production costs, eating away at profits. Wakayama sent a plaintive memorandum to his Mitsui superiors: "If we produce more, our losses will increase." He concluded that Shibaura employed far too much manual labor and too few machines. "There is no profit in stubbornly clinging to old customs at a time when machines are able to do 20 to 30 times the work of a manual laborer with greater precision and ease."[13] Wakayama tried to steer Shibaura toward shipbuilding, using his naval connections to secure contracts, and he followed up on his commitment to add new machinery and facilities. This brought a surge of activity to the Works, but Wakayama died suddenly in 1899 before his plans had revealed much potential. In the three years of his tenure, the company continued to run in the red, and discussion of selling the Works continued at Mitsui's top level.

Wakayama tried to lead Shibaura down the same path toward technical modernization chosen by Kawasaki, Mitsubishi, Yokosuka, and Kure during this period, but he did not change the social organization of factory life as he imported new machines. Ōtaguro Jūgorō and Kobayashi Sakutarō, the former a young Mitsui protégé made Director of Shibaura in 1899 at age 34, the latter in turn a protégé of Ōtaguro, finally took decisive steps in 1900 to inaugurate a new era of direct control at Shibaura.[14] Ōtaguro saw Shibaura's fundamental problem in human as well as technological terms; he recognized that new machines would only be effective with improved control of labor. In the early 1900s, Ōtaguro reduced the product line, focusing on electric motors, and introduced more sophisticated machinery, but his major concerns were to raise efficiency and assert stricter discipline. He fired technicians who did not come up to his standards of diligence and loyalty, reorganized the company's divisions, and took firm steps to eliminate the powerful oyakata. He fired several of these men, who supervised and in fact "employed" the regular workers in each shop, and who were notorious for biting off large chunks of job contract wages.[15]

These changes directly challenged the structure of indirect management, at Shibaura called the "village-headman" system, where oyakata stood, as had Tokugawa village leaders, between higher authority (the company, the domain) and the workers or villagers. Yokosuka management two decades earlier had failed in a similar attempt, suggesting that a few firings could not change a management style deeply rooted in Meiji social structure. The oyakata provided informal, if arbitrary, benefits and care to their followers. Would the workers not object to their elimination? Part of Ōtaguro's cleverness was, as he eliminated the abuses of the arbitrary labor boss, to substitute for some of the lost oyakata functions. He moved with some care as he began a savings system and a program of injury compensation, loosened requirements for overtime and night work, and eliminated fines for tardiness.[16]

Ōtaguro and his sidekick, Kobayashi, appointed Factory Director in 1900, together erected a new structure of control in place of the "village headman" system. Its two supporting pillars were closer staff direction of production and the integration of foremen, functional equivalents of the old oyakata, more directly into the staff hierarchy.

They gradually imposed tighter staff supervision between 1900 and 1907. Most important was a new hierarchy of control in each of the 6 separate workshops (machine finishing, wiremaking, wood-pattern cutting, metal casting, boilermaking, and foundry work). Before 1900, at Shibaura as everywhere else, staff presence on the shop floor was limited and ill-defined, with just a factory supervisor in each shop and several technicians below him. Technicians were university graduates with excellent qualifications, but they could not keep order in the factory. Ōtaguro moved to expand the corps of supervisors, clarify their jobs, and put them in closer touch with laborers. In August 1900, he placed a work director at the head of each shop and put two levels of staff assistant below him. In 1905, the term *work director* was changed to *factory director,* and, in 1907, a third rank of staff assistant was inserted in each shop. At the same time, Ōtaguro forced staff employees in the factory to put in the same hours as the workers (6:30 a.m. to 5:30 p.m.). He simply began to enforce a rule that required staff to do this. Prior to this, factory supervisors apparently wandered in closer to 8:00 a.m., a practice not conducive to close control of work.[17] Through these reforms, management began to control work at Shibaura directly.

Critical to the success of this program was the integration into this new company hierarchy of the foremen who replaced the oyakata-village headmen. Ōtaguro tried simultaneously to strengthen the ties between foremen and staff and sharpen the distinction between the foremen (all of worker origin) and the regular workers under their control. In 1902, Shibaura formed an outing club for staff and foremen. In addition, the company began to offer some forms of company "welfare" to its employees. It probably intended in part to compensate workers for the loss of informal oyakata care, but the goal of cultivating the loyalty of foremen seems even more prominent. Shibaura consistently applied different standards of treatment for technicians or white-collar personnel (*shokuin*) and factory workers (*kōin*), often excluding the latter altogether. The scope of a wide range of benefits varied greatly with status. From 1893, the company made a dining hall available to technical and office staff but not to workers. Also, with the Mitsui takeover in 1893, managers offered a bonus of 1 month's wages twice a year to all salaried employees, raised this to 2 months' in 1903, and changed it to a percentage of profits in 1908. None of these bonuses included factory workers. By 1912, however, the profit-sharing plan covered foremen; among factory personnel, only they received about 1 month of extra pay per year.[18]

Anxious to retain those employees seen as valued members of the firm, Shibaura developed a program of retirement pay, as well as an aid program for injured or sick employees, and benefits for the survivors of deceased employees. In all cases, the company was fairly generous to its white-collar men. Workers received pay for time missed only in cases of work-related injury, and the amount depended on the severity of the injury; but staff employees took home full pay for the first 60 days of *any* illness and half pay for the next 30 days. In 1903, managers further introduced a clear separation between foremen and unranked workers in separate programs of injury compensation. The foremen gained more generous benefits, and all payments were made to depend on tenure.[19]

Policy toward white-collar personnel or foremen, and the mass of regular workers, who numbered 700 by 1905, addressed fundamentally different concerns. Rather than encouraging the regular men to identify with and remain with the company over the long term, as in the case of foremen and supervisors, Shibaura looked primarily to short-term goals of exacting efficient labor and tightening discipline.

Kobayashi Sakutarō manipulated pay raises and bonuses for shop-floor workers to encourage productivity. He began to give out semiannual raises to these men, restricted to so-called diligent workers whose output was of high quality. He also held out promise of promotion to those whose skill merited it. Kobayashi claimed that particularly skilled workers could rise to foreman rank or higher.[20] To improve discipline, Kobayashi first reformed the widely abused attendance bonus, based on *days* of attendance. Workers previously could register in the morning, quietly leave at midday, and still maintain a perfect record. Diligent workers who missed a day or two because of a true illness were penalized.[21] This abuse was symptomatic of a deeper problem. Staff supervision remained superficial. Oversight did not penetrate to actual evaluation of the results of work. The immediate solution to the bonus problem was to use an hourly rather than a daily attendance calculation. A man on the job for over 1,600 hours in the winter half-year received the bonus; in the summer 1,690 hours qualified him for this extra. This forced supervisors to keep a closer watch on workers and more effectively encouraged disciplined work habits. By 1912, it also included a twist designed to reward long service, one of the first signs of Shibaura interest in regular workers who were skilled, diligent, *and* loyal. Those with less than 3 years' tenure received 6 days' extra pay, and the bonus gradually increased with further years on the job. Ten or more years' tenure brought 150 days of extra pay to the worker exceeding the minimum attendance standard. A diligent, healthy worker with 10 years' seniority who came to work each day in 1912 would receive 10 months' extra pay.[22]

A change in the relation of payday to the day off also took aim at the twin goals of tighter discipline and greater productivity. Kobayashi found inefficient the custom of placing payday just before the two days off each month, to avoid the problem of low attendance after payday. "The workers get drunk [on the day off] and so, even upon returning the next day, they cannot work effectively. Two days are thus lost."[23] In 1911, Shibaura separated holidays and paydays. The factory closed every Sunday, but retained the old paydays, the 1st and 15th of each month. Longstanding customs were not broken easily, and for some time Shibaura continued to be troubled with high absenteeism after payday. According to Kobayashi, this gradually subsided, resulting in greater productivity and higher rates of saving among workers.[24]

Managers took limited additional steps to encourage longer tenure and foster among the regular workers a sense that they, too, belonged at the company. These consisted mainly of changing informal practices of the nineteenth century into systematic welfare programs. Sometime before 1912, Shibaura instituted a savings plan, and, in 1902, the company made explicit an existing customary program of injury compensation, in which workers injured on the job were treated at company expense.[25] By 1912, the company had set up a mutual-aid fund, supported by worker contributions, to provide sick pay or condolence money for illnesses or deaths not related to work.

Shibaura's labor policy between 1900 and 1910 pursued three basic goals: greater control over the work process, more efficient labor, and cultivation of foremen who identified their fates with the company. The attendance bonus, severance pay, injury compensation, and condolence allowances rose with worker tenure—evidence of some wish to slow turnover among regular workers as well—but the company did not encourage these men to feel themselves members of the enterprise as it did foremen or staff. Measured in yen, these changes appear to have succeeded. The company had lost money steadily between 1893 and 1899, but the 7 years of red-ink operation ended in 1900, the year Ōtaguro began his reforms. The company recorded a tiny 7,000-yen profit. In the decade that followed, profits rose and remained fairly consistent even during the slow years after the Russo-Japanese War.[26]

Shibaura was typical of the large, wealthy firms of the era. In 1903 and 1908, Mitsubishi's Nagasaki Shipyard adopted efficiency-based wage systems in many workshops to raise productivity, and the cost of new ships per worker dropped between 1907 and 1911. Management also attempted to limit oyakata power and draw foremen into a closer relationship with the company. Semiannual bonuses and a savings plan for foremen both commenced between 1900 and 1904. In 1908, Mitsubishi stopped contracting jobs to oyakata, a practice that still covered 20 percent of the workers, and new regulations of the same year gave the company more control over hiring, firing, and wage-setting. Foremen still retained a great deal of informal authority in these decisions, but they now operated within a company framework. Measures aimed at the unranked worker also took a form similar to those at Shibaura. In 1897, the shipyard implemented Worker Protection Regulations covering medical costs of work-related injuries, and it set allowances for missed days, crippling or fatal injuries, and for retirement pay. In 1909, Mitsubishi revised and extended these programs, raising injury benefits and broadening allowances to cover family illnesses, marriage, and births. The company also founded a small pension fund.[27]

Other Keihin-area firms moved less systematically than Shibaura in a similar direction. Ishikawajima managers made a clumsy attempt to draw oyakata closer to the company in 1906 by offering them better wages, while at the same time asserting greater control over workers with a hierarchy apparently based on military organization. Managers here lacked the sophistication of their Shibaura counterparts, and a strike resulted. Regular workers called the wage hike for oyakata unfair and discriminatory. Upper-level foremen did try to persuade the strikers to return to the job, indicating that Ishikawajima had already convinced some top foremen to identify their interests with the company, or at least separate them from the regular workers.[28]

In the early 1900s, the Uraga Dock Company also took some steps to favor foremen and encourage them to cast their lot with the company. At some point prior to 1911, Uraga created a mutual-aid program which offered generous benefits to foremen. Depending on the severity of an injury, foreman benefits were 25 to 100 percent higher than those for regular workers. This, and perhaps other undocumented policies, did lead some foremen to remain at Uraga. By 1921, exactly one-half of all foremen and supervisory foremen (*kōshu*), but less than 5 percent of regular workers, had been with the company since before 1900; only the foremen settled down at Uraga between 1900 and 1921.[29]

Complementary to the assertion of direct control of the workplace, Shibaura and several other enterprises began to sponsor formal vocational training programs and even general education for the men who entered the factory. In the face of inadequate public vocational training, a short supply of skilled men, and their frustrating mobility, companies implemented education programs in the hope that men given the benefits of free training would remain to constitute a small future corps of skilled workers and foremen. They reinforced hope by careful screening of the trainees and by a contract which bound the worker (upon pain of forfeit of a deposit) to stay with the company for some years upon completion of the training.

The Mitsubishi Shipyard at Nagasaki established a tuition-free training school mainly for children of the company's workers. Trainees enrolled after completing elementary school. The first class entered in 1899 with 42 students. Older trainees with no education followed a separate curriculum.[30] Yahata Ironworks in North Kyūshū, geographically isolated from other metalwork enterprises and facing a shortage of skilled workers, established a similar 3-year training program in 1910. It required the carefully screened applicants to stay with the company for 6 years after graduation. Yahata paid tuition, but in theory required anyone who quit within 6 years to repay tuition and give up separation pay.[31]

The shortage of skilled workers prompted firms in the Keihin area to build ties with local schools. The Uraga Dock Company sponsored vocational training courses at three nearby elementary schools beginning in 1906 and 1907. The Dock Company at first hired select graduates from this course—16 in 1909, 1 in 1910, and 8 in 1911—but, in 1910, it established a more intimate tie with the schools, sending all newly hired trainees (*minarai*) to a 3-year course. In daily classes after work, from 4 to 9 p.m., the youths studied Japanese, math, science, and English, in addition to industrial design and production. The curriculum stressed the design of tools, machines, and blueprints, and the use of wood and metalworking tools and materials. Uraga looked to ferret out the brighter workers and put them on a fast track which promised promotion someday to foreman. The company paid close attention to trainee progress, giving special raises to boys with excellent academic records. At times of general pay increases, the amount of a trainee's pay raise would depend upon his scholastic record.[32]

Both Shibaura and Ishikawajima were sponsors of a similar program founded in Tokyo in 1905. For Ishikawajima, "because workers stayed for a short time, training of skilled workers was a major problem."[33] Shibaura took the initiative in dealing with this problem. The company believed that "skilled workers were indispensable, but workers at the time generally had low levels of education, skill, and character, and were in great need of reform." Kobayashi Sakutarō therefore joined with leaders of the Tokyo Chamber of Commerce, the Tokyo Higher Industrial School, and the Tokyo District Workers' School to establish a special training program. Participating enterprises were to send workers in proportion to the company's financial support. Only three companies joined at the start. Shibaura sent 20 workers, and the Tokyo Gas Company and Ishikawajima sent fewer than 10 each.[34]

Shibaura selected men to attend this 1-year, twice weekly afternoon course from among those between the ages of 13 and 40 with 3 or more years' experience at the company and good attendance records. If over 20 applied, higher-paid workers had priority. Shibaura paid workers for time spent in classes, but required any who left the company without permission during or after the training period to return their pay. Participants were required to remain with the company for 5 years after completing the course. For Shibaura, the goal of this limited program was consonant with other labor policies, as the company sought above all to "cultivate high-quality foremen."

The capitalist managerial elite of the late Meiji era also dealt with ideas. Prodded by a quiet but persistent undercurrent of official skepticism, business leaders sought to justify their rapidly growing economic and political power. They began to articulate a coherent ideology of paternalism, both to counter government pressure for a factory law and to justify their new institutional framework of labor cultivation and control. Out of heated debate and political struggle concerning a factory law came a cross-fertilization of concepts regarding the so-called "labor problem." Eventually, both advocates and opponents of a law defended paternalism as a progressive concept which took the best of Japan's past and applied it to insure an economically and socially healthy future. Reform-minded bureaucrats in the Industrial Bureau of the Ministry of Agriculture and Commerce and the Health Bureau of the Home Ministry began to press seriously for a factory law in the

1890s, and they won a victory of sorts in 1916 when the rather weak Factory Law took effect.[35] Over these decades, capitalists gradually evolved a sophisticated defense of paternalism as the special Japanese key to solving the labor problem, and government officials gradually accepted the view that paternalism and factory legislation could be compatible supports of a healthy, orderly industrial society.

Concern for social order, narrowly and broadly conceived, lay at the heart of the bureaucratic push for a law. The government feared that industrialists left to their own devices in the management of labor would undermine social and political order in factories and in society at large. Oka Minoru, chief of the Industrial Bureau and the most active proponent of the law, asserted that inadequate facilities and overwork caused excessive labor turnover inimical to the interests of industrialists themselves. Therefore, "a law is necessary to provide for the orderly development of industry."[36] Soeda Juichi, a high-ranking Finance Ministry official who supported a factory law, spoke of a broader anxiety in 1896 when he early on raised the specter of a British disease:

> We cannot find security in the fact that our nation's people are rich in compassion. If the state does not take some slight role in employer-employee relations there will be no way to protect the interests of the employed, and as a result there will be increasing cases of social illness, disturbance, and struggle.

Soeda's fear was perhaps a bit extreme. Certainly his rhetoric was grand:

> If we leave things as they are today, we will see a process producing extreme social illness much like that which befell England at the beginning of this century. . . . We will have unavoidable problems ending in social evils such as strikes. . . . I hope we can solve this problem before it develops and save ourselves from the fate of Europe.[37]

In response to such declamations, leading industrialists defended the very "compassion" that Soeda and others felt inadequate or obsolete. Legislation would not pave the way toward future industrial success; it would stir up a hornet's nest of social problems and destroy the beautiful old customs of obedience and loyalty which brought order to Japanese industry. The most stubborn opponents of a law were textile industrialists, but leading figures involved in the heavy industrial activities of the Mitsui and Mitsubishi zaibatsu also raised voices in opposition. They asserted that time-honored "beautiful customs" (*bifū*) of obedience and loyalty from below matched by sympathetic understanding from above would suffice to solve problems such as resistance to factory discipline, low morale, or poor health. A law, on the other hand, would legally sanction the interests of workers, thereby undermining the emotional basis of the old, integrated social order, and stimulating conflict.

Masuda Takashi, president of the Mitsui Trading Company, and for many years a board member at Shibaura, argued in 1896 that only education, and most certainly not an arbitrary law, would prevent troubled labor relations. Masuda's objective was to avoid a cold, Western-style labor relationship and preserve warm Japanese social customs, even in the modern era. Without these, he concluded, Japan would end up no better off than the West.[38] Elaborating in a similar vein, Shōda Heigorō, director of the Mitsubishi Nagasaki Shipyard stated his conviction, in 1898, that a factory law would bring "great evil" as it sowed seeds of self-interest and led workers to oppose managers on the basis of their new legal power.[39] Twelve years later, Shōda had sharpened his sense of the need to preserve the special Japanese customs which made the law not only unnecessary but harmful. This statement of 1910 offers a succinct summary of the managerial ideology of Japanese paternalism:

> Since ancient times, Japan has possessed the beautiful custom of master-servant relations based firmly on a spirit of sacrifice and compassion, a custom not seen in the many other countries of the world. Even with the recent progress in transportation, the development of ideas about rights, the expansion of markets, and the growing scale of industrial society, this master-servant relationship persists securely. This relationship is not weak like that of the Western nations, but has its roots in our family system and will persist as long as that system exists. Because

of this relationship, the employer loves the employee and the employee respects his master. Interdependent and helping each other, the two preserve industrial peace. . . . Today, there exist no evils and we feel no necessity [for a factory law]. We cannot agree to something that will destroy the beautiful custom of master-servant relations and wreak havoc on our industrial peace.[40]

While Masuda and Shōda, in the late 1890s, stood in the main stream of industrial opinion against a factory law, by the time of the 1910 article Shōda's opposition was a minority opinion among influential capitalists. Most had come to accept factory legislation as inevitable. Several developments lay behind this major shift in opinion. An unprecedented wave of strikes and labor disputes in heavy industry in 1906 and 1907 strengthened the government position that "beautiful customs" *by themselves* were an inadequate guarantee of healthy industrial development.[41] Improved working conditions in large factories had eliminated much of the practical reason to oppose a law. Compliance with the law would no longer seriously affect hours of work and the age of workers, two major points of controversy in the 1890s. Further, in remaining areas where the proposed law would have had major impact, textile interests worked through the Seiyūkai party to force the government to revise it. The final version granted a 15-year grace period before the most controversial clause, a prohibition on night work for women and children, took effect. Also, the industries most affected by the law as it stood in 1911 were those with the least political clout—small match factories, silk reelers, and weavers. The state ignored their protests.[42] Finally, on the ideological level, a changed perspective among bureaucrats on the relationship between "Japanese customs" and the law helped business interests accept the law. In the debates of the late 1890s, most advocates of a factory law saw it as a *substitute* for antiquated old paternal customs destined to wither away as modern industry advanced. By 1911, most government leaders had modified the reasoning behind their support of the law. Rather than a substitute for, they now saw the Factory Law as compatible with, or even inextricably linked to, the continued survival of "beautiful customs." Bureaucrat

Soeda still supported the Factory Law, but he had changed his view of the place of "old customs" by 1907:

> The old, beautiful customs existing in Japan are concepts of mutual love and respect from employer and employee. This master-servant relationship is not an evil feudal remnant but a benefit gained from feudalism. Will not these beautiful customs, namely compassion from above for those below, and respect from below for those above, be greatly helpful in harmonizing labor-capital relations?[43]

By the time the Factory Law passed both houses of the Diet in March 1911, Masuda of Mitsui and Shōda of Mitsubishi had for some time been speaking of "warm Japanese social customs" or the "beautiful custom of master-servant relations based firmly on a spirit of sacrifice and compassion" as the basis for the smooth development of Japanese industry. They were just two of many.[44] By 1911, bureaucrats had joined these industrialists in their approval of such customs as a vital partner to legislation. This important convergence of business and bureaucratic perspectives regarding the value of "beautiful customs" represented the spread and acceptance within Japan's government and business elites of the notion that paternalistic management, based on "warm master-servant relations" and supplemented by a factory law, was one key to solving the social problems of industrialization and control of the factory.[45]

Roughly one decade into the twentieth century, then, paternalism as ideology had sunk its roots. Top business leaders used it to fend off or weaken labor legislation in public forums; in addition, the men dealing with everyday problems of labor management used it to reinforce their policies of direct control and education. Shibaura managers used the language of paternal concern in speaking to those foremen, in 1904, whom the company was seeking to integrate more effectively into the management hierarchy. Kobayashi Sakutarō told several foremen discontented with low wages, compared to those of new workers hired during the Russo-Japanese War:

Shibaura doesn't think of you as regular workers. You are chosen and are part of the Shibaura family. Of course, those that are hired from outside get high pay, but these are temporary people. Even when the war is over, you will still be working at Shibaura as part of the family. It wouldn't do to think of yourselves in the same category as these new temporary people.[46]

In similar fashion the company announced its new education program, also aimed mainly at foremen, in 1905:

In order to develop the skill and knowledge of our workers, to improve the quality of our products and the personalities of our workers, and to encourage educated and disciplined workers, we have joined together with several enterprises. . . . We believe that this action was undertaken out of devoted loyalty to our country and reverent affection for our workers. We thus expect that those who are chosen to attend this school will, with careful attention and mindful of the company's motivations, faithfully bear the above in mind and not falter for even one moment.[47]

THE LABOR RESPONSE

The multi-faceted drive to control labor directly evolved through a continuous dialectic of management-labor interaction. While new policies, training programs, and ideology to some extent molded the factory labor force, workers were not simply malleable objects. They greeted the new departures of the early 1900s with a mix of acceptance and resistance, which in turn shaped the labor relationship.

A wave of unrest broke across Japan's mines, arsenals, and shipyards following the Russo-Japanese War and reached a peak in 1907. Overtime work ended as the war boom subsided, and higher prices diminished real income further. While bread-and-butter issues precipitated most of these strikes, hostility to the assertion of direct control over production often fueled them. At Ishikawajima, for example, skilled regular workers and lower-level foremen opposed upper-level foremen or staff over changes in customary work routine seen to be unfair or arbitrary.[48] Ishikawajima managers had crudely pulled oyakata into the company at worker expense and brought on this dispute. At the Mitsubishi Shipyard in Nagasaki, the several labor disputes of this era took place in reaction to the strict new structure of control which replaced the indirect oyakata system. Despite several similar disputes elsewhere protesting the switch to direct control in the early 1900s, many workers accepted changes such as those implemented at Shibaura. To the extent that limits placed on arbitrary oyakata power brought more systematic treatment, even if under close company control, workers welcomed the reforms. Most likely such an attitude spared Shibaura from disputes of the type that took place at Mitsubishi. If managers were careful in offering compensation to workers often glad to see arbitrary oyakata stripped of their authority, resistance came later, if at all.[49]

More effective supervision through closer integration of the office and technical staffs with the foremen, and the elimination of the independent oyakata, had been achieved in some respects by the eve of World War I: Shibaura cut down oyakata power and integrated foremen into the management hierarchy with no open worker protest; some Uraga foremen began to stay with the company for relatively long periods beginning in the early 1900s; and, at Mitsubishi, most top-level foremen (*kogashira*) in about 1910 had been with the company for over 20 years, and most regular foremen for 10 to 15 years.[50] But managers did not draw all foremen securely into a company, convince them to identify their fates more with the firm than with their subordinates, and pull them out of the ranks of working-class society into the lower-middle or managerial class. One sees only tentative movement in this direction. Preferential treatment, bonuses, wage increases, or company welfare benefits introduced new tensions into the relationship of foremen to both workers and company. At times, the foreman became the lowest ranked company "official" (*yakutsuki*) in the enterprise structure of control, anxious to suppress or mediate any conflicts. Often, however, foremen leaders of the work group remained in close, sympathetic contact with unranked workers. The work process still required foremen to exercise much independent judgment and authority; it still placed a premium on skill acquired through long experience. The leadership of foremen played a central role in the early Yūaikai labor movement. These men were still workers, with considerable authority, willing to lead others in action against the company.

Events at Shibaura between 1912 and 1915 throw the Janus-like character of foremen into sharp relief. The success of the Yūaikai in gaining a foothold at the company eventually brought on a second major reform of labor management at the Engineering Works.

Suzuki Bunji, dedicated social reformer and self-styled champion of Japanese laborers, had founded his Friendly Society, the Yūaikai, at a meeting of 13 men in the basement of a central Tokyo church in August 1912. By 1916, the Yūaikai, adhering to a vision of gradual social reform and labor unionism within the existing political and economic order, had grown into a stable national organization of about 15,000 members. While Suzuki insisted in these years that the Yūaikai was an organization for social reform, not socialism, he also insisted upon the need for workers to "awaken" and assert themselves as full-fledged members of society. While the early Yūaikai did not advocate social revolution, it did promote worker "self-revolution" and class-consciousness. It did not champion strikes, but it did work to cultivate among workers a sense of community and the strength that unity would bring.[51]

Shibaura was one of the earliest centers of Yūaikai activity. By the end of 1912, 33 of the 260 Yūaikai members were Shibaura workers. As the organization grew in 1913, it formed a regional branch in the southern part of Tokyo (Jōnan). The Shibaura factory was the largest single component of the branch, and, as Shibaura workers continued to sign on, the Yūaikai decided to form a separate Shibaura local. Roughly 10 percent of Shibaura's 1,500 employees were members of the local, founded on March 1, 1915. By September 1916, the Shibaura local numbered 353 workers of a total work force of 2,252, and membership reached 500 by the end of 1917.[52] Of significance equal to quantity was the quality of the membership. Highly skilled workers, in many cases foremen, dominated the early Yūaikai. These were the men capable of attracting new members and holding their allegiance, as one Shibaura worker attested. He joined the Yūaikai "because most of the skilled workers in his factory had joined that branch and he wanted to be counted among their number, partly to benefit from learning their expertise."[53]

Managers at Shibaura were typical in viewing these Yūaikai locals with serious concern, in large part because of the prominence of the union members within the factory. After the sustained attempt of the early 1900s to encourage skilled workers, especially foremen, to identify with the company, Shibaura managers faced an unpleasant possibility. With the growth of the Yūaikai, skilled workers and even foremen might offer their primary commitment to an outside organization dedicated to protecting the interests of the workers and raising their status, at the expense of company interests. Shibaura therefore responded swiftly to the formation of the separate Shibaura branch of the Yūaikai, although the group organized only one-tenth of the company work force, by initiating a costly new labor policy in early 1915. They took this step knowing that profits for 1914 had been down significantly from 1913 and that 1915 promised only slight improvement.[54] They nonetheless felt it necessary to go the Yūaikai one better by expanding some existing programs, offering more attractive benefits to all workers, and giving foremen a special stake in the company.

On June 1, 1915, exactly three months after the Yūaikai local had been founded, Shibaura announced a wholesale renovation of its personnel policy. Management introduced a revised set of factory regulations including 16 chapters and 137 articles covering all aspects of work.[55] The company broadened and increased coverage offered for illness or injury. A worker permanently crippled on the job would receive 360 days' pay. Shibaura set up an infirmary with one full-time doctor and two nurses and organized a mutual-aid society for all workers, supported by deductions from pay and a company contribution. Significantly, a committee dominated by foremen administered the fund.[56]

Shibaura also formally established a retirement fund in 1915, supported by a donation of up to 5 percent of profits each half year. The company set aside a sum for each worker in proportion to his daily wage and attendance record during each 6-month period, and it returned the total plus interest upon retirement, at age 60. Fired workers received the amount accumulated to that point, and Shibaura paid a bonus, which increased with tenure, at the time of firing or retirement. Voluntary leavers forfeited their shares. The principal in the fund expanded from 20,700 yen in 1916 to 870,000 yen in 1920.[57]

The company also revised its education policy, and for the first time gave significant attention to worker education within the firm, setting up an Education Section. In addition to orientation for all new employees which stressed their importance to the enterprise, this section administered a new training program. Shibaura expected the trainees (*kyōshūkō*) to form a future corps of skilled workers and chose them with care from among technical-school graduates. Their 6-month to 2-year in-company course of study (separate from the Workers School program described above) emphasized "character and personality development," as well as technical education. In-company training programs were not adopted at many enterprises until the 1920s, and Shibaura was a local pioneer in this respect.[58]

Perhaps the most important innovation was the Foremen's Council (*kumichō kai*). The foremen, considered as worker representatives, began to meet monthly with company officials. Through the exchange of ideas the Council was supposed to encourage harmony in the attitudes and actions of workers and the company. Topics for discussion included pay as well as work duties, aid, and treatment of workers. The freedom to discuss wages distinguishes this group from most later Factory Councils.[59] It indicates that the company hoped the Foremen's Council would play an important role.

The workers did not demand any of these new policies. No strikes had taken place. The mere fact of Yūaikai growth at Shibaura stimulated reforms which extended or deepened policies of a decade earlier. The company gave a leading role to foremen, offered welfare benefits to all workers, and expanded programs for training a hand-picked group of loyal, skilled workers. The Yūaikai had promised similar benefits such as mutual aid and education. Shibaura quickly responded to the emergence of a working-class organization transcending the company framework, hoping to nip this vague future threat in the bud by extending the scope of its paternalism and allowing some participation through the Foremen's Council. The stormy history of labor relations at Shibaura in the 1920s will reveal limits to the success of this effort, but many of the later conflicts took place within the framework established by company policy. The foremen led none of them. Although not all firms imitated the Shibaura policy before the 1920s, this case indicates that, with substantial effort, a company could draw these men successfully into the lower ranks of a hierarchy of supervision.

At first glance, company-sponsored education programs, at Shibaura and elsewhere, did not fare as well. A good many men spurned the promise of a career on the fast track at a big firm, and the attempt to educate and retain skilled workers disappointed management expectations. Shibaura sent about 950 men to the Tokyo Workers' School between 1905 and 1938.[60] By 1939, the 1-year course had produced 700 graduates for a respectable 75 percent completion rate, but, at least in the early years, many graduates peddled their improved skills elsewhere, ignoring both a contractual obligation and the company pleas for loyal service.[61] Kobayashi Sakutarō, the Shibaura labor manager most intimately involved in the creation of this program, offered this informed description of company training in 1908:

> Recently, at a certain factory, the company established a suitable system of education, but workers [in the program] who have not completed the required number of years are leaving the company in a rush. One cannot expect the practice of talent pirating to result in the production of satisfactory products. Already in Tokyo the situation is such at all factories. Therefore, when it comes to selecting talent, if one does not carefully research the worker's character and will, the selection will not succeed.[62]

Training programs everywhere faced these problems. Most graduates of the rival Hitachi Engineering Works' school either left before finishing a similar course, or took their valuable skills soon after graduation to factories in Osaka or Tokyo where the pay was better. Managers often complained to the school administrators about the low commitment of the graduates. The Mitsubishi school enrolled 406 students in its first six classes, which graduated between 1904 and 1909. Of the 406 entrants, 185 (46 percent) actually stayed until graduation day, and, by 1912, only 78 of these workers (42 percent of the graduates and 19 percent of the entrants) remained in Mitsubishi employ at either the Nagasaki or Kōbe yards. Thirty-six percent of the 78 were regular workers, the rest foremen or staff personnel. At Yahata, only 791 (13 percent) of the 6,521 graduates produced at the company school between 1910 and 1935 remained with the company in 1935. The attrition cannot be due to retirement since the oldest graduates would not have been over 45 in 1935. Most important in view of the school's explicit goal of training foremen, by 1920 graduates only accounted for 3 percent of the foremen and 6 percent of the sub-foremen at Yahata.[63]

The lack of commitment to the company of trainees at Hitachi, Shibaura, and Mitsubishi is all the more noteworthy because these figures predate the World War I boom which brought with it tremendous competition for scarce skilled workers and high turnover. Education programs promising future glory as foremen and seeking to draw the graduates into a close, long-term relationship with the company met a skeptical response. Companies did not change the behavior of young workers who still believed that skill and advancement came through experience accumulated at a variety of factories.

Even so, continued scarcity of skilled men and continued high turnover, as well as inadequate public vocational training, encouraged continued private-sector training of skilled blue-collar workers. Such training remains characteristic of Japanese industry today, one sign that these programs at some point began to turn out numbers of committed, skilled employees sufficient to justify their existence. The few training schools of the very early twentieth century were significant as precursors of an approach to the training of labor which in later years proliferated and covered a broad range of workers.

In similar fashion, the flowery rhetoric of paternalism in the early 1900s persisted, later to exert considerable impact, despite a lukewarm initial reception. Shibaura trainees betrayed the "reverent affection" of the company and, in Kobayashi's words, "left in a rush." The language and ideology of paternalism did not impress working men of this era for good reason; the early glorification of beautiful customs of paternal care had little grounding in actual practice. It was rather the dissonance between the reality of long hours, insecure jobs, confiscatory "savings plans," and minuscule or nonexistent injury compensation, and the abstract presentation of an ideal, paternal labor-manager relationship that impressed them. In fact, precisely because of labor displeasure with this dissonance, managers began to give substance to what had been empty statements of the paternal ideology, and make of paternalism a more potent ideology and policy of control in later years.

A company document from the Mitsubishi Shipyard at Nagasaki in 1909 explains that major expansion of injury benefits and allowances for illnesses, marriage, or births came in response to a new belief among some workers that they had a "right" to such benefits. By implementing such programs before they were actually demanded, Mitsubishi sought to preempt any direct assertion of worker rights.[64] Similar concerns motivated the Uraga Dock Company as it set up a medical clinic in 1912 and the Mitsubishi shipyard at Kōbe in 1916 as it thoroughly revised its regulations for worker aid, a savings fund, and apprenticeship. The Factory Law was not a completely toothless document, and its provisions required some of these changes, but both companies went beyond the minimum demands of the law. They felt compelled to show that paternalism was not forced upon them by the government. A grudging retreat, or outright evasion of the law, would only encourage workers to demand such benefits as their legal right, in the company view.[65] Just as Shibaura moved to head off the Yūaikai in 1915, so these firms moved to head off the articulation of an independent interest in, or right to, "paternal" benefits.

One well might ask if such managers, acting to soften even the whisper of conflict, or mute even the faint murmur of a claim to labor rights, were not moved by irrational paranoia. The story of labor at Yokohama Dock Company in these years yields a different suggestion. It provides an important contrast to the shadow-boxing at Shibaura, as it depicts a far less subtle dynamic of change in the labor relationship. The Dock Company style was consistent from the 1890s through the mid-1920s. Yokosen either ignored or repressed labor activity, exhibiting none of the cooptative instinct so evident at Mitsubishi or Shibaura. In response, Dock workers vigorously criticized both the absence of substantial paternalism and the arbitrary nature of labor control, winning changes as they did so.

The Dock Company was a stronghold of the early Yūaikai in Kanagawa. In early 1915, the Yūaikai founded a separate Yokohama branch, dominated by Yokosen workers who rapidly built a solid organization. By September 1915, the Yokohama branch could boast 713 members, including 300 of the 1,200 employees at the Yokohama Dock Company.[66] In August 1916, the Yūaikai contingent at the Dock Company demonstrated to the rest of the work force that organized labor could take effective action on a wide range of issues.

Managers had only recently begun to assert direct control over work at Yokosen, with a new policy transferring authority to hire and fire from shop-floor supervisors to the dockyard's central office. Workers welcomed this as a step which, in theory, could end arbitrary treatment by direct supervisors, but they charged the company with failing to live up to the new policy. The 1916 dispute began when an unpopular supervisor, Uchiyama, "arbitrarily" fired a lathe-section foreman and Yūaikai member, Hasegawa Hatsutarō, on August 9. Uchiyama had a reputation for high-handed behavior. A few days earlier, he had fired one of

"Yokohama's most prominent skilled workers," Ōkawa Torakichi, for going on a pilgrimage to a temple, and before that he had "fired another excellent worker, Ozawa Kintarō, for sloppy work, a totally unfounded charge." Hasegawa had been with the company for 16 years, Ōkawa for 23.[67] Outraged at Uchiyama's actions, a group of 50 in the lathe section, most if not all Yūaikai members, met in a local restaurant on the evening of August 13. What reportedly angered them most was that shop supervisors such as Uchiyama did not have official authority to fire these men, according to the new company policy.[68]

The men who deliberated that evening formulated demands for the reinstatement of the fired workers, a pay raise, and several other reforms, and they asked leaders from the nearby Yokohama Yūaikai Seamen's Union and the Yūaikai headquarters in Tokyo to help them negotiate with the company. But the lathe workers ran out of patience in just four days, and, before the company issued a formal reply, they went on strike. Within a day, on August 16, 1,200 of the 1,420 Yokosen workers decided to join them. The company immediately rejected all the demands and "fired" the lathe workers who had originally submitted them.[69] That evening, Suzuki Bunji arrived in Yokohama, hastily called back by telegraph from a trip to Kansai. He used his considerable influence to help the workers negotiate a favorable settlement. The 10 demands themselves, and their resolution, serve as a barometer of the climate of labor relations at Yokosen.

(1) Dismiss the lathe shop supervisor, Uchiyama. *Accepted.*

(2) Allow the workers to elect the new supervisor. *Compromise:* The Company would appoint a successor, but promised to choose a skilled worker for the post.

(3) Institute semiannual meetings between management and foremen to resolve future differences. *Accepted:* The company agreed such meetings would be useful, and proposed they be held more often.

(4) Repair plumbing facilities. *Accepted:* The Factory Law to take effect September 1, 1916 would require these changes in any case.

(5) No firing of a worker by a shop supervisor on his own initiative, unless a crime is committed or company property damaged. *Accepted:* The company agreed such arbitrary action was inappro-

priate. If it occurred in the future, workers were to appeal to the head technician.

(6) Reinstate Hasegawa and Ōkawa. *Accepted:* The company replied that, since they were never "officially fired," they need only report to work as usual the next day.

(7) Grant a 10-percent pay raise to cover inflation. *Compromise:* Yamada of the company and Suzuki reached a "gentleman's agreement" that the company would implement a raise in the near future.

(8) Implement a policy of yearly pay raises based on skill and experience. *Accepted:* With the provision that the word *diligence* be added as a criterion. Pay raises would be given out twice a year. However, even if they had experience, workers deficient in skill would not merit an increase. The company promised to be as fair as possible but would not guarantee a raise for every worker.

(9) Establish a system to notify the family in case of an accident at the company. *Accepted:* This was required by the Factory Law.

(10) Decide the wage of a newly hired worker within 5 days. *Compromise:* This is not always possible because a task appropriate for testing a worker is not always available immediately. The trial period will be kept as short as possible. [70]

The beautiful custom of care for the worker apparently did not insure that Yokosen would notify his family of injury or provide him decent toilet facilities. The shipbuilders therefore demanded these reforms, guaranteed by the new Factory Law, when the company did not offer them as part of a paternal package (Demands 4, 9). Likewise, the attempt to curb the independence of shop supervisors was not part of a well-monitored, comprehensive program of direct control at Yokohama, so the workers demanded an end to arbitrary, unauthorized personnel decisions (1, 5, 6) and a closer relationship between management and the foremen (3). On these issues, Yokosen workers acted entirely within the framework established by typical management rhetoric and policy of this era. On the wage issue, however, labor sought to stretch this framework. The Yokosen workers wanted to transform the unreliable, periodic pay raise common even at the turn of the century into a more systematic, seniority reward. And, on the matter of choosing supervisors, the workers directly challenged the right of the company to decide who was boss (2).

Finally, the very fact that workers organized by the Yūaikai had raised all these demands and won most of them indicates that the imposition of new forms of direct control and training, justified by an ideology of paternal care, at the very least could not proceed without reference to worker demands or desires. The tone of the labor relationship at Shibaura in 1915 differed from that at Yokohama in 1916, but the spirit of the demands at Yokohama Dock was similar to that of the 1915 reforms at Shibaura, and the underlying tensions were the same. Workers had pushed management, either directly or indirectly, to modify employment practices, including the nascent seniority wage and the treatment of foremen. The labor relationship would continue to evolve out of just this process of conflict and compromise.

THREE

Failure of the First Attempt: 1917–1921

The dispute at Yokohama in 1916 was one of several dozen similar incidents at major heavy industrial firms between the turn of the century and the middle of World War I. Together these constitute an important chapter in the making of the Japanese working-class movement, but their cumulative impact nonetheless left intact the emerging new structure of management control. Managers at Yokosen, Shibaura, or Mitsubishi in 1915 or 1916 could reasonably expect that a strategy of direct control, paternal rhetoric and a bit of paternal substance, and cultivation of a small, committed corps of favored skilled men would bring sufficiently smooth, efficient operation to their firms. Events of the five years following the dispute at Yokohama shattered this expectation. In the surge of disputes and union activities that began in 1917, the initiative in the factories passed to the workers, and, for the first time, a genuine sense of crisis spread among Japan's managerial elite.

A complex of international and domestic changes combined to render inadequate the labor management policies developed in the decade prior to World War I. The war stimulated unprecedented industrial expansion in Japan, but the boom of 1917 to 1921 also brought labor shortages and soaring inflation. In addition, the Russian Revolution, the victory in battle of the democratic allies, and the creation of the International Labor Organization together generated a newly favorable climate for labor organizing. The political and economic impacts of these events were inseparable. Inflation made union activity necessary and attractive; the labor shortage and the desire of owners to avoid costly strikes made it often successful. These twin economic and political effects of World War I brought two related sets of "labor problems" to light: an old "labor force" problem, still unsolved despite the policies of direct control, periodic pay raises, paternalism, and company education, and a new, menacing "working-class" problem. By the end of World War I, the effort to deal with a still mobile, uncommitted labor force, and a growing labor movement, had touched off a scramble back to the drawing board among top politicians and bureaucrats, as well as managers.

The labor-force and working-class problems reached a peak in 1921. That autumn, an observer from the recently formed Kyōchō-kai scrutinized employment practices and labor relations at the Uraga Dock Company in unusual depth and detail. The Kyōchōkai itself was an important semi-private organization founded in 1919 in response to the new labor problems of the day. It proposed to study and help eliminate the causes of labor-capital tension by promoting cooperation and harmony (*kyōchō*) in the work place and society. Major capitalists, such as Shibusawa Eiichi, and top bureaucrats and politicians, including Home Minister Tokonami, supported the organization.[1] Together with information concerning other workers and companies in the region and some national statistics, the Kyōchōkai survey of Uraga offers a revealing glimpse of management policy and thinking as well as the attitudes and behavior of workers during the unsettled years of the war and its aftermath.[2]

THE LABOR-FORCE PROBLEM
DISCIPLINE, TURNOVER, AND WAGES

Ill-disciplined, independent-minded workers had troubled managers since the nineteenth century. Kobayashi at Shibaura had addressed the problem in some of his reforms of the early 1900s. Dealing with the men on the shop floor brought constant headaches for the hard-driving factory director, and he was not pleased with the impact of his reforms, as we learn from a series of magazine articles in 1908 where he vented his frustration at the Japanese worker. The increasing numbers of well-educated young workers were uppity and did not know their place. When not promoted rapidly, they would quit and move from factory to factory like nomads. Older, uneducated laborers were no better. They were proud and unteachable men who relied only on past experience. "Teaching them anything is like trying to teach a cat to chant the *nembutsu*," he fumed. Ironically (viewed from the era of Japan as Number 1, land of the diligent and efficient), a trip to America showed Kobayashi a useful model with which to contrast the hopeless Japanese worker. The American, he discovered, followed rules, came to work on time, never loafed, and would everyday seek to double his prior output. "One cannot easily find such attitudes among Japanese." American workers were docile. "They carry out a job well after just one order . . . and the job of a supervisor is easy. . . . In Japan things don't get done without constant instructions and the lot of a supervisor is difficult." And the Americans saved pennies earned by diligent sweat. "There is no such idiotic saying as that of the Edo artisan: 'Never sleep overnight on your money.' Everyone, no matter what his income, works hard and tries to save."[3]

The managers at Uraga Dock Company in 1921 would have agreed with Kobayashi's views of a decade earlier. The relation of worker and employer at this large shipyard began in a context of wary scrutiny, as hiring procedures at Uraga (and throughout Japan) brought to bear tough sanctions in the effort to keep order in the factory. Several years prior to 1921, Keihin-area shipbuilders began to exchange information regarding job applicants with local work experience. The Mitsubishi Nagasaki Shipyard, together with the Sasebo and Kure Naval yard in western Japan, had set up a similar exchange in 1911. Uraga required a reference from the previous employers of each new worker and checked the background of inexperienced recruits, and local shipyards exchanged the names of voluntary leavers with the agreement that companies

not hire those marked as troublemakers or those who left against
company wishes. By 1921, this had done little either to reduce
mobility or suppress union activities.

Of greater interest, Uraga had each new worker sign a formidable
oath, witnessed by a guarantor, either a relative of the applicant or
a worker of at least sub-foreman rank. The applicant pledged to
serve the company with loyalty, strictly to observe company rules,
and to accept the punishments specified in Uraga regulations for
the infringement of any rule. The use of a written document represents a break with earlier artisan practice. Preindustrial apprentices had typically entered their 7- or 10-year commitment on the
basis of no more than an oral agreement, but Uraga required a
signed oath which specified sanctions for violation of company
rules and spelled out clearly the worker's obligations.

The strict 1921 Work Rules reflect the ongoing distrust of those
shipbuilders actually hired. Frequent labor disputes between 1907
and 1921 had taught Uraga that workers were unreliable men who
required constant supervision. In their emphasis on punctuality
and tight regimentation of factory life, the Work Rules exemplify
one common response to the discipline dimension of the labor-
force problem. The paid work day ran from 7 a.m. to 4:30 p.m.,
but workers had to enter the gate by 6:50 a.m. to begin preparation for work, and they could not leave until 4:40 p.m., to allow
time for cleanup. Uraga would not admit latecomers to work.
Probably to hamper union organizing, the company required all
meals to be taken within the shipyard and did not allow workers
to meet outsiders during work hours or leave the yard on private
business. Foremen were to note officially all worker comings and
goings in a register provided by the Worker Section (Shokkō-ka).
The rules forced all workers below foreman to submit to a body
check at the gate, and workers could not remove objects (tools,
parts, and so forth) from the factory without the shop director's
permission slip, to be shown to the guard at the gate. Rules further
stipulated that all workers leaving early due to illness or injury
present to both the head of the Worker Section and the guard

a permission slip, unless ordered to leave immediately by a doctor.[4]

Strict work rules, punitive hiring contracts, and Kobayashi's earlier cynicism reflect the frustrations of an organization—the large factory—unable to generate efficient, committed service from its members; but they do not tell the whole story of worker values or behavior. When they saw a chance to benefit themselves or their families, working men were willing to apply themselves, to study, and to sacrifice. Even Kobayashi grudgingly recognized the will to work for independence and security as he wrote from the company perspective. Shibaura often lost contracts to "shrewd workers," he complained, because they pulled up the floorboards of their homes, installed a small engine, and started in business for themselves:

> The products aren't that different from what can be produced at a factory with modern facilities, but large factories cannot take in work as cheaply as these places. While one admires their cleverness, on the other hand the prevalence of such makeshift production slows the progress of more modern enterprise.[5]

A Yūaikai organizer named Uchida Tōshichi was one of many such "shrewd" men active in Tokyo before and during World War I. In 1908, age 21, he secured a post as a temporary employee at the Naval Arsenal in Mita, Tokyo. Although he soon became a regular worker at the arsenal, he decided that to rise in the world he would have to polish his skills. In order to learn a trade, he began to spend time after work, from 4:30 to 9:00 p.m., at the shop of a local metal-casting oyakata. After two years, he was a fairly proficient hibachi-maker, and, beginning in about 1910, he filled orders for hibachi in his spare time. "I somehow felt that this hibachi work was a guarantee for the future, and I kept at it, all the while buying as many of the necessary tools as I could." Early attracted to the Yūaikai, he succeeded in organizing a small branch at the arsenal as early as 1913, an activity that eventually cost him his job in 1916. Uchida was cut from the traveler mold. He changed jobs several times, and, more important, he was always ready to do so, as he quite righteously tells us:

> I recognized that I was a determined person who would not retreat one step from what I felt to be the correct path. Therefore, I was resigned to the fact that, at any time, I might come to a confrontation with a superior and lose my job. For this eventuality I had all preparations ready to be able to turn out hibachi at a moment's notice.[6]

In 1939, he finally established his own small metalworking factory.

Although not as intent upon attaining the security of self-employment, Saitō Tadatoshi displayed similar zeal for self-improvement and education in this era. Born in Akita prefecture in far northern Japan in 1896, Saitō began his career as a Tokyo worker in 1914 (after breaking an oral commitment as a blacksmith's apprentice back home). He too attended evening school between 1914 and 1919, while working at a variety of Tokyo factories. At age 18 in 1914, he began commuting to the Tokyo Metropolitan Workers' School. In 1915, he switched from the foundry to classes on machine work, this time at the Tokyo Industrial Arts School. His work day at the Army Arsenal in Koishikawa ran from 7 a.m. to 5 p.m., and his classes kept him busy from 6 to 9 p.m. In 1919, while a worker at Ishikawajima, he entered the Labor Problem Study Group organized by members of the Home Ministry's Tsukishima Report survey team. He also began a 2-year course in politics and economics at Senshū University's night school.

The determination of Uchida and Saitō was probably exceptional. Both went on to become leaders in the labor movement of the 1920s, Uchida on the right, Saitō on the left. Yet, they were typical in their search for self-improvement, an attitude found among numerous workers in this era which infused the early Yū-aikai movement. Men who believed they were gaining something threw themselves into their work or study. Kobayashi's scorn for the lazy, unruly, nomadic worker, and the strategies adopted to change or, at least, control such men, including the tough work rules at Uraga and the strict hiring procedure, tell us more about the Japanese factories of this era than about the workers. By the end of World War I, companies had yet to convince the determined self-improvers such as Saitō or Uchida, or the owners of tiny workshops who competed with Shibaura, that the route to a better future lay in a career at a large factory.

The continued attraction of the traveler lifestyle was a second, related aspect of the labor-force problem. Some firms at the turn of the century or before had seen high turnover as a problem. In addition to the selective regular raise, one dimension of labor policy at Shibaura or Uraga was the emergence, in the early 1900s, of a few policies favoring senior workers, but a handful of allowances rising with seniority did little to slow mobility. In management eyes, high turnover remained at the heart of the labor problem on the eve of World War I, and the subsequent expansion only fueled the travelers' wanderlust.

Frequent job-switching was reported nationwide. Yearly turnover rates of around 75 percent were the norm in most industries during World War I. A survey carried out in Kyoto revealed that yearly turnover among the city's 1,200 to 1,700 machine-industry workers ranged from 82 to 87 percent per year in 1916 and 1917, and the Factory Inspection Report for 1919 found the nationwide machine industry separation rate to be exactly 75 percent.[7]

At Shibaura, a few policies between 1900 and 1910 had sought to encourage long service among regular workers, but turnover exceeded 90 percent per year during the Russo-Japanese war and it fluctuated thereafter in response to changing economic conditions rather than management policies, it would appear (Table 3). The years of lowest turnover, 1909, 1914, and 1915, were slow years at Shibaura and in the machine industry generally. The industry production index dropped in each of these years, while it rose in almost every other year in this period (see Appendix). With the war, turnover at Shibaura once again began to climb, and, from 1916 to 1918, it ranged between 60 to 70 percent each year, slightly below the national average.

These turnover data must be handled with care. While turnover rates of 60 to 90 percent per year imply considerable job-switching, they are somewhat below figures reported for the United

Table 3   Shibaura Blue-Collar Turnover, 1904–1927

Year[a]	Total Workers[b] (a)	Total Hired (b)	Total left or fired (c)	Yearly Turnover (%) $\frac{(b+c)/2}{a}$
1904[c]	779	450	289	47
1905	778	787	747	99
1906	860	567	485	61
1907	929	611	271	47
1908	853	357	433	46
1909	958	155	271	22
1910	1,031	367	294	32
1911	1,123	499	407	40
1912	1,144	400	379	34
1913	1,438	653	359	35
1914	1,517	314	235	18
1915	1,241	116	392	20
1916	2,264	1,890	867	61
1917	3,188	2,499	1,575	64
1918	2,792	1,798	2,051	69
1919	2,795	780	777	28
1920	3,172	1,148	771	30
1921	3,123	478	528	16
1922	3,104	739	758	24
1923[d]	1,667	522	1,959	74
1924	2,356	1,478	789	48
1925	2,868	1,004	492	26
1926	3,087	705	486	19
1927	2,675	20	432	8

Source: Shibaura seisakujo eigyō hōkokushō, 1904–1927. Category labeled *shokkō, rōekisha,* or *kōnin.*

Notes: [a] Year runs from 12/1 of previous year to 11/31 of year noted in company reports.

[b] Total at 11/30 of that year.

[c] Only 7/1–11/30/1904.

[d] Earthquake, 9/23, brought on most of these firings.

States at the time when managers in this country first began to complain of turnover as a major problem. The best American survey focused on 105 plants with roughly 225,000 employees between 1913 and 1915. Two-fifths of these factories had yearly turnover rates greater than 100 percent.[8] In addition, a yearly rate of 75 percent is not likely to mean that three-fourths of those employed on January 1 quit over the following 12 months. Certain positions probably turned over several times. It is conceivable (if unlikely) that, in a work force of 100 men, for example, 10 unskilled positions turned over once each month, while the other 90 posts saw no turnover at all. This would produce a yearly turnover rate of 120 percent, despite the continuous presence of 90 percent of the men.

At best, turnover figures are suggestive indicators of possible trends over time or comparisons across societies. The Japanese work force appears less mobile, in the aggregate, than the American force during World War I. But, within Japan, turnover measured at the national or company level seems to have intensified dramatically during the war. Perhaps most important to a study of management policy, observers uniformly conceived it as a frequent occurrence, and official sources invariably saw it as a problem. To probe more deeply into the nature of worker mobility and the managerial response, we must turn to other sorts of evidence: figures on the age and seniority breakdown of a company's work force, long-term rates of worker retention, individual work histories, and the testimony offered by workers, labor inspectors, or managers.

For individual firms, the greatest problem posed by expanding work forces and high rates of turnover was the difficulty of retaining a sufficient critical mass of skilled men. A national survey of all factories covered by the Factory Law in 1919 revealed that only 11 percent of nearly 300,000 machine-industry workers (and 12 percent of all 1.3 million industrial workers) had over 5 years' experience with a single employer. Figure 1 illustrates the Uraga situation, somewhat more settled than the national average. Sixty-eight percent of all Uraga workers had 5 years' tenure or less; 88 percent had been with the company for 10 years or less. The labor force was somewhat more stable here in 1921 than it had been at Ishikawajima in 1902, when four-fifths of the work force were 5-year men or less. But the skilled adult travelers were still prominent.

To sense this concretely, compare figures on the tenure and the age of Uraga workers in 1921 (Figures 1 and 2). While 2,136 of the Uraga men were over 30, just 512 employees had more than 10 years' seniority. Three-fourths of the men over 30 must have entered Uraga as adults (over 20) within the past decade. Although the Kyōchōkai survey discusses the problem of integrating experienced recruits into the Uraga force, none of the abundant sources on Uraga mention *inexperienced* adult recruits in this era. These men probably brought work experience gained elsewhere to the shipyard. Further, national surveys of the 1920s indicate that over 90 percent of 30-year-old industrial workers were married, so men with families were among those on the move. Put another way, at most 512, or 18 percent, of Uraga's 2,835 men aged 25 or more had been with the company continuously for the 10 or more years since they left school. The remaining 82 percent had spent a portion of their working lives elsewhere.[9]

Cohort data from Shibaura Engineering Works allows us to study persistency of employment over a longer period. Table 4 reveals that, of all employees hired between 1904 and 1908, less than 3 percent spent the following 25 years at Shibaura. This rose a bit between 1909 and 1913, when between 3 and 6 percent of each cohort remained with the company for 25 years. Of all those hired in the decade 1904–1913, 3.2 percent spent what amounts to an entire career at Shibaura. These data, as well as similar sets covering shorter periods at Yahata and Mitsubishi, suggest that we are dealing with two types of workers. In addition to the travelers, a small minority of the blue-collar force at these firms did consist of "company men" even in World War I, and at Shibaura their numbers rose slightly over time. But contrast these figures with the postwar retention rates of nearly one-half of a cohort over a 23-year span. The likelihood that a skilled man hired in 1913 would spend his entire career at Shibaura was of a different order of magnitude.

Not all the attrition of these early cohorts was voluntary. We must assume that, in contrast to the postwar group, limited to teenage school graduates, the prewar set of newly hired men

Figure 1   Tenure Distribution of Uraga Workers, August 1921

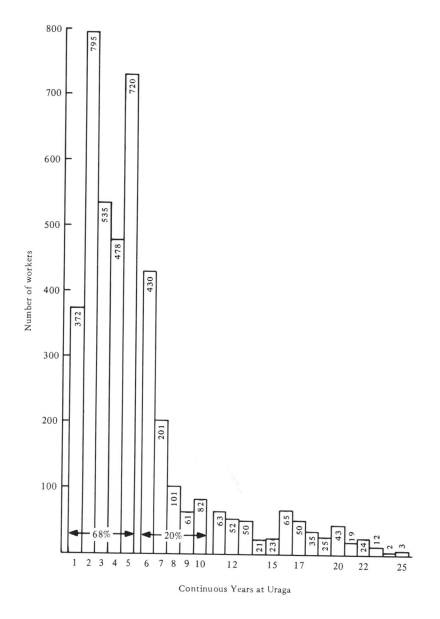

Source: Kyōchōkai, *Uraga*

Figure 2 Age Distribution of Uraga Workers, August 1921

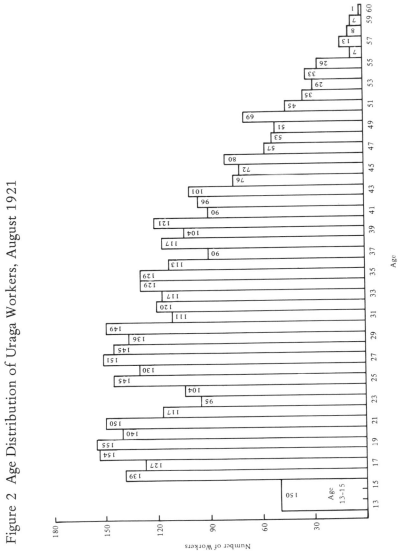

Age

Number of Workers

Source: Kyōchōkai, *Uraga*

Table 4 Length-of-Service Awards to All Shibaura Employees

	Year of Hiring	Year of 25-Year Service Award	Number Hired (a)	Number Given Award (b)	Percent Remaining 25 years (b/a)
Prewar	1904	1929	467[a]	12	2.6
	1905	1930	854	17	2.0
	1906	1931	651	10	1.5
	1907	1932	752	21	2.8
	1908	1933	461	2	0.4
	1909	1934	187	6	3.2
	1910	1935	394	16	4.0
	1911	1936	538	32	5.9
	1912	1937	669	23	3.4
	1913	1938	843	47	5.6
Total			5,816	186	3.2

		Tenure in 1980	Number Hired (a)	Number Remaining in 1980 (b)	Percent Remaining 21–23 years (b/a)
Postwar	1957	23 yrs.	290	135	46.6
Tōshiba[b]	1958	22 yrs.	309	139	45.0
	1959	21 yrs.	328	130	39.6

Sources: Prewar award figures from Shibaura seisakujo 65 nenshi, pp. 183–185. Hiring figures from Shibaura seisakujo eigyō hōkokusho, 1904–1913. All postwar figures from Tōshiba Personnel section.
Note: [a]The 1904 figure is for hiring in the second half of the year only, so the true retention rate is lower than 2.6%.
[b]Postwar figures are for middle-school graduates (see p. 398).

included numerous experienced adult travelers. With Shibaura's retirement age set at 55, anyone hired over age 30 would have retired before becoming eligible for an award. In addition, mortality was higher in prewar Japan, and Shibaura dismissed large numbers after the earthquake and probably during the Depression.

How much higher would retention rates have been if we could factor out these involuntary causes of separation? Assuming the age distribution of the Shibaura hirees was similar to that of men at Uraga in 1921 (the best available proxy), we find that around 42 percent of those hired between 1904 and 1913 would have retired before 25 years on the job. Applying mortality rates provided in prewar Japanese life tables, we find that around 17 percent of the men 30 and under were likely to have died. Subtraction of all these individuals from the full entering group of 5,816 produces an adjusted or "real" retention rate: the ratio of those who worked 25 years (186 men) to those who possibly could have done so (2,199). About 9 percent of this group remained for their entire career, over twice the unadjusted rate, but still far fewer than the nearly 50-percent retention in the postwar cohorts.[10]

What of the roughly 2,000 remaining Shibaura workers (41 percent) among those hired? How many were travelers who left on their own, and how many were fired between 1904 and 1939? The best we can say is some of both. There are no reliable breakdowns of reasons for leaving before the 1920s. One survey of available data from after 1921 (see Chapter 4) reveals tremendous variety in the proportion of voluntary separations. These account for as many as 70 percent, and as few as 20 percent, of several large samples of men who left their jobs. The statistics do not sing in harmony. But supplemented by qualitative evidence, which does sound a consistent note, the Shibaura and Uraga data do suggest that the traveling worker, polishing his skills through movement from job to job, remained dominant as the 1920s began.

The survey team which carried out the pioneering study of work and living conditions in 1919, the Tsukishima Report, asserted that "few workers failed to count five previous jobs by age 30"[11] (Table 5). The labor market was not yet segmented; the

Table 5 Turnover at Four Tsukishima Factories in 1919

	Mean No. of Workers (a)	(b) Accessions	(c) Separations	Turnover (%) b/a	c/a
Factory A	326	—	223	—	68
Factory B	3,456	3,103	2,771	90	80
Factory C	80	59	62	74	78
Factory D	101	—	62	—	61

Source: *Tsukishima* Report, pp. 228–229.

Tsukishima Report indicates that workers moved between large and small factories, free of attachments to particular enterprises. And the report at Uraga shows clearly that, even in early 1921, well after the boom had ended and new job opportunities were hard to find, the traveling habit persisted. Between January and August, 1921, three workers left Uraga voluntarily for every one hired. The Tsukishima study examined turnover for several factories on the island of Tsukishima, including the Ishikawajima Shipyard (Factory B), and it offers rare documentation of the careers which produced the low statistical rates of long-term employment, by offering profiles of several typical men:

Worker A: 32-year-old lathe operator; at age 18 in 1906, he entered a casting factory in Nagano as a lathe trainee; in 1908, he was fired for striking, came to Tokyo and worked 6 months at Ozaki Casting Company, 1 month at Ashio Copper Refinery, 6 months at Tokyo Fukagawa Casting Company; in 1909, he moved to Kure Naval Yard; in 1916, he worked at Shibaura Engineering Works, and, since 1917, he has been employed at Ishikawajima.

Worker B: 27-year-old lathe operator; at age 16 in 1908, he entered Iwamizawa Rail Factory in Hokkaidō as a lathe trainee; in March 1909, he moved to Tokyo Shimbashi Casting Factory; in April 1910, he quit this job and spent 2 years moving from shop to shop in Shiba ward, Tokyo, with side trips to Osaka, Kōbe, and Hiroshima, picking up much expertise; in 1912, he opened his own machine shop in Shiba Ward with 3 lathes but failed after 4 months and started working for Ishikawajima; in September 1914, he entered Muroran Ironworks in Hokkaidō, but enlisted in December; discharged in 1917, he worked at the Hitachi

Mine Refinery in Ibaraki; in 1918, he entered Tokyo Iwabushi Ironworks; in 1920, he entered Tokyo Niigata Ironworks' Tsukishima factory.[12]

The attitudes and policies of employers provide another perspective on the still widespread tendency to switch jobs and travel,
in search of better pay or the opportunity to gain in skill. The
Factory Inspection Report of 1919 stated that "intensity of worker turnover remains unprecedented, despite discussion of all possible methods for keeping workers in one place."[13] Most of these
methods focused on wage policies, such as bonuses for seniority,
mid-year or year-end bonuses, and regular pay raises. Yet, companies experimenting with any such wage policy to encourage long
service faced an apparently insoluble dilemma. Wages that favored
loyal, senior people by definition discriminated against newly arrived job-switchers. So long as economic conditions made job-
switching easy, and experienced workers saw movement as the
best way to advance in skill, wages penalizing skilled job-switchers
would be self-defeating: they would not attract the best workers.
Skill rather than seniority, therefore, had to remain a fundamental
determinant of a worker's income in this era, despite varied efforts
to change matters. This, in turn, encouraged or allowed mobile
workers to continue moving.

The importance of skill began with hiring. As they had for decades, companies set initial wages on the basis of the skill an experienced applicant brought to his job. Uraga used a 1-week test to
determine the appropriate starting day wage, during which it paid
a flat 1 yen per day. Each new employer gave Saitō Tadatoshi informal tests. The Koishikawa arsenal evaluated his performance on
the lathe and set his wage at 40 sen per day. At Ishikawajima, the
tōmoku supervisor offered him a 50-sen day wage after a brief
evaluation.

Individuals bargaining in this extremely open labor market were
usually at a disadvantage even when times were good. The further
adventures of Uchida Tōshichi illustrate the weakness of a lone
individual in the absence of independent wage scales or measures
of skill, such as those a craft union could provide. Uchida quit his

job at the Mita Naval Arsenal after 8 years in 1916. He applied to Nippon Electric Company (NEC), introduced by two friends who worked there. After a 4-day trial period, the company offered him a job at 60 sen a day, but this offer insulted Uchida, a rather proud and stubborn man. It was a mere 2 sen more than the pay of his friends at NEC, whose skill, he was sure, did not approach his own. His daily rate at the arsenal had been 82 sen. But, when the company raised its offer to 65 sen, he swallowed his pride and accepted.[14] Uchida's initial day wage exceeded that of his two friends, who, of course, were his seniors at NEC. Clearly, a skilled applicant would receive higher wages than workers with less skill but more seniority. Yet, with no independent standards for skill in various crafts, Uchida could not bargain to maintain his previous wage rate, and it would seem that NEC was trying to strike a balance between the wages of skilled men such as Uchida and senior men such as his friends. The traveler took risks as he moved from job to job, and, when the labor market ceased to favor workers, companies would be able to treat job-switchers less kindly.

While the initial wage decision depended on skill, managers made some effort to keep these workers by linking subsequent increases, allowances, and bonuses to seniority. The granting of periodic raises to some of those who remained with a company was one critical practice which became fairly common by the end of World War I. Uchida described the situation at the Mita Naval Arsenal between 1912 and 1916:

> At that time [1912] at the arsenal, it had been established that pay be raised twice a year. . . . Some workers wanted to get in good with the bosses and get pay raises or promotions. At *Obon* season [August] and the New Year they would compete to give gifts to their superiors. . . . This toadying and gift-giving had great influence on the pay raises.[15]

Saitō Tadatoshi also saw his pay go up several times during his 2 years at the Army's Koishikawa arsenal during World War I, but neither he nor any other Ishikawajima workers received pay hikes between 1919 and 1921.[16] Very likely the end of the wartime boom and a slack job market led managers there to conclude they could retain sufficient skilled workers without the pay raises.

The semiannual pay raise was, thus, common but far from universal by 1921. Managers in arsenals, factories, and shipyards granted them selectively, in principle based on skill, in practice often based on petty bribery, and always subject to changing economic conditions.[17] The impact of this wage policy on the work force as a whole was to maintain a distribution of wages reflecting the relative importance of skill and rank as opposed to seniority. Juxtaposition of the tenure (seniority) distribution of the work force at Uraga with the wage distribution makes this point graphically (Figures 1 and 3). If income reflected tenure, wages would cluster at the low end and drop off sharply, as did the number of long-term employees. The wage curve, instead, has one major cluster in the center, covering 67 percent of all workers earning from 1.2 to 2.2 yen a day, and two smaller peaks at the low and high ends of the scale. Each peak coincides precisely with the average day wage for regular workers (1.6 yen), trainees (.7 yen), and foremen (2.7 yen). These broad rank designations determined the general range of a man's wage. Company evaluation of his skill determined where the traveler landed within each category. The cumulative impact of the periodic pay raise was limited. Turnover remained too intense for wage policy to shape a wage system based on seniority.

Managers also tackled the turnover problem by granting *promotions* in part on the basis of seniority. Table 6 indicates that Uraga supervisory foremen, foremen, and sub-foremen were usually workers with long tenure, while 94 percent of regular workers had 10 years' tenure or less. Yet, merely staying at Uraga did not guarantee promotion, for some 150 men had been with the company for over 10 years and were still regular workers. Conversely, skill and experience acquired elsewhere allowed a few workers with very little seniority to climb quickly, if not immediately, over senior men into high ranks. Two of 11 supervisory foremen, 19 of 161 foremen (11.8 percent), and 175 of 635 sub-foremen (27.6 percent) had been with Uraga for 5 years or less. Skill, experience,

Figure 3 Wage Distribution, Uraga, June 1921

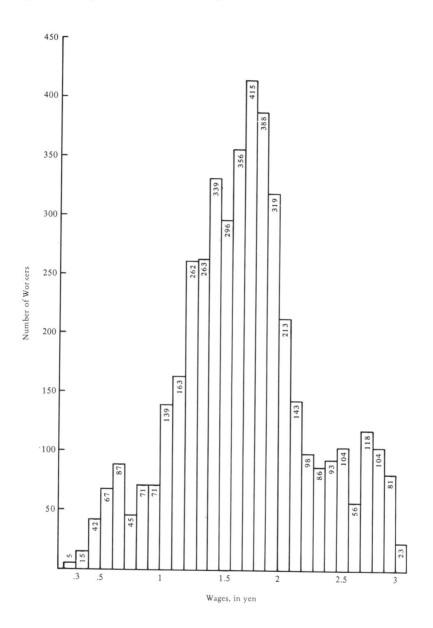

Source: Kyōchōkai, Uraga.

Table 6   Worker Tenure by Rank at Uraga, August 1921

Tenure in Years	Rank											
	Supervisory Foreman		Foreman		Sub-Foreman		Regular		Trainee		Coolie	
1–5	2	18%	19	11.8%	175	27.6%	2,003	73.5%	609	97.6%	102	87.9%
6–10	1	9	34	21.1	247	38.9	565	20.7	15	2.4	13	11.2
11–15	1	9	29	18.0	97	15.3	82	3.0	0		0	
16–20	4	36	49	30.4	97	15.3	67	2.5	0		1	0.8
21–25	3	27	30	18.6	19	2.9	8	0.3	0		0	
Total No.	11		161		635		2,725		624		116	
Mean tenure (grouped)	15.27 yrs		14.15 yrs		9.36 yrs		4.76 yrs					

Source: Kyōchōkai, *Uraga.*

and performance all influenced the decision to promote workers to leadership positions. Promotion on the basis of seniority was not a firm rule.

Finally, most companies used bonuses and allowances that rose with seniority to encourage skilled workers to stay in place. About 10 major shipyards, steel mills, and arsenals initiated seniority bonuses (*kinzoku shōyo*) during World War I. These typically offered several days' extra pay once a year to workers with more than a minimum level of seniority. The amount rose for workers with longer tenure in some cases.[18] Very small mid-year and year-end bonuses for blue-collar men also spread to many of these same enterprises during and just after World War I. As managers usually offered them only to workers with over one year on the job, these bonuses would serve to some extent as an incentive for newly hired workers to stay with a company.[19]

Work rules and hiring contracts indicated that solving the labor-force problem meant imposing discipline as well as slowing turnover. All these wage policies, the periodic increase, the bonuses, and the allowance, reflected this dual managerial concern as they sought to encourage diligent, disciplined labor as well as reward long service. Bonuses in particular were part of the continuing effort to control work more directly, tighten discipline, and encourage efficiency. Only men considered models of conduct were eligible and in many cases a good rate of attendance was a prerequisite.[20] At Uraga, various wage extras served as incentives to skilled, diligent workers. The 1921 report describes four different bonuses. In half-year periods when the company recorded a profit, the board of directors usually decided to distribute a bonus on the basis of each worker's record. Uraga offered a further special bonus at year's end to workers with outstanding records of skill or conduct, workers who acted as "models" for others, workers who made great contributions in times of crisis by preventing accidents, and workers who caught thieves, or attained other special achievements. Uraga offered a "technical bonus" to workers making a discovery or invention that contributed to company profit or aided the company in some other manner, and also offered a perfect attendance bonus: 5 to 10 yen for 6 months' perfect attendance, 3 to 6 yen for missing 3 days or less in 6 months, 1 to 3 yen for missing only 4 or 5 days.

In addition, the continued use, and indeed the spread, of piecework, incentive, and job wages was a response to this efficiency or discipline dimension to the labor-force problem. These payments rewarded the skilled, strong, fast, relatively young worker more than his senior counterpart. In the system of indirect management of the nineteenth century, oyakata commonly bid for specific jobs and distributed the revenue to their workers. By the early twentieth century, as companies replaced the oyakata with foremen who were direct company employees, this type of oyakata contracting was rare. In order to avoid the abuses found when contracts were given directly to oyakata, managers closely linked the job wages of the 1900s and 1910s to output, using them as incentives to individual workers as well as the work group. Some companies adopted simple payment by the piece. The more complex Rowan or Halsey premium systems, in use at a few enterprises as early as the 1890s, spread also. By 1922, the majority of heavy industrial firms offered output wages alone or in combination with day wages, although payment entirely by result was less common.

Companies in the Tokyo area were typical in their reliance on wage incentives to stimulate diligence. Piece, premium, or job wages typically produced one-fifth to one-half of a man's income. While employed at the Koishikawa arsenal, Saitō Tadatoshi made parts for artillery shells. The output portion in this case was simple piecework, calculated to serve as a group incentive. If 20 lathe workers produced 1,000 pieces in a day, the entire group would split the piecework rate for those 1,000 pieces; the foreman would distribute it. Saitō's pay at that time was 40 sen per day, and the piecework extra he received generally came to another 40 sen. A 50-sen-a-day worker, he recalls, would receive closer to 50 sen a day extra for the piecework, regardless of individual output. The foreman distributed the total in proportion to the individual's day wage. At Ishikawajima in 1919, as well, about one half of Saitō's daily income of 1 yen came from output wages.[21] At

Nippon Kōkan in 1919 and 1920, worker income derived from three components, base pay (a day wage), two forms of incentive pay, and extra allowances.[22] At Uraga, piecework or job wages were less significant, accounting for an average of 25 percent of a supervisory foreman's income and only 10 percent of a regular worker's take-home pay in August 1921. Here, the foremen were still able to keep a disproportionate share of the "profit" (Table 7).

Ironically, the continued reliance on output wages throughout heavy industry served to reinforce oyakata-like authority and independence among the foremen, undermining other management efforts to rein these men under control. The foreman was usually responsible for setting the job rate, and for distributing the premium to group members on the basis of day wages and his subjective judgment of performance.[23]

The labor-force problem was, thus, actually a cluster of related problems: loose discipline, inefficient labor, and job-switching. Strategies to solve these could be contradictory. In an era when the traveler was still king, sustained attempts to slow turnover and recruit a stable work force militated against efforts to attract the most skilled, efficient labor. The case of the Uraga Dock training program goes to the heart of this dilemma.

Formal worker training at Uraga dated back to 1906. In fifteen years it did little to change established patterns of behavior. First, Uraga failed to attract a sufficient number of trainees, despite recruiting visits by company personnel to local schools in March of each year, just prior to graduation. The 1921 report stated that, when Uraga sought 200 recruits, it was fortunate to sign up 100 men. Potential trainees preferred the nearby Yokosuka Naval Yard, which offered higher initial pay, greater job security, and training during work, not after hours as at Uraga. The competitive job market worked against the program from the start. Second, Uraga had problems retaining trainees during and after the 3- to 5-year program. Most left for a better offer at the Naval Yard or for "personal reasons." During the period from April 1920 through December 1921, trainees left the program at an annual rate of 13

Table 7　Uraga Day Wages and Total Income, 1921

	Rank					Coolie		Average
	Supervisory Foreman	Foreman	Sub-Foreman	Regular Worker	Minarai	Male	Female	
Average Day Wage	2.95 yen	2.72	2.16	1.63	0.73	1.19	0.73	1.62
Average Daily Income	3.93	3.09	2.37	1.81	0.81	1.36	0.81	1.80
Day Wage as Percent of Income	74.9	87.9	91.0	89.9	89.9	87.1	90.5	90.10
Days Worked per Month	25.4	24.4	22.5	20.5	21	21.4	20.6	21.1
Monthly Income Average	100.70	75.40	53.40	37.25	17.06	29.22	16.60	37.92

Source: Kyōchōkai, *Uraga.*

percent, which comes to well over one-third of a given cohort over the entire 3- to 5-year program.

Uraga offered a number of incentives, both positive and negative, to discourage dropouts and keep trainees at Uraga after the program ended. It granted a regular pay raise, increasing trainee wages twice a year during the training period. The raise varied with an evaluation of performance, but, upon graduation, a well-regarded trainee was receiving 1.7 or 1.8 yen a day, a bit more than the average for an older, experienced worker at Uraga. A bonus of 3 days' pay was given for each month of perfect attendance. Negative incentives included a temporary 1-day pay cut of 10 percent for any trainee who skipped a class and, more important, a compulsory savings plan. The company in essence confiscated 3 days' pay from each worker every month and kept the funds in individual, interest-earning accounts. It returned this money only upon trainee completion of all obligations, and these included a commitment to stay with Uraga a full 5 years after training ended. Uraga gave money forfeited by voluntary leavers to the company's mutual-aid society, but this was an unpopular program.

These incentives were ineffective, although the savings plan exacted a considerable penalty from the disloyal trainee. A worker who completed a 5-year course and then left Uraga would lose roughly 166 yen, equivalent to 4 months' pay for an average skilled worker earning 1.6 yen a day.[24] Yet, many graduates left Uraga to work elsewhere. Their skills were generally superior to workers trained on the job in hit-or-miss fashion, and they commanded high wages at other shipyards. A graduate who would receive 1.8 yen a day starting at Uraga reportedly could earn at least 2.4 or 2.5 yen at another company. The temptation to leave was understandable.

These trainees were local boys. After a period of traveling, many decided to head back to Uraga and seek a good wage near home. "Among the leavers [the 1921 report tells us] were some who returned to Uraga after two or three years." How was the company to greet these delinquent, stray sheep?

Their skills on returning are greatly advanced, and this is welcomed openly by Uraga. Workers who move from place to place polishing their skills learn most effectively, and there is no comparison between their skill and that of those who stay all along at the company. However, when these people return, it is very difficult to offer them a wage commensurate with their skill, given the desire to maintain a balance between them and their former classmates.

If it paid these men what their skill warranted, what would the company say to those "loyal" workers who had remained at Uraga and yet received lower wages? Uraga apparently opted for long-term work-force stability at the price of losing a few skilled men, a choice whose significance would emerge in later years. The report observed that returnees were upset at the relatively low wage offers and left again.

The contradiction is clear. The paternal company philosophy and labor-management strategy required that Uraga reward loyalty and seniority with a gradually increasing day wage for workers who stayed. Yet, effective business competition required that the company seek, reward, and retain skilled workers. What was Uraga to do when skill and loyalty failed to coincide, when the loyal worker was perhaps the unambitious laggard and the skilled worker a "disloyal" traveler, perhaps even a union member? This dilemma remained unsolved in 1921. In practice, the entire system of wage payment from wage setting upon hiring, to subsequent day-wage raises, to contract work and incentive pay, to bonuses, was closely tied to the skill, productivity, diligence, and rank of a worker. Uraga even based decisions to fire on a hard-headed concern with skill and productivity. Company rules in 1921 specified the following order of priority in cases where firings were unavoidable: first, fire the unskilled and those with little prospect for improving their skills; second, fire the weak and sickly; third, fire those over 55, with exceptions made for workers with special skills. Payments linked to seniority were only one part of an overall wage strategy designed to keep skilled workers and encourage efficient production. Even when managers offered some benefits linked to seniority, they were sure to consider skill and diligence as well. A context in which this situation could change eventually emerged in the economically depressed 1920s, when both the loyal and the skilled tended to cling to jobs in short supply. Ironically, as mobility decreased, the workers became more interested in wages rewarding their efforts at a single company, while managers felt less need to grant them.

THE WORKING-CLASS CHALLENGE

Organized labor in 1916 was moderate to a fault, and the dramatic increase in labor disputes of that year and the next caught the Yūaikai and Suzuki Bunji by surprise. These disputes inevitably drew in the unions and transformed them as well. By 1921, labor unions, not only the Yūaikai, by then renamed Sōdōmei, but many other independent or semi-affiliated smaller groups, were boldly taking the lead in strike activities, even though such action was illegal, and despite a drastic slump in the economy beginning in the spring of 1920.

Yūaikai members took part in many of these disputes, although the union itself did not openly advocate or lead strike actions before 1919. Encouraged by a favorable economic context, the union rank and file became decisively more militant than the cautious leadership. The "old guard" leaders were forced to respond to this more assertive rank and file and at the same time deal with a group of radical, intellectual union activists attempting to push the organization in a new direction. These pressures transformed the Yūaikai from a Friendly Society to an open supporter of labor unions.

Suzuki Bunji began to speak more openly of the need for true labor unions as early as 1916, but, under his leadership, the Yūaikai responded to the spread of strike activity in 1917 with uneasy caution. Suzuki warned workers not to strike, stressed moderation, and disavowed any Yūaikai connection with the strikes occurring throughout Japan. This was, to some extent, a tactical necessity. The Yūaikai could easily be targeted as an "outside" agitating force vulnerable to Article 17 of the 1900 Police Law.

By 1919, however, a combination of pressure from the rank and file and younger, more radical activists at Yūaikai headquarters forced a major redefinition of the Yūaikai mission. As early as 1917, some of the more radical young men at Yūaikai headquarters had affirmed strongly the right of workers to strike.[25] Then, a controversial national convention in the autumn of 1919 formally inaugurated a new age of assertive unionism. The group changed its name, replacing Yūaikai with the name Dai Nihon Rōdō Sōdōmei Yūaikai (Friendly Society Greater Japan Federation of Labor). Eventually, the terms Greater and Friendly Society were abandoned, the former too imperialistic, the latter too moderate, and the Japan Federation of Labor (Sōdōmei) was born.

Against this background, a flowering of labor organization took place between 1919 and 1921 both within and without the Sōdōmei-Yūaikai structure. These organizations varied from moderate mutual-aid societies to aggressive local or factory unions.[26] Their leaders were constantly involved in moves toward mergers and larger regional federations and continually thwarted by ideological rivalry. The union movement by 1919 had reached a new stage. Unions more often took the lead in strikes and actively sought to organize on a large scale.[27]

By 1921, strong factory-based unions were in place at Shibaura, Ishikawajima, and the Yokohama Dock Company, as well as at a host of other heavy industrial firms nationwide, and the creation of an industrial federation seemed to be a logical next step. Shibaura managers in 1919 sponsored a company union to counter the still growing Yūaikai-Sōdōmei contingent there. This "yellow union" ironically changed colors and led a controversial strike in 1920, but the old Yūaikai union refused to support it. In the wake of this disastrous display of factionalism, Shibaura workers were unable to build a united front until late 1921, when they created a single, independent, company-wide union. The Shibaura Labor Union which emerged was a solid group. It claimed the allegiance of half the 3,120 Shibaura workers and remained a significant force until the late 1920s. In similar fashion, workers at Ishikawajima and Yokohama Dock Company built strong unions on a foundation of workshop organization between 1919 and 1921. The stumbling blocks in both cases were factional disputes between small, horizontal unions of varied ideological persuasions, and one solution was to create a single company-wide union absorbing all the local factions of outside unions. The result must not be confused with so-called "company" or "yellow" unions, for these company-wide groups were independent organizations interested in broader industrial federation and determined to confront managers within the factory or shipyard.

The vitality and coherence of the activity of the men in these and similar unions was in large measure responsible for the shedding by the Yūaikai of its Friendly Society skin and the emergence of the Sōdōmei by 1921. The challenge posed by angry, combative workers, often younger men with little work-place status and little use for the paternal warmth offered mainly to foremen, forced managers to rework a wide range of important labor management practices. The extent of the labor movement impact is underlined by the fact that, even where the union movement was relatively slow to organize men with obvious discontents, as at Uraga Dock, labor disputes or merely the threat of unrest sufficed to bring a defensive reaction.

Strike or dispute actions had a direct impact on wartime wage policies. In several major firms, workers gained bonuses by demanding them. The Mitsubishi Nagasaki Shipyard bonus of 1917 came in response to a demand of 13,000 striking workers, and extension of such a bonus to workers was a demand of the Shibaura strikers of 1920.[28] In both cases, far more generous semiannual bonuses had been part of white-collar wages for decades. Here, as in the railroad disputes of the 1890s, workers demanded and won benefits previously reserved for staff. In many other cases, as at Uraga, managers avoided a firm, written commitment to pay such bonuses, for they hoped to be able to retract them if the boom came to an end. This was true also of the wide variety of "temporary" allowances—housing, rice, lunch, or inflation allowances—extended to workers during the inflationary war years. Rather than add to worker day wages, managers offered temporary and, in theory, retractable benefits, but worker pressure eventually led companies to incorporate the benefits into the regular daily wage. At Yahata, the "temporary wartime allowance" of 3.25 to 25 yen per month became part of the day wage as a result of a strike in 1920. Incorporation of temporary allowances into base pay was a common demand of this era. Finally, retirement pay was another benefit extended to workers, not as paternal benevolence but as a response to labor agitation.

But, even more than wages, the substance and rhetoric of paternalism changed in the face of the working-class challenge. Managers in heavy industry had been speaking of beautiful customs of paternal care and worker obedience since the 1890s, but these remained little more than figures of speech in many cases before World War I. By the end of the war, most heavy industrial firms had implemented a fairly substantial number of benefits in addition to wages. This more substantive paternalism was a direct, self-conscious response to the rise of the labor movement and the spread of radical ideas among workers, an attempt to satisfy worker demands without recognizing independent labor unions.[29] As the labor movement continued to grow, it forced management to alter, between 1918 and 1921, the tone and, to some extent, the content of its paternalism.

The decision of many major enterprises to establish specialized personnel or labor sections reflected serious concern with labor management and the labor movement. These sections played a major role in the elaboration of company welfare programs. The Mitsui, Mitsubishi, and Sumitomo zaibatsu concerns all created independent personnel or labor sections in their head offices between 1917 and 1921. Shibaura was a leader in the Kantō region in this respect, for it had established an Education Section in 1915 and had revised its entire labor management policy. Uraga established a Worker Section (Shakkō-ka) at some time before 1917, and by 1917 the section had a staff of 15 employees.[30] When disputes arose or a major change in labor policy was at issue, top executives still became involved, but, with the creation of these new divisions, the "managers" charged with day-to-day labor administration became a middle-level group of labor specialists.

At Uraga, this section in principle made all decisions concerning wages and work conditions. The men in 1917 reportedly trusted the Worker Section employees and welcomed its activity because one staff member, Kosugi Rokusaburō, in charge of worker protection, was a Yūaikai member.[31] By 1921, the Worker Section had further expanded into a division with three sections. In contrast to other area shipyards, Uraga gave the Worker Division a great deal of authority. At Yokohama Dock Company, the report said, each factory head in fact still retained the power to fire workers. At Ishikawajima, most authority over personnel decisions rested in foreman hands throughout the 1920s. Uraga was different. It required the factory director to consult with the Worker Division on all disciplinary matters, and workers reportedly trusted the head of the division more than the shop-floor supervisors.

The Uraga Dock Company moved quickly and one step ahead of its competitors in creating a powerful Worker Division and a fairly extensive range of welfare programs for workers. This policy reflected the management philosophies of company presidents Machida (1912–1919) and Imaoka (1922–1934). Imaoka, especially, had great interest in labor problems. As Executive Director in 1921, he was deeply interested in strengthening company contact with the workers. Even during the post-World War I depression, when other companies were cutting back all operations not directly involved in production, Imaoka expanded the Worker Division, had it carry out a range of surveys, compile statistics, and study ways to avoid labor problems.[32]

Uraga strove to encourage a sense of hierarchy and division between regular workers, sub-foremen, and foremen, so as to lead the foremen and sub-foremen to feel themselves privileged members of the company and weaken unity among workers. Regulations of 1919 on travel at company expense set daily allowances for food and lodging at different levels for the three ranks, 1.6 yen, 2.5 yen, and 3.3 yen respectively.[33] Managers organized foremen into their own mutual-aid society, and the sub-foremen in various workshops also had their own mutual-aid groups by 1921. These organizations served as vehicles for negotiation in times of labor disputes, and the company viewed them favorably. The regular workers had no separate organization, a source of resentment which surfaced in the labor disputes of the 1920s. In 1921, Imaoka was studying the idea of forming a factory council at Uraga, but he felt it would be safest to start with smaller shop committees and build up to a factory council.

Favoritism shown to ranked workers had first appeared in Uraga policies of the early 1900s, and the fact that foremen tended to side with the company in disputes after 1910 indicates that this treatment was effective. The same cannot be said of policy toward either regular workers or sub-foremen, which helps explain Imaoka's interest in the factory council idea. As World War I ended, managers at Uraga were well aware that an appeal for loyal worker service to the company would ignite no sparks of emotion. When they urged workers to make greater efforts, they spoke explicitly in terms of loyalty to the nation, not the Uraga Dock Company. In 1919, the company obtained orders from the Japanese Navy for a light cruiser and a destroyer and issued the following notice to all employees:

> The skill and spirit of service of our employees has been recognized. . . .
> The recent war has clearly shown that a nation's strength lies in its industry, and in the future we want you to consider yourselves not mere employees of a profit-making company but participants in a national enterprise.[34]

In another attempt to link work at Uraga to service to the nation, the company formed an unnamed organization of workers in 1921, whose main purpose was to "serve the Emperor." The group was actively soliciting members as the Kyōchōkai reporter collected his data, and he noted that "quite a few" workers joined the society.

This high level of concern with labor management was no accident. Eight labor disputes took place at the Dock Company between 1907 and 1921. The many company welfare programs, including sale of inexpensive rice, injury compensation and medical care, awards for long service, recreation and housing programs, a variety of mutual-aid organizations, a savings plan, and a pension fund, were usually countermeasures adopted and modified as direct or indirect responses to worker complaints.[35]

The company's savings plan, its one all-inclusive mutual-aid society, and a pension fund all evolved in a context of interaction with dissatisfied workers. The savings program caused a prolonged strike in 1915. As part of the settlement, Uraga substantially modified the confiscatory aspects of the plan, and changed it further in later years due to continued protests. As of August 1919, all workers belonged to the new Savings Association created in 1916 after the strike. One-half of a man's semiannual bonus went to the association and was deposited with the national postal savings system. In order to withdraw the money, one still needed the permission of the factory director. When incomes declined due to a drop in overtime in the postwar depression, this restriction too became the object of widespread complaint. The company at some point in 1920 or 1921 decided to allow free withdrawal of funds, and workers took advantage of this new freedom. At the time of the Kyōchōkai report, very few workers still kept money in the savings association, which, at the end of 1920, had contained a peak of 7,986 yen.[36]

In the summer of 1916, the company set up a pension fund, supported in part by compulsory deductions from worker pay. The deducted funds earned no interest. Uraga also modified this plan under pressure, as workers complained bitterly over what they saw as confiscation of their pay. In response, the company established a new mutual-aid society using the disputed wage deductions, and it agreed to pay interest on the money. Uraga also assumed the full burden of support for the pension fund, and promised to pay 3.6 percent yearly interest on that fund as well. The mutual-aid society gave workers control over a part of the company's overall welfare program. All employees were members of the society, beginning with the company president. A committee chosen from staff and workers in equal numbers ran the society.

One-half of 1 percent of each worker's monthly wage was put into the fund. The society paid benefits to a worker or his survivors in cases of firing, injury, retirement, the military draft, death, death in the family, and natural disaster. In 1916, the aid society had funds of 11,728 yen, 10,000 donated by the company. By 1921, the total had reached 48,546 yen.[37]

The complementary pension fund began in 1916 with a mere 2,636-yen principal. It remained controversial even after the company agreed to pay interest, for a worker received his share only if he met the rather restricted conditions of accumulated seniority (15 years) or a medically certified reason for stopping work. Voluntary leavers received nothing from the fund.[38] In November 1921, Uraga made several changes in the rules governing the fund. Some favored the company. Uraga increased its freedom to decide how much to contribute. It would set the amount between 1 and 5 percent of the worker's monthly wage, depending on the economic situation. It was, in fact, paying in 2 percent of each worker's wage. Also as of November 1921, the company discontinued interest payments on the principal of the fund. On the other hand, Uraga agreed to grant voluntary leavers one-half of the total accumulated in their names, in cases where the company decided this appropriate, and it gave each worker the right to examine the fund records to see how much money had accumulated in his account.

The most interesting of these changes was a slight modification in wording which reflected a far more important change in management policy, a company response to a new attitude among heavy industrial workers. Managers at Uraga were sensitive to the "trends of the times." They sought to satisfy or anticipate the new worker demands for rights by redefining the labor relationship as a relationship of equals:

> Until now [November 1921] the wording of the [pension] fund has tended to make everything seem to be the benevolent gift of the company. Now all such paternalistic language is to be taken out of the regulations. For example, the term "to bestow" money [*keiyo*] is to be replaced by the term "to pay" [*kyūyo*].

The Uraga workers were ready enough to accept welfare benefits which, by 1921, included free medical care in certain cases,
housing, and entertainment, in addition to the pension plan,
mutual-aid society, and savings fund, but they did not accept
these unconditionally. The company modified or reformed welfare programs in response to or in anticipation of worker resistance or dissatisfaction. Out of this give and take, Uraga's
labor management policy slowly became more systematic and
generous. And what managers once thought of and described as
company benevolence was now the fulfillment of a company
obligation to its workers, the simple "payment" of money.

This change was by no means isolated or accidental. As the
labor movement grew in size and became more effective and aggressive, the political, bureaucratic, and industrial elite responded
with growing concern. Since 1918, Home Minister Tokonami
actively had been encouraging capitalists to organize company
unions amenable to management calls for cooperation, in which
workers would be granted a measure of respect and equality. In a
similar spirit, he and others in the government encouraged introduction of factory councils. The formation of the Kyōchōkai in
1919 was another manifestation of this new interest in labor
problems. Uraga's interest in a factory council and modification of
the wording in company regulations, and the Shibaura attempt of
1920 to form a company union to compete with the Yūaikai,
must be seen in this context. They reflected a common concern.[39]

At the same time, other industrial leaders responded to Tokonami's urgings or to the Kyōchōkai with skepticism or even hostility. By encouraging "cooperation," company unions, or factory
councils, it was said, the government was recognizing the existence
of two opposed entities which had to cooperate. Some capitalists
saw this as a dangerous idea giving sanction to union activities.[40]
At Uraga, management moved slowly and was just "studying"
the idea of a factory council in 1921. Only in the following
several years did managers actually create factory councils or company unions at a fair number of companies. The unprecedented

shipbuilding disputes of the summer and fall of 1921 motivated many companies to move from study to creation of various in-company organizations designed to promote cooperation and to accept the need to grant some increased respect or equality to workers.

Labor relations were in a state of flux in 1921. Managers had not yet solved the problems of maintaining a stable, skilled work force, retaining valuable men trained at company expense, and asserting discipline and direct control over workers, although these had been recognized as problems since the turn of the century. They viewed workers with suspicion, and men in the factories in turn offered no special commitment to particular companies. Companies made some effort to link wage payments, bonuses, or allowances to seniority and cultivate this commitment, and these changes would persist and take on greater importance in time, but skill and diligence continued to be the major factors determining wages, bonuses, or promotions.

Despite two decades in which talk of paternalism and beautiful customs dominated public discussion of the labor issue, and despite efforts to encourage a sense among workers of identification with the enterprise, by 1921 an aggressive young labor movement which transcended single enterprises and attempted to organize by industry forced management to reevaluate and revise the "paternal" approach to labor. Uraga policies were part of this revision, but, when the company changed the wording of its pension fund rules in late 1921, it was by no means clear that such cosmetic measures would suffice. Consider, for example, the following dialogue between strike group representatives and managers at the Yokohama Dock Company, also from the fall of 1921. Management's professed view of the company as a paternal, benevolent institution concerned above all with its workers stands in stark contrast to the worker perception of the company as insincere and cold blooded.

[The meeting took place at the company office at 1:30 p.m. on September 28, 1921. Itō Masayoshi, Iwasa Seizō, and Shiga Kōju represented

the workers, while Tōjō and Miyanaga, two company directors, spoke
for the company.]

Itō: Today the three of us have come as worker representatives with
this petition.

Managing Director Miyanaga: The four demands, you mean?

Itō: That's right.

Miyanaga: Does this demand for a 20-percent daily wage increase mean
an average increase of 20 percent for all the workers?

Iwasa: Our wages average 1 yen 60 sen. Out of 1,000 people, if there is
one getting 3 yen, the rest are getting around 1 yen 40 sen. With
days off, one month is 25 days and, with a wife and children, we
can't make ends meet. This is why we have asked for a pay raise.
With the present severance pay, if one of us is fired, he is reduced to
poverty [one demand was for higher severance pay].

Miyanaga: We want you to understand the company's situation. As you
are well aware, the economy, especially the shipbuilding industry, is
facing a severe depression. The question of how to support the workers in this situation is one that troubles us greatly. Because of the
shipbuilding depression there have been many layoffs, and, aware of
your anxiety about this, the other day we announced that we would
not carry out any large-scale layoffs. As for ship repairs, which this
company has been engaged in since its founding, in good times we
were able to charge the shipowners a good price, but today the situation is so bad that, even if we offer a price below cost, they won't
take it. Shipbuilding revived briefly after the war and we were able
to make some profit, but now we are making no profit and are taking
orders at a loss.[41] In this depression, we are taking on such orders because we do not want to have to lay off you workers. Recently we
accepted two orders from NYK and one from elsewhere, and in all
these cases the company accepted them below cost. Putting thought
of profit aside, we are making great efforts to secure as much business
as possible. We understand well your plight, but, even at present pay
levels, the situation is as I have described, so we would hope to have
your understanding on this point [the pay raise]. You also raised
demands regarding severance and retirement pay. As I have already
noted, out policy is to avoid layoffs at all costs in the hopes that this
will reduce your anxiety, so we would like to gain your understanding on these points also. As for the fourth demand, you use the term
"expel" [*haiseki*]. Does that mean you want us to fire them?

All three: That's right.

Miyanaga: You want us to fire the three factory heads. However, the decision to take action against those who break company regulations does rest with these people. Although we hope to avoid such situations, every day two or three people are fired for breaking company rules, and there was nothing exceptional in the case of these three. Thus, it would be difficult to take action [and fire the supervisors who had fired three union members, ostensibly for breaking rules]. As for what the company will do in the future, we feel it would be best to work to harmonize [*sotsū*] your desires with those of the company and work from a position of mutual understanding. We are presently studying ways to promote your welfare. In due time, we are hoping to implement these plans. Thus we would like to gain your understanding regarding both the company's present position and future plans and have you pass this on to your fellow workers.

Itō: Are you saying that you will absolutely not lay off any workers?

Miyanaga: I can't promise "absolutely" but . . .

Miyanaga and Itō (together): Insofar as possible [*Narutake to iu koto*].

Itō: In that case wouldn't it be better to decide on severance pay and relieve our anxieties in that way?

Miyanaga: Our thinking is that it would be even kinder to take the policy of avoiding layoffs rather than getting involved in the severance pay issue.

Itō: So you mean to say that there is no necessity to decide on severance pay? If your policy is not to lay off workers, well, this is a bit of an extreme example, but in that case wouldn't it be just as well to set severance pay at 10 or 20 thousand yen?

Miyanaga: I didn't say that there was no need. We are now considering the issue of severance pay.

Itō: You say "insofar as possible," but does that mean that in the eventuality of a layoff you will handle it as in the past?

Miyanaga: We are now also considering the possibility of increasing the level in the future.

Iwasa: Isn't what you are saying merely that, if you accept our demands, your profit will be narrowed? For us this is a matter of life and death.

Miyanaga: You say "our profits are narrowed," but in fact, not only are we not expecting any profit, but the company is going so far as to take orders at a loss [to operate at a loss].

Executive Director Tōjō: I'm the one responsible for estimates of material, labor, factory, and office expenses. It would be fine if we could take in some profit, and previously we would add a bit to our overall estimate, but now we subtract a certain percent from the estimate.

Miyanaga: As the director has just said, the times are very hard and we wish you would report on our situation [to the other workers].

Itō: We have already heard at length from Mr. Yamaguchi on this point and understand it well. In any case, we regard the fact that the company will not now announce its intention to change the present severance pay as an indication of the company's total lack of sincerity regarding this entire affair. Let's go back and report this to all the others.

Miyanaga: You say that we are insincere, but as I have already explained the company is striving to promote your welfare and guarantee your security, and we'd like you to report this to the others.

Iwasa: The other day a worker named Tsukui, who was working in one of your manufacturing shops, was fired for going to another shop and talking to a worker there. You said that this was a violation of company rules, so he was fired. But this is something which other workers are constantly doing, so, if you seize on such little things to fire workers, and since we are now in the midst of a time of great unemployment, if you look for such little matters and fire someone everyday, pretty soon you'll have fired all the workers. Therefore, all your kind words are just the attitude of a man who stands laughing after having strangled seven people. We'll go and report this situation to all the other workers.

Miyanaga: If we were trying to get rid of 5,000 workers we wouldn't go about it that way.

Tōjō: Actually the number of workers is declining naturally due to a variety of circumstances, and sometimes we are even hiring new workers to make up for this.[42]

Clearly the Yokosen strikers had no use for empty declarations of understanding and sympathy. Masumoto Uhei, the government representative for Japan to the I.L.O., echoed this point in remarking that "workers view the shipyard as a place that, even if it provides work, by no means does so with the workers' interests at heart."[43] Yet, imbedded in the language of the Yokosen strikers is a set of concerns going beyond a simple wage increase, concerns that echoed the railway workers of the 1890s and would remain to shape the labor relationship of the future. The company lacked sincerity. It refused to promise job security. It refused to raise severance pay. The men at Yokosen got angriest over these issues. They wanted a secure place in the company, or at least the social security of decent severance pay. They were demanding better terms of membership, not rejecting the notion that a company should in good faith take care of its workers.

Those who gained such security could, it seemed, be induced to change their attitude toward the firm. Shibaura and Uraga both offered special terms of membership to foremen, and in these and similar companies the foremen, by 1920 or 1921, identified their interests with the company as well as with the labor movement and worked to insure peace within the factory. A company such as Ishikawajima, on the other hand, adopted more of a hands-off policy and the foremen remained close to the workers. This, in fact, helps explain the strength of the labor movement there.

Disputes at Yokohama and Uraga Dock Companies, and throughout Japan, as well as the earlier management response to the Yūaikai seen at Shibaura, describe a labor relationship in which workers pressed for more systematic benefits and more "equal" treatment, and managers occasionally adopted new personnel policies in response. Many of these workers demanded from the company more substantial forms of company paternalism, but, by World War I, they increasingly viewed such treatment as their right, not a paternal gift. Further, the common demands for an 8-hour day, a share in profits through bonuses (Ishikawajima in 1921), or election of foremen (Shibaura in 1920) went beyond the paternal framework. Some workers sought not just more substantive "good treatment," but a labor relationship based on recognition of worker rights. Almost all new management policies of the World War I era at the Mitsubishi Shipyard in Kōbe were adopted as responses to labor activity. Workers demanded and, at least for a brief time, gained bonuses, systematic pay raises, pay raises given to all without reference to skill, and sale of rice below cost. On a more abstract level, the Mitsubishi workers wanted respect for themselves as individuals and as a group, not paternal benevolence, unless, perhaps, managers were to redefine paternal benevolence to include respect for the dignity of workers.[44]

The management response to this new labor assertiveness during and just after World War I was not particularly confident or consistent. Only after several years did a new set of effective management initiatives emerge. A group of 74 Tokyo factory owners and managers in the machine industry who met in March 1920 were quite uncertain of their response. They were almost ready to concede that paternalism without unions could not work.[45] They discussed lockouts or blacklists but rejected these as impractical. The financial loss suffered by a company during a lockout made that tactic unsuitable, and the establishment of an effective blacklist would be impossible in practice. Several owners advocated recognition of unions. They reasoned that, in the present chaotic situation, managers or owners had no clear opponent, no opposite number with whom they could negotiate, so that the recognition of labor unions would serve their own interests. One owner, whose workers were at that moment out on a strike led by the Japan Machinists Union, went so far as to advocate recognition of large horizontal unions. He felt that, with several small unions present, the worker representatives disagreed among themselves, making negotiations impossible. With one large union as an opposite number, the capitalists would be able to negotiate with more certainty, to accept or reject demands as they wished, and avoid bitter labor-capital antagonism.[46] Whatever the merit or logic of this argument, it contrasts sharply with earlier management attitudes. The strength workers in heavy industry were able to muster between 1917 and 1921 had forced managers in Tokyo and throughout Japan to rethink their approach to labor. In the 1920s and 1930s, they almost always chose to confront or coopt unions, rather than recognize them, but they also remade the system of paternal management in policies concerned with hiring, job security, wages, and welfare.

Part Two

Workers, Managers, and the Interwar Employment System

FOUR

Travelers' End? Hiring and Long-Term Employment

In 1931, capitalists and managers from firms large and small joined together to defeat a trade-union bill decisively in the House of Peers, and the uncertainty of the Tokyo owners one decade earlier seemed a relic of the distant past. By the end of the 1920s, managers had contrived to banish almost all strong, independent unions from major shipyards, machine factories, and steel mills. Only a few maverick industrialists still believed unions necessary or desirable. To this extent, the managerial elite had overcome the working-class challenge. In addition, a sustained decline in labor turnover raised the possibility that managers had solved at least this part of the labor-force problem. Still, earlier tensions remained; the interwar labor relationship evolved within a framework of continued management concern with efficiency and control, and continued labor concern with status and security. Common career patterns changed some in this era of economic stagnation. More men than before hoped to remain with their first employer from initial hiring to maturity as a skilled worker, rather than travel broadly. But labor demands for job protection were not met, so that long-run employment prospects remained insecure and impermanent.

GETTING STARTED

A few managers had experimented with systematic hiring programs in response to both labor-force and working-class problems before the 1920s. They had sponsored vocational training
and sent selected men to night school in the early 1900s. In the
1920s, these strategies became standard procedure at virtually all
large firms. The result was a hiring system in which a minority of
inexperienced young boys regularly entered a firm each year as a
favored group expected to become future workshop leaders and
career employees, while managers drew the majority of factory
laborers from a pool of mobile, often unemployed adult wage
earners.

Those firms hiring inexperienced youngsters recruited them
directly from the elementary or middle schools upon graduation
in March or April. Therefore, one way to get a rough indication of
the frequency of school-graduate hiring is to compare hiring rates
for March or April with those for other months, when school grads
were not being hired. The figures indicate that, in the 1920s, such
recruitment took place to a limited extent, while the most important means to meet labor requirement was to hire older, experienced men year round, as business demanded. As a basis for
comparison, consider figures for typical years in the 1960s and
1970s. In Table 8 a clear peak in the post-World War II hiring rate
comes at the end of the school year in March and April. One-
third of all hiring in the manufacturing sector nationwide (35 to
36 percent) took place in these two months. While prewar figures
are limited, there are nationwide data available from the machine
industry in 1922 and 1924. No comparable sharp peak can be
found, but 1922 hiring was above average from February to April,
and, in 1924, hiring increased slightly in early spring. March-April
hiring in these two years accounted for 26 and 24 percent of all
hiring, below the 32 percent figures for 1967 and 1978, but above
the 16.7 percent expected if hiring were distributed evenly year
round. In a perfectly even case, one-sixth of all hiring would take
place in any 2-month period. In the 1920s, one-fourth of hiring

Table 8   Average March and April Hiring Rates
(as % of total work force and total year's hiring)

Prewar Machine-Industry Accessions (a)
1922:

% of work force		March-April % of Year's Hiring
March hiring	5.3	
April hiring	5.1	
March-April total	10.4	
Year's total hiring	40.7	25.6

1924:

% of work force		March-April % of Year's Hiring
March hiring	4.7	
April hiring	4.9	
March-April total	9.6	
Year's total hiring	39.9	24.1

Postwar Manufacturing Industry Accessions (b)
1967:

% of work force		March-April % of Year's Hiring
March hiring	4.0	
April hiring	6.9	
March-April total	10.9	
Year's total hiring	31.4	34.7

1978:

% of work force		March-April % of Year's Hiring
March hiring	1.4	
April hiring	3.8	
March-April total	5.2	
Year's total hiring	14.6	35.6

Sources: (a) Nihon ginkō, *Rōdō tōkei,* 1925 edition, appendix.
(b) Rōdō shō, *Yearbook of Labor Statistics,* 1967, p. 22; 1978, p. 20.

came in March and April, while, in the 1960s, the proportion was just over one-third.

These numbers suggest that the common postwar policy of school-graduate hiring was already practiced by the few large firms which, by the late 1920s, provided training programs for new employees, including classroom education as well as on-the-job training. Keihin-area examples include Uraga from before 1921, the Yokohama Dock Company from at least 1926, and Ishikawajima from 1928. Similar programs were started elsewhere in the country in the 1920s, although this was not universal. Even Shibaura, usually in the forefront of new trends in labor management, had no formal in-company classroom program for new workers until 1933. Such programs very likely account for part of the springtime bulge in hiring, although a natural process of job-seeking by new graduates is probably important as well.

A variety of qualitative and company-specific evidence indicates how limited these programs were. A 1927 survey of machine, ship-building, and metal industry labor finds that hiring (and leaving) rose slightly in the spring (Table 9), but the thorough explanation offered by the authors of that report looks to factors other than school-graduate hiring. The report notes that turnover for males rose in February and April and from June through August. "However, one of the factories surveyed had especially high turnover. It both hired and fired an unusually large number in February and April. If we disregard this factory, turnover never exceeded 2 percent monthly." The report accounts for the remaining examples of relatively high spring and summertime turnover, found in all industries and regions, by noting "increased illness in the intense heat of summer and increased job-switching in the good weather of April and May, when workers tended to move to smaller factories in search of higher wages."[1] If deliberate policies of hiring recent school graduates were widespread and statistically important, we would expect the report to have mentioned these.

At one company for which good data are available, Nippon Kōkan, hiring of workers took place year round with no spring peak, in sharp distinction to hiring of white-collar employees at the company. From 1915 to 1931, NKK hired 26 percent of a sample of 149 white-collar staff in April alone, and the steelmaker signed on exactly one-half of this group in the March-to-May springtime period. Hiring of the blue-collar force in the sample was entirely different. Of 391 hired over the same 16-year period, only 8.7 percent were hired in April, 23 percent in the three spring

Table 9 Turnover Survey at Three Machine Factories,
         11/1925–10/1926

Date	Hired		Fired		Total		Turnover Rate	
	Male	Female	M	F	M	F	M	F
11/1925	84	15	44	17	128	32	1.8%	7.1%
12/1925	14	16	82	6	96	22	1.3	4.8
1/1926	46	15	44	7	90	22	1.3	4.8
2	167	32	65	15	232	47	3.2	10.4
3	79	23	54	12	133	35	1.9	7.7
4	142	32	109	37	251	69	3.5	15.1
5	95	5	68	13	163	18	2.2	4.0
6	109	29	69	29	178	58	2.5	12.8
7	93	9	80	17	173	26	2.5	5.7
8	95	5	68	10	163	15	2.5	3.3
9	65	13	65	13	130	26	1.9	5.7
10	53	8	135	17	188	25	2.6	5.6
Total or Yearly Avg.	1,042	202	883	193	1,925	395	2.4	7.3

Source: Kikai kōgyō (1927), p. 43

months, figures virtually identical to the 8.3 percent and 25 percent one would expect in a situation of totally even year-round
hiring.[2] The sharp difference between figures for blue and white
collar is a strong sign that management had a well-established recruiting program for the high-school and college graduates entering white-collar jobs, while it had no such program for laborers.

For management, hiring of experienced workers who would
require little company investment in training made business sense,
and it was more common than hiring of untrained school graduates.
Experienced workers were available. According to a 1926 survey
of the shipbuilding industry, recruiting was done in the vicinity of
shipyards and naval arsenals, primarily from among unemployed
men. "Because of surplus labor and great unemployment, it is easy
to find the needed workers from among the unemployed in these
locations."[3] Companies relied on introductions by workers already
at their factories to locate recruits from this ready pool.[4] When

Uraga needed new workers, it posted an announcement within the company grounds and gave preference to men introduced by present employees. In 1921, 70 percent of the Uraga work force was drawn from its home base of Kanagawa prefecture. As they had since World War I, Uraga and its competitors then made sure the applicant was not a labor-union activist. By 1926, the managers of major shipyards communicated news of fired union members or union leaders rather effectively and "those who have joined union or strike efforts [were] unlikely to be hired by other shipyards."[5] The next step was a rigorous health examination. After the enactment of the Health Insurance Law in 1927, this protected the company against claims made for prior injuries or illness.[6]

The skilled applicant who passed the political and health tests was hired for a 1-week trial period. As in earlier decades, a company set wages on the basis of work performance during the trial week.[7] Finally, most applicants hired in this manner began as temporary employees with a 3-month, 6-month, or 1-year contract. Only after that period would a company give some new workers "regular" status. A company either fired the others or renewed their contracts for another short term.[8] This appears to be a major new hiring policy of the 1920s. The difficulties of trimming the bloated work forces of the war boom, recounted below, led managers to move cautiously in subsequent hiring as well as firing.

This hiring procedure was open to abuse, as it had been for decades. One Shibaura worker complained about the situation at his company:

> Do you want to work here? Well, come try applying. First, you've got to pass a bothersome skill test. Then they want to know about your ideas. They fear an increase of awakened workers most of all. . . . But if you come in and bow your head low and work like a slave they'll gladly take you. Of course, the surest way is to bring about 30 yen to Naitō or someone else in the Worker Section. . . . There's no place where these "commissions" are as effective as at Shibaura.[9]

Whether a commission was necessary or not, applying with experience was the dominant route to employment in heavy industry throughout the 1920s and early 1930s. Mariko Kōsaburō, who entered the Ishikawajima shipyard in 1928, estimates that, for every 100 men hired, 70 to 80 would be experienced workers signed on as demand warranted. Professor Hazama Hiroshi supports Mariko's recollection, writing that companies hired most new workers in this era from among experienced workers. He cites a survey of the machine industry in Osaka in 1921 where 70 percent of newly hired workers were experienced.[10] An example of such hiring in response to demand is found at Uraga in 1927 where the work force increased by 293 workers, or 12.8 percent, between July and September, after orders for four new ships were obtained.[11]

Even so, the 20 to 30 percent of the workers hired without prior experience, those recent graduates of elementary or middle schools who entered special programs for company trainees or apprentices, were a group of considerable significance. The spread of programs for them was a sign that companies increasingly saw education and cultivation of a corps of skilled workers as a major priority. Earlier managerial strategies to retain, control, and motivate labor were increasing in sophistication and scope.

With the possible exception of the Mitsubishi Shipyard in Kōbe and perhaps one or two other giant firms, these trainees remained a minority of those hired, and training programs were no more successful in retaining workers than in earlier decades, despite a depressed job market.[12] Companies continued to give close attention to their young trainees. At Uraga, regulations of 1926 provided for the same confiscatory savings plan for trainees as had those of 1921. Also, a 1924 revision of the rules for trainee application procedures added the requirement that "trainees be persons intending to work [at Uraga] for a long time." On the positive side, Uraga still gave the trainees pay raises more regularly than other workers.[13] Despite such incentives, the 1927 report on shipbuilding labor concluded that none of the worker-training programs had good records. "There is a fair amount of turnover even during the trainee period, and this continues unabated even after training is over. . . . In general, 35 to 40 percent of trainees remain after their program ends. Over half go elsewhere."[14] Of course, this investment was not wasted from an industry-wide or long-term perspective, as "most trainees move between major shipyards and many return to the company that trained them after working elsewhere for a while."[15]

These "regular hiring" programs of the 1920s only became the dominant route to employment in a big factory in later years. The evidence available does not support the claim that companies relied on "new recruits [school graduates] exclusively or almost exclusively in the 1920s."[16] This suggestive forerunner of employment policies of the 1950s or beyond tells only part of the story of labor relations in the 1920s, for the forerunners were only a minor, and not even a new, part of the picture.

At the center of the picture were managers interested first in obtaining skilled workers when needed with a minimum of effort and investment, second in insuring that these workers were ideologically safe, and third by keeping many on only as "temporaries," in maintaining a low-paid, easily fired, yet skilled work force. Finally, they took some boys as favored trainees in the hope of creating a corps of key workshop leaders, and the trainee as career employee took on new importance in management eyes. The technology imported in this decade was more complex than before, and national economic woes made efficient production a top managerial priority. As a result, the training effort was more extensive in the 1920s than before. The training programs included classroom education plus on-the-job-training, and some companies founded new schools, but company education itself was not new.[17] The trainees continued to put this company investment to work for other employers, even with jobs hard to find.

STAYING PUT: JOB SECURITY AND THE LABOR MOVEMENT

The Japanese economy trod a rocky path in the 1920s. "Traveling" became a risky and difficult matter for the skilled adults for whom frequent movement and "polishing of skills" (*ude o migaku*) had long defined the ideal career. In hard times, the security of a place in a large firm was more attractive than before, and at times labor managers tried to seize the advantage by encouraging these formerly elusive men to stay; but the business climate that increased the value of a secure job led these same firms to cut back and fire expensive skilled labor. Managerial efforts to elicit long-term service were, thus, inconsistent, while labor was hard-pressed to enforce its desire for job security. Out of conflicting economic pressures and labor-management confrontation over jobs, a newly attractive pattern of long-term or career employment began to take shape and compete with the "traveler" pattern in the 1920s, but we must not exaggerate the extent of this change. Insecurity and short-term commitment (on both sides) continue to dominate our story.

A series of economic disasters in Japan and abroad, one natural, the others man-made, buffeted labor in the 1920s. The prosperity brought by World War I continued briefly after the Armistice, but, in April 1920, the boom ended abruptly. The stock market plunged, as did the market in silk, Japan's major export commodity. Many banks failed. The golden era of the wartime *nouveau riche* had come to an end. No longer would white-collar employees at the Yokohama Dock Company receive *semiannual* bonuses of 14 months' pay. The volume of machine-industry production peaked in 1920 at 880 million yen, falling to 568 million yen the next year. Employment fell at an equally drastic rate; shipbuilding workers numbered 95,000 at the peak in 1918 and only 42,330 in 1923.[18]

Before recovery could begin, the Washington Conference on disarmament of 1922 dealt a severe blow to heavy industry, so dependent on military procurement. Layoffs were common in shipyards and machine factories throughout Japan, but workers did not go quietly. The Yokohama Dock Company and Ishikawajima Shipyard both faced (and overcame) strikes to prevent firings in 1921 and 1922. Then, on September 1, 1923, the Great Kantō Earthquake brought economic activity in the Tokyo-Yokohama region to a virtual halt. For years thereafter, people dated major personal events in relation to the earthquake, much as contemporary Europeans defined their view of the past in relation to the

Great War. All the companies under study in this work suffered major damage and laid off many workers, and union activists were prominent among those fired. Union activity in the region took second place to a struggle for survival.

Heavy industry showed only ambiguous signs of recovery in the mid-1920s. Output in the machine and shipbuilding industries hit bottom at 392 million yen in 1923 and then rose gradually to nearly 682 million yen by 1929 (a total still well below the 1920 peak, not exceeded until 1934). Machine and shipbuilding industry employment plunged from 305,239 in 1922 to 229,475 in 1923, the year of the earthquake, and was slow to rise thereafter. These industries gave work to 236,051 people in 1926 but slipped to 232,799 in 1927, the year of the financial panic which caused the failure of many smaller banks and manufacturers.

The Great Depression proved an unambiguous disaster for Japanese heavy industry. Employment fell to 190,000 in 1929 and 168,000 in 1930. The value of machine and shipbuilding production slid from 682 million yen in 1929 to 615 million yen in 1930, then to 443 million yen in 1931.[19] Most Keihin employers fired large numbers of workers, and hiring at all levels was at a standstill. Even the university elite felt the crunch. A popular movie of the time concerned the plight of a jobless college graduate. Its title, *I Went to College But . . .*, became a cliché of the era. Anzai Mitsuru, who graduated from the Kyoto Imperial University Law Faculty in 1932, estimates that at best 10 percent of his classmates got the jobs they wanted. "The rest took work as policemen or anything, like *rōnin*." He worked at Tokyo Fire Insurance from 1932 to 1936, and then he entered Ishikawajima in the Labor Section.[20]

The balance sheets of the cases under study reflect national trends closely. The Ishikawajima Shipyard and the Yokohama and Uraga Dock Companies all recorded their highest profits in history during World War I. Profits did not return to these levels until 1937 or 1938. Both the Ishikawajima and Yokohama yards lost money in the year of the earthquake, 1923, and during the Depression. Uraga fared somewhat better, but its profits throughout the

1920s reached only half the World War I levels. The total of current and accumulated profits at Shibaura peaked in the second half of 1918 at 4.18 million yen and remained at nearly 4 million yen until the earthquake, which inflicted a 7-million-yen second-half loss on the company. By early 1926, total accumulated profits again rose above 2 million yen, but Shibaura did not once record a profit from 1927 to 1932 and did not exceed the 1918 peak until the first half of 1939. Nippon Kōkan, the largest steelmaker in the region, recorded a tremendous 6.7-million-yen profit in 1918, but only reached the 1-million-yen profit mark three times in the 1920s. The company lost money in 1930 and 1931, although its recovery was faster than that of the shipbuilders or Shibaura. In 1933, profits climbed to over 7 million yen, and they kept rising until the 1940s.[21]

Employment at these companies followed the profit trends, as work forces contracted at most firms in the 1920s, and then expanded in the early 1930s (Table 10). As the NKK recovery suggests, the Japanese experience in the Great Depression was rather different from that of the United States or most European nations. Japan's recovery came earlier than recovery in the West. Finance Minister Takahashi's deficit-spending policy had just the pump-priming effect Keynesian economic theory would have predicted, had it been fully elaborated in 1932. As Japan started along the path of military expansion in China with the 1931 Manchurian Incident, military spending rose, and heavy industrial enterprises were among the chief beneficiaries.

Despite recovery, the labor market only gradually shifted from one of tremendous oversupply to one of labor shortage. The large pool of unemployed skilled workers as the recovery began allowed a buyer's market to continue for several years. Also, individual companies behaved cautiously. They were anxious to avoid the chaos of high turnover and pirating of skilled workers that accompanied the World War I boom, as well as the subsequently bloated payrolls of the 1920s bust, and they tended therefore to designate many of their new employees "temporary." The temporary worker received a yearly contract renewable at company discretion and

Table 10 Average Work-Force Size, 1920–1937

	1920–1921	*1930–1931*	*1936–1937*
Shibaura	3,150	2,450	5,000
NKK	2,000	2,400	5,100
Yokohama Dock	4,800	1,600	5,000
Uraga Dock	4,300	2,170	3,225
Ishikawajima	3,000	1,800	?

Sources: Shibaura seisakujo 65 nenshi, p. 169; *Nippon Kōkan 30 nenshi,* pp. 381–382; Kyōchōkai, *Yokohama sōgi,* 1921; Yokohama dokku shashi, p. 173; Yokohama Dock Personnel Office records, Uraga company Archives, A-20, Chart on employees; Kyōchōkai, *Ishikawajima sōgi,* 1921; *Ishikawajima 108 nenshi,* p. 405.

fewer benefits than his regular co-worker. This hiring policy created a buffer group of dispensable men in case the recovery itself proved temporary. It also encouraged the regular worker to stay with his company, as he realized a new job elsewhere would probably be offered on temporary terms.

The fear of a short-lived recovery dissipated as the expansionary economy of the mid-1930s became the overheated economy of the late 1930s. Profits at all the cases under study exceeded the World War I heights by 1937 or 1938, output measured in yen rose sharply, and an acute labor shortage developed by the late 1930s. The machine industry, which had employed a mere 168,000 in 1930, required the services of 1.28 million workers in 1940.[22] Industry also began competing for its workers with a military draft which had been expanding rapidly since the war with China began in 1937.

The simple scarcity of jobs in the 1920s and their abundance in the late 1930s naturally influenced the attitudes and behavior of skilled workers. With heavy industrial enterprises nationwide laying people off in the 1920s, and early 1930s, workers would cling to jobs they had rather than risk quitting and seeking new jobs, and the emergence of a dual structure of higher wages at the larger companies and lower pay at smaller places also kept men from moving as freely as they had in earlier decades.[23] Conversely, the labor shortage of the mid-to-late 1930s brought an increase in job-switching, but a decade of bad times and some new management policies had changed matters somewhat. Turnover rates never approached the heights of the World War I boom.

The decline in labor turnover of the early 1920s was dramatic. During World War I, turnover in heavy industry had been roughly 70 to 90 percent per year, and in some cases it exceeded 100 percent.[24] Professor Hyōdō Tsutomu gathered separation rates from the Mitsubishi Kōbe shipyard, the Kure Naval Yard, and the Sumitomo and Yahata Ironworks over the period 1914 to 1930. Yearly separation rates declined from a range of 40 to 100 percent during the war to roughly 5 percent a year by 1930.[25] Unfortunately, other statistics from the 1920s were recorded on a monthly basis, making comparison difficult, but they indicate that, by 1926, turnover in heavy industry ranged from less than 1 percent to about 2.5 percent per month. Simply multiplying these rates by 12 probably exaggerates yearly turnover, since the same jobs may have changed hands several times. Yet, even multiplying by 12, the resulting yearly turnover rates are only 12 to 30 percent, far below the levels of World War I.

The drop in separation rates, coupled with a decrease in new hiring, led to a rise in average worker tenure. A 1919 nationwide survey of over 285,000 machine-industry workers reveals that only 11 percent claimed 6 or more years' seniority, while the rest had been at their jobs 5 years or less. No comparable nationwide information is available for the 1920s, but a survey of male workers at an unnamed large machine factory in 1926 suggests that, due to a combination of less hiring and less movement, the tenure pattern had changed. Nearly one-third (32 percent) of the workers could boast of 6 years' seniority or more. Our one shipbuilding source on this point, the Uraga Dockyard, depicts a similar shift toward more workers with higher tenure between 1921 and 1925 (Table 11).[26]

The great difficulty facing the historian is to sift out and weigh the factors responsible for this shift in worker behavior and the tenure structure: the stagnant job market, and management policies to discourage job-switching. Contemporary observers

Table 11: Distribution of Uraga Dock Workers by Tenure,
         1921 and 1925

(%)

Year	1–5 years	6–10	11–15	16–20	21+	Total=100%
1921	68	20	5	5	1.4	4,274 workers
1925	40.7	37.6	11.9	5.4	4.3	2,424 workers

Source: Kyōchōkai, *Uraga,* 1921, 1925

noted the influence of both, but they differed in assessing their importance. A 1927 survey of conditions in heavy industry states that managers had come to see high turnover as a drag on efficiency and a cost to their companies. Therefore, they devoted considerable effort to reducing turnover and encouraging long-term employment. The report cites severance pay, retirement pay, and pensions, all rising with seniority, as well as expanded company welfare facilities and "standardized treatment" of workers as the most common policies to this end. One machine manufacturer reported to be typical offered a 25-yen bonus to workers staying for 5 years (15 yen to women), and retirement or severance pay averaging nearly 40 days' pay for each year with the company. A 10-year employee fired by this firm would be entitled to 336 days' pay, and the yearly increments increased gradually with seniority, thus raising the stakes. After 10 years, each additional year brought 60 days' extra severance pay. Similar policies were common for shipbuilding and metal-industry enterprises.[27]

As we recall, however, that all these programs were present at Uraga and other firms during World War I, to little evident effect, it appears that a 1926 investigation of the shipbuilding industry was more accurate in stressing the decisive role of the slack labor market. Yoshida Atsushi, a researcher for the Kyōchōkai, took note of company allowances linked to tenure but did not expect them to be effective:

Shipbuilding workers are in excess supply. If a worker leaves his job, there is no telling when he will find another, and for this reason turnover is extremely low. However, if good times return, first the so-called "reserve army" will be absorbed and then, when a labor shortage ensues, the pirating of workers and the movement of workers in search of higher wages will reach surprising proportions. [28]

Yoshida had the still recent experience of the World War I labor shortage on which to base his judgment, and his conclusion was in part confirmed when "good times" did return to shipbuilding in the 1930s.

The sharp economic reversal of 1920 coincides precisely with the decline in turnover, and the job shortage that resulted provides the single most convincing explanation for decreased mobility. [29] But certainly factors other than the depressed economy played some role in reducing mobility in the 1920s. Company training programs and regular promotions or raises must have convinced some young men or adults, aware of the poor job market but nonetheless interested in "traveling," to stay put. [30] These programs to train workers or reward seniority were not innovations of the bad times of the 1920s. Pension funds, seniority bonuses, and a range of welfare and some education programs had been implemented in much of the industry during World War I or immediately thereafter in response to the labor force and working-class problems. During the 1910s, they were unable to slow turnover, and, in the 1930s, they could not prevent a sharp rise in job-switching; but, in the 1920s, they very likely had a marginal impact on decisions to stay with or leave an employer. They encouraged workers to view longer-term employment as an attractive alternative, one indeed to which many workers gradually decided they were entitled, but they could not cause long-term employment to emerge *in practice* as a career pattern, for they were only one part of managerial strategy in this decade.

The policies that encouraged tenure were not applied consistently or systematically. Managers occasionally discontinued welfare programs. They suspended annual or semiannual pay raises in bad years and always used them selectively. Of most importance, employers were ready to fire when business was slow, and seniority was no guarantee of exemption. To the contrary, they more often fired the older worker with seniority, but very likely declining skills as well.[31] Throughout the decade, managers fired workers and reduced work-force size. As a result, the chance of finding members of a given cohort of workers at the same company after 5 or 10 years was about the same in 1920 as it had been earlier. Information on Mitsubishi and Yahata between 1913 and 1924 indicated that 20 to 30 percent of the workers stayed for over 10 years.[32] Data from NKK and Uraga Dock Company present a slightly more fluid picture of the 1920s (Tables 12, 13).

Of the NKK workers hired between 1921 and 1923, after the depression began, only 12 to 17 percent were still with the company in 1933. Nearly half (48 percent) of the workers hired between 1924 and 1933 had either left or been fired by 1933.[33] If atypical, these figures probably reveal a situation of greater long-term employment than average.[34] The company histories that present the information do so only because NKK felt it had a good record of loyal service from its workers. The very low level of long-term employment among NKK workers hired in the 1920s is found despite a sharp drop in yearly turnover at the company over the same period (Table 13). One cannot rely only on turnover data.

The Uraga statistics cover just 1921 through 1925, but, in the absence of other company-specific information, they are worth analyzing (Table 12). Less than one-fourth of the workers hired between 1918 and 1921 remained at Uraga over this 4-year span. Attrition was high among experienced cohorts also. The entire work force contracted by 43 percent, from 4,272 to 2,424, and a good number of these separations were involuntary. Uraga fired 450 workers in two actions in 1925. Despite these cutbacks, 37 percent of the 1925 work force had been hired in or after 1921. Even during this recession, the worker's attachment to his job was not great enough to allow an "orderly" work force reduction relying upon a simple hiring freeze, firings, and attrition.

The separation ratios at Uraga can be adjusted to eliminate the effect of the overall 43-percent drop in work-force size by reducing each 1921 cohort by 43 percent, and comparing the adjusted cohorts to the 1925 groups. The adjusted figures show that separation was particularly frequent in less experienced cohorts. Workers with over 5 years' experience in 1921 were far more likely to remain at Uraga over the next few years.

The Uraga and NKK figures show that long-term employment was definitely the experience of a minority of workers hired at both companies in the 1920s. The data offered below (Table 27) for Mitsubishi, IHI, and Toshiba blue-collar workers of 1955 to 1980 reveals a tendency toward relatively long-term employment in post-World War II Japan. Roughly half of most cohorts remain with the company after 5 years, and close to 40 percent usually remain after 10 years. The NKK and Uraga data do not admit this interpretation for the 1920s or early 1930s. Less than 20 percent of the NKK workers lasted their first 10 years. Less than 25 percent of the inexperienced cohorts of Uraga workers remained for a mere 4 years. Turnover fell, but long-term employment did not result from new policies favoring senior men.

Insecurity remained the defining feature of jobs in heavy industry in the 1920s. The statistics indicate that, for a segment of the skilled male work force (perhaps one-fifth to one-third), long-term employment was both desirable and possible, but these men coexisted with a larger group of transient skilled workers, and their status was far from permanent. The varied and opposed objectives of powerful managers and relatively weak laborers worked together to stunt the growth of long-term employment. A management ideology and some policies encouraging loyal service, and labor efforts to protect jobs, were counterbalanced by a lingering fondness for traveling and a managerial push to "rationalize" operations in hard times. Managers desperate to survive wanted efficient and productive labor. If this meant the continuation or elaboration of policies to encourage tenure in some cases, at other times it meant readiness to fire workers, reduce wages or fringe benefits, and manipulate pay structures to raise output. It did not mean job security.

Table 12 Persistency of Employment, Blue-Collar Males, 1918–1941

a) Nippon Kōkan Kawasaki Works

Year hired	No. hired	Tenure in 1933 (July)	No. Remaining in 1933	Percent Remaining
1918	3,090	15	116	3.8
1919	1,227	14	76	6.2
1920	1,220	13	63	5.2
1921	386	12	47	12.2
1922	884	11	135	15.3
1923	801	10	142	17.7
1924	801	9		
1925	297	8		
1926	209	7		
1927	430	6	1,390	52.1
1928	385	5		
1929	197	4		
1930	27	3		
1931	9	2		
1932	167	1		
1933, Jan–June	148	0		

Year hired	No. Hired	Tenure in 1941 (December)	No. Remaining in 1941	Percent Remaining	Remaining since 1933
1918		23	83	2.7	72
1919	same	22	52	4.2	68
1920	as	21	58	4.8	92
1921	above	20	48	12.4	—
1922		19	103	11.7	76
1923		18	129	16.1	91

Source: NKK 20 nenshi, pp. 272–273; NKK 30 nenshi, pp. 380–382

Table 12 (Continued)

b) Uraga Dock Company

1921 Tenure	Number of Workers	(Adjusted Number)[a]	1925 Tenure	Number of Workers	Percent Remaining	(Adjusted Percent Remaining)[a]
			1	89		
			2	598	895 or	
			3	75	= 36.9% hired since 1921	
			4	133		
1 year	372	211	5	92	24.7	43.6
2	795	451	6	135	17.0	29.9
3	535	303	7	130	24.3	42.8
4	478	271	8	140	29.3	51.6
5	730	414	9	294	40.3	71.0
6	430	243	10	212	49.3	86.9
7–11	508	283	11–15	288	56.7	100
12–16	211	120	16–20	132	62.6	110.3
17+	213	121	21+	106	49.8	87.8
Totals	4,272			2,424	(35.79 = 1,529/4,272)	
				(1,529 were present in 1921)		

Source: Kyōchōkai, *Uraga Reports*
Note: [a]See pp. 140–141 for explanation of adjusted figures

Table 13   Yearly Turnover at Nippon Kōkan,
1918–1933, Blue Collar

Year	Hired (a)	Fired (b) or Left	Avg. Employed (c)	(%) Turnover (a+b/2/c)
1918	3,090	1,844	2,771	89.0
1919	1,227	1,943	2,475	64.0
1920	1,220	1,607	2,134	66.2
1921	386	886	1,529	41.6
1922	884	531	1,692	41.8
1923	801	821	1,894	42.8
1924	801	586	2,018	34.4
1925	297	333	2,003	15.7
1926	209	237	1,965	11.3
1927	430	151	2,125	13.7
1928	385	198	2,346	12.4
1929	197	173	2,437	7.6
1930	27	212	2,358	5.1
1931	9	197	2,155	4.8
1932	167	153	2,155	7.4
1933 (Half)	148	53	2,210	9.0[a]

Source: NKK 20 nenshi, pp. 272–273
Note: [a]1933 turnover was 4.5% for 6 months, or a 9% yearly rate.

For workers, on the other hand, job security became a major objective for the first time in the 1920s. By defending their jobs, workers helped lay the groundwork for the later emergence of long-term employment. They joined in frequent if rarely successful efforts to prevent layoffs. As an important result of these disputes with managers hoping to streamline the work force, they created an atmosphere that made firing difficult, and, by the Great Depression, some managers expressed great reluctance to fire.[35] Most still laid off hundreds when they had to (Table 14).

The authors of the survey of the machine, shipbuilding, and metal industries in 1927, quoted above, recognized the importance of conflicts over job security:

Recently, workers have become more aware (*jikaku suru*) and organized, and factories have generally had to clarify rules regarding firing and revise work rules, setting clear standards for firing and separation pay. This issue has been the major one behind recent disputes and is invariably included in the demands in some form.[36]

Such disputes took place throughout the decade and throughout the nation. In Kyūshū in 1922, the Yahata Iron workers successfully carried on an "anti-employment struggle" which prevented the Steel Works from firing any regular workers.[37] In the Keihin area, Shibaura, NKK, Yokosen, Uraga Dock, and Ishikawajima all experienced labor disputes over the firing issue, and the lines of conflict were similar in almost all cases.

The wrangling over jobs at Yokohama Dock Company was typical. At the start of the decade, the company readily fired excess workers, who responded by defending their jobs. By the end of the decade, this response bore partial fruit; the company consulted with a fairly strong union and moved with considerable circumspection in dealing with excess or idle workers.

Less than two months after the bitter strike of October 1921, Yokosen managers sent a note to 260 workers which read in part, "With great regret, due to the prolonged depression, we have no choice but to fire you."[38] When the Yokohama Shipbuilders Union, a Sōdōmei organization centered on the Dock Company, began unsuccessful negotiations on behalf of those fired for higher severance pay and a promise of absolute preference in any new hiring, the company responded with a forthright denial of any paternal duty to look after its employees:

> While we sympathize with the difficult plight of the fired workers, we cannot take responsibility for their poverty. We have neither the obligation nor the capacity to raise the severance allowances or meet the other demands.[39]

The shipbuilders union collapsed after another unsuccessful strike in 1922, but in 1924 workers formed a new union, the Kōshinkai, with company support. The group dedicated itself to fairly moderate goals of unity, better working conditions, and

Table 14 Firing in Heavy Industry, 1925, 1930-1931

a) A list of large-scale firings in heavy industry in 1925

Month	Company	Number Fired	Work Force Size Before Firings
January	Mitsui Bussan Tama Shipyard	220	1,600
February	Yokohama Zinc Galvanizing Co.	100	?
March	Uraga Dock	300	2,400
	Tobata Casting	118	?
	Kobe Steel's Harima Shipyard	300	?
April	Army Arsenals	2,748	18,000
	Navy Arsenals	1,697	49,000
	Tōkai Electric Wire	200	?
May	Osaka Ironworks Hiroshima Factory	300	1,000
June	Mitsubishi Nagasaki Shipyard	1,600	6,768
	Kawakita Electric Engineering	300	422
October	Mitsubishi Kobe Shipyard	300	7,000
	Uraga Dock	150	2,100
November	Yokohama Dock	600	3,000
December	Miike Engineering	150	?

Source: *Kikai kōgyō*, 1927, pp. 18-19

b) Firings at Shipyards in late 1930 and 1931

Company	Number Fired	Work Force Size Before Firings
Ishikawajima	600	2,300
Yokohama Dock	2,400	5,000
Fujinagata Shipyard	500	2,000
Asano Dock	300	1,500

Source: *Kōaikai jūnen shi*, 8/1933, p. 65

greater social status, plus one utopian objective, the "creation of an ideal society."[40] When rumors surfaced in the local press that hundreds of workers were to be fired in the fall of 1925, the Kōshinkai faced its first major test. The company, for its part, "feared worker action or disturbances and wanted to implement the firings without any trouble."[41] The disputes over layoffs and severance pay of 1921 and 1922 had influenced company stategy; managers decided to tread carefully and negotiate with the union before announcing the firings.

Factory Director Yamashita and Hara Ichirō, the head of the Kōshinkai Union, negotiated over severance pay in the last two weeks of November. Hara claimed that the union rank and file accepted some layoffs as inevitable. The members were upset only at the low severance pay proposed by the company. He feared they would break with the union leadership if this offer were accepted, and a dispute would perhaps result. The Kōshinkai leaders later did have trouble maintaining rank and file support, so Hara's threat may not have been a mere tactical ploy. It worked in any case. The company raised its severance pay offer, and the union leaders and membership accepted it. On November 30, the Dock Company fired 246 regular and 237 temporary workers, selected by management because of their relative inefficiency (*nōritsu no agaranai*). It fired 108 staff members the following day.[42]

The union was not powerful or aggressive enough to resist firings. It could only negotiate over severance pay. Yokosen managers were quite ready to fire workers when necessary, but they took a more conciliatory stance over time. Similar issues and potential disputes surfaced repeatedly until 1931, and negotiations continued to take place, always against a backdrop of rank-and-file or temporary-worker discontent. In the 1925 negotiations, the union did secure severance pay for temporary as well as regular workers, but, in March 1927, it could only secure an ambiguous promise of efforts to continue the severance allowance, if possible. In June 1927, union leaders pressed Yamashita to raise the temporary workers to regular status, but he would only promise to select some skilled, senior temporary workers for promotion.[43]

Behind the consistent union defense of temporary workers was the continued assertiveness of these relative outsiders in demanding better status. Angry letters to the union magazine regularly expressed the discontent of temporary workers, first employed as a separate category in 1922. Consider these two voices from 1926:

We have been raising our voices against the unfair temporary system at each opportunity for years now . . . to no avail. We are workers and we are skilled. Must we continue to be treated like day laborers?

There is no real difference between temporary and regular workers. We are human beings too, and we are as skilled or more skilled than many foremen.[44]

A variety of tensions at the Dock Company peaked in March 1929 and brought on a successful 10-day strike. The wage issue dominated, but concern for job protection surfaced as well. In its settlement, the company promised to give regular worker status after one year to all temporary workers able to pass a physical exam.[45] While it broke this promise, Yokosen did set up what it called a "secondary-skill" system in August 1929 to avoid firing idle workers. This innovation came in response both to years of union prodding over job security and protection of temporary workers, and the surprising unity of the March strike.

An "idle system" had been in effect since at least 1927. The company did not fire an idle worker, but told him to stay home and gave him 60 percent of his day wage. A worker actually lost well over 40 percent of income, given the large portion of pay derived from output wages and overtime, and the union opposed the system.[46] The Kōshinkai tried to negotiate a change in 1927 but gained merely a promise to keep idle workers to a minimum in the future. Then, in August 1929, after the strike, Yokosen announced a policy to use idle workers effectively and reduce their numbers, without firing. First, each shop would determine the "secondary skills" of all workers, and the Labor Section would compile the results. Second, all workshops were to report any excess or shortage of workers each day. The Labor Section would use the secondary-skill information to shift excess workers to shops where they were needed and could contribute. Shifted workers were given a 20-sen-per-day raise to compensate for any loss in output pay resulting from the switch to less familiar work. Evidence for subsequent months is sketchy, and it appears the system was hardly used, but, even as a blueprint, it offers evidence of management concern to reduce idle workers and avoid firings.[47]

In 1930, the company continued to avoid outright firing, even of temporary workers, despite the Depression. In July, Yamashita approached the union and asked for cooperation in recruiting voluntary "retirees" from among the *temporary* workers. They were to receive the severance pay levels usually reserved for regular workers. Only fear of provoking a labor dispute or worker antagonism can explain reluctance to fire outright even temporary workers, who at the Dock Company were signed to short-term 3- or 6-month contracts renewable at company discretion.[48]

The union refused to cooperate. Only a handful of "voluntary retirees" came forward, and, on July 21, the company fired 60 workers. On July 31, a group consisting of 1 representative per workshop conducted a symbolic walkout. The 30 representatives visited city, prefectural, and NYK officials to present their case. The fired workers formed a "struggle group" to press for better severance pay, but, lacking strong, sustained union support or close contact with the remaining workers, the struggle collapsed.[49] The balance of power shifted decisively in favor of management with this failure and with the deepening depression. In January 1931, the Dock Company fired 500 more workers after "negotiations" with the union. The company claimed this was a reduction from an original plan to fire 800, and it required the union to accept, in exchange for this "concession," a shorter work day and a proportionate reduction in day wages.[50] The memoirs of one Dock Company staff employee claim that, by May 1931, the company had fired 1,600 workers and 170 staff members.[51] Other sources give different totals, and we can only be sure that between 1929 and 1931 managers fired between 1,000 and 2,400 workers, and many white-collar employees.

Despite these mass dismissals, the actions of Yokosen shipbuilders had altered managerial behavior over the course of a decade. In 1922, executives denied responsibility for looking after workers, but, by the late 1920s, they trod softly and with some hesitation before firing, in 1927 offering some pay to idle workers, and in 1929 drawing up elaborate plans to protect jobs. The Depression rendered meaningless any such promises of job security, but the direction of change, under continuing union pressure, had been toward somewhat greater job security.

Organized workers elsewhere in the region fared no better in similar efforts to defend jobs. In April 1926, 450 of the 1,950 steelworkers at NKK's main Kawasaki plant went on strike to protest dismissal of an unspecified number of workers. The strike lasted a full 21 days, but management was unmoved. It revoked none of the dismissals. [52] After Uraga fired 300 men in March 1925, the Kōaikai union at the Dock Company merely set up an Employment Introduction Center to help dismissed men find jobs. In contrast to the Kōshinkai, Uraga's Kōaikai was a weak company union. Continuing rank-and-file concern with job security, evident in frequent letters to the union magazine, produced only half-hearted negotiations over rumored or actual dismissals in the bad years of the late 1920s and the Depression. [53] The company almost always succeeded in firing when it so desired. Union demands raised here and by the similarly passive Ishikawajima Jikyōkai union generally concerned merely severance pay levels, the number and selection of those fired, or, at Ishikawajima, a plan to provide 60 percent of wages for two months after dismissal. [54] Even so, a more militant attitude among the rank and file occasionally led to stiff defense of jobs and some gains for labor. Pressure from below moved the Kōaikai to help 360 temporary workers fired in December 1926. The union won severance pay for dismissed men over 55, the immediate rehiring of 50 workers, and a promise to rehire the rest by spring. [55] Also, workers at the small Yokohama factory of the Uraga Dock Company consistently acted on their own in defiance of management and union leadership. In late 1929, they mounted an unsuccessful "Movement for Rehiring" on behalf of 24 men, but, in September 1930, when Uraga fired about 60 of the 100 workers still at the Yokohama plant, the remaining shipbuilders struck and won the rehiring of 33 of these men, 18 as temporaries.

The political issue of union membership or support often lay behind small-scale dismissals in the 1920s. Here, labor was even less effective than when simply defending jobs threatened by recession. The Shibaura Engineering Works in 1925 fired 18 men, all leaders of the more-or-less anarchist Shibaura Labor Union, centered on the company's Tokyo factory. The company history of 1939 frankly recalled this as a move to clear out the "bad elements" (*furyō bunshi*). The union led a strike from July 9 to 21 demanding the rehiring of these workers. The action failed, despite solid support at the Tokyo plant, in part because workers at Shibaura's impressive new factory in the Tsurumi district of Yokohama, who favored a Hyōgikai-Communist union, did not support the Tokyo contingent. Shibaura refused to rehire the 18 workers, denied that the firings were politically motivated, and refused to promise not to dismiss workers in the future.[56] The union continued to call for job protection over the next six years as Shibaura slowly closed down the Tokyo plant and shifted operations to Tsurumi. A strike in March 1930 did win a promise not to fire any Tokyo workers specifically because of the move to Tsurumi, but Shibaura made no broader pledges of job security.[57]

If Kantō-area enterprises offered no long-term promise of job security, neither did a good many workers evidence strong commitment to their employers. They acted to defend their jobs, but they continued to move when they saw opportunity or felt the need to do so. Voluntary quitting (as opposed to dismissals) still accounted for a large portion of job turnover (Table 15). Of particular interest are the Mitsubishi and Yahata statistics, limited by definition to workers at large factories. These indicate that voluntary separations accounted for from one-third to two-thirds of all separations. In the only exceptions, 1924 at Nagasaki and 1927 at Yahata, management took an ax to the work force and fired thousands. Otherwise, despite the poor job situation and seniority-linked inducements to stay, many left on their own. According to the 1927 report on the shipbuilding industry, they usually ended up at other large factories.[58]

Workers at the Yokohama Dock Company were, of course, among the movers. Yokosen's Kōshinkai union published a short union history in 1928. The introduction explains the motive behind writing a "history" only four and one-half years after the

Table 15   Reasons for Separation, 1914–1932

	Years	Category	% of Voluntary Separations		% of Involuntary Separations (Fired)	N=100% Number Leaving
			Gave Notice	No Notice		
(a)	1924*	Tokyo Industrial Workers	31		15	11,821
(b)	1924	Osaka Machine Industry	70		30	8,993
(c)	1925	Industrial Workers, National	25		54	72,391
(d)	1932	" " "	20		65	4,435
(e)	1923	Mitsubishi Nagasaki Shipyard	31		35	929
	1924		8		84	2,109
	1925		41		22	286
(f)	1925	Yahata Ironworks	60	4	8	1,612
	1926		53	4	8	1,683
	1927		33	1	40	1,991
	1928		51	3	5	1,060
	1929		49	2	5	1,016

Note: Wherever possible, separations due to death, illness, retirement, and draft are not included, so in these cases the total percent is less than 100.

*34% who lost their jobs due to the 1923 earthquake are not included.

Sources: (a) NRUS, p. 192, cites Tokyo shi chūō shokugyō shōkai jo. Zenshoku betsu ni yoru shitsugyō jijō, 1924.
(b) Hazama, p. 507, cites Osaka shi shakai bu, Rōdōsha kōyō jōtai, 1926, p. 156.
(c) NRUS, p. 196, cites Naikaku tōkei kyoku, Shitsugyō tōkei chōsa hōkoku, 1925.
(d) NRUS, p. 204, cites Naimu shō, Shakai kyoku, Shitsugyōsha seikatsu jōkyō chōsa, 1935.
(e) Hyōdō, p. 420, cites Mitsubishi Nagasaki zōsenjo, Shokkō karkei shōtōkei.
(f) Hyōdō, p. 420, cites Yawata seitetsu jo, Yawata seitetsu jo kōjō rōdō tōkei, 1924–1929.

founding of the union, and in so doing it offers a workers' perspective on commitment to the company:

> We are all workers. We try to sell our labor to the highest buyers and have no choice but to go wherever they may be. If we are here today, we may have to move to another factory tomorrow. We have to move constantly and work constantly. We live from hand to mouth. Therefore, union members are continually entering and leaving. There is turnover. While many workers have been at Yokohama Dock Company since the union's founding, there are also many who have entered the union since then. There must be quite a few workers who want to know how the Kōshinkai was founded and what it has done.[59]

The scarcity of jobs did not transform the foot-loose travelers of earlier decades into immobile company men. By the early 1930s, a decade of job scarcity had taught some of the new generation of workers to value the job they had over the one they could perhaps get somewhere else. Mariko Kōsaburō, a welder at Ishikawajima shipyard, is surely one such man. He entered the company as a 19-year-old trainee in 1927 and was still there in 1980, serving as advisor to the company president. Yet, as he recalls those around him in the early 1930s:

> People would stay with Ishikawajima for a while and become fairly skilled, and their pay would go up, but there were some who felt they weren't getting enough. They would leave for a while, a lathe worker or some other kind of worker, and work some place else for three or four years, and then come back. When they did, their pay would be much higher . . . Those who left and came back would sometimes get a better wage than those who had been there the whole time.[60]

Managers in the 1920s pursued a double-edged policy. They continued to value and encourage long service, and they offered some seniority benefits to reduce costly voluntary separations, but they remained willing and usually able to fire when they had to. Workers were less likely to switch jobs at a moment's notice than during World War I, but less than one-fifth of the 1923 cohort at NKK remained 10 years later. At the same time, workers did unite and act either to defend jobs or bargain over terms of separation. Put simply, managers wanted to keep workers when times were good, and workers wanted to stay most when times were bad.

In this complex stand-off of the 1920s lay potential for the fairly long-term employment evident since the 1950s. Neither Uchida Tōshichi, leaving the Mita Arsenal in a rage at the unfair practices there, nor the restless workers at Ishikawajima, nor those who were "continually entering and leaving" Yokosen moved simply because traveling was the noble or proper thing to do, as the proud metalworker had proclaimed in his union magazine at the turn of the century. Poor treatment and low wages emerge as the more compelling motives. It is a treacherous undertaking to sort out the balance between such motives and a positive belief that moving around was in any case a good thing for a worker. The two are not mutually exclusive. But the undeniable presence of negative sentiments suggests that workers could be induced to change their orientation to the firm. Indeed, the tone of the Yokosen strikers of 1921 (or 1929, discussed below) suggests they wanted to change it, but that a precondition would be that managers change their approach to the worker.

Such change was a long time coming, and the pressure of organized workers did indeed prove to be the heart of the matter. The Keihin shipbuilders, engineers, or steelworkers could not win long-term, not to mention permanent, jobs in the 1920s. They often saw the older, senior, more expensive men lose their jobs first. Union activities at best limited the extent or moderated the impact of firings, but even these gains take on fair significance with hindsight. Bad times, combined with the political weakness and legal vulnerability of unions, gave managers the power to fire almost at will, but the negotiations over layoffs, and union willingness to strike over jobs, even in a depression, remained characteristic of Japanese labor relations. In the 1920s, this tension over job security led some companies to exercise caution or even moderation when faced with the need to fire, so as to avoid labor disputes. This sort of interaction would eventually produce far greater job security when the balance of power shifted to favor labor two decades later.

The 1930s brought only greater political power to management. Almost all unions in major factories were destroyed or weakened fatally by the start of the decade, and they mounted no comeback thereafter. The quick recovery of heavy industry, however, gave to workers a sort of economic power. By 1934, almost all skilled men thrown out of work during the Depression had been rehired, and scattered labor shortages were reported. By 1937, an acute scarcity of skilled labor afflicted the economy.[61] For managers in the 1930s the problem was no longer how to cut back without a dispute, but, once again, how to keep senior skilled men and find young new workers.

As recovery gave way to tremendous expansion, hiring continued to take place year round. Only three of a sample of 23 NKK workers hired between 1934 and 1939 were hired in March or April. NKK hired the others evenly throughout the year, and, as in the 1920s, adults were a more important source than recent school graduates. These workers averaged 25 years of age at hiring.[62] Even so, the practice of hiring some inexperiened men and training them for the long term continued and even spread. In the 1920s, mid-career entrants were usually experienced workers, but, by the mid-1930s, it had become impossible to fill new jobs with a combination of experienced older workers and young school grads. Locating and training inexperienced workers of *all* ages became and remained a major concern of factory managers.

Uraga Dock Company responded in the mid-1930s in typical fashion by expanding its worker-training program. A memorandum of February 1936 complained that replacing the 100 men recently retired, or about to retire, would be difficult. The solution was to recruit well-qualified young adults and place them in a new Special Trainee Program. Previous training programs had been limited to teenage school graduates, but now "male adults aged 20 to 24 who have fulfilled draft obligations, are well disciplined, healthy, strong, and want to work at the company for a long time" would be eligible for the new program. They would follow a 3-year training course and receive semiannual pay raises which, although contingent upon skill, achievement, scholastic record, and behavior, would be given out separately from the raises for regular workers. Especially excellent trainees would receive a bonus of 15 days' pay at the end of each 6-month term. The company hoped this program would secure a new source of skilled, long-serving workers. Under labor-market pressures, it offered to these recruits essentially guaranteed, regular pay raises and fairly large bonuses, benefits not offered to most previous Uraga workers.[63]

Despite such innovations, the persistence of the older ideal of skill acquisition through traveling posed continued problems for large companies. At a meeting of city officials, business leaders, and educators in Kawasaki, in August 1937, convened to discuss problems of worker training and recruiting, the head of the municipal Social Affairs Office remarked that "many workers would rather enter a small local factory than a big place like Shibaura, because they can learn a wide range of skills there." Such machinists still felt that independent acquisition of skill, rather than entry into a large enterprise, was the first step in a proper career.

For some, further advancement also dictated movement in search of better wages when the opportunity arose. Big companies had no use for such men, in public pronouncements; they had no choice but to grit their teeth and hire them, in private practice. The NKK representative at the meeting, after it was pointed out that wage differences often led workers to shift jobs, retorted, "We don't want to have anything to do with those workers who would jump from one place to another for a bit more money. Workers who will stay no matter what are better."[64] Companies such as NKK and Uraga therefore attempted to attract and keep needed workers by offering systematic training, better guarantees of seniority pay raises, and other bonuses. As was the case with similar policies during World War I, such measures were insufficient to slow turnover in the face of a growing labor shortage. In 1938, a prominent labor analyst wrote:

Entrepreneurs will offer anything as bait to attract workers, from higher pay to payment of worker debts on their behalf. A worker with even a little skill is constantly ready to move and doesn't give full attention to his job. Because conditions are worse at small places, their workers are always ready to seek work at a large factory. . . . However, if a large factory expands and suddenly needs many more workers, it has no choice but to pirate them from both small local factories and other large competitors. As there is not one large factory today doing military related work which has a surplus of workers, the people thus "stolen" are pirated once again. Factories are constantly competing for workers.[65]

If some workers preferred small factories for the freedom they offered, others were anxious to leave for major companies, or leave one big company for another.

The reemergence in the late 1930s of such mobility *between* large factories is a signal that policies to retain workers, some dating back to World War I or the 1920s, were of limited impact. Managers tried to keep their own workers in place, even as they raided competitors. As a result, less than half the workers in large heavy industrial enterprises in 1938 had spent their entire careers with a single employer, even though most of them had only recently entered the work force[66] (Table 16).

From 75 to 85 percent of all workers in these industries had been working for 5 years or less.[67] The metalworkers were fairly settled, but in shipbuilding two-thirds of all workers had switched jobs at least once. This movement had intensified in the late 1930s. Among those hired most recently, in 1937 and 1938, an even higher proportion were job-switchers. One interesting sidelight is that workers in industries dominated by small-scale factories, nail or rivet manufacturers, farm-tool makers, or bicycle manufacturers, were not significantly more mobile. In all cases, large and small, from one-half to two-thirds of all workers had changed jobs at least once.

Company information on job-switching for the 1930s is hard to come by. Fortunately, figures for the Uraga Dock Company's Yokohama Factory are available for 1939. These cover only those workers defined as skilled, 48 of a total work force of 169. All 48 skilled men were over 30 years old, the people any company

Table 16 Extent of Job-Switching in Heavy Industry, 1938

Industry	Workers Hired Before 7/1/1937		Hired Between 7/1/37–2/1/1938		Total % Changed Jobs Once or More	Total % Never Changed Jobs	Total Number of Workers
	One or more job change	Never changed job	One or more job change	Never changed job			
Metal Refining	33.7%	66.3	49.7	50.3	45.3	54.7	97,653
Rolling Mills	50.3	49.7	58.1	41.9	58.2	41.8	48,624
Electric Wire	48.2	51.8	52.5	47.5	49.6	50.4	9,366
Gas, Steam Eng.	53.5	46.5	70.4	29.6	58.5	41.5	39,624
Electric Machine	44.2	55.8	58.5	41.5	48.6	51.4	46,211
Shipbuilding	63.4	36.6	72.8	27.2	66.0	34.0	88,317
Rolling Stock	67.9	32.1	66.6	33.4	67.6	32.4	24,895
Total					57.3	42.7	345,690

Source: Rōdō tōkei jitchi chōsa (1938).

would hate to lose—experienced skilled workers in the prime of their careers. Yet, 20 (42 percent) of the 48 left the company between December 1, 1938 and November 30, 1939. Uraga could only find 9 replacements, although management wanted to increase substantially the number of skilled workers at the factory.[68] The loss of 42 percent of the factory's skilled workers in a single year took place despite two new benefits recently offered: a perfect attendance bonus of 1 extra day's pay per month, announced in March 1937 "in order to increase all employees' spontaneous motivation to work and to encourage efficiency," and a "temporary allowance," very likely a response to inflation in lieu of a raise across the board, of 10 sen per day to regular workers, 12 sen to sub-foremen, and 14 sen to foremen, extended in May 1938.[69]

While turnover and job-switching rose, NKK data offered above (Table 12) show that most workers who kept their jobs throughout the 1920s remained with the company in the 1930s, even though opportunities to change were present. Seniority-linked benefits and (one imagines) the simple fact of inertia (settling into a neighborhood, getting married, getting older) in time became powerful inducements to cast one's lot with NKK for the long haul. And, throughout heavy industry, although one-half to two-thirds of all workers, most of them recent entrants to the job market, had indeed changed jobs once as of 1938, a sizeable minority had never changed jobs. The workers of the time, in large companies as well as small, included significant contingents of both travelers and organization men.

In the late 1930s, as in the 1920s, the organization men were a minority. While almost half the factory workers in this nationwide survey had never changed jobs, most had been working less than 5 years. They were not yet permanent or long-term employees. The interwar era did witness the emergence of an ideal of long-term employment for company-trained youth or even experienced older men, to compete with the traveler ideal, as managers continued or expanded programs to encourage efficiency and long service, and a decade of hard times buffeted labor. This career pattern gradually became more attractive than before World War I, when a man who "clung to a job" at one place was ridiculed as weak and unimaginative. But dissatisfaction with unfair treatment, the inherent attraction of moving, the inability of labor to defend jobs at the big firms in the 1920s, and the return of opportunities to move in the 1930s, together insured that short-term commitment (or insecurity) and traveling would persist as important elements in Japanese working-class life.

FIVE

The Wage Tangle

By the end of World War I, Japanese managers offered an impressive array of enticements to seniority. Promotions, wage hikes, bonuses, and welfare programs such as retirement pay all favored senior workers and theoretically encouraged long-term employment. These benefits had emerged largely as a piecemeal response to the persistence of high turnover, although, in a few cases, organized workers had demanded and gained them. When the job market contracted and turnover fell sharply in the 1920s, these practices, *insofar as they persisted,* gradually began to reshape the wage and benefit structure. As more workers stayed put, or tried to, seniority and status within a firm rose in significance.

These enticements were never conceived as seniority benefits, pure and simple. The tangled web of wage policies addressed problems of efficiency and discipline, in addition to turnover. Indeed, as the prolonged recession took care of turnover, managers focused more and more on the productivity dimension, narrowly defined, and devised a variety of newly sophisticated incentive- or output-pay schemes, often adapted from the great American contribution to productivity, scientific management. In the face of a surplus of skilled labor, companies viewed costly seniority benefits with less enthusiasm than before. They often retreated from commitments to seniority bonuses, regular pay raises, or retirement funds, while introducing new incentive-pay formulae. The 1920s reveal labor

pushing both to expand or at least maintain the security of seniority-linked pay and benefits, and to reduce or eliminate the uncertainty and pressure of efficiency-based wages. Worker success in
these endeavors was limited, but out of such give and take the
interwar wage structure developed.

FIGURING WAGES: OUTPUT, SKILL, SENIORITY

Payment by result and payment by the day both went into the
wage envelope in the 1920s. By World War I, the former category
included individual piecework and a range of premium wage systems, all of which set standard times for a job and then used a
formula to calculate the premium due the worker, or group of
men, who bettered the job time. The United States had been the
source of most such schemes since the 1890s, but, with translation of Taylor's *The Principles of Scientific Management* in 1913,
just two years after American publication, and with the overwhelm-
ing need to cut prices to compete internationally in the 1920s,
managers throughout heavy industry looked with new interest to
incentive or output wages as part of their salvation.

The three Keihin shipyards, NKK, and Shibaura all experimented
with new incentive wages throughout the 1920s. Early in the decade, Shibaura paid some workers by the job and others by the day.
It set the job rates after careful time-and-motion studies, a tech-
nique imported from the United States. The company adopted a
more complex wage system at its new Tsurumi plant in 1925
under the tutelage of productivity expert A. K. Warren of General
Electric, who served Shibaura from 1924 to 1931 as a technician
and company director. Shibaura used hourly pay, piece-rate pay,
and the Halsey premium system at Tsurumi. In 1929, management
introduced a new incentive scheme called the "job wage" (*shigoto
kyū*), and it further expanded this in 1932. This complex system
remained basically unchanged until 1945.[1]

The workers at Shibaura lost no love for these wage arrangements. One man wrote the union magazine:

> Most all of you were likely told by a boss on entering the company that "day wages are low here, but instead everything is done on a contract basis" . . . So the contract system is implemented and we all have to work like horses pulling carts till we're blue in the face.[2]

Another griped:

> The unit price is always changing . . . They give prizes to the top producers and encourage competition to raise efficiency, which lets them lower unit prices. They always make the top output level into the standard and work to lower the unit price.[3]

Wage issues were indeed prominent in the several Shibaura disputes of the 1920s, discussed below. These complaints appear to reflect the shop-floor consensus.

Nippon Kōkan was no less enthusiastic in embracing the incentive-pay notion. From the time of its founding in 1912, the company followed practices of other leading enterprises, especially the arsenals, with regard to wages, paying a so-called incentive increment in addition to the base wage. At first, this was simply X yen paid for Y output, but, as operations became more complex, the possibilities of running up a huge wage bill forced NKK to put an upper limit on the increment. The company history reports that "this nullified its incentive effect, so, in the mid-1920s, NKK switched to a more sophisticated increment system, both Rowan and Halsey, which set more appropriate standards. This system continued relatively unchanged until the war ended."[4]

Tomiyasu Nagateru entered the Wage Section of NKK's Personnel Division in 1933 and soon became a wage specialist. He describes NKK's incentive-wage system, introduced in the company's rationalization drive of 1925–1928.[5] A small minority of the workers, perhaps 10 percent, received individual piecework wages. But NKK calculated the output pay for the vast majority of workers on a group basis and then distributed this to the group members. A work group at a particular furnace, for example, would receive a monthly premium calculated as the product of the group's total day wage, the total days worked, and a "premium factor." This last would be the quotient of the amount of time "saved" divided by the standard time for the job (for a 50-hour job done in 40 hours, the premium factor was 10/50 or 0.2).

The distribution of this premium was no simple matter. Each worker received a monthly "point total" calculated as the product of several factors: days worked, an overtime multiplier, a status multiplier, a responsibility multiplier, and an attendance multiplier. By totaling the work group's points and dividing this total into the premium value, each point received a monetary value. The individual's point total was then multiplied by the yen value of each point, resulting in an individual share of output wages. The following hypothetical example should clarify matters. Points would be calculated by rank as follows (Table 17). Assuming the group accumulated 1,000 total points in a month and the group premium for the month was 500 yen, each point would be worth 0.5 yen (500/1000). The output wage due a worker would then fall into the following ranges, as each worker's total points were multiplied by 0.5 yen.

- Foreman   27 to 32.4 yen/month
- Sub-Foreman   23.6 to 28 yen/month
- Regular   15 to 18 yen/month
- Trainee   4.3 to 4.4 yen/month

This system was notoriously difficult for workers (and perhaps readers) to understand, and its effectiveness as a direct incentive can be questioned. The connection between individual exertion and the output premium was not great. The major determinants of a worker's output wage would be individual rank, the total value of the group premium, and the number of days worked by each individual. Seniority had very little to do with this output pay. Rank was a partial reflection of seniority, but many men with long tenure never rose above regular rank, and they received no more output pay than others. Group output and days worked were unrelated to individual seniority. Based upon practices common at other steel mills or arsenals, the NKK incentive-wage system was designed to strengthen work-group solidarity, raise output, and

Table 17 Premium Point System at NKK, ca. 1933

	10-hr. Days	×	(2 hrs/day) Overtime Multiplier	×	Status Multiplier	×	Responsibility Multiplier	×	Attendance Multiplier	=	Total
Foreman	25		1.2		1.5		1.1–1.2		1.1–1.2		54.45–64.80
Sub-Foreman	25		1.2		1.3		1.1–1.2		1.1–1.2		47.19–56.16
Regular	25		1.2		1.0		1.0		1.0–1.2		30.00–36.00
Trainee	25		1.2		0.6		0.6		0.8–1.0		8.64–10.80

reward group leaders. Such group premiums, sometimes with less complex distribution systems, were common.

Ishikawajima differed from NKK by distributing output pay in proportion to the day wage. In this case, the incentive portion would reflect seniority to the same extent that day wages did. The Shibaura and Yokosen systems were closer to NKK in ignoring seniority, but precise judgment on the frequency of either method of distributing incentive pay is impossible.[6] We can only be sure that several of the major Keihin factories paid little heed to seniority as they distributed the incentive premiums, and, insofar as incentive wages constituted a significant portion of total income in these cases, take-home pay would vary with little regard for seniority. At NKK, the incentive portion of a worker's total wage remained over 50 percent throughout the prewar era. At the Yahata Ironworks in 1928, 55 percent of average monthly income derived from similar incentive wages. When Mitsubishi Electric adopted a new "scientific" wage system in 1925, modeled on practice at Westinghouse Corporation, an average of 40 percent of all worker income resulted from incentive wages.[7] The Yokohama Dock Company's Kōshinkai union surveyed wages at other Kantō-area factories in early 1929 in preparation for wage negotiations. The union found that a somewhat lower but nonetheless significant portion of wages derived from incentive pay: 20 percent at the Asano Shipyard, 26 percent at Niigata Ironworks and at Tokyo Gas Company, 29 percent at Shibaura and Ishikawajima, and 40 percent at the Ikegai Ironworks.[8]

Even with a substantial portion of total income derived from output wages, the day wage (often called the base wage) accounted for 45 to 80 percent of income in these cases. If it indeed rose periodically as an inducement and reward to skilled men, it was likely to reflect seniority in some measure. In fact, the day wage was at best a muddied mirror in its ability to reflect seniority. Informed observers of the 1920s did not describe day wages as a function of seniority, for several good reasons.[9] Workers in the 1920s assumed they deserved the regular raises first implemented years earlier, but managers all along insisted that skill and performance be considered in setting the level of an increase. In the 1920s, especially, they did not in fact give these so-called "regular raises" (*teiki shōkyū*) regularly, they did not give them to all workers, and favoritism often influenced decisions.

All these features were prominent at Yokohama Dock, where company rules specified that "skill, performance, attendance, and character" determine the amount of an individual's pay raise. Workers with poor records received lower raises or were passed over entirely. By the mid-1920s the Dock Company had created a complex program of semiannual raises. It gave these out in June and December to a limited number of men. Low-paid workers (below 2 yen a day) were eligible once a year, the medium group with wages between 2 and 2.5 yen qualified each year and a half, and high-priced men pulling in 2.5 yen or more had a chance every 2 years. The pay hikes for the bottom group ranged from 0 to 8 sen a day, and the company made sure that not all the eligible workers actually took home raises. Management allotted each workshop a semiannual "raise budget" and the workshop supervisor set maximum, minimum, and standard raises. The standard was always high enough to insure that the money ran out before all workers received a standard raise. One personnel section manager recalls, "Announcement day was tense. . . . Some were pleased with their raises, others weren't. We also made exceptions. Good workers could get extra raises, even when not eligible."[10]

The uncertainty inherent in this system disturbed Yokosen workers, but they did not challenge management policy effectively until the 1929 strike. Through most of the decade, their union meekly accepted company wage decisions. For example, in May 1925, the Kōshinkai union leaders discussed how to approach the expected June raises. Factory Director Yamashita had promised the union a raise but had given no details of the amount or scope, and some union leaders favored making specific demands. Yet, the majority, by a 17 to 5 vote, decided that, because the late Executive Director Tōjō had promised only to raise wages yearly and said nothing about the amount, the union had to accept whatever levels were offered.[11] In June 1926, an anonymous worker revealed much about the workings of the pay-raise system as he voiced his discontent:

> Our greatest present problem is the issue of regular pay raises. Before the earthquake, all workers except those with very bad records got one pay raise a year, even if these were divided into two levels. After the quake, we and the company both worked like crazy and the company got back on its feet. . . . Yet the company did almost nothing for us . . . just a small bonus hardly worth mentioning. We should get regular pay raises once or twice a year like the Naval Yards and other shipyards. At present, the company treats us like cows. Raises are given out only to a mere 10 percent, called model workers. [12]

To this worker the grass seemed greener at "other shipyards," but, in fact, the situations at the Uraga Dock Company and Ishikawajima were similar. Uraga gave out bonuses "when business is good, in accord with a worker's performance." [13] Uraga's Kōaikai union in 1924 also asked for more regular pay raises and reached agreement with the company that pay hikes be offered quarterly, the amount not to exceed 10 sen per day. The company selected only workers with superior skill for the raises, and many received no increase in a given year. This system changed little in following years, and in July of 1928 discontented boilermakers asked the union to negotiate for a 20 percent pay raise for all those with day wages under 2.4 yen who had not received any raise for 4 years or more. Four hundred workers of a 3,400 man work force reportedly fell into this category. The compromise reached did not satisfy everyone:

> The Kōaikai is about to set up a cooperative store. Great. We need it to live. I got my first pay raise in 6 years recently. Two whole sen per day. At this rate, my next raise will be in 1935. [14]

Ishikawajima gave out raises to regular workers in April of each year in the late 1920s. These varied from 0 to 5 sen per day, depending on a management evaluation of skill and performance. As at Yokosen, a "raise budget" was given to each workshop, to be distributed at the discretion of the foreman. The system favored the handful of trainees at the company apprentice school, who received 10-sen raises twice a year while apprentices and more rapid advancement later as well. This was the small group of workers offered *steady* seniority benefits to encourage long service.[15]

In machine factories as well as shipyards, skill and performance were crucial. Ikegai Ironworks in 1927 gave pay raises ranging from 3 to 20 sen per day on the basis of attendance and work record, but by-passed a few workers entirely.[16] These pay hikes were typically irregular and limited in scope. At Ikegai, a major demand in a strike in December 1926 was for a 30-sen-per-day average pay raise, "because no pay raises have been given out for several years."[17] And at Shibaura:

Semiannual pay raises are a basic premise of the present factory system, but this is merely nominal, almost wholly ignored. Not a few workers go 5 or 10 years without pay raises. Sometimes, when granted, the raise is so low as to not even buy a pack of cigarettes. . . . Assume a worker starts at age 20 with 1 yen a day and gets 10 sen raises each year. He'll have 2 yen a day by age 30. But a 1-yen raise over 10 years is mere dreaming.[18]

It's been so long I've lost track of when the last pay raise was. This company is really cheap. After 2 or 3 years we get just about 5 or 6 sen a day as a raise. A worker who slaves and in one year cuts his life expectancy by 5 may get 10 sen, while the worker who runs errands for an executive's mistress gets 15 sen.[19]

As this last fellow suggests, the decision-making process at Shibaura, and surely elsewhere, was open to abuse. The raises of December 1922 were especially controversial:

What's going on with the pay raises? . . . People who never missed a day and worked hard got zero, while guys who stood around and loafed got raises. What are the standards? Skill? Conduct? If there's no chance for a raise, we may as well fool around.[20]

In November last year the Personnel Section ordered a survey of worker attendance and skill . . . as preparation for a pay raise. Apparently we all got point ratings. Who gets good points? The worker who bows and scrapes to supervisors, who pretends to be hard at work when a boss comes by even when there's no work to be done. . . . I got no raise and was surprised. I haven't missed a day or been late, and I can do my job well, but I didn't get a sen. Maybe they don't like me because I won't call something black white just to please the bosses. . . . Discontent was all about after the pay raise. One worker asked a shop supervisor what the standards were. The answer: "I don't know." All of us who got no raise selected representatives to talk with a supervisor on the 13th. He told us that we were not only lazy but impudent and didn't follow orders. . . . Asking around later, we found out that the real decisions were made not by the personnel office but by the shop supervisors. Even many of those who got raises are upset. [21]

The combination of day wages loosely tied to seniority, with a variety of output wages, meant that older men in heavy industry actually received less total pay than their younger or middle-aged (and often less senior) co-workers (Table 18). The 1927 survey of the machine industry noted that, "since many workers get output pay, their income drops with age and loss of strength." [22] Together with the Shibaura worker who complained that the "basic premise" of semiannual raises was betrayed in practice, most workers felt their wages ought to rise with seniority and ought to reflect increasing skill. For some fortunate men this was the case, but complaints and union protests would be common so long as managers routinely excluded many workers each year, granted widely varied amounts, and suspended raises altogether in some cases.

WAGES AND THE LABOR MOVEMENT

The labor movement was a force shaping wage practices in the interwar years. [23] The workers who expressed opinions or tried to influence wage policies spoke to a pair of critical, related issues. On the one hand, they sought to limit the uncertainty of output wages. Their other major goal was to make the link between seniority and the day wage more systematic through regular pay raises. Managers worked with fair success to maintain freedom to suspend wage hikes when necessary and manipulate both day and output wages to stimulate production, but pressure exerted by organized workers of varied ideological persuasions was important.

Table 18 Total Daily Income for Male Heavy Industrial Workers
in Tokyo, 1924 and 1927, in Yen

Ages	Shipbuilding 1924	1927	Machine Industry 1924	1927	Metal Processing 1924	1927
21–25	2.82	2.96	2.82	2.77	2.59	2.46
26–30	3.06	3.27	3.37	3.43	2.90	2.82
31–35	3.18	3.47	3.72	3.76	3.04	3.04
36–40	3.25	3.59	3.79	3.99	3.12	3.25
41–45	3.34	3.57	3.86	4.04	3.07	3.17
46–50	3.45	3.54	3.70	3.93	2.91	3.05
51–55	3.35	3.40	3.26	3.61	2.67	3.06
56–60	3.23	3.30	3.26	3.26	2.59	2.57
61+	—	2.07	2.75	2.94	2.15	2.32
Average[a]	3.00	3.18	3.09	3.19	2.66	2.72

Sources: *Tokyo rōdō tōkei jitchi chōsa*, 1924, pp. 240–241, 244–245, 250, and 1927,
pp. 223–227, 237–243, 256–259.
Note: [a] Ages 13–20 have been omitted because the 1924 figures are incomplete. The
average given, however, includes these young workers.

It spread the notion that wages rewarding seniority were more just
than output wages, and in a very few cases led directly to change.

Most of the major Keihin unions addressed the incentive-pay
issue at some time in the 1920s. Members of the radical Kōrō
union based at Ishikawajima, with members in several other nearby
factories, often grumbled over the insecurity of incentive wages in
the early 1920s. One Kōrō member revealed his low regard for factory labor generally as well as the wage system, as he complained
in December 1921 that unit prices were being cut, income was falling, and workers had no choice but to "sell their daughters as factory workers."[24] His union officially took up the incentive pay
issue with a stand at its third annual convention in 1924 against
the exploitative "two-tiered" (*ni jū*) wage system of base wages
overlaid with incentive pay, but the union could take no effective
action to change the wage structure.

Organized labor at NKK took slightly bolder steps on this front,
as it faced managers intent upon using "rational" incentive wages
to bring efficiency to the steel mill. Spurred by a pressing need to

lower costs to compete with foreign steel entering Japanese markets, NKK jumped wholeheartedly onto the bandwagon of the "rationalization" (*gōrika*) movement of the mid-1920s. To NKK managers rationalization meant reducing expenses by ending material waste, adopting more sophisticated technology, encouraging efficiency, and both reworking the wage structure and reducing wages. The rationalization program pleased management. From 1925 to 1928, production rose 50 percent, productivity per worker increased 38 percent, from 45 to 73 tons per month, and costs per ton fell 25 percent. Behind this success story were pay cuts and output wages forced upon all employees between 1923 and 1928, implemented partly on the basis of time-and-motion studies.[25]

NKK workers were not pleased. The Sōdōmei in 1927 claimed 600 members among NKK's 2,100 workers, and this union felt the "pay raise" announced on September 1, 1927 was a sleight of hand.[26] It incorporated the first 10 percent of worker output pay into the base wage, in the name of income security, but a union survey found the net result to be a monthly loss in income of from 5 to 10 yen. The union petitioned NKK to redesign the "pay raise" so that no loss of pay would result, and in a settlement mediated by police, who prevented a strike, they gained this guarantee. NKK workers were to this extent able to soften the impact of rationalization measures, but Sōdōmei power at the mill then declined. On September 1, 1931 the company announced a 12-percent cut in unit prices. By this time, the union only claimed 200 NKK members, but it was able to gather 1,746 of the 2,150 workers at a meeting on September 10 which resolved to demand restoration of the pay cut, revival of a perfect-attendance bonus, and improvement of several welfare facilities. When negotiations proved fruitless, the union called a strike, but police immediately arrested the strike leaders, and NKK fired 10 of them. The settlement mediated by the Kawasaki police chief in the wake of the short-lived strike left intact the cut in the unit prices. In addition, regular pay raises and attendance bonuses would not be revived "until 5-percent dividends once again became payable on preferred stock."[27]

At the Shibaura Engineering Works, wages were at the heart of work-place discontent and disputes from the early 1920s until 1931, and here too fluctuating, uncertain output pay was a special concern for this entire period. Shibaura men raised these issues with greater persistence and aggressiveness than any workers in the region, but in the end they were no more successful than their counterparts at NKK or Ishikawajima.

In the early 1920s, workers were upset with the rate-cutting and wage insecurity inherent in the incentive and unit price wage system. In March 1924, a group of Shibaura Labor Union members demanded higher severance pay, linked to tenure, a "tenure allowance" to be given all workers on a regular basis, and guaranteed minimum incentive pay of 70 percent of day wages. Managers refused all the demands, and the workers were angry, if unable to act. "The next time [manager] Sekiguchi tries to use this illogic with us, we'll give him a taste of violence."[28] None ensued, but discontent over incentive pay remained. A plate metal worker in 1924 wrote:

> We are human beings, upright producers, and as humans have various rights. Yet capitalism still treats us as machines, as commodities, especially through the contract and incentive-pay systems. These exploit us more than anything, as previous contributors to this magazine have said. . . . The company sets a very low base pay and then attaches a unit price to each job. . . . We have to work like crazy to supplement the low base pay and take home a sufficient income. Then our high output levels are made the new standard, and the unit price is lowered. No matter how hard we work, pay doesn't go up. . . . The company thinks, if they add the output part to our base pay, we'll fool around and won't work hard.[29]

Anger over a host of issues, prominent among them the wage system, finally boiled over in the 90-day dispute at the Tsurumi plant in autumn 1927. Alleged company mistreatment of an injured worker sparked the dispute, but the Tsurumi union used the incident to raise a host of demands. A work stoppage on August 25, followed by the firing of 59 workers, led to a strike beginning August 31. A meeting of all 1,300 workers on September 1 decided on 15 demands. At the top of the list was a reformed wage system: full pay even when a job was not finished within the standard time allotment; discussion of the setting of standard times with workers; no reduction of standard job times once set; distribution of both incentive and day wages on the same day with a clear breakdown on the envelope; and conversion of incentive and allowance pay into a fixed wage. Also among the demands were calls for a semiannual pay raise of at least 5 sen per day and a raise in the tenure allowance of 3 days' pay for each month of seniority.

The wage issue remained on the workers' agenda even when the 15 original demands were reduced to 5 in a late-October union meeting. The union realized too late that its 15-point program was impractical (and in fact inconsistent, calling for both reform and elimination of incentive pay), and the prolonged dispute never approached success. In late September, union leaders called a "cease fire," as support crumbled in the face of company intransigence. Management fired 26 workers on September 23, in addition to the original 59, and sent several others threats of firing in the mail. Work resumed, but union activists continued to rally support, and, on November 15, a general meeting of 400 Tsurumi workers resolved to resume the strike. The company, under police pressure to settle the incident and anxious to resume normal operations, agreed to give severance pay of 24,000 yen to the 84 fired workers, to pay 3,500 yen to cover strike group expenses, and to loan 3 days' pay to all workers. A final settlement was reached on November 21.[30]

The location of this dispute at the Tsurumi plant is significant. Criticism of the incentive-wage system at Shibaura from before 1925 came from workers at the Tokyo factory, who in 1923 and 1924 were solidly behind the unaffiliated but semi-anarchist anti-Communist Shibaura Labor Union. The large new Tsurumi factory farther down the coast in Yokohama commenced operations in 1925, and a branch of the Hyōgikai labor federation, closely allied to Japan's Communist movement, had gained a strong foothold among the workers by 1927. Despite the separate location, the opposed ideology, and the marked lack of cooperation between workers at the two plants (Tsurumi workers did not support a 1925 Tokyo plant strike; Tokyo workers reciprocated in 1927), the wage demands raised by workers at both factories were almost identical. These demands represented a consensus among workers that transcended union or party platforms.

Several months prior to the 1927 strike, workers in two chapters (workshop branches) of the Tokyo factory's Shibaura Labor Union also took up the wage issue, presenting a petition which called for restoration of an April 12 reduction in unit prices. These workers surrounded their shop supervisors and threatened violence, using the so-called "group attack" tactic (*shūdan kōgeki*).[31] The company fired 6 leaders of the "attack," and the two chapters decided they lacked the broad support necessary for a strike. Negotiations continued over the modification in the incentive-pay system, to no avail.[32]

In 1929 and 1930, workers at the Tokyo plant again took exception to the incentive-wage policy, as the company tried to institute a more "rational" wage system based on its experience at the Tsurumi factory. Casting-shop workers held meetings and campaigned unsuccessfully to raise the output rate in October 1929.[33] Another group of the Tokyo factory workers formed a separate union, as the Shibaura Labor Union lost support with its increasingly shrill anarchist stance. Yet the new Shibaura Dōshi Renmei voiced the same complaints: "When a rush job comes, we work like crazy. The unit price fixer says the time standard was too high and cuts it after the fact. This happened late last year and happens often."[34]

By 1930, the workers at the Tokyo plant were deeply divided among themselves. Of 1,407 workers, 338 belonged to the old Shibaura Labor Union, 404 had joined the new Dōshi Renmei, aligned with the Sōdōmei and Social Democratic Party (Shakai Minshūtō), and 60 owed allegiance to the Kantō Metalworkers Council (Kantō Kinzoku Kyōgikai), a remnant of the now-outlawed Hyōgikai. The one issue capable of temporarily uniting these factions and the 615 remaining unorganized workers turned out to be a threat to wage security. When the company announced a reduction from a 9- to an 8-hour day and a corresponding pay cut on March 1, 1930, the three unions formed a joint committee which agreed on 5 demands. The committee gained the support of all the workers at the factory, who stopped work on March 4 to back up the strike committee in its negotiations. The demands, not surprisingly, opposed the pay cut, the introduction of the new "job wage" in use at the Tsurumi plant, and all reductions in unit prices, as well as any firings as the company shifted operations to the Tsurumi plant.

The company attempted to soothe discontent over the pay cut and the new wage system:

> Workers on contract pay should be able to avoid a loss in income [due to the 12 percent day-wage cut] through their efforts. As for those on fixed wages, we are considering the matter seriously. . . . This [job wage system] is based on the Warren system practiced in the United States in which the commission rate or unit price is set according to each individual's skill. It is presently in use at Tsurumi, and the results are truly good. It will not decrease your incomes.

The opposition, as expressed at a meeting of 800 workers on March 5, focused on the manner of setting the job rate. "The job rate is not based on an individual's day wage. *It does not reflect length of service.* And yet, even if efficiency is raised, the company takes the profit."[35] Shibaura workers were demanding wage reforms that would have established a species of the "seniority wage" system: regular pay raises for all, a tenure allowance, and a higher, fixed day wage to replace the incentive wage.

After a week of fruitless negotiation, the fragile worker alliance dissolved. The three factions differed in their willingness to take a firm stand, and, after much stormy debate, the joint committee decided not to strike. It accepted the following promises and lamely announced a "cease-fire, not a defeat." The company guaranteed that the new incentive system would not result in less than 80 percent of prior pay levels for 6 months after its adoption. No firings would be made specifically because of the move to Tsurumi, although the company would not promise never to fire. The unit price would not be reduced in cases where a worker's income increased due to diligence or cleverness.[36]

Labor broke the cease-fire in February 1931 in the last major dispute of the prewar era at Shibaura. Fear of firings during the move to Tsurumi precipitated the strike, virtually a rerun of the 1930 dispute. Workers raised similar demands over the contract wages and regular semiannual pay raises. Similar factional strife doomed the strike, and it was called off after two weeks. In a reply issued during the strike, the company stated that it would not promise semiannual pay raises of at least 5 sen a day but would "give regular raises to the extent our financial situation allows."[37] As at NKK, the Shibaura bosses were willing to link day wages to seniority only if the bottom line was black. Most important, they remained convinced throughout the 1920s that, for efficient production, a substantial portion of wages must derive directly from output.

The regular raise, an important undercurrent in these Shibaura disputes, was the second major goal of working-class action on wages in the 1920s. Workers at Ishikawajima were typical in their displeasure at irregular increases in the day wage, but their Kōrō union was unable to force change even during its period of considerable strength, from 1921 to 1926. Then, in a violent last stand in the summer of 1926, which turned the tide decisively against radical labor activity in this bellwether center of union strength, Kōrō broached the regular pay raise and related issues for the last time.

The firing of 3 union members in late July brought tensions to the surface. The Kōrō union was facing a serious challenge from the conservative, anti-union Nogi Society which claimed the allegiance of nearly half the yard's 2,000 workers, so Kōrō attempted to use the firing issue to build its strength versus the Nogi Society.[38] The union claimed that "the company wants to lower your day wage and unit prices, but first must squash the union."

Kōrō gathered 60 representatives of all workshops on August 3. They demanded the rehiring of the 3 fired workers and also called for a 20-percent pay raise and regular semiannual pay raises. On August 5, the union added demands for an end to both cuts in the piece rate and pay deductions for output quota shortfalls. But the union claimed only 600 members, and its leaders did not want to press to the point of a strike. The company was clever enough to sense this fear. By accepting some demands, it satisfied some of the workers, and thereby further divided and weakened the union. Management agreed to improve sanitation facilities, reduce tardiness fines, offer vacation pay, and "consider favorably" the regular pay-raise and unit-price issues. In late August, the company announced formation of a factory council and charged it with recommending a decision on these outstanding matters.

By mid-September, the most radical members of the Kōrō union, centered in the Ishikawajima Automobile Factory at a separate nearby location, had turned against the council idea and what they regarded as a betrayal of this settlement. These workers insisted that the council decisions be binding on the company and that elections to the council be open and unrestricted, and they resubmitted demands for regular semiannual pay raises, regular semiannual bonuses, a 20-percent pay raise, an end to the fine system, and a retirement program. About one-half of the shipyard workers supported the Auto Section demands and began an on-the-job slowdown on September 13. This spread to cover two-thirds of all workers by the 16th.

Ishikawajima responded firmly. It fired 44 strikers on September 14, 26 more on the 15th, and another 21 on the 16th. It mobilized foremen antagonistic to the union to break the strike by encouraging their subordinates to return to work. Officials of the Hyōgikai labor federation, to which Kōrō belonged, feared that a prolonged disturbance would only destroy the union, and it sued for peace. In the settlement, the company agreed that only 43 workers would actually be fired; the others would be taken back and given one-half pay for the time missed and, the company promised, would not be discriminated against in future "irregular (*futeiki*) pay raises." Thirty or so auto factory workers remained angry at a settlement they felt had been imposed from outside, but the union accepted the company terms. This was the last major dispute at Ishikawajima until after World War II. The future belonged to Kamino Shinichi and his Nogi Society.[39]

Managers at Ishikawajima had maintained their freedom of action. Pay raises would remain irregular and at management discretion; workers would have nothing to say about output wages. But the Kōrō demands over wages and welfare facilities gathered the support of from one-half to two-thirds of the Ishikawajima work force during the dispute. As at Shibaura, the most radical workers raised those demands which, if implemented, would have produced a "seniority pay" system of regular raises, regular bonuses, and retirement pay.

The far more moderate Kōaikai union clashed with Uraga Dock Company management over pay issues several times in the late 1920s, and here too workers sought above all to make irregular pay raises into regular management practice. In a parallel effort, they demanded that occasional bonuses be made part of the wage system, and in 1928 they won slightly higher bonuses. The issue had been raised earlier, in January 1927, when the region's proletarian paper denounced the year-end bonus of 3 yen, about 2 days' pay, as an insult and called on workers to ignore the Kōaikai and demand a bonus of 2 months' pay. In June 1928, the Kōaikai finally took up the bonus issue and negotiated an increase to nearly 5 yen per worker. This was a short-lived victory. The December 1928 bonus was once again 3 yen for a regular worker.[40]

The more critical issue of pay raises came to a head in July 1928, against a background of rank-and-file discontent over infrequent limited raises and the weak union response. On July 7, union leaders finally resolved to demand that workers with day wages under 2.4 yen who had not received a pay raise for 4 or more years should receive an appropriate raise. They claimed that 400 workers fell into this category. The union also demanded a further increase in the semiannual bonuses, just raised in June, to roughly 10 yen per worker. The third demand was for payment of 50 percent of the full severance pay to voluntary leavers.

On August 7, the company denied the last two demands:

"Bonuses depend on our business each half-year. Ishikawajima and NKK don't have bonuses." Severance pay would remain at 33 percent of the full level for voluntary leavers, limited to those with over 3 years' tenure. Uraga accepted the demand for a pay raise. "Each shop supervisor will investigate the reasons why some have not received pay raises, and all will be given considerable raises, except those in special circumstances. Raises will be given out in two stages, separate from the usual 'selective pay raises.'"

The union claimed a great victory. It had forced management to adhere to the principle of regular pay raises. Discontent continued among the rank and file, with criticism of the union capitulation on the bonus and severance pay, and in the following months the shipbuilders waited in vain for the promised raises, which never came. They protested this "betrayal" by the company to no avail. The Kōaikai weakness against management was real, although its leadership was strong enough to resist the challenge from within that followed.[41]

Uraga workers continued to complain about wages in 1929 and 1930, but no effective action resulted. Machine finishers protested arbitrary differences in pay raise amounts in the May 1930 issue of the union magazine. They also expressed anger because, "the distribution of contract pay doesn't match the work done. Who will put out in such a situation?"[42] In October, another worker threatened: "Our union is moderate and doesn't want to strike, but we cannot remain silent if our members are fired, wages cut, incentive pay increments abolished, pay raises and bonuses withheld. In that case we will be like a sleeping lion awakened."[43]

The lion slumbered on, although Uraga fired many of these men in 1930 and 1931. In the 1920s, few Japanese shipbuilders, steelworkers, and machinists were able to defend what they clearly felt to be fundamental interests, which, if successfully protected, would have established basic elements of the "Japanese employment system": secure jobs, regular raises, and regular bonuses. Managers at Uraga and elsewhere were not interested in creating a wage system tightly linked to seniority. Skill remained the key word for them.

In May 1929, the Kōaikai had raised the issue of semiannual pay raises, and the company replied:

> Raises will be given only to workers whose present wage is judged to be low compared to their skill, and in other special cases. There will be *no general pay raise* in view of the present business situation [this before the Great Depression], and we hope to gain your understanding, since you are different from other Keihin-area workers and have a special relationship to the company.[44]

The story of wages and the union at Yokosen in the 1920s ties together these several threads in the interwar wage tangle, with an interesting difference. In this one case, labor prevailed. In the wake of the strike of March 1929, management compromised some in the implementation of output wages and even more in the calculation of a predictable day wage reflecting seniority and age. Yokosen cooperated with labor in designing a so-called "rational" wage structure based on a social as well as an economic definition of the "rational wage."

The Kōshinkai was a meek organization through most of the 1920s. The union had exacted a company promise of yearly pay raises in lengthy negotiations in spring of 1925, but won no commitments as to how many workers would receive how much.[45] Until 1929, it never approached calling a strike, but, throughout this period, the temporary and some regular workers consistently favored a tougher union stance, and, on several occasions, grumbling in the ranks brought on the defeat of union leaders and their replacement by a supposedly more aggressive crew.

Then, beginning in the summer of 1928, Yokosen began an efficiency movement, changing the incentive-pay system and reducing overtime. Management felt that, with efficient work, the overtime and wage bills could be reduced, and overtime perhaps eliminated. In early 1929, management set up a Work Inspection Committee, composed of supervisors and technicians, to reform the incentive-pay system and improve productivity. Yokosen hired Araki Tōichirō, a young efficiency expert just back from study in the United States, as a consultant to direct this effort.[46]

Unhappiness with these changes gradually spread among the workers and in the union. As early as August 1928, Kōshinkai leaders opposed the new company departures, requesting a raise in day wages to make up for the loss of overtime and a guarantee of semiannual pay raises for all workers. Yet the union soon withdrew the requests, ostensibly because of the impending coronation of the new Shōwa Emperor. Its members reacted to this display of weakness by electing new officers to lead the union in January 1929.[47]

Events moved swiftly thereafter. The new leaders prepared demands to replace those abandoned in the fall by surveying conditions at other companies in the region, organizing preparatory strike committees in all workshops, and secretly seeking assurance of support from the Sōdōmei and other unions. They chose March as the best time to present the demands and possibly go on strike, as two ships ordered by the Navy were scheduled for completion in early spring. On March 5, the union convened a meeting of 238 workshop representatives to ratify a petition containing 7 demands, and, on the 7th, it presented these to the company with lengthy explanations attached. Both the demands and their justification deserve close attention.[48]

In a long preamble, the union stated its basic support for rationalization intended to raise efficiency and strengthen Japanese industry. But, to gain labor cooperation, the company would have to create a "secure psychological environment for the workers" by promoting factory safety and guaranteeing a stable livelihood (that is, higher wages). The 7 demands reflected this reasoning closely.

(1) A 50-sen-per-day raise for all workers. This would benefit lower-paid workers the most and guarantee a basic standard of living for all workers. Able to lead more "human" lives, they would make greater contributions. Income at the Dock Company was said to be about 20 percent below that at other major yards. (The company later disputed this figure.)

(2) An end to all overtime work, assuming the full pay raise is granted. Overtime was neither desirable nor necessary. Workers only sought it because day wages were too low. It

disrupted worker family life and was an example of the lack of management respect for workers as human beings. With better day wages, work would get done efficiently and overtime would be unnecessary.

(3) A minimum wage of 2.2 yen per day, for reasons similar to 1, above. It would also help eliminate imbalances between workers in various shops.

(4) Promotion of all temporary workers to regular status after 6 months. Such a policy would demonstrate management respect for workers and create a secure environment.

(5) Higher severance and retirement pay for regular workers, extended to temporaries as well. Similar reasons.

(6) Company assumption of a greater portion of the health-insurance burden.

(7) Union responsibility for recruiting and hiring new workers, because "workers can judge workers best." This would eliminate hiring of unqualified people and would involve workers directly in the efficiency drive by giving them responsibility for finding good workers and a stake in the outcome of their decisions.[49]

In these demands, the shipbuilders sought reform of the wage structure as a prerequisite to creating a factory community in which they would cooperate gladly, working hard and efficiently.

The Kōshinkai did not expect a favorable response. It set up a strike fund, and the union's cooperative store prepared for the rationing of necessities to strikers. The company offered a compromise in its March 13 reply: a 15-sen-per-day raise; abolition of overtime as requested; an investigation of the minimum-wage issue; a pledge to make physically qualified temporary workers into regular workers after 2½ years' employment; a slight raise in severance pay; and acceptance of the insurance demand. The union responded by resubmitting the original petition in the form of demands, now phrased in less polite, curt language. The company then sent a lengthy appeal to each worker, stressing the weakness of its financial position and the sacrifice it had made to obtain orders at any price, stating in detail its positions, and offering to discuss the wage issue further. Five years of frequent negotiation and discussion with the Kōshinkai, originally a company creation, led the company to expect that this problem, too, could be negotiated.[50]

The workers refused to negotiate. On March 14, the entire work force gathered in the open area in front of the ship carpenters' workshop. Union leaders declared a strike, and the assembly quietly left the yard. As in the shipbuilding strikes of 1921, each workshop constituted a branch of the strike committee, and the union organized a large variety of support committees.[51]

The strike lasted 10 days. The workers remained united, and many local unions offered aid. Negotiations began on March 22, focused on wages. The union wanted a guaranteed average worker income, day plus incentive wage, of 3.05 yen per day, and proposed a 2.2-yen average day wage and a higher incentive pay rate to realize this. This was 57 sen higher than the union calculation of a pre-strike 2.48-yen average income, and it represented no retreat from the original demand. The company was ready to offer a total of 3 yen a day, but it would not admit the day and incentive proportions of this amount as bargaining issues. The two sides reached a compromise on March 24, by agreeing to form a Rational Wage Committee, charged with devising a new "rational wage." In the meantime, a temporary allowance would be issued to guarantee an average income of 3 yen per worker.[52]

The unofficial mediation of the Kyōchōkai brought about this solution and kept the Wage Committee together through the following months of intense negotiating. The committee was composed of 9 worker and 9 company representatives.[53] Although the company chose the slate of 18 workers from which the 9 worker representatives were chosen, and required that 3 of these be foremen and 3 be sub-foremen, the creation of a committee of equal worker and management representation with power to *decide* upon a new wage structure was probably unprecedented in Japan. The outcome of 5 months of hard bargaining was equally unusual.[54]

The committee decided to set the new average day wage at 2.21

yen, 1 sen greater than the worker demand of March 22.[55] Based on the results of a Kyōchōkai cost-of-living survey, *day wages were based on standard living expenses* incurred by a worker of normal ability. "Because there is great variation in what is considered standard, items such as cultural expenses and nonessential expenses are to be met by the incentive-wage portion."[56]

Management had accepted the principle raised explicitly here and implicitly in other labor demands for regular raises and less resort to incentive pay: wages ought to reflect worker needs. Sixty-five percent of day wages would depend solely upon a worker's age and seniority, for a careful survey of the company work force had found age to be the best proxy for family size and thus need. For the average Dock Company worker, a 34-year-old with 5 years' tenure, this portion would be 1.4 yen, 65 percent of the 2.21 yen average day wage. This would vary by 1 sen per year of age and year of seniority above or below the average, so that a 40-year-old worker with 11 years on the job would receive 1.52 yen as the age-based portion of the day wage.[57] The company determined the remaining portion of the day wage by a rank addition (30 to 60 sen for foremen, 10 to 30 yen for sub-foremen) and a work-point addition. It gave each worker 1 to 15 points depending on the difficulty of his job, 1 to 15 points depending on a skill evaluation, and 1 to 15 points depending on attendance and diligence. Each point was assigned a monetary value, and the sum of a worker's age, rank, and point additions produced the exact wage. In this fashion, difficult negotiation between labor and management produced a major, much publicized innovation: a day wage explicitly linked to age and tenure and implicitly reflecting worker need.

Management still retained considerable discretion. The committee agreed that future raises would continue to be given every 6 months to only 30 percent of the regular workers. The amount would be calculated from the work points for skill, diligence, and job difficulty used in the day-wage calculation. Incentive wages also remained a significant portion of total pay, on the average around 27 percent. These incentive wages were for the most part calculated as payments to a work group. The company then distributed them to individuals in accordance with a ratio "decided for each worker on the basis of his skill and rank." One important concession was a promise to workers that no income would be lost as the Work Inspection Committee and the efficiency expert Araki reformed the incentive pay system, although the company asserted that incentive pay would depend solely on individual effort and output. From the time of the 1929 settlement until the early war years, the Yokohama Dock Company wage structure changed very little.[58]

The pay system negotiated at Yokosen in 1929 differed in important respects from that prevalent a decade earlier in Keihin shipyards and factories. When traveling was common and relatively simple, the skill a man brought to his job played the major role in setting his initial pay and inviting or discouraging subsequent raises, and the ubiquity of piecework reinforced the importance of skill and efficiency. In 1929, systems of pay by result were still common, and usually more sophisticated, and performance still figured in setting pay raises, but a decade of hard times for travelers had decreased the importance of skills traded for pay in an open market, and increased the weight of company-specific factors. Under the Yokosen system, attractive to labor for its predictability, and in less explicit or systematic fashion at other companies, the day wage came to depend less on the job and skill level, and more on seniority and rank. While the semiannual raise and other seniority benefits predated the 1920s, their impact had been limited. Recall the problems faced by Uraga just after the war; when turnover was intense, the company rewarded the traveler's skill at the expense of the loyal, senior worker, or else lost the traveler to a competitor. As mobility decreased in the 1920s, an enduring change in this wage structure began to unfold, as pay slowly came to adhere more to characteristics of membership in the firm, seniority, and rank, and less to independent attributes of skill. This shift had only begun in the 1920s. It would take on critical importance over time as both government policy in World War II and the intense wage battles of the early postwar era reinforced this evolving structure and developed from it a more predictable, less capricious wage system.

However portentous this change, we must not exaggerate and see in it the simple creation or crystallization of a seniority-wage system in the 1920s, as a number of scholars have done. Their interpretation misreads both the interests of labor and management and their power.[59] A significant portion of the wage package derived from output, and the day wage was contingent upon several factors other than seniority. Company evaluations always influenced the size of the raise; arbitrary judgments or favoritism were common sources of complaint. In bad years, no one took home a raise, and, even in good times, not all the regular men got them. One finds only the slow beginnings of the seniority wage pattern in these years; managers tried to discourage mobility among "key skilled workers" (*kikan kō*), and the promise of a pay raise each year was part of this effort. Even if promises were not always kept, the typical senior skilled man was often better paid than his newer, less-experienced counterpart, and he expected this. The 1902 case where a 7-year man outearned (in day wage) a 15-year buddy would have surprised managers and offended workers by 1930.[60] Many factors, chief among them the decline in job-switching, brought this state of affairs into being. Seniority in and of itself did not bring the senior men higher pay, for managers were interested in raising productivity in a steady fashion more than in raising wages. They felt workers could not be motivated to produce without substantial, direct wage incentives, and they would not give out raises without carefully taking skill into account. Workers were interested in the long-term stability of their income, and, throughout the decade, they pushed for regular pay raises and stable incentive pay, but the simple fact that managers were far more powerful weakened the relationship between seniority and wages.

Potential for a more thoroughly "seniority" wage remained. The tight job market went some way toward fulfilling this potential, and, where workers were strong enough to demand a voice in wage determination, and management was willing or forced to listen, something close enough to a seniority wage could account for at least part of income. A strong union convinced management to listen in Yokohama in 1929. At the Kure Naval Yard, managers decided to listen while the noise level was still low, but the labor movement was indirectly responsible for Kure's pioneering experiment with a livelihood wage. In 1923, Godō Takuo at the Naval Yard justified a new policy of offering raises in simple accord with age and tenure: "If things are left as they are with no effort made to stabilize worker livelihood, the result will be the spread of dangerous ideas (*shisō no akka*) and an invitation to social disorder."[61] These cases were exceptional in the 1920s, and the Yokohama Dock wage system was the object of widespread interest for this very reason.[62] Yet, their number would increase with further pressure from workers or the government.

For most of the 1930s, any such pressure was absent. Although managers were certainly concerned with the rise in turnover by the middle of the decade, they took few new steps to strengthen the link between seniority and the day wage or reduce the importance of output wages. Union calls for regular pay raises or more stable incentive pay no longer troubled them. If they felt pay rewarding seniority encouraged long-term employment, they still viewed incentive or output wages as essential to induce efficient labor, particularly as orders increased. Business logic dictated reliance on both day wages, which rose as the result of several factors in addition to seniority, and on incentive wages, designed to stimulate hard work. As a result, wage practices in the 1930s remained fairly similar to those that had evolved in the previous decade. Managerial evaluation of skill remained important in the distribution of raises, incentive pay continued to account for a significant portion of wages, and income still fluctuated from month to month and year to year.

Nippon Kōkan and one unnamed steelmaker with 260 workers are the best documented Keihin cases. A report compiled in the summer of 1935 focused on a small group of workers at each company over a 3-month period, and it offers an unusual chance to examine the interwar wage system.[63]

The researchers found that NKK gave out raises in the day wage with fair regularity between 1933 and 1935. Most men received raises of 2 or 3 sen per day each year.[64] This would insure a gradual and steady, if slow, rise in day wages for most workers. The system at Uraga Dock Company remained more selective and perhaps more typical. Until 1937, 20 percent of the workers became eligible for a raise every 3 months. In 1937, the pool of eligible workers was increased to 25 percent each quarter, but not all these eligible workers actually received raises. Management limited pay hikes to "those who have worked 6 months or more, or in special cases less than 6 months, and have made great progress in skill and diligence."[65]

Compared to Uraga, NKK gave out a more dependable seniority raise to its workers. It is hard to determine which approach was more common, but Yokohama Dock Company gave out raises in a manner similar to its competitor in Uraga, and consistent management concern with efficiency here and elsewhere leads one to expect a fair degree of selectivity in the "regular raise." Shibaura and Ishikawajima sources are silent on this point, but one additional, very small statistical sample sheds some light on the impact of seniority upon the day wage. A survey conducted in the Keihin region in 1951 gathered figures on age, experience, seniority, and day wages from 37 machinists and shipbuilders. Calculations for the 13 men in the group who began to work before 1945 reveal seniority to be a better predictor of day wages than either age or experience.[66] The sample suggests that, however selectively raises were implemented, over the long run day wages of the 1930s tended to reflect seniority more than other factors.

Ten of the 13 workers entered the labor force in the 1930s. In the absence of similar data from earlier periods, these results raise the possibility that a similar strong relationship between day wages and seniority obtained earlier. Yet, good reason exists for concluding that the day wage did, in fact, correspond more closely to seniority in the 1930s than before. A generally buoyant economy allowed managers to honor customary practice and give out raises with fair regularity, and the desire to prevent job-switching, once again atractive and possible, encouraged the practice. We have seen that, in the 1920s, frequent business setbacks prevented this, with disputes over wage hikes one result. While tentative, the evidence implies that the day wage of the 1930s was a bit more closely tied to seniority than before.

Of course, the day wage was still only one component of income. In 1935 at NKK, it accounted for 46 percent, while 54 percent derived from incentive wages. At the smaller Kawasaki steelmaker, the proportional breakdown was 55 percent day wage and 45 percent incentive pay (Table 19). The still notoriously complex NKK system involved three different incentive calculations. It was commonly believed that few NKK managers fully understood how wages were calculated![67] At Yokohama Dock Company, incentive wages accounted for an average of 20 to 24 percent of a worker's total monthly income from 1935 to 1939.[68] In both cases, the proportion of income derived from output pay had not changed from the 1920s.

When this portion of income is considered, the relationship between seniority and pay weakens. Table 20 documents this for NKK. It ranks workers by day wage, the component most likely to reflect seniority. In each month, the incomes of 3 or 4 of the 8 NKK workers were either higher or lower than day-wage rank would have predicted. One worker in each month, worker A in July and August, and D in September, had the second highest income, although only the fifth or fourth highest day wage. Similar "irregularities" can also be found in data for workers at another, nearby steelmaker.

Such "irregularities" arose because attendance and the amount of work available to a work group also had a major impact on income. In several cases, workers with relatively low income were those with poor attendance records, not low day wages. In other cases, even workers with low day wages received a fat monthly pay envelope because their shops were very busy and their output pay high. The survey team noted this to be true of NKK's worker D in August and September, and worker A in July and August. The relationship between these two determinants of income, attendance

Table 19 Wages of 8 Workers at Nippon Kōkan, July–September 1935: Average Monthly Wage, by Component

Worker	Fixed Day Wage	Basic Wage	%	Added Wage	%	Incentive	%	Extras	%	Total Income	%
B	1.75	59.39	43.2	49.04	35.7	29.10	21.2	—	0	137.53	100
F	1.48	54.46	57.9	30.51	32.4	9.10	9.7	—	0	94.06	100
E	1.42	41.95	45.4	40.32	43.6	6.70	7.2	3.430	3.7	92.40	100
D	1.40	26.05	29.8	57.77	66.2	3.50	4.0	—	0	87.32	100
A	1.38	32.80	35.0	40.85	43.5	12.71	13.5	7.446	7.9	93.81	100
C	1.30	43.81	55.3	30.81	38.9	3.67	4.6	—	0	78.29	100
G	1.25	31.54	49.3	23.80	37.2	4.92	7.7	2.666	4.2	62.93	100
H	1.20	39.61	55.2	20.58	28.7	10.60	14.8	1.000	1.3	71.79	100
Avg.	1.40	41.20		36.80		10.04		1.817		90.024	
%		46.4		40.8		10.3		2.1		100	

Source: NRUS, VII, 165.

Table 20 Wages of 8 Workers at Nippon Kōkan, July–September 1935:
Actual Monthly Wage (yen)

Worker	Day Wage	July			August			September		
		Income	Days	Day Avg.	Income	Days	Day Avg.	Income	Days	Day Avg.
B	1.75	139.59	30	4.65	134.53	30	4.84	138.47	27	5.13
F	1.48	94.84	30	3.16	93.44	31	3.01	93.91	30	3.13
E	1.42	95.80	28	3.42	92.75	24	3.86	88.64	22	4.03
D	1.40	83.09	21	3.96	56.40	10	5.64	132.46	21.3	5.75
A	1.38	99.68	30	3.22	121.66	27	4.51	60.09	13	4.62
C	1.30	78.43	30	2.61	73.77	28.5	2.59	85.68	29	2.92
G	1.25	67.07	25	2.68	57.58	20	2.80	67.33	26	2.59
H	1.20	86.70	30	2.89	64.77	31	2.09	63.91	31	2.06
Avg.	1.40	93.15	28	3.34	86.86	25.1	3.63	91.31	24.9	3.78

Source: NRUS, VII, 165.

and shop workload, was probably not accidental. Worker A showed up on only 13 days in the month after his 122-yen windfall.[69] Worker D was able to pull in a reasonable 56 yen with just 10 days' work in August because his workshop group was so busy. Unfornately, we cannot find out if his attendance dropped in October after he earned 132 yen in September. While insufficient as proof, these cases at least suggest that a selective work ethic, informed by a sense of how much a man needed or expected, remained part of working-class culture; if a steelworker greatly exceeded his normal pay one month, he would reward himself with a few extra days off the next month.

Because the output portion of income was so dependent on attendance and the group's level of activity, the link between seniority and income was tenuous. Monthly variations of over 15 percent in take-home pay were common, found in the cases of 5 of the 8 NKK workers, 10 of the 13 workers at the smaller steel mill. The income of 2 workers in 1939 at the neighboring Tsurumi shipyard, later bought by NKK, fluctuated even more radically, and in this case the instability led to a dispute.[70]

	Feb.	*Mar.*	*April*	*May*
Worker A	¥126	170	86	146
Worker B	132	127	115	153

Worker income was not steady from month to month in the 1930s, despite the fixed day wage which bore some relation to seniority.

Nor did seniority raises mean that income rose steadily over the long run. For individuals who stayed the entire period covered in the NKK survey, income was higher between 1928 and 1930 than in the early 1930s. Not until 1935 did the income of most return to 1928 or 1929 levels. The report cited Worker F as typical. He entered NKK as a trainee in 1928 with a 1.35-yen day wage and an average income of 77.9 yen per month. His average monthly income fluctuated considerably over the following years: 84.1 yen in 1930, 61.9 yen in 1932, 81.1 yen in 1934, and finally 94.1 yen in 1935. His day wage had registered a slow but steady 13-sen rise over these 7 years, but income rose and fell with the business fortunes of his employer, not with his increasing seniority. In heavy industrial enterprises of the 1930s, skill, output, attendance, and long-run business trends all combined to influence income. A day wage that rose to some extent together with seniority and status in the firm was a significant development of the interwar era, but it could not guarantee steadily climbing income.

STATUS AND SECURITY
THE MEANING OF NON-WAGE BENEFITS

The same dual managerial strategy that dictated wage policy in the 1920s and 1930s shaped non-wage benefits as well. Employers manipulated promotions or bonuses for two reasons: to keep senior men from leaving and to prevent the rest from loafing. Programs of retirement or severance pay and mutual aid had similar twin goals, but, when times were bad, the management commitment wavered, while labor sought to preserve these benefits. As had the regular raise and the secure job, the bonus, the retirement fund, and the mutual-aid society became part of the Japanese worker's notion of "just" treatment through a decade of implicit or explicit negotiating.

In Japanese industry of the high-growth era and beyond, nearly automatic promotions with "no functional connotation whatever" have served to keep up worker morale and perhaps slow turnover.[71] Scholars tempted to read the present back into a "traditional" past have described prewar foremen as simply "seniority foremen," promoted to their posts without reference to skill or leadership ability, to reward and further encourage long tenure. Hazama Hiroshi is typical in evaluating the prewar foreman rank as "an honorary label given for long service," but this is only half the story. Seniority and advanced age were usually necessary for promotion to higher rank, but they were by no means sufficient. The post was more than an honor. Skill was critical as well.

The foremen and sub-foremen in the interwar era were indeed relatively old and senior. A sample of 48 NKK foremen and sub-foremen in 1939 shows the mean foreman age to be 48, mean sub-foreman age 43. The 1935 survey found that all NKK foremen had over 10 years' seniority, sub-foremen around 7 to 8 years on the job.[72] But NKK work rules in 1935 also read "foremen must have at least 3 years' seniority and be selected from among sub-foremen. Sub-foremen are selected from highly skilled regular workers."[73] At Ishikawajima, also, "skill was a major factor in promotions, in addition to attitude and the ability to get along with others."[74] Seniority by itself was no guarantee of promotion at the Yahata Iron Works, where 43 percent of all workers with tenure of over 20 years, virtually a full career in that era, had not yet been promoted beyond regular worker.[75] Competition for advancement was fierce, and for good reason. In most firms, foreman wages were from 50 to 100 percent higher than those of regular workers.[76] Output-wage distribution at NKK and the "rational day wage" of 1929 at Yokosen both worked to give foremen and sub-foremen substantially higher incomes than regular workers. In addition, the foreman possessed authority to make important decisions concerning wages or hiring in heavy industry. Responsibility as well as higher pay came with the post.

A further difference separates the chancy promotions of the prewar era from those of the 1960s and later. The number of steps on the promotion ladder was far greater at Hitachi in the 1970s than in most major heavy industrial firms in the 1920s; the Hitachi hierarchy included 3 ranks of foremen and 8 grades of skilled workers below that, while most prewar companies simply divided adult workers into 3 ranks: foreman, sub-foreman, and regular workers. Eighty percent of all employees in a major 1927 survey fell into the "regular" slot.[77]

For blue-collar workers in prewar heavy industry, promotion was at best an uncertain incentive to remain with a firm. The company gave these boosts on the basis of skill, to senior workers to be sure, but it never promoted many senior men. The promotion ladder was simple and short, so an enterprise could not offer promotions as more or less automatic, periodic morale-boosting rewards. The only possible promotions, to sub-foreman and foreman ranks, came late or did not come at all. A worker who doggedly remained at Yahata Ironworks in hopes of becoming a foreman

was as likely as not to be sorely disappointed. In part an inducement to keep workers from moving, promotions were also prized
carrots dangled to elicit diligent efforts from workers competing
to rise in the firm.

The promise of a semiannual bonus could also theoretically lead
a man to choose steady service over job-switching, and, during the
1910s and 1920s, many companies did in fact begin to include
workers in bonus programs previously limited to staff. Here again,
the motives were complex, the impact limited. As with so much
of management policy of World War I and the years thereafter, the
labor movement directly or indirectly stimulated this change, and
managers implemented bonuses grudgingly, in small amounts, with
an eye to discipline as well as seniority.[78] The gulf between staff
and worker bonuses was immense throughout the interwar years.
Semiannual profit-sharing bonuses offered to machine or metal
industry blue-collar men were generally worth 10 days' to 2 weeks'
day wages, about 15 or 20 yen. NKK steelmakers took home such
payments twice a year, and company records reveal the vastly different treatment of white-collar staff[79] (Table 21).

Other companies offered workers no semiannual bonuses at all.
The Shibaura company history, quick to point out all examples of
company benevolence, makes no mention of such a bonus. Shibaura denied the labor demand for one-third of the staff bonus in
1920. A fair number of major shipbuilders in the late 1920s offered
no semiannual bonuses to men below the rank of sub-foreman,
and shipbuilding bonuses in general were much lower than in the
machine or metal industry. Two to 5 yen for a regular worker was
most common.[80]

Attendance bonuses, on the other hand, were widespread. In
one typical program, a shipbuilder of regular rank gained 7 yen for
6 months' perfect attendance, and 2 yen if he missed 5 days or
less.[81] In some cases, the two types were combined; a worker's
attendance would determine the size of his semiannual bonus.
These bonuses served to promote diligence more than long-term
service. A Shibaura worker lamented that many refused to take
the day off on May Day for fear of spoiling their attendance

Table 21 1935–1939 NKK Staff and Worker Bonuses (Staff does not include executives)

Period	Staff			Workers			Worker Bonus as % of Staff Bonus
	Bonus (mos.)	Salary (avg.)	Bonus (yen)	Bonus (days)	Day Wage (avg.)	Bonus (yen)	
1935 1st half	7.5	75.8 yen	568.5	12	1.57 yen	18.84	3
1935 2nd half	7.5	78.3	587.25	12	1.53	18.36	3
1936 1st half	7.5	76.3	549.7	11	1.64	18.04	3
1936 2nd half	6.0	74.7	485.4	10	1.49	14.9	3
1937 1st half	7.5	76.6	566.8	12	1.54	18.48	3
1937 2nd half	8.0	75.2	601.3	13	1.54	20.02	3
1938 1st half	8.5	78.5	667.45	14	1.50	21.0	3
1938 2nd half	8.5	77.15	665.81	14	1.46	20.44	3
1939 1st half	8.5	72.3	651.9	14	1.45	20.3	3

Source: 1935–1939 minutes of executive meetings.

records, a good indication that the bonus functioned as the company hoped.[82] But, when times were bad enough, the mass of idle or unemployed provided incentive enough to keep attendance up among the fortunate employed, and many shipyards abolished their attendance bonuses in the late 1920s.[83]

Ironically, these small bonuses extended to workers could further stimulate the desire for treatment equal to that of staff. Even at Ishikawajima, the company union quietly worked out an agreement in the late 1930s whereby worker bonuses increased.[84] The tremendous gap between staff and worker payments made the bonuses as likely to sharpen awareness that a worker was an outsider, not entitled to full benefits, as to "bind" him closer to the company.

Retirement or severance pay, mutual-aid societies, and, later, health insurance programs, were the major non-wage benefits offered by management in heavy industry.[85] If conscientiously implemented, these and some other company welfare programs could have served to encourage long tenure. In the baldest cases, managers usually gave retirement pay in reduced amounts to voluntary leavers, and they used forced, long-term savings programs to keep workers "hostage" to the firm. In theory, extensive company welfare also would have generated good will and worker dependence upon the company.

Listed in a sentence or two, the total range of company "benevolence" appears impressive, and workers appreciated, indeed expected, these non-wage benefits, but company welfare programs in heavy industry did not simply generate the long-term commitment or the good will often credited to them. They frequently lacked substance, were cut back or abandoned when business needs so dictated, and could exacerbate rather than reduce tension within an enterprise. When employers changed a provision of an important benefit, workers often protested this denial of their "just" reward.

Many companies made no formal distinction between retirement and severance pay (*taishoku* and *kaiko*). In all cases, these allowances started with the first, second, or third year on the job and increased with seniority. A fund labeled "retirement" would provide a sum to a worker fired far short of retirement age. In addition to rising with seniority, these allowances worked to discourage mobility by reducing the amount paid to voluntary leavers. At the Mitsubishi Shipyards, voluntary leavers received from 20 to 50 percent of full retirement pay, set at 150 days for a 10-year worker, 420 days for a 20-year man. Shibaura voluntary leavers received nothing prior to 1920 and from one-third to two-thirds of full benefits thereafter.[86]

Most companies first offered retirement programs during World War I, in 1916 at Uraga Dock Company and NKK, in 1915 at Shibaura, as part of a strategy to lower turnover as well as respond to worker demands.[87] Then, as the labor market shifted in favor of the employer, management support for retirement funds waned. The principal of the Shibaura Worker Retirement Fund stood at over 1 million yen in 1921 but dropped gradually throughout the decade. Management enthusiasm declined together with profits, and a 10-million-yen loss in 1931 wiped out the entire fund of over 492,000.[88] In the 1920s, the company did not need the retirement-pay incentive to keep a critical mass of workers from quitting.

Two factors combined to bring about a revival of many worker retirement funds in the 1930s. An expanding economy and new job opportunities once again led companies to design policies to keep workers from switching jobs. Also, the government began plans for a Retirement Fund Law in 1931. Industry leaders uniformly opposed this law, and their chief argument was that existing practice took sufficient care of retiring or fired workers. Circumstantial evidence suggests that companies took steps to improve their existing, occasionally dormant retirement programs in order to lend credibility to such an argument, for the Home Ministry advocates of the law were not easily fooled.[89] For whichever reason, Shibaura revived its Retirement Fund in 1934, after a 3-year hiatus, and contributed from 8 to 17 percent of profits to the fund each year until 1938.[90] In 1937, Shibaura established a detailed set of Retirement Fund Regulations in accord with the new Retirement Fund Law. The company put 2 percent of each month's pay into a postal savings account for each worker, held the account books, and reserved the right to withhold half the balance from voluntary leavers.[91] The Ishikawajima Shipyard in 1934 for the first time instituted a formal retirement fund covering workers. The title of the fund was identical to the term used in the then pending Retirement Fund Law, a clear sign of its influence three years before it took effect.

Management thus established and expanded retirement funds during World War I and in the 1930s, but the more common practice in the 1920s was for workers to resist cutbacks in existing programs or push for new ones with less success that they had enjoyed during the war. These actions were not wholly in vain. The 1926 shipbuilding report noted that, "in the wake of the 1921 shipbuilding wave of unrest, the level of severance pay has risen considerably and is now quite high."[92]

A dispute at Shibaura in June 1924 centered on welfare issues. Workers demanded, in addition to an 8-hour day, the restoration of severance pay, retirement allowances retroactive to before the earthquake, restoration of the mutual-aid society, and modification of the attendance bonus. The company refused to commit itself formally to any of these programs, while maintaining "it had always been a Shibaura tradition to give more than the legal minimum in severance pay." The workers failed to gain any of their demands.[93] Strikers at the Uraga Dock Company's small Yokohama Factory in August 1926 demanded higher retirement/severance pay of 30 days for the first year on the job and 24 additional days for each additional year. This would have raised severance pay well above the industry average. When Uraga fired all 132 workers, the strike collapsed, and the men offered to withdraw their demands in return for rehiring.[94]

One isolated successful effort to improve severance pay came in 1929 at NKK. The 48 employees at the small Osaka plant went on a slowdown, angry at NKK retraction of a promise to extend retirement/severance pay to voluntary leavers. Several days of negotiations resulted in agreement to extend the allowance as promised.[95] Successful or not, worker pressure in the 1920s helped establish and reinforce a belief that retirement or severance pay was part of the system, to be denied at management peril.

Mutual-aid societies offered sick pay and medical expenses for injured workers as well as gifts or condolence money for births, marriages, or deaths. In 1927, "almost no large factory in Japan was without one."[96] Ideally, such organizations, in addition to cooperative stores or health insurance unions, would create a positive workplace atmosphere, increasing the worker's sense of security, belonging, and participation, as well as his dependence on his employer. In fact, companies did not support these societies consistently, for they too could turn into arenas of conflict, with workers demanding greater company generosity, greater control, or both.

Uraga established a mutual-aid society in 1916 with capital of 11,728 yen, and this grew to 56,264 yen by early 1923. The earthquake destroyed the society. Earlier, in December 1920, the company had put an end to sales of rice below cost to workers.[97] Several years later, the more aggressive among the workers began a movement to revive the aid society, complaining that the company was obligated to pay allowances to staff and workers who had left the Dock Company since the earthquake and charging the company with hiding the society's funds.[98] Uraga revived the aid society for workers only, whereas it had included staff in the pre-1923 version, but complaints continued. In 1929, one worker insisted to no avail that the union demand full control of the society because workers paid the entire bill and had the ability to run the organization.[99] Uraga preferred to keep control of its welfare programs and could safely ignore these occasional complaints.

Both Shibaura and Nippon Kōkan likewise elected to retain control of aid and insurance programs as far as possible. NKK discouraged any worker involvement in welfare administration, so as to block the Sōdōmei effort to penetrate the company. It extended benefits unilaterally, as a sign of company generosity. NKK always maintained strict control of both the mutual-aid society founded in 1916, which also ran a thriving cooperative store, and the Health Insurance Union founded in late 1926.[100]

For Shibaura managers, too, union activity at both major factories posed a threat that would have been greater had the unions controlled substantial aid programs. High on the union agenda for both 1924 and 1926 was "asserting control over the company mutual-aid fund."[101] Workers made some progress in 1924. When Shibaura created a new mutual-aid society, to replace an older organization dissolved in the wake of the earthquake, workers could elect one-half of the directors, and they used the opportunity to pack the society with union activists.[102] Management disbanded the society in 1926, ostensibly because the new Shibaura Health Insurance Union, mandated by law, duplicated many of its services. But the old mutual-aid society had, in fact, offered benefits not provided by the new Insurance Union, and the fear of a labor takeover of this welfare program was likely an important company motive.

At Yokohama Dock, such fears became reality. In November 1926, the Kōshinkai union, at this point still supposedly a company pawn, began to run its own welfare activities, founding a successful consumer cooperative. By the end of the year, sales were already 13.3 yen per month per worker. The average worker was thus spending a significant portion of his income, which ranged from 50 to 100 yen per month, at the cooperative.[103] The cooperative presented a problem to the Dock Company. While it relieved the company of a financial burden, it moved in an unwelcome direction. Uraga and Shibaura workers never translated complaints about company welfare, or calls for union control, into action, but Yokosen workers used welfare programs for their own ends. The Yokohama Dock Cooperative Store provided crucial assistance to the union during the 1929 strike. Kōshinkai officers also took leading positions in the Health Insurance Union and strove to keep worker premiums from rising. In the 1929 strike, the Kōshinkai forced the company to increase its contribution toward insurance costs, while worker contributions remained the same.[104]

Throughout these years of shifting management policy, the labor interest was consistent. An Ishikawajima man called for a program of injury compensation in 1922. To pass the hat and collect aid after the fact was all wrong, he argued. "There should be a more rational system, and the company should shoulder the burden."[105] Seven years later, a shipbuilder at Uraga echoed this chorus and invoked the great theme of prewar labor, the call for "human" treatment:

> We're humans too. (*Oretachi datte ningen da.*) The amount given to sur- vivors of a worker killed on the job is an insult. The company owes us a guarantee that, if we die working, our family can live.[106]

Creating or expanding these corporate welfare programs was not high on the management agenda in the 1920s. Often workers fought unsuccessful battles to keep or to enlarge those programs already in operation. Welfare programs experienced two signifi- cant growth spurts, first during World War I, and again in the mid- 1930s.[107] Management used welfare benefits to attract and to keep workers when jobs were plentiful and turnover high, and to offer an alternative to the labor movement when it was powerful. In the 1920s, retrenchment took priority. The first NKK company his- tory, published in 1933, devoted only one sentence to welfare ef- forts. In its contrast to the glowing descriptions of worker benefits in later histories, it captures nicely the spirit of management policy: "To the extent that finances have permitted, we have pro- vided various facilities for staff and workers for relief, sanitation, and moral education."[108]

In wages as in welfare, the key practices associated today with the Japanese factory were slowly evolving out of the wrangling of workers and managers. The yearly pay raise and the mutual-aid society had first appeared in the late nineteenth century at a few companies, initiated by managers anxious to attract and satisfy some skilled workers. From World War I into the 1920s, these practices were transformed into labor-movement causes. They came to be part of the worker's notion of fair or equal treatment. Workers pushed for the founding, continuation, or expansion of welfare programs and on occasion sought to control them. In disputes over wage levels and retirement or severance pay, labor demanded explicit linkage of seniority with wages, secure output pay, and expanded benefits for all workers including voluntary leavers. Workers failed in most struggles for lack of power in a hostile environment, not confusion over their objectives. To the extent that they succeeded, wage or welfare practices considered part of the Japanese employment system slowly took root, to reach full growth, together with job security, in a later era when the political and economic balance had changed.

SIX

The Enterprise Community
Companies, Unions, and the Working Class

The shipbuilding strikes of summer and fall 1921 marked the most profound labor upheaval to shake the nation until 1946. In the wake of these and other disputes, managers moved adroitly to separate workers from their unions, and, by the end of the 1920s, a full decade prior to the Pacific War and the formal dissolution of all unions, organized labor in big business was on the defensive, if not defeated. Cognizant of this successful managerial campaign, one influential perspective on the Japanese factory identifies this decade as the time when a cozy "enterprise community" emerged in most big firms. Between 1918 and 1931, managers of large companies supposedly came to see themselves "as looking after all aspects of their employees' lives, including their families. The employees, for their part, had the deeply engrained attitude of committing themselves to the care of the managers or the firms."[1] Respect, trust, and good will reportedly characterized the management view of labor, and the workers committed themselves to the firm with reciprocal dedication, for "Japanese industrialists' view of man (like Robert Owens' for that matter) made them believe in the *efficiency* of benevolence in evoking loyalty, and of trust in evoking responsibility."[2]

While unions certainly fared poorly in the Keihin factories and shipyards of the 1920s, workers and managers created few if any such communities. Our alternative to this rosy view of paternalism, dependence, and cohesive community in the factory must explain managerial ability to overcome unions without exaggerating the harmony or stability that resulted. Disputes disrupted all the Keihin firms more than once in this decade. In some cases, these were isolated incidents punctuating longer periods of relative calm. Elsewhere, undercurrents of discontent broke to the surface regularly in union activity, for managers were reluctant to make far-reaching concessions to labor. The desire for fuller membership in the enterprise, implicit in many of the demands for job security, wage stability, and company welfare support, offered managers an opportunity to create stable, harmonious enterprise or factory communities by skillfully and decisively meeting worker expectations and winning over their leaders. This did not happen. The few concessions offered—job security and wage hikes for good workers in good times, limited welfare programs, and some advisory factory councils—brought at best an uneasy peace to the shop floor. Despite the weakness of organized workers in big firms, a "labor problem" continued to loom significant in the calculations of the bureaucrats and businessmen who sought to mobilize the nation for war in the 1930s.

THE GOVERMENT ROLE

In the 1920s, bureaucrats and politicians discussed labor issues extensively yet took few positive legislative steps. The state influenced the labor movement most in its decisions on when not to act; it came to quietly tolerate moderate labor activity, in an application of the candy-and-whip (*ame to muchi*) theory of social control. Repression of the left wing of the socialist and labor movements continued as before, for the elite hoped to channel labor activity in a less threatening, moderate direction with its selective tolerance. In the 1930s, in contrast, advocates of extensive social and economic controls, including control of labor, came to dominate the bureaucracy, and the state moved toward widespread intervention in labor matters.[3]

Policy toward the union movement and toward strikes began to change with Hara Kei's Seiyūkai party cabinet of 1918-1921. Hara left it to the bureaucracy, particularly the Home Ministry, to revamp the administrative approach to labor through a changed interpretation of Article 17 of the 1900 Peace Police Law. Citing the vaguely worded prohibition of "incitement to strike," authorities could easily turn the law against unions, but under Tokonami Takejirō the Home Ministry stopped using Article 17 against "healthy" unions, those organized vertically on the enterprise level and amenable to management calls for cooperation and harmony.[4] Tokonami actively supported formation of such unions, badgering or cajoling industrialists to create them.

While the government, beginning in 1918, tolerated both moderate unions and strikes that did not transcend the enterprise framework, the result was only limited breathing space for organized workers. Others within the bureaucracy challenged the Home Ministry stance. The hard-line Justice Ministry advocated unrestrained repression to deal with the social movement. In place of Article 17, those authorities bent on repression turned to other legal means. Strikers could be and were arrested for disturbing the peace, rioting, sedition, slander, or other criminal and civil charges.[5] A battle over labor policy continued unabated within the bureaucracy throughout the 1920s. It pitted the Home Ministry, especially the relatively liberal Social Bureau created in 1922, against not only the Justice Ministry, but also the Agriculture and Commerce Ministry and even, on occasion, the more conservative Police Bureau within the Home Ministry. The Social Bureau pushed for abolition of Article 17 and enactment of a Labor Union Law and Labor Dispute Arbitration Law. While the Imperial Diet abolished Article 17, already more or less a dead letter in practice, in 1925, it never approved a Labor Union Law. It did pass an Arbitration Law in 1926. While applied only six times before 1945, the law was significant insofar as it served to sanction unofficial third-party mediation. The police, especially, became increasingly active in dispute mediation in the late 1920s and throughout the 1930s.

Shifting government policy gave workers the de facto right to strike for economic ends by the mid-1920s, but the Justice Ministry was able to apply a new anti-violence law to many incidents emerging out of labor disputes, and informal mediation by the Police Bureau of the Home Ministry was generally unfavorable to workers in the 1920s. Union activity never gained legal protection. Even if authorities did not arrest strikers, managers were likely to fire them, and workers had no legal recourse. Union activists and strikers remained extremely vulnerable. With jobs scarce and employers exchanging information on labor activists, the decision to lead or join a strike, or even to become involved in a union, meant grave risk for the worker and his family. Strikes of the 1920s were serious affairs, especially when compared to the predictable, relatively safe Spring Offensives of the 1970s or 1980s.[6]

The political impact of the more tolerant policy of the 1920s was real. The Social Democrats and Sōdōmei gained a de facto legitimacy as the voice of labor. Katō Kōmei's government in 1924 implicitly recognized organized labor by allowing unions (instead of the government) to choose the Japanese "worker representative" to the I.L.O. each year, and, by the early 1930s, the most prominent leaders of the Sōdōmei and Social Democratic Party served together with businessmen on several advisory committees to the Home Ministry dealing with social issues. But, viewed from the shop floor of large firms, government policy had little direct effect. Politicians and bureaucrats essentially allowed businessmen to tackle their own problems, intervening only when disputes got out of hand. Tokonami and the Social Bureau of the Home Ministry encouraged cooperative, vertical unions or Factory Councils as a solution to labor troubles, but a Factory Council Law never left the drawing board. Management was free to impose its own settlement on labor, following government advice if it so chose.

Two exceptions were the Factory Law Revision of 1923 (effective 1926) and the Health Insurance Law of 1922 (effective 1927). The new Factory Law raised the minimum sums for death benefits, injury compensation, and sick pay. It forced companies to offer ill or injured workers 60 percent pay for 6 months and 40 percent thereafter, instead of 50 percent pay for 3 months and 33 percent thereafter. A 1927 summary of conditions in the machine industry claimed this brought about changed policy at many companies. In several cases surveyed, the company offered only the legal minimum, a clear sign of the law's impact.[7] The Health Insurance Law, drafted in 1921 by the Labor Section of the Agriculture and Commerce Ministry, protected workers in cases of illness and injury on or off the job and applied to all enterprises covered by the Factory Law. A company could either allow direct government administration of the insurance program or create its own Health Insurance Union run by a committee of workers and managers. Committees would be composed equally of worker and management representatives, and the company would contribute at least 50 percent to the insurance fund. The rest of the funds would come from wages, up to a 3-percent maximum deduction from monthly pay. Disputes frequently arose over the issue of who would bear insurance costs, and a 1927 survey of 326 Health Insurance Unions revealed that, in 135 cases, the employer shouldered over half the burden.[8] While these laws influenced labor management practice by forcing enterprises to expand welfare programs, most other major changes in the labor relationship prior to 1930 grew out of the unmediated interaction of workers and managers.

COMPANIES AND UNIONS

The stories of company and union at NKK, Shibaura, and the three Keihin shipyards present the full range of variations on the dominant theme in big factories of the 1920s—the ousting of organized labor. Nippon Kōkan was fairly quiet. The Sōdōmei fared poorly, and management control remained firm. Slightly more discordant notes sounded at Uraga and Yokohama Dock, where managers respectively learned of the potential and the danger in cultivating company unions. The Kōaikai at Uraga began as a moderate group and remained docile, but managers at the

Yokohama Dock Company could not keep a tight rein on a succession of company-sponsored unions. The last of these rather nastily bit the hand of its feeder before it retreated in the 1930s. Only at Ishikawajima and Shibaura were confrontations sustained and violent. Unions of the radical left and right contended for power at Ishikawajima; managers nurtured an ultra-nationalist union which fought a fierce and finally successful battle with the leftist Kōrō union. In unleashing the Jikyōkai, Ishikawajima was toying ,with a potentially dangerous species of right-wing, anticapitalist ideology which, fortunately for the company, did not find a broad base of support elsewhere. Radical unions also found numerous supporters at Shibaura, but the company took a hands-off approach, letting union factionalism and government repression weaken, then destroy the unions. These five cases describe the withering of the aggressive young labor movement in big firms which had emerged after World War I as a seemingly powerful new social force.

Steelmaking in prewar Japan was grueling and dangerous. Twelve-hour days, 6 days a week, took their toll, and a steelworker's value to the company declined rapidly past age 40.[9] A morbid pun of the day had it that "at Nippon Kōkan you trade your life for money." The Japanese version makes a play on the two meanings of the word *kōkan:* "steel pipe," as in Nippon *Kōkan,* and "trade." (*Nippon Kōkan wa inochi to kane no kōkan kaisha*). It is therefore not surprising that, during World War I, just after the company was founded, "discipline and order were lacking among the workers."[10] Rather more surprising is the limited success of union organizers at NKK in the 1920s, even though the company was a major target of their efforts.

The Sōdōmei made progress at NKK in the mid-1920s. The Yūaikai had gained a foothold there in the 1910s, and the Sōdōmei built on this base to recruit 1,000 members from the 2,000 workers at the company by early 1926. This contingent formed the core of the Kanagawa Metalworkers Union founded in February 1926, and this Sōdōmei union reached the height of its power in the following year. An ineffective wildcat strike in opposition to several firings took place in 1926, apparently without union support, but, in 1927, all 2,500 workers joined the now 600-member union contingent in a 19-day dispute over wages. With the local police mediating, NKK agreed to guarantee prior income levels under a new wage system. On the strength of this victory, union prestige and membership increased.

The company response to the Sōdōmei advance was low-key but adroit, a model of "soft" but determined union-busting. As in the several World War I disputes at the mill, managers strove to keep emotions down with a flexible stance during the dispute, while moving carefully behind the scenes. Whenever possible, NKK recruited new men from the prefecture of the company's director and co-founder, Imaizumi. Once the steelmaker had established this route, it could be fairly sure that new workers would not be troublemakers, but personnel managers still gave careful attention to the ideas of all workers and to signs of prior interest in the labor movement. While the Sōdōmei was strong, NKK appears to have avoided an open challenge, preferring to chip away slowly at union strength. With high attrition of workers, and thus union members, close attention to new hiring was effective. Even at the time of the 1927 dispute, union strength had declined from 1926, and the boost offered by that victory proved short-lived. By 1928, only 300 NKK workers were Sōdōmei members, and, in 1931, only 200 members remained. By this time, the company felt able to move decisively against the union, and, when a dispute over a pay cut took place, NKK immediately fired 10 strike leaders. The union continued to decline thereafter.[11]

NKK maintained a vigilant watch over worker activities well into the 1930s. It canceled a field day scheduled in 1932 out of fear that a gathering of all workers would provide an opportunity for labor organizers or agitators.[12] On May Day each year, labor managers scanned attendance lists and checked the homes of those reported absent. In 1933, Tomiyasu Nagateru of the personnel section went on one such mission and discovered 2 absent NKK workers at a rally in Ueno Park. They were fired immediately.[13]

This series of anti-union measures seems only part of the

explanation for the rapid decline in union strength at NKK. Other companies adopted similar strategies with less success. Yet, neither management nor labor-union sources reveal any additional insights; the situation at NKK remains opaque. Perhaps it was just the thorough screening and checking of new workers that put an end to union growth. It also may well be that the brawny, relatively unskilled steelworkers, mainly migrants of rural origin, working longer hours than men at any other major Keihin factory, were not initially interested in the labor movement and had no energy left at the end of a day to find out more about it. Immigrant steelworkers in America were also notoriously difficult to organize, and the parallel between the preponderance of immigrants in their ranks and of rural migrants among NKK workers is intriguing.[14] The nature of the steelworkers and of steel work in both countries may have retarded labor organizing more than any single management policy.

Unlike many passive company unions in Japan, the Kōaikai at Uraga Dock was not organized by management. Regular workers, frustrated at their lack of influence, founded it in 1921 as an independent organization. The Kōaikai initially was less ready to cooperate with the company than were the non-union foremen and sub-foremen, who had their own separate organizations.[15] Even so, the Kōaikai was never a radical group, and it slowly became quite moderate.

Initial goals were the raising of worker consciousness, skills, morale, and status through united action, and the promotion of mutual-aid activities.[16] Within several months, the union had enrolled 400 members among the 3,000 Dock Company workers, but it took several years for the Kōaikai to enroll the entire company work force, a good indication that, despite its moderate platform, the union did not enjoy active management support. The company waited and watched, while the union grew on its own.

The Kōaikai gradually expanded both membership and activities. In May 1922, it began to operate a cooperative store. The company had earlier eliminated sales of inexpensive rice to workers, so the co-op was well received. It expanded considerably by the summer of 1923, at which point 1,000 workers had joined the union. Management then decided to recognize the Kōaikai informally as labor representative in negotiations over working conditions. This strategy proved quite successful. The Kōaikai provided a means for workers to express their discontents, and the company made sufficient minor concessions to give the union a measure of legitimacy. The Kōaikai also served company interests by working to prevent the expression or penetration of more radical ideas. By early 1925, almost the entire work force of 2,200 belonged to the union.[17]

In 1923, the union negotiated successfully for improved treatment of trainees, elimination of fines for losing identification badges, and permission to go to public offices on lunch break and come back late if the appointment required it. Through these little victories the union defined its role at Uraga. In the years following, the Kōaikai continued to negotiate with management over similar issues, especially reduction of the extensive list of fines in the company work rules. Problems raised were as minor as better food in the dining hall or the supply of lockers for workers.[18] When the union broached stickier subjects, such as pay raises, it made little headway and soon retreated.

The Hyōgikai also attempted to gain supporters at Uraga, building on a base provided by a few unionists remaining at the Dock Company from the Yūaikai era. While the Kōaikai actively sought to prevent this influx of "Communist" elements, with fair success at the main shipyard, it could not prevent radical gains at the company's Yokohama factory. By the summer of 1926, 100 of the factory's 132 workers were Hyōgikai members, and they led an unsuccessful strike for higher pay, better injury and severance pay, and an end to the temporary-worker system.[19]

Neither was the Kōaikai fully successful in mobilizing all its members to support the union leadership and company goals. As union leaders drew closer to the company, they lost touch with low-level regular workers. Newly hired, younger members complained about do-nothing leaders, and, in late 1925, the union gave more power to workshop representatives so as to involve rank-and-file workers more directly.[20] The change was not effective. A steady undercurrent of tension and calls for more aggressive union action persisted for several years. Workers wrote to the local progressive paper, the *Hantō Jichi,* to express their gripes: a weak stance on bonuses and pay raises; weak defense of jobs; failure to end the fine system; and a lack of concern for temporary workers.[21] The conflict within the union came to a head in January 1929 when the *Hantō* faction ran a slate against the incumbent leadership in union elections. The discontented minority was sizeable, but its challenge fell short; dissident candidates received from 30 to 50 percent of the votes.[22]

As it established a relatively secure working relationship with management, it lost the support of the rank and file, and new tensions emerged. The dissidents in this case were unable to dislodge the leadership or form a separate organization. One factor that helped the Kōaikai retain its position was the decision to join hands with the Yokohama Dock Company's Kōshinkai as the first step in the creation of a regional alliance of shipbuilding workers. The Busō Renmei (Busō Federation) was launched in May 1925, and, while its concrete achievements were limited at first, it bolstered union leaders at a time of internal conflict.[23] Uraga managers were no doubt pleased. The frequent disputes of the 1910s were just an unpleasant memory; the cultivation of the Kōaikai had brought a degree of labor peace to the yard.

The assertive company unions at Yokohama Dock neatly reverse the Uraga experience. Rather than moving from independent to cooperative entities, they began as company creations and later asserted their independence. Not until the 1930s did management arrive at a solution to the problem of the disobedient company union.

Strikes were yearly events at the Dock Company from 1916 through 1922. Both managers and workers viewed them as battles, and rules of war applied. When a strike began, company executives and top managers would form a strike headquarters parallel to that of the union. They would secretly create an "information section," charged with infiltrating worker headquarters to glean whatever information it could. Which foremen or supervisors were being denounced, by whom? Where and when were demonstrations scheduled? What outside groups were arriving in Yokohama, to what end? Finally, they sought workers ready to desert the strike, invited them to secret nighttime meetings, and offered sake or other bribes in exchange for a promise of a return to work.[24]

By late 1921, management concluded that a long-range strategy of pacification was also necessary. The company had fired 260 workers, mostly union members, in November. The Shipbuilders Union could mount no effective resistance, but it did not collapse with this defeat, and the dockyard atmosphere was tense as the year drew to a close. Management decided to break the impasse by forming a company union to oppose the Shipbuilders Union. The first attempt, christened the Jishinkai, never materialized. In December, the company formed a second group, the Machine Technicians Alliance (Zōki Gikō Rengōkai), with somewhat better results. Yokosen designated staff supervisors in all machine shops as "union branch leaders," and the union quickly enrolled 1,700 members, including 400 defectors from the Shipbuilders Union. The group spoke in its bylaws, written on company stationery, of restoring peace and moderation to the work place while raising worker status. Yet, in an apparent bow to democratic ideology, the union also referred to "securing worker rights."[25]

To the dismay of Dock Company managers, after just two months the leaders of this "yellow union" concluded that, to gain these rights, particularly job security, they would have to join hands with their ostensible enemy, the Shipbuilders Union. The company proposed in early 1922 that the new union take responsibility for distributing severance pay, and union leaders quickly deduced that dismissals were imminent. If they went along quietly they would look like fools; even leaders of a company union had to maintain a pretense of independent defense of the worker interest. Alliance leaders therefore approached the Shipbuilders Union with an offer of joint action, accepted on condition that the Machine Alliance join the Sōdōmei and adopt a more aggressive program. By February 20, final agreement resulted in the formation of a new union, the Yokohama Shipbuilder and Machinist Federation, with 4,200 members.[26]

The rest of the story is an unhappy one for the union. A bitter and unsuccessful strike in late February and early March for better retirement and severance pay and a guarantee of no firings for one year brought only the firing of 65 union leaders and the final destruction of the expanded Shipbuilders Union.[27] The attempt to use a company union had failed, but a hard-line approach enjoyed brief success, and for two years no union activity took place at the Dock Company. Even so, management did not feel secure in its control of labor. In March 1923, the company could only induce one-third of the work force to sign a pledge to honor a new set of work rules.[28] By 1924, perhaps confident that they had learned from past errors, or else just convinced a cooperative organization of workers had to be formed, managers once again decided to create a company union. Once again a wayward child was born.

In its first year, this Kōshinkai union followed company orders. Factory Supervisor Yamashita was the union advisor, and he attended all union meetings, closed to the rank-and-file members. Yokosen distributed money to union leaders for parties to promote good will, and the union cooperated in arranging the dismissal of temporary workers.[29]

All 4,100 Dock Company workers were members, however, and gradually discontent with the weakness of the union spread among them. The rank and file voted into office a new set of union leaders promising more aggressive action in October 1925. The Kōshinkai began to act in concert with Uraga's Kōaikai, forming the Busō Federation, and it joined many Yokohama unions in the 1926 May Day. By the summer of 1926, a more strident tone dominated the union magazine: "Even a beggar's child is 3 years old at age 3. The more we are oppressed, the more we'll resist."[30] The union declared:

> The era of preparation is over. The passive era is over. The foundation is laid and we will now begin an era of real, aggressive action

on all fronts, political, consumer, labor federations, further organizing.[31]

Tensions within the union continued even after this new departure, leading to a second leadership change in 1926, but workers still protested that: "the rank and file is not heeded"; "union shop representatives are not attending executive committee meetings as they should"; "the union is divided into two camps, the foremen and the regular workers, and this is behind our lack of strength"; or finally:

> What's wrong with our leaders? The union seems to be asleep. There are plenty of issues such as pay and the temporary-worker problem. The differences between us should not obscure our true unity. The new Shōwa era is a time for action.[32]

The union met these calls with a decisive shift in policy in 1927. It finally took up the temporary-worker, wage, and health-insurance issues, longstanding concerns of the rank and file, at its third annual convention in the spring of 1927. In addition, the union gained control of the health-insurance union in 1927 by electing its leaders to the Insurance Union Committee.[33]

Throughout these years of the union's transition and gradual shift to the left, the company sought to keep the union under control by negotiating on a wide range of issues, handling the Kōshinkai as Uraga had dealt with its Kōaikai. Yet, when push came to shove, the Yokohama union responded positively to the rank and file, raised controversial issues, and finally embarked on a well-planned strike. In 1925, the union negotiated over severance pay, using the threat of wildcat rank-and-file action to exact compromise. In 1927, it raised the temporary-worker issue, and Factory Director Yamashita promised to "consider" promoting "skilled temporary workers" to regular status after a fixed period. In 1928 and 1929 came the major struggle over wages. By 1930, jobs were the principal concern once again, and the Kōshinkai bargained without success for a no-firing promise and protection of temporary workers.[34]

The attempt to erect a stable work-place order and a cooperative

environment through cultivation of a company union appeared to
have failed utterly with the outbreak of the March 1929 strike.
Yet, within two months, the situation began to change, in part
because of the management response. By meeting the workers
halfway and bargaining in good faith over a new wage system,
managers dispelled much of the accumulated tension. Kōshinkai
union leaders continued to warn that the rational wage concept
could be dangerous:

> Basically this is an effort to raise productivity without increasing pro-
> ductive facilities but lowering working conditions and getting more
> work out of us.
>
> Although various contract schemes . . . have raised output, they have
> also raised the injury rate.[35]

However, the wage issue in fact had been settled with a real compromise, and the union could not seriously raise it again.

In addition, the Kōshinkai found itself isolated in the expanded
Busō Federation, and this did much to weaken the union. The federation had, from the start, been anxious to draw in other shipbuilding unions in the region, and, in May 1929, the Kōaikai and
Kōshinkai unions welcomed Ishikawajima's Jikyōkai into the federation.[36] Although the Kōshinkai and Jikyōkai could agree on certain anti-capitalist positions, stating that "true rationalization will
begin by denying 10,000 yen bonuses to executives and halving
their salaries, as well as stopping dividend payments to parasitic
stockholders," the Kōshinkai was unwilling to join in patriotic
declarations of unqualified support for Japanese industry, and not
ready to back a "movement to build an industrial nation," or to
"overcome the present crisis through hard work and sacrifice."[37]
In 1929, it had the strength to reject a proposal to join an even
broader right-wing alliance, but, with right-wing nationalism on
the rise among workers as in society at large, the Kōshinkai was
ousted from the federation by the Jikyōkai and Kōaikai in 1931,
only to rejoin it in 1933 after converting to the nationalist principles of the "Japanist" labor movement. This interlude of ideological confusion and conversion fatally weakened the Kōshinkai.

In addition, during the early 1930s, the company took steps to limit union activity, while encouraging the Kōshinkai leadership to change its position and rejoin the Busō Federation.[38]

With the help of the right-wing labor movement, the company finally disinherited this wayward child. When Mitsubishi Heavy Industries bought the Dock Company in 1935, it dissolved the Kōshinkai, after arranging for the arrest of 3 workers expected to oppose the move. In its place, management created a factory council in early 1936, in line with Mitsubishi policy, to give advice on matters of efficiency, welfare, and working conditions.[39] After two difficult decades of union organizing and disputes, the Dock Company had established a measure of non-union stability.

The labor relationships at both Ishikawajima and Shibaura were distinctly more contentious than at NKK, Uraga, or even Yokosen. A persistent spirit of radicalism infused worker activity, and managers required more than simple company unions to combat this. At Shibaura, both anarchist and Communist labor unions enjoyed substantial support, and unions of one sort or another were active from 1913 to 1931. While the company did not officially welcome or even recognize organized labor, neither did it destroy these unions primarily through its own policies. Government repression and union factionalism were the major obstacles to labor success at Shibaura.

Strikes or major disputes disrupted the Engineering Works six times between 1920 and 1931. With the exception of the 1927 strike at Tsurumi, all the incidents took place at the Tokyo factory. While the company took a harsh stance in each instance, firing the strike organizers, and also used the excuse of the 1923 earthquake to dismiss a number of union leaders, management did little else between strikes to repress the union or offer alternatives to the workers, except to create a Worker Mutual Aid Society in 1924. An observer commented in 1931 that Shibaura had always followed a hands-off policy of minimal interference in worker private lives and had limited effort to prevent union activities within the company.[40]

This management posture enabled organized labor to maintain a presence throughout the 1920s, but the breathing space also allowed the emergence of destructive factionalism. The anarchist union in Tokyo offered no aid to the Hyōgikai union in Tsurumi in 1927, and the Tsurumi workers were equally unsympathetic in the 1930 and 1931 disputes in Tokyo. At Shibaura in these years, labor-management harmony was in short supply, but the workers at Shibaura were equally unable to create a community of their own interests at the *enterprise* level. Unions, built upon workshop units, did not transcend the particular factory, and workers were divided among themselves. While for several years a single union was strong at each factory, even this community broke down at the Tokyo plant in the late 1920s, when three different unions contested for power.

Government repression played a major part in eliminating union strength at Shibaura, for the Hyōgikai Labor Federation was outlawed on April 10, 1928 as a Communist organization, effectively destroying the union branch at the Tsurumi plant. Finally, the company decision, taken in 1923 and realized in 1931, to close the cramped and increasingly outmoded Tokyo factory and shift all operations to Tsurumi dealt a fatal blow to the anarchist, Tokyo-based Shibaura Labor Union, which already had lost much support as it became increasingly radical and divorced from rank-and-file sentiment.

Only after the failure of unionism at Shibaura did the company take measures to introduce alternative organizations. It did not establish a factory council until 1936. Also in the 1930s, Shibaura made some effort to promote nationalist sentiment on behalf of smooth labor relations; it founded a Nogi Society branch and a moral-education group in the early 1930s. In addition, management established a Personal Problem Discussion Center in 1935.[41]

Managers at Ishikawajima relied even more heavily than had their Yokohama Dock counterparts on the anti-union unionism of the ultra-nationalist labor movement to bring stability to the shipyard. The intense clash of left- and right-wing unions at Ishikawajima makes this a distinctive and important case. The Kōrō union advocated a self-described socialist program and affiliated with the

Hyōgikai federation. The intensity of its rhetoric and strength of its organization was met by a reaction of greater strength. Ishikawajima eventually succeeded in ousting the Kōrō union from the shipyard, but only after five years of bitter work-place struggle between 1921 and 1926.

Ishikawajima workers founded the Kōrō union in the spring of 1921, and, bolstered by the determined strike of that fall, union leaders and rank and file quickly came to espouse a spirited anti-capitalist ideology. For one anonymous man writing to the union magazine in 1922, socialism was the only system that promoted the interests of workers. Wage bargaining was useless; the higher production costs would only return in the form of higher prices to hurt workers. The factory council, too, was an "idiotic scheme" to deceive workers. Revolution, he concluded, although the term was censored, was the only true path to liberation.[42] Another man wrote in March 1922:

> We live unfree lives, shoulder an unnatural burden, and suffer under an irrational system. We are oppressed victims. Where is our value as humans? Racing to the factory on icy mornings, rushing home under the stars, we have no chance to enjoy life. We live an inhuman existence.[43]

This worker and others at the shipyard then took this common theme of "humanity denied" one step further. He attributed his plight to the capitalist economic system, under which the propertyless were destined to remain forever propertyless. By 1924, Kōrō had revised its platform to include a declaration that "we will resist absolutely the violent oppression of the capitalist class with courageous actions."[44]

Kōrō radicalism naturally troubled management. Of equal concern was the determined and successful union drive to expand its organization beyond the confines of the Ishikawajima shipyard, a union goal from its earliest days. After the 1921 strike, many of the fired workers gathered to form a separate central local of the union, and workers fired by Ishikawajima in subsequent strikes also joined this local. When members of this group later found work in other nearby factories, they organized some of those workers as well, and in this fashion Kōrō founded 9 or 10 locals in addition to the Ishikawajima contingent. Three collapsed in the wake of the 1923 earthquake, but, as of early 1925, the union had 6 locals outside the shipyard. Saitō Tadatoshi, by now a committed Marxist and experienced labor organizer, played a major role in the creation of the new branches.[45] The next logical step in the Kōrō drive to organize an industrial union in the Keihin region was affiliation with the Hyōgikai, committed to a similar Marxist program and to industry-wide organization.[46] After several months of negotiations, Kōrō, the Kantō Ironworkers Union (Kantō Tekkō Kumiai), and the Watchmakers Union joined to form the Kantō Metalworkers Union (Kantō Kinzoku Kumiai), in August 1925. The new union claimed 3,800 members at over 70 factories, and the Ishikawajima-Kōrō group was by far the largest single contingent. The union named Saitō chairman and joined the Hyōgikai.[47]

Parallel to its industrial organizing activities, Kōrō protested Ishikawajima company policy. In October 1921, the union led a remarkably effective 5-week dispute over pay and other issues which ended in a stand-off. A May 1922 strike over harassment of union members was in a sense the final incident in an 8-month dispute dating back to the October strike. Antagonism between union members and strikebreakers continued throughout this time, as did chronic short slowdowns. The May strike failed after just 7 days, due to a split in union ranks over strategy and a changed economic climate. In October 1921, a destroyer lay half finished in the shipyard, and the company was worried about meeting the contract deadline. In May 1922, the Washington Disarmament Conference was history. As a manager explained to the foremen:

> This union is an annoyance to the company. It wants to oppose us on anything and everything. Since other good workers are kept from work on its account, we must get rid of the bad workers. They are like weeds that grow out of control if left alone. We must root them out, one by one, and carry on in this depression with only the workers who are ready to work for the good of the company.[48]

The Kōrō union led two more major disputes during its period of ascendance at Ishikawajima. A July 1924 incident arose over an announcement of a 30-minute extension of the work day at the company's auto factory. All 237 auto workers were members of one of Kōrō's best-organized and most radical branches. They forced the company to retract its announcement and also to agree that all work after 3:30 p.m. would be considered overtime. Previous closing time had been 4:00 p.m. The 1926 dispute ran from early August through mid-September and involved, at its height, two-thirds of the shipyard's 2,000 workers, but it ended in defeat for Kōrō.[49]

In addition to the disputes of 1921, 1922, 1924, and 1926, all of which disrupted normal operations to some degree, the union raised a host of smaller issues during these years which it settled through negotiations.[50] Labor relations at Ishikawajima in the first half of the 1920s were extremely unsettled, and for management the destruction of Kōrō was of top priority from the time of the 1921 strike. Beginning in late 1923, the outlines of an anti-union strategy gradually emerged. Kamino Shinichi, a skilled machinist, and Matsumura Kikuo, a Vice-Admiral in the Navy who entered the company in December 1925, were the chief architects of this policy.[51]

Kamino began his career as a typical traveler, entering the Kure Naval Arsenal in 1902 at age 15, and working at the Kawasaki Shipyard and Sasebo Naval Yard before entering Ishikawajima in 1918. He then settled down and remained at Ishikawajima until his death in 1933, age 45. He also followed a fairly typical pattern in his early flirtation with socialism, and in 1918 he organized a socialist study group at the Ishikawajima yard. His career then took a decisive turn, during a company-sponsored trip to Europe in 1920 for the purpose of studying turbine-engine manufacture. The cases of white, colonial discrimination toward Asians which he observed on the trip, especially in Shanghai, apparently convinced him that workers of the world would never unite because differences of race and nationality were far too basic. He returned to Japan an ardent nationalist. All Japanese must cooperate to build a strong industrial nation. Benefits for all people would follow in time. "There cannot be morality in the world without nations," he concluded. By the time of the 1921 strike, Kamino was a fierce opponent of the labor-union movement, which he saw as a betrayal of the nation. He did all in his power to break the strike.[52]

In late 1923, Kamino formed a Technical Study Group at the Toyokawachō company dormitory, but in 1924 the group dissolved due to internal conflicts and antagonism toward Kamino himself. As the official "dorm father," however, he had a ready corps of disciples. Determined to create an organization for the spread of his ideas, he was able to regroup his followers into one of the first factory-based Nogi Societies in Japan.

The choice of General Nogi, a hero of the Russo-Japanese War who followed a feudal custom by committing suicide when his "lord," the Emperor Meiji, died, was a careful one. Kamino astutely realized that even workers who cared little for the company or the fate of "Japanese industry" could be intensely devoted to their immediate superiors. The loyalty of General Nogi to the Emperor Meiji stood as a symbol of a spirit of personal loyalty which Kamino felt had to be *created* in Japan's factories. The Society dedicated itself to raising national consciousness and devotion to the *kokutai* (national polity) while building character and a (non-union) spirit appropriate to "men of industry" (*sangyōjin*). Most leaders were foremen or supervisors. The Society held monthly meetings at which it collected dues and provided dinner, this last reportedly a major attraction to many.[53]

The Ishikawajima Nogi Society had the strong backing of the military establishment, which had been promoting these groups in villages since 1915. Araki Sadao and other prominent leaders of the Imperial Army were at the head of the Society, and they gave lectures to the Ishikawajima group, regarded as an important test case in the attempt to reach Japanese labor with a nationalist message.[54] When Vice-Admiral Matsumura entered the company in 1925 as an advisor (Director in 1926, Executive Director in 1932,

President in 1933), he became an active supporter of the Society.

Despite this high-powered backing, the Nogi Society did not win over a majority of the shipbuilders. Kamino complained that most young workers were easily infected by "dangerous ideas" and that many left the Society, and Kōrō of course did all in its power to resist the Nogi Society. Kamino decided that to change the union movement he would have to join it and create a brand of unionism appropriate to Japan. A moralistic "Society" was not sufficient to root out socialism, so, in October 1926, he and the company founded the Jikyōkai labor union, with Nogi Society members as its core.[55]

October also marked the emergence of a coherent, multi-faceted company strategy to cope with labor unrest and Kōrō. In addition to the Jikyōkai, strongly supported by Matsumura and the company, Ishikawajima set up a Military Reservist Association, an Efficiency Study Group, and a Factory Discussion Council. Kōrō protested all these developments, and, at the founding ceremony of the Jikyōkai union, attended by 500 workers, 300 Kōrō and Hyōgikai members stormed the hall, broke windows, and set off a wild melee. This was only one of several violent clashes between the two unions, and eventually Kōrō was defeated. Centering its drive on the machine division where Kamino enjoyed great prestige, the Jikyōkai soon claimed 1,500 members, far more than the declining Kōrō contingent.[56]

Several factors account for the Jikyōkai success. Kamino's personal charisma and forceful message attracted support. Mariko Kōsaburō, who entered the shipyard as an impressionable teenager in 1928, recalls:

> I had no particular political feelings when I entered the company. Then, as I was exposed to Kamino, I gradually came to feel, "Ah, that makes sense. . . . Yes, that's how it ought to be." He stressed the Shanghai story [of colonial racial discrimination] and convinced me that the idea of workers uniting against capitalists was empty. . . . Even as a child I had heard, "Communists are bad," but I didn't really know why. After

entering the company, I had this notion confirmed, and was told how dangerous leftists were.[57]

One element of Kamino's ideology was fervent anti-communism, best seen in his effective rewriting of the history of the 1921 strike, which became a plot directed by Soviet Russia through Katayama Sen in his retelling, but Kamino's self-styled "Japanism" (*nihonshugi*) involved more than anti-communism. At its core lay the notions of loyalty, sacrifice, *fusion* of the interests of labor and capital, and rejection of mere cooperation. He felt the nation desperately needed these ideals. At a time when Japanese felt their nation to be isolated and under pressure from other imperial powers, Kamino's appeal could be powerful:

> We must put aside stress on rights for a time and go back to *giri* (obligation) and *ninjō* (human feeling). Only an immoral fool would demand pay raises or better treatment in such a depression as this. If the father is poor, so must be the child. We must accept lower pay, work as hard as we can, and, with labor and capital united as one, overcome this adversity. . . . Japanese workers must work for the sake of the nation and abandon concepts of labor and capital.
>
> Labor-capital fusion (*yūgō*) is not the same as labor-capital cooperation or harmony (*kyōchō*). *Kyōchō* assumes a prior conflict which may reemerge at any time. *Yūgō* asserts a fundamental unity of purpose. Workers, technicians, and capitalists are of one mind and spirit, fused in an inseparable solidarity. This gives birth to tremendous power. This alone can move Japanese industry forward.[58]

In its insistence on the equality of workers and capitalists, Japanists had an element in common with mainstream union ideas. The Jikyōkai phrased this in emphatically nationalist terms, as Kamino claimed that workers and capitalists performed equally important functions on behalf of Japanese industry and the nation, but the claim of equality was nonetheless present.[59] The total Jikyōkai message was effective. In October 1926, several top Hyōgikai leaders from Ishikawajima, including Nishiyama Nisaburō, succumbed to the union's ideological appeal or some other inducement, signing on with the "Japanist" movement in an apparently sudden conversion which dealt Kōrō a grave blow and still puzzles historians.[60]

Another source of Jikyōkai strength lay in the concrete benefits it could offer workers, with company support. A cooperative store providing inexpensive daily necessities began sales in December 1927, and the union founded a health clinic in 1928. By 1931, this had become a small hospital, open to workers, family members, and local residents. The union also found jobs for fired workers, usually with companies who needed to replace union activists fired for striking.[61]

Finally, Kamino integrated the union hierarchy of workshop leaders with the company hierarchy of foremen and sub-foremen. This allowed him to build on the loyalty felt by some workers to their immediate superiors, as he earlier hoped to do with the Nogi Society.[62]

Kamino did not want the Jikyōkai to remain a single-company union, which he associated with the unacceptable principle of cooperation. He sought a broad alliance of patriotic workers in "Japanist" unions. Jikyōkai rules never limited membership to Ishikawajima workers, and the union recruited members from other companies.[63] Kamino's maverick position was that

> when one speaks of unions in Japan today, one speaks of either socialist unions or company unions, and there is not a single union in the nation that is firmly and correctly established.[64]

The first concrete sign of the desire for a broader base was participation in the Busō Federation in 1929. Within a year, the Jikyōkai pushed aside the Yokohama Dock's Kōshinkai and took control of the Federation, turning it into a leading edge of the "Japanist" labor movement. The Federation in 1930 and again in 1932 actively promoted the Scrap-and-Build Movement for a law to require replacement of old ships. With its promise of jobs, together with military and industrial revival, the movement was another "pocketbook" factor behind Jikyōkai success. In 1932 and 1933, the Federation spearheaded a National Defense Fund Movement in which participating unions donated all wages earned on a designated day to the Army or Navy for purchases of necessary equipment, especially aircraft. The Japanist movement also allied itself with Yasuoka Masahiro and his Golden Pheasant Association (Kinkei Gakuin), as well as several of the so-called new bureaucrats, including Gotō Fumio.[65]

The ideology of the Jikyōkai and Japanist labor movement included anti-capitalist and anti-big-business overtones. While Kamino praised Matsumura of Ishikawajima as an exceptional capitalist whose major goal was to serve the nation, he denounced as unpatriotic parasites the "bad capitalists," who showed up to work at mid-morning and left by 2 p.m.[66] Perhaps company managers were playing with fire at places like Ishikawajima, Uraga, and Yokosen, by encouraging this far-right wing of the Japanese labor movement, but, as events unfolded, at least until 1941, these companies gained far more than they lost by their embrace of ultra-nationalist unionism. Japanese industrialists had the strength to resist or dilute any concrete plans of the right to restrict or regulate their activity.

Under Jikyōkai guidance the Busō Federation in 1930 became the Japan Shipbuilders Labor Federation (Nihon Zōsen Rōdō Renmei) in an effort to broaden its base. This organization in turn participated in founding the Japan Industrial Labor Club (Nihon Sangyō Rōdō Kurabu) in 1933, a group created to oppose the Sōdōmei's moderate Japan Labor Club (Nihon Rōdō Kurabu). Seeking to organize a broad national movement of "patriotic workers," the Industrial Club set an ambitious long-term goal, the elimination of conflict from capitalist society. The group called for the organization of councils for workers and managers in factories throughout the nation. It expected the councils to build a new labor relationship of mutual trust and respect. In 1934, the club had 15,000 members in 15 unions. The Jikyōkai was the largest single union, with 3,400 workers enrolled, including 110 in small factories near Ishikawajima.[67] This movement of "Japanist" labor unions had its beginnings at Ishikawajima in the 1920s and eventually became an important source of support and concrete ideas for the Sanpō movement of the late 1930s.[68]

Kamino Shinichi and Matsumura Kikuo ended years of open work-place conflict at Ishikawajima through the Jikyōkai union movement. Kōrō, a strong industrial union with support in several factories, was unusual. It called forth an equally unusual response, an alliance of nationalist labor unions of the right. These few radical-right labor organizations were strong in several factories, such as Ishikawajima, where Hyōgikai unions had earlier been powerful, raising the possibility that capitalists of this era needed such allies in order to defeat the radical left.[69] Direct confrontation of leftist unions by ultra-nationalist groups was not common in interwar Japan; rather, it nicely serves to delineate more typical patterns. As most unions were more moderate and limited to single companies, so were the measures taken against them. While hardly ever a quick, easy, or final solution, repression coupled with creation of a factory council, a company union, or some other subservient in-company organization often brought a degree of stability to the large factory.

The 1920s brought decisive confrontation between union and company in heavy industry. Even where the union movement made little progress, at Nippon Kōkan, the company had to make a determined, cautious, and systematic effort to oust the Sōdōmei, and management remained on guard for years thereafter. A moderate company union could serve to promote stability, as at Uraga, but tensions within the Kōaikai union were not easily resolved, and at the Yokohama Dock Company similar tensions led to an aggressive push from lower-level workers that culminated in a major strike. A more settled labor relationship did not emerge until the 1930s, despite the introduction of several company-led unions. Finally, years of open confrontation characterized both Ishikawajima and Shibaura. In the former case, the company had to encourage and manipulate ultra-nationalist ideology to regain control on the shop floor. Calls for company loyalty or the provision of company, as opposed to Jikyōkai, welfare were not sufficient. At Shibaura, only government repression of the Hyōgikai overcame the union movement at the new Tsurumi plant, a factory proudly presented to the world in 1925 as the "model factory of the East."[70]

By 1931, all five companies had eliminated unions, and the fate of organized labor at other major factories was similar. In an important study of the prewar factory, Hyōdō Tsutomu attributes this to managerial promotion of the "factory council system."[71] As he sees it, in the 1920s, a sustained offensive against union penetration of large companies led managers to express a measure of respect for workers, and, through creation of factory councils, they won the allegiance of enough workers to overcome organized labor by the end of the decade. Particularly numerous in the Kansai area, these councils were designed to function as substitutes for autonomous unions, to be easily controlled by management and committed to company goals, while offering workers a chance to express their views. While managers usually allowed workers to elect council members and sometimes permitted discussion of wages or work conditions, they always limited the councils to an advisory role. Initial labor hopes for using such councils as springboards for union growth proved illusory, and unions turned against the councils. In the end, Hyōdō asserts, management successfully removed union activists from large enterprises and created a fairly stable new system (*taisei*). In the factory-council system Hyōdō sees the emergence of a distinctive Japanese pattern of labor relations.

The experience of heavy industry in the Keihin area reveals factory councils to be only one part of the story of labor's defeat. Ishikawajima was the only case studied to experiment with one in the 1920s. Most of the other firms initiated them in the 1930s. In 1924, a fairly high point in the movement to create factory councils, one survey finds that 30,000 of a total of 300,000 machine-industry workers belonged to such councils, while 80,000 belonged to labor unions.[72] In an important recent study of factory councils in zaibatsu firms, Nishinarita Yutaka draws a similarly divided picture. Forty-eight shipyards, arsenals, steelmakers, machine and metalworking factories, including most of the very largest firms in the country, did introduce factory councils between 1919 and 1928. But he also counts at least 35 heavy industrial firms with over 500 employees nationwide that did *not* form councils over this period.[73]

The use of councils to cope with labor antagonism was clearly part of managerial strategy. The factory council perspective is helpful if we define the term broadly and recognize that councils achieved only an uneasy peace. Our definition of these groups must encompass functional equivalents to those actually labeled "factory councils" (*kōjō iinkai*). A weak union such as the Kōai-kai certainly behaved in the manner expected of a factory council; it worked as a safety valve. It offered a forum for the airing of worker complaints and the ironing out of minor difficulties which otherwise might have built up to a major confrontation. Yokosen managers briefly achieved similar results with their company union, the Kōshinkai, between 1924 and 1927, and Ishikawajima relied on both the Jikyōkai "union" and a factory council after 1926. Statistics that simply count unions and councils underestimate the significance of the council system, broadly conceived.

The councils or their equivalents were not static; they represented no simple, one-shot solution to the labor problem. This is the most important qualification to emerge from investigation of several cases in detail. Amid ongoing disagreement over the status and treatment of labor, these institutions developed in a variety of ways, especially after the government raised worker expectations in 1924 by recognizing moderate labor unions in its administrative practice.

The Osaka and Tokyo army arsenals and the five major naval shipyards, which together employed between 50,000 and 75,000 men in the 1920s, were among the first to introduce councils, in 1919. But workers at these government enterprises put in longer hours at less pay, with fewer benefits, than their zaibatsu comrades, and the Sōdōmei successfully began to organize unions in all these work places in 1924. Managers responded with cautious toleration, concluding that mere councils were not sufficient to pacify the work force, and, after 1924, a period of quiet annual bargaining began between these Sōdōmei groups and management at several of the arsenals and naval yards, focusing mainly on hours, benefits, and union recognition. These unions never engaged in, or even threatened, dispute activity, and they made no noticeable progress on these key issues. "Bargaining" essentially meant ratifying a set of demands at an annual union convention, presenting these to the arsenal management, and then accepting whatever reply came back as the settlement for that year.[74] These groups appear to be something less than independent unions, but something more than factory councils. Despite their moderation, the state felt compelled to dissolve them by fiat in 1936.

A Sōdōmei union also coexisted for several years with a factory council at Sumitomo Electric Wire Company, despite determined managerial efforts to keep it out. In this case, as at Ishikawajima, the radical right eventually emerged to help destroy the union. In 1929, 100 Sumitomo workers bolted the Sōdōmei to form an ultra-nationalist society at the company, the Kokushikai. Within a year, it had won 5 of the 13 worker seats on the factory council, and Sōdōmei influence declined thereafter.[75]

Even when a council-like entity remained unchallenged at a plant, implicit or stated labor expectations that it play a meaningful role could apparently spur further development. Nishinarita's study of the Mitsubishi shipyard in Kobe is the only work to examine in depth the operation of a zaibatsu factory council over a sustained period. It shows that the Mitsubishi councils became ever-so-slightly more union-like as the 1920s progressed. By 1926, Mitsubishi felt compelled to allow discussion of hiring, dismissals, wages, hours, and allowances in council meetings for the first time. Almost 10 percent of the 300-odd agenda items each year between 1926 and 1931 concerned such issues. As before, discussion of company welfare facilities accounted for just over half of all council business. Among the Keihin shipyards, the movement of the Kōshinkai company union in 1927 from its original council-like status to an independent posture was a far more dramatic example of a transformation similar to that at Mitsubishi.

Managers approached the labor problem more delicately in the 1920s than earlier, and factory councils or functionally similar organizations were a key part of their strategy. They occasionally spoke of offering greater respect to workers. Even if their words often spoke louder than their actions, by creating, tolerating, or manipulating a variety of worker organizations they did change the labor relationship. The period during and after World War I was a time of frequent, sustained confrontations in large shipyards, machine factories, steel mills, and arsenals, and the formation of many aggressive unions. By the years of the Great Depression, arguably a far greater disaster for workers in these same plants, our picture is one of occasional disputes against a background of tension, with unions hardly a factor. Managers achieved this relative peace through their total control over formal decision-making in almost all factories, but in no case was this a simple matter. Not councils alone, but repression of radical unions, encouragement of nationalist ideology, and a constant, vigilant watch over worker ideas and behavior were needed to maintain order in the factories of interwar Japan.

ATMOSPHERE AND ATTITUDES

Careful exercise of this control allowed managers to bring a degree of non-union stability to factories by the 1930s. Not far beneath the surface, reciprocal hostility and suspicion remained at the heart of the labor relationship throughout the interwar era. A variety of sources shed light on these tensions, between workers and the rest of society, workers and their direct superiors, and at the intersection of the general and concrete, between workers and the company.

Concern for dignity, respect, and treatment as a human being and an equal, continued to characterize worker thought.[76] When denied this respect, workingmen directed anger and resentment toward supervisors, managers, or capitalists in the abstract. The publication of the Shibaura Labor Union abundantly documents this attitude, not because Shibaura workers were uniquely sensitive to these issues, but because the magazine was unusual. Influenced by anarchist thought, the union leaders exercised little editorial control. The union magazine became an open forum for ideas, gripes, and proposals from the shop floor. The editors actively encouraged members to contribute, and they devoted major parts of each issue, especially from 1922 to 1924, to letters submitted by workers from all over the factory.

Of course, workers who contribute to a union magazine are a self-selected group, no matter how open the editorial policy. One would not expect to find the Shibaura loyalists among these men. Certainly the anti-capitalist, anti-company tone ought to be discounted some before taking these views as typical of all workers. Yet, few working men of this era left behind reflections on factory life in diaries or other sources, and labor-union magazines, however imperfect, are one source of insight into the attitudes of some workers. Certain themes recur throughout the pages of these publications, whether from the left, center, or right, and these are especially worth noting.

Some men combined their demand for human dignity with a sense of the working-class political mission:

> We will struggle with a spirit of opposition born of our experience and true feelings. We are poor workers who produce everything for society. But what do we get? A struggle for our livelihood, no matter how hard we work. All we produce is taken from us. They say they're human. We, too, are human. We will live as human beings. We will unite with the strength overflowing from the depths of our being. We will go forward with that unity.
>
> Human beings are different from dogs, horses, or pigs because we think. That makes us human and makes our revolution necessary.[77]

Others demanded equality and dignity more concretely:

> Last year, the foremen used the same gate that we workers did, but, since we reflect poorly on the honored foremen's character (*jinkaku*), they all went crying to the company asking to be allowed to use the same entry as staff employees. The company pacified them with an entry separate from ours. Then, with the foremen no longer passing through our gate, the company began strict body checks of workers leaving work. The guards, on orders to be sure, happily carried out their obnoxious task without a second thought. They [reference is vague] think we're all robbers.[78]

Still others framed the plea for a human existence in stark economic terms. One man described a visit to the home of a friend who had been ill for ten days:

For this he's been working 20 years, since before I was born. Lying sick, covered by a thin bedding in a 6-mat room where 6 people live [about 3 feet by 6 feet per person]. Is this the value of a human life? ... To be in danger of destitution after missing 10 days' work. I'll never forget the haggard expression of his wife and children as I entered their home. Compensation for 20 years' work! [79]

Publications of other unions, more tightly controlled by the editors, were often filled with exhortations to unity and tales of union victories or struggles, but most offered some space for letters of similar import. An Uraga worker abstractedly lamented the degradation of the human spirit brought on by the rampant materialism of modern society.[80] Another complained bitterly that union leaders had failed to secure even the most minimal facilities to protect worker dignity:

[When we work the night shift], there is no place to eat a meal except on the ground under the stars. No water, not to mention tea. A dog's meal, it would be, in most homes. I have to lie to my wife and kids, tell them things are better, out of shame.[81]

Finally, a "song" from a 1928 issue of the Busō Federation magazine reflected the dock-worker's sense of dignity and humanity denied, pleading in the final refrain, "Don't turn away from the worker you love, from his evening interrogation at the gate."[82]

One phrase summed up the labor attitude toward society and toward the company: "Workers are human, too" (*Warera rōdōsha, datte, ningen de aru*). Before and during the interwar era, variations on this phrase appear in the letters and statements of countless workers from all sorts of unions, leftist, moderate, or right-wing. They constitute a call for a measure of social equality, admission to the mainstream of society and the enterprise, and membership on "human" terms.[83] By the 1910s, some organized workers phrased these demands in terms of democratic rights, and some change in management treatment, or at least rhetoric, ensued, but, throughout the 1920s, as in the late nineteenth century, workers were acutely aware of their outsider status and equally anxious to be made insiders.

Antagonism between workers and their immediate superiors provoked some of the most intense expressions of this desire for respect and equality. Reciprocal affection of boss and worker had been one of the mythic "beautiful customs" of Japanese factory life since the turn of the century, but even Kamino Shinichi saw the need to shore up the ties between shop supervisors or foremen and their subordinates in building his anti-union movement. He astutely realized that, in a large shipyard such as Ishikawajima, this relationship must be cultivated and recreated constantly, and he strongly felt that most firms barely made efforts to do so.[84] As a result, the arrogance and abuse of petty power created widespread resentment. An Ishikawajima worker in 1921 complained:

> When a worker is upset about something and can't hold it in, he goes to a supervisor (*gishi*), who replies, "What's going on?" stamps his foot, and breaks in two the piece you've just finished. If you get angry and talk back, you're called impudent and fired.[85]

Another shipbuilder in 1922 was even more direct: "You can't trust any supervisors, division chiefs, section chiefs, whatever, so don't be fooled."[86]

The issues at stake were often small, but the sentiments were felt deeply nonetheless. A Shibaura man in 1923 was angry at the supervisor of the electric distributor section:

> He is a real dishonest bastard who thinks he's a god. A worker was sick and went home to the country for a while. He submitted a doctor's note, but, "If you give a country doctor some money, he'll write whatever you want." So saying, the supervisor threw it out.[87]

And, in October 1929, workers at the Shibaura Metal Plate Shop were upset that announcements of Sunday work were never posted by Friday, as they were in all other shops:

> The idiot supervisor wouldn't discuss the issue. So we stopped our machines and gathered by the watchman's post. Misawa, a former supervisor, tried to appease us. No one responded. We wanted to rough him up, but didn't. He finally apologized. Next time, we'll smash his head flat in the press.[88]

Occasionally a worker would frame his specific annoyance with discontent at more general social inequality. One Shibaura worker wrote:

> The bunch that went to school is no smarter than us. They had the money, so they went to higher schools, were made our superiors, and now lord it over us. All they do is wander around the factory all day, but they get more pay than we do. . . . We're treated like fools, but we're human too. The executive, the division chiefs, and the factory bosses are humans just like us. [89]

Another brought together dislike for supervisors with a hearty condemnation of the hypocritical notion of company as community:

> One day, a supervisor got hold of me and asked whether I thought community life was important. "In order to live in this community, everyone must take responsibility. If you only do what you want, or freely do whatever comes to mind, we can't maintain a community." All this talk about community spirit is amusing. I can't recall ever voting for a foreman. . . . The motto here is supposedly, "We all eat from the same pot." Since none of us have ever shared a meal with any of the big shots, it's no wonder the message doesn't get across. [90]

Workers, even union leaders, were not in principle opposed to the community concept, as this Yokosen union leader tells us in 1930:

> The only way to raise efficiency is first to set up a better factory and then to create a more harmonious work-place atmosphere. At present, upper-level employees look with scorn upon their inferiors, especially the technicians who parade around "supervising" operations while leaving the real responsibility to foremen and sub-foremen. [91]

His outlook suggests that Kamino Shinichi was correct to believe in the *potential* for assiduous social engineering to bring greater harmony to the work place. At the same time, the ubiquity of complaints over treatment and low status suggests that the desire for respect and the calls for membership rarely met a sympathetic response from above.

Information on actual behavior of workers and their bosses supplements and supports these insights gained from letters to labor publications. In addition to the disputes and strikes discussed above, one extraordinarily direct type of action was the so-called "group attack," found at Shibaura and, it seems, at other factories of the time. This was a relatively unplanned confrontation initiated by workers intending to settle a score on the spot by intimidating their outnumbered superior. The first evidence of such an event comes from Shibaura's general manager, Sekiguchi, as reported in the union magazine in 1922:

> If you have something to negotiate about, why don't you come in a group of four or five? It's extremely disturbing when a large crowd gathers at the washroom, makes a big fuss, sings XX [censored] song and forces its way past the reception desk. If only you'd stop that kind of behavior, I'd be glad to discuss anything with you any time. But, when you gather in such a large group and raise a fuss, it really causes trouble.[92]

A Shibaura worker in 1925 offers a detailed description of this tactic:

> Group attacks! These are our sharpest weapons. The facts tell us how effective they are. Look! Last month the group attack began in the plate-metal shop, then spread to the foundry and rounded-metal shop. All three stopped work. [Company president] Ōtaguro came out and, in the face of our unity, surrendered. . . . Next was the group attack in the electric-distributor shop. Our brothers suffering there under the unit-price system took matters in hand. When the whistle blew they all gathered, formed a committee and cried XXX [censored]. Negotiations began on the spot. They sang the XXX song as usual. Sounds of shouting rather than engines. The guard came, was threatened with violence and left. The result was a victory. . . . Next was the March 12 uprising, beginning at one machine and spreading to stop work at the entire factory. Negotiations were prolonged. The guard, the company dog, came but was forced to retreat. The staff supported us from afar. After half a day the demands were accepted.[93]

Union sources in September and October 1926 at the Tokyo plant and November 1927 at Tsurumi reported other group attacks.[94] With the exception of the 1927 disturbance, none of these incidents received the attention of the popular press, the police, or the central government, so far as available documents reveal. Even when Shibaura appeared to the public to be operating smoothly, intense confrontations took place within the factory.

More routine forms of behavior such as daily attendance and diligence at work provide further insight into the labor commitment to the company. One Shibaura worker advised:

> Loaf! If all there is in life is the sweat of factory labor, we'd be better off as horses or cows. The harder we work, the fatter they get, the thinner we get. We have to enjoy while we can. There's no point in sweating our guts out for the profit of capitalists. Don't believe the propaganda that hard work is its own reward. [95]

Apparently not all the men followed such advice, although some wished to:

> Nowadays, people say that to work like crazy is "serious" or "clever." I have something to say to them. This is not a human existence. . . . The person who gets drunk, oversleeps, comes late to work, talks back to an abusive boss, takes off whenever he wants a vacation. . . . This person is overflowing with human vitality. Why, then, do we compromise our spirits with the times? I'm no hero. Because it's the only way to get by in this city where we make machines, more machines, to oppress us further. [96]

The times, it seems, were changing. More and more workers believed, or at least were being told, that hard work was a virtue in itself. [97]

A 1926 survey of the shipbuilding industry provides the best overview of attendance and highlights the limits to this lamented compromise with the discipline of the machine. Attendance still varied inversely with fluctuations in income. In good times, plentiful work and overtime tired workers and increased their pay, leading to lower attendance. In slow times, when managers would not have minded a few no-shows, attendance reached its highest. As before, attendance rose on the several days before the cutoff date for monthly wage calculations, and peaked on payday itself. It was lowest on the days after the cutoff date, after payday, and after vacations. While Shibaura had abandoned the practice two decades earlier, the strategic placing of payday before the day off persisted at most shipyards.[98] Workers were still uncomfortable with factory discipline and did not "understand" that work done at the beginning of the month was as valuable as that done at the end.[99]

Negotiations between union and management at Yokohama Dock in 1927 offer an indirect hint at the attendance problem. The union feared that a survey of worker efficiency would be used to justify firing older workers, but Factory Director Yamashita assured them the survey was intended only to discover and fire workers absent without excuse for months at a time.[100] The few company attendance rates available are consistently low: 70 percent attendance at the Uraga Dockyard in August 1921, 82 to 83 percent at Shibaura's Tokyo plant in July 1925, 77 to 84 percent attendance in mid-September 1926 at Ishikawajima, and 85 percent at the Tsurumi plant in September 1927. Company representatives at the time called the Tsurumi figure about average.[101] Attendance and the commitment it implies were qualitatively different in these years than in the late 1950s or after when workers at Mitsubishi's Yokohama Factory (former Yokohama Dock) averaged a startling attendance rate of 96 to 98 percent.[102] The artisan unwilling to sleep overnight on his money and the undisciplined worker little committed to his company remained part of the working-class community of the 1920s.

From the other side of the time clock, work rules offer a glimpse of management treatment of workers. Throughout the prewar era they continued to reflect deep distrust.

The 1927 survey of the machine industry notes that factories commonly prohibited smoking, talking on the job, moving from shop to shop or assembling without permission, as well as less surprising prohibitions on gambling, producing goods for personal use or sale, any form of resistance to an order from a superior, or any sign of on-the-job union activity.[103] At the Uraga Dock Company, strict order and discipline were still the major concerns. The

1926 rules instructed company guards to be especially sensitive to worker comings and goings, to any hints of unrest, gambling, arguments, or theft. Guards were to be sure that workers entered through the workers' gate, staff and visitors through the main gate.[104] Article 2 instructed the men to work hard and loyally, keep order, behave well and strive to improve conduct, respect machinery and property, and follow company rules, all in a spirit of mutual friendship and harmony. While the work day began at 7:00 a.m., workers were not normally allowed into the yard after 6:50 a.m. Uraga still subjected all the shipbuilders to body checks at the gate and did not allow them to meet outsiders or leave for personal reasons during working hours. Poor attendance or conduct were punishable with firing, and loafing, drinking, sleeping, reading, talking, or singing on the job all brought fines to the unfortunate offender.[105] All together, Uraga subjected 51 actions to punishment while 11 merited reward, and the pages of the Kōaikai monthly at Uraga reflected widespread discontent with this punitive set of rules. Excessive use of the fine for substandard work aroused particular union opposition in 1927 and 1928.[106]

Another side to the management perspective was the belief that workers were fundamentally lazy and needed constant prodding. Poor attendance offers one good reason for this attitude, expressed in a 1924 speech by Imaoka Junichirō, President of the Uraga Dock Company from 1922 until his death in 1934, and President of Yokohama Dock Company as well for part of that time. This prominent spokesman for the shipbuilding industry remarked:

> I don't believe that Japanese workers are *that* lazy. It's just that workers in the Tokyo area are a bit special and have a tendency to loaf. At our factory [Uraga Dock] we tried a riveting competition. We were working 9-hour days and had several merchant ships in the docks and lots of materials, so we put together a large number of riveting teams. The results were truly surprising. Whereas, on an average day, one team would drive 300 or 350 rivets, in that one 9-hour day, each team drove over 2,500 rivets! That experience taught us to just what extent the

workers normally loaf on the job. . . . It's not enough just to put the worker in front of the machine.[107]

The punitive work rules, the preoccupation with discipline and control, the prevalence of wage incentives, and the belief that "workers normally loaf" together complete our picture of the managerial image of labor. The worker was a donkey responsive to carrots and sticks: lazy, irresponsible, undependable, to be controlled by a tight web of punishments and rewards, output pay for good work, and fines for bad work.[108]

This image, and the reality of worker behavior which supported it, can be delineated with great clarity for the 1920s. As we move to the 1930s, the quality of the shop-floor atmosphere in large factories becomes rather elusive, for the absence of unions, union publications, or frequent disputes deprives the historian of many of the sources that documented the previous decade. Of course, this absence in itself indicates that confrontations were less frequent than in the 1920s, but the available evidence suggests that the same currents ran beneath the surface throughout the interwar era.

Company use and abuse of output wages were still sensitive issues. The imposition of longer hours sparked a dispute in 1939 at NKK's Tsurumi Shipyard, but constant manipulation of unit prices was the deeper issue behind the 8-day slowdown that included 3 days of a 90-percent effective work stoppage. Elsewhere in the heavy industrial factories of the region in 1939, disputes over job rates took place at Ishikawajima's new Yokohama Engineering Works and an unnamed Kawasaki firm.[109]

Discipline and diligence remained problems throughout the 1930s. The 1939 Tsurumi dispute began when the company announced that the 3,000 workers would have to remain on the job right up to the 7:00 p.m. quitting time and could not leave the shipyard until 7:10 p.m. When the foremen angrily protested, managers explained that, at present, work in effect stopped at 6:30 p.m. and that the only way to insure a full day's work was to enforce strictly the rules on quitting time.[110]

At the Yokohama Dock Company, recalls one manager who entered in 1935, older workers were a superstitious lot: "If they felt their luck was down, or the omens were bad, they would stop part way through the day and go home." Younger workers were no better: "For each day of attendance at the training school one got 7 sen in a school supply allowance. This was a greater motive to attend than the desire to study. Students tried to anger the teacher to the point of calling off a day's lesson, or they would sneak out a window or door when the teacher was facing the blackboard."[111]

Stricter discipline was one result of the Mitsubishi takeover of the Dock Company in 1935. "Previously, if one finished a day's task early, one could loaf for the rest of the day. That came to an end."[112] Despite tighter control, tension and fear remained at the heart of life at the Dock Company. On payday, wage envelopes were brought in boxes to each workshop. One personnel employee described the scene:

> The *hanagata* (stars) of the shipyard society, the caulkers, riveters, drillers, with brilliant colorful tattoos covering their backs, naked to the waist, would crowd around the wage box in menacing fashion. It was a strange feeling, encircled in that way. Payday for those of us in the personnel section was always a tense day. It was with great relief that I would hand over the last envelope. The head of the wage section would make sure we all had eel for lunch that day [eel was a food thought to impart stamina].[113]

One key to keeping these various tensions under control was the integration of foremen into the company hierarchy and careful attention to satisfying these shop-floor leaders. They still had great power; a Yokohama Dock technician of this era recalls being scolded by a foreman for "interfering" when he tried to inspect the latter's work.[114] Successful cultivation of "human relations" between staff and foremen was essential, and the failure to satisfy foremen was often the cause of those disputes that did get out of hand. The 1939 dispute at Tsurumi began only when foremen decided to resist the company. They were able to gather support in all workshops and quickly organize an effective work stoppage, despite the absence of a union or other organized base. In the aftermath of the incident, observers criticized the company for "losing control" over these key shop-floor leaders.[115]

Such failures became increasingly rare in large factories in the 1930s, and greater attention to the promotion of positive human relations may have been one reason. In 1933, the head of the Labor Section at one major company was quoted as exhorting new workers, in a typical speech, to:

(1) Take care of your body. It's your capital.

(2) *Remember that you're part of a large organization. Try to get along.* If you mess up, it affects others.

(3) Constantly polish your skills. Make yourself the best worker in the shop. Make yourself indispensable.

(4) Always try to improve yourself, morally as well as in skill. Be courteous. Remember that you don't work only for money and we don't view you only as a source of labor, but as a person.[116]

One can almost hear the tattooed Yokosen shipbuilders laugh at such advice, and this speech did not necessarily reflect the treatment actually accorded workers. Exhortation did not eliminate tension or solve problems involving discipline, diligence, or attendance. Yet the gradual spread of such attitudes carried with it the potential for a labor relationship built more on trust and respect, less on suspicion and fear.

THE WORKING CLASS, 1921–1932

Although workers, viewed with suspicion and treated with contempt, responded in kind, Japan's steelworkers, shipbuilders, and machinists did not sustain the labor movement in the big factories of the 1920s, or generate anything resembling a revolutionary threat. The heavy industrial workers of 1921 were seldom able, in later years, to translate their resentments or interests into effective action, or to build organizations capable of defending those interests. No rash of strikes comparable to that of 1918 to 1921 greeted the far more serious Depression of a decade later. Why not? What happened to the working class in heavy industry over this decade?

A sense of working-class community and separateness did remain, with some roots reaching back to the nineteenth century. This class feeling was expressed in daily life and in union statements. A midwife, the wife of a Yokohama Dock worker and Kōshinkai member, offered to attend births in worker families for one-third the regular fee.[117] Ishii Kumazō, a worker at Uraga for the entire decade and for several years chairman of the Kō-aikai union, was certainly no radical, yet, as he reminisced about his career in 1935, he expressed great pride in the union and its members: "better than the men of the 'western clothes' class." Even on the far right of the labor movement, this sense of separation was acute. A leader of the National Defense Fund movement at Ishikawajima complained in 1933 that "well-dressed ladies and gentlemen never contribute. These people who prosper from capitalism feel patriotism is something for others." At the Yokohama Dock Company, one worker sitting on the Rational Wage Committee of 1929 revealed that the language of socialist exhortation had percolated to the shop floor. He worried that each side had its own definition of rational, and he warned that union members must not be fooled: "The Kōshinkai must back its people on the committee and not forget its class position."[118]

Workers in large factories did organize and take concerted actions through the 1920s. Although failures far outnumbered successes, the facts that unions existed, that workers in different factories communicated with each other and on occasion cooperated, should not be overlooked. Union membership in prewar Japan never exceeded 7.9 percent of the industrial work force, but this figure is quite deceiving. It does not mean that the cases studied here, where unions were often present, were atypical. We must break the 7.9-percent figure down by sector. In 1927, 73 unions, 16 percent of all those in the nation, were found in the machine industry, and, in 1930, roughly half of all machine-industry workers were union members (Table 22).[119] Union membership at

Table 22 Union Membership in the Machine Industry, 1930–1933

Year	Machine Industry Union Membership (a)	(b)	a/b	(c)	a/c	(d)	a/d	(e)	a/e
				Various Calculations of Total Machine Industry Employment and Unionization Ratios =					
1930	99,683	250,657	39%	205,308	49	164,075	61	241,848	41
1931	95,353	220,654	43						
1932	92,689	168,338	55						
1933	88,559	187,757	47			220,485	40		

Sources: (a) *NRUS*, p. 426, cites Naimu shō, Shakai kyoku, *Rōdō undō gaikyō* and *Rōdō undō nempō*.
(b) *Japan Statistical Yearbook, 1930–1933.*
(c) *NRUS*, p. 154, cites *Kōjō tōkei hyō*, 1930.
(d) *Rōdō jitchi chōsa*, 1930, 1933.
(e) *NRUS*, p. 74, cites Sōri fu, tōkei kyoku, *1920–1945 National Survey.*

NKK, Shibaura, and the three shipyards fluctuated throughout the decade, but, in any given year, from one-half to two-thirds of the workers at all five companies belonged to unions, making them roughly representative of the heavy industrial sector. In addition, the frequent turnover among union members meant that far more than 7.9 percent of all workers, or 50 percent of machinists, were part of a union at some point in their careers. According to one union activist in 1927, just 8 percent of those joining the Sōdō-mei's Osaka Federation in a given year remained until the following year. The pool of men with labor-union experience of some sort, but no longer union members, was far greater than the total membership at any point.[120]

These unions were capable of cooperation, as the formation of the Busō Federation indicates. During the 1929 Yokohama Dock strike, the Ishikawajima and Uraga unions put aside clear ideological differences with the Kōshinkai and resolved not to accept any Dock Company work that might be contracted out to their companies during the strike. In Yokohama, both the Seamen's and Longshoremen's Unions helped guard against strikebreakers.[121] Unions exchanged information regarding management policy. The 1924 Kōshinkai magazine contained a detailed list of naval orders obtained by major shipyards throughout Japan in an article discussing the prospect of future layoffs.[122]

Despite continued feelings of separateness and the persistence of national federations, by the early 1930s, almost no independent unions survived in large factories. The union movement as a whole further expanded in the 1930s, reaching its prewar numerical peak in 1936, but most union and dispute activity shifted to smaller factories. Also, the total number of workers grew even faster than the unions, so that the unionized proportion of the work force peaked in 1931 at 7.9 percent. Even as the union base grew in size, it shrank in significance. The unions of the 1930s did not do well in firms or sectors most critical to Japan's economic future. Unions and strikes were rare at the major firms that spearheaded the tremendous expansion of heavy and chemical industries as Japan geared up for war. In large factories, no lasting institutions grew out of the vigorous young labor movement of the late 1910s and early 1920s.

Three factors partially explain this failure. A decade of economic stagnation kept the union movement on the defensive, and made strikes and organizing activities difficult. The number of disputes centered on "active" demands, mainly wage increases, reached a peak in 1919 and declined throughout the following decade. Defensive strikes against pay cuts or firings increased throughout the 1920s.[123] We have seen that few of these were successful. During the wartime expansion, with labor in short supply, workers had the upper hand, but, in the 1920s, managers could afford to wait, to fire strikers, and to move against union leaders.

Second, the liberal reinterpretation of Article 17 of the Peace Police Law and its eventual abolition signaled a shift in government concern, but repression of the labor movement continued. Between 1921 and 1925, the Police Bureau of the Home Ministry often arrested strikers when union activity was behind a dispute, and authorities did not spare moderate unions, including the Sōdōmei, if they were involved. After the 1925 repeal of Article 17, administrative regulations provided sanctions for continued repressive measures, and the number of workers arrested in strikes actually *rose*. Laws restricting assembly, "dangerous meetings," or seditious publications served to hinder the labor movement as well.[124]

After March 1924, the government directed much of this repression against the left wing of the labor movement, especially the Communist Party and Hyōgikai, and this served to promote centrist unions at the expense of those on the left. The Kenseikai's first cabinet, led by Katō Kōmei with Wakatsuki Reijirō as Home Minister, began this policy by explicitly tolerating "orderly disputes" and intervening only in strikes at public enterprises or when "professional agitators" were involved. Yet, the police occasionally discovered professional agitation in moderate unions; they arrested Sōdōmei leaders at NKK in 1931. Also, informal police mediation of disputes became increasingly common in the late 1920s, and the police usually sided against labor. Finally, company repression of labor-union activity was common and effective throughout this decade. Managers fired union leaders when they felt it necessary, and the workers had no legal recourse.

Third, ceaseless factional strife weakened labor greatly. In Kanagawa, the Sōdōmei in 1922 claimed 11,660 members, including the Yokohama Dock workers. Another 7,110 formed a consciously anti-Sōdōmei group, and they too were plagued by anarchist-bolshevist controversy. Still another 10,170 workers were in neutral or independent unions such as the Shibaura Labor Union. The situation only worsened as the years went by. The Sōdōmei itself split in two in 1925 as its left wing set up the rival Hyōgikai. In Kanagawa, 19,460 workers were in the Sōdōmei camp, 10,788 in the Hyōgikai.[125] The damage wrought at the company or factory level by this factionalism is seen clearly at Shibaura, where enthusiasm for union activity and a host of grievances with the company offered great potential to labor organizers. The failure of the several unions at Shibaura to cooperate destroyed the labor movement there.

These blows struck the Japanese labor movement when it was still young. In 1920, when the postwar depression began, most labor unions were only two or three years old. Professor Nimura Kazuo suggests this unfortunate timing as a cause of the weakness of the prewar movement. While his argument is reasonable, all these problems faced the workers of industrial nations in the West. Depression, determined and often violent repression, and factional strife also afflicted the American and European labor movements when they were young. The final factors that hindered the prewar Japanese labor movement were the values and the organizing style of the working class itself.[126]

That harmonious enterprise communities were rare in prewar heavy industry does not mean that the workers were in principle against their creation. To the contrary, respect, treatment as an equal, and *membership*, remained fundamental values for Japanese workers.[127] Laboring men were committed to the enterprise not as it was but as it ought to be. A shipbuilder at Yokohama or Uraga in 1927 expressed his desire for membership in the mainstream of society very concretely. "I want to provide a livelihood for my family. I want my wife to be able to afford cosmetics." A Yokohama Dock electric worker expressed his desire for membership in the company with a glowing description of the Endicott Johnson Company in the United States. The company president there "recognized that without workers there would be no company, without the company no workers." An interdependent community of mutual need and mutual benefit was the result.[128]

The desire for membership in both society and the company invited acceptance of company organizations advertising sincere concern for worker welfare. It offered sterile soil for nurturing a union movement uniting workers from different companies. A pamphlet distributed during the 1930 Shibaura strike called for the cooperation of workers at other major electric engineering firms. It warned of danger in a complacent belief that "my company is big so we're safe." It fell on deaf ears.[129] A Kōshinkai union member noted that troubles at the Kawasaki shipyard in Kobe, including layoffs, had allowed the Yokohama Dock Company to obtain an important order. He expressed appreciation to the Mitsubishi NYK shipping line and the Yokohama Chamber of Commerce for their help in securing the order, and concluded that "this is an important chance to construct an excellent ship and show what we can do for [the city of] Yokohama." This worker appears more a local booster than a company man, but his undisguised enthusiasm for proving himself as a member of the local community far outweighed his sympathy for the fired workers at the Kawasaki shipyard.[130]

A structural characteristic of the working-class movement also hindered the union cause. The workshop, not occupation, craft, or industry, continued to be the basic unit of organization. This was true in successful disputes such as the 1929 Yokohama Dock strike, as well as unsuccessful actions such as the 1926 Ishikawajima dispute. Labor leaders recognized the need to go beyond the workshop and build industrial unions or unions uniting more than one company. The Kantō Metalworkers branch of the Hyōgikai (including Ishikawajima's Kōrō) attempted to join all factory locals into a regional unit in 1926. The union soon abandoned as unworkable this plan to build an organization capable of industry-wide action, for the "factories where day-to-day struggles take place must be the basic unit of the union movement."[131] The Shibaura Labor Union welcomed a proposal for merger offered by the 800 member Hitachi Employee's Union. "This will be our last chance to forge horizontal links and escape from an endless cycle of internal disputes." But the two groups never realized the merger.[132] The desire for industrial unions could not overcome the impediment of workshop-based unionism.

Due to working-class values and social structure, unions and workers channeled their energies into struggles that never went beyond company-specific issues. Even the successor to the outlawed Hyōgikai, which had been the most active proponent of industrial organization and industry-wide demands and actions, decided in 1929 to devote its primary energy to work-place struggles.[133] The issues that drew support and resulted in disputes were particular to the company: no firings this year, change the company wage structure, raise severance pay. But these issues could in theory cross company lines. Common grievances were abundant, and similar sources of complaint are seen in all the factories studied, but a strong movement transcending particular companies did not result. Despite the fact that three major electrical-engineering firms were located close by Shibaura in Tokyo, the attempt to arrive at a common platform of wage and job security demands in 1931 never went beyond distribution of leaflets calling for unity.[134]

The essence of the Japanese labor relationship of the interwar years was insecurity for the worker and sharp status distinctions between white and blue collar. This was a social and economic relationship of mutual distrust, antagonism, and weak commitment. Companies built stability upon authoritarian control and skillful use of council-like organizations which had some appeal for men hoping to be treated with respect. Yet, concessions were never generous or substantial enough to eliminate a fairly high level of dissatisfaction and tension. If managers spoke of their

enterprises as communities or families, the workers were not full
members. Their jobs and wages were insecure, their status low.
The separate entrances for workers and the body checks at the
gate, found at all of the companies studied, were important symbols of their status. If the enterprise was a family, then workers
were servants using a separate entrance; if a community, workers
were misfits liable to steal or cause trouble.[135]

Despite insecurity and discrimination, the working class did not
sustain itself as a major force. It did express worker interests. The
desire for dignity, human respect, and membership was clear.
Workers voiced it concretely in struggles over job security, wage
security, and company welfare. As these struggles combined the
defense of economic interests with idealistic demands for "human"
treatment, they expressed precisely the complex interests of
Japanese workers, but the workers and their organizations lacked
the power to win these struggles. Ironically, the character of the
working class kept disputes within the company, hindered the
establishment of a sustained, horizontal movement, and helped
keep the balance of power tipped in management favor. For this
very reason, a "Japanese employment system," so called, could
not emerge. So long as far greater power lay in management hands,
jobs would be insecure, wages would depend greatly on diligence,
skill, and output, sullen resentment would pervade the work place,
and an uneasy stalemate would continue. The failure of the labor
movement in large factories in the 1920s and the insecurity that
defined the prewar version of Japan's employment system were
two sides of the same coin.

Part Three

The Government and Wartime Labor Relations

SEVEN

Permanent Jobs and Regulated Wages

By the 1930s, a loose but distinctive bundle of practices marked Japanese factory life. A man's pay rose periodically, in theory at least roughly reflecting seniority, and some blue-collar men enjoyed a variety of welfare benefits and company training programs. A number of those so favored expected to remain on their jobs for most of their working lives. During World War I, a combination of labor-market and labor-movement pressures contributed to the elaboration of these practices; in the stagnant 1920s, unions consistently but vainly sought to reinforce or defend earlier gains. Limited in scope, open to exceptions, and capricious in implementation, these practices nonetheless constituted a recognizable structure of interrelated parts.

The Japanese invasion of China marked the beginning of a shift toward a more predictable, less capricious version of this labor relationship. The government baldly directed much of its drive to control labor and the economy at mobilizing productive resources for war. However ironically, given the disastrous economic impact of the war, this effort included attempts to eliminate what some bureaucrats saw as the fundamental insecurity, and the corresponding low morale and poor productivity, of an employment system dominated almost entirely by the imperatives of the profit-making enterprise. To say this is not to glorify the reforming impulse of the wartime bureaucracy, merely to note its presence and begin to study its impact. We shall see that contradictions permeated the programs to control and reform labor relations. The study of wartime labor is, on one level, a study in the pathology of authoritarian intervention in the economy. Yet, on another level, significant changes took place, sowing seeds of a far-reaching postwar transformation of the labor relationship.

TOWARD THE BUREAUCRATIC INITIATIVE

The Japanese government, including both prefectural police officials and bureaucrats and politicians in Tokyo, gradually emerged in the 1930s as an active force intervening to regulate the relationship of workers and managers; to some degree, the government bureaucracy replaced organized labor as the force pushing managers in the direction of a "Japanese system" of labor management. Bureaucrats with interest in or jurisdiction over labor matters had their own notion of a healthy labor relationship. They believed workers deserved job security and wages sufficient to meet their needs, and they defined this as a wage linked to seniority. They also insisted that differences of opinion be settled through amicable discussion and cooperation. The 1938 National General Mobilization Law (Kokka Sōdōinhō) was the major symbol and source of new government authority to control labor relations toward these ends, as it gave the state broad powers to "control human and material resources" in time of war. The first labor regulations based on this law appeared in 1939, a set of detailed ordinances limiting worker mobility and controlling wages, but the government played some part in shaping labor relations during several preceding years of gradually increasing involvement.

One sign of a newly activist government approach to labor was the enactment of laws concerning workers. The major piece of labor legislation of the mid-1930s was the Retirement Fund Law, first discussed in 1932 and approved by the Diet in 1937. The law signaled some shift in the government role, but also indicated the limits that characterized this role until almost the end of the war. As finally enacted, the law required all enterprises of over 50 employees (such firms employed 62 percent of the nation's workers) to set up funds for retirement or severance pay. The law established minimum levels according to years of seniority and the reason for leaving the employer. Typically, advocates of the law saw it as building upon, and strengthening, existing practice. They pushed it as an alternative to the "foreign" notion of unemployment compensation. Opponents, primarily industrial leaders and business federations, accepted this argument in principle but were determined that existing retirement or severance-pay programs not be expanded by the law. Any legal restrictions on labor management practice were anathema to them. Industrialists were especially adamant that a worker leaving an employer on his own receive less than a fired worker, and management lobbyists prevailed on this point. They also won a provision allowing companies with existing retirement funds of sufficient scope merely to set up an emergency reserve fund while administering the company program as before.[1]

The Retirement Fund Law exerted impact in three ways. It stipulated levels of pay that tended to exceed standard practice in large enterprises, in the case of fired workers with short tenure.[2] Further, retirement funds were far from universal prior to this law. Two surveys conducted in the 1930s indicate that, at most, half of all major companies had their own programs before the law took effect, so that the law brought creation of many new retirement funds.[3] Even before it took effect, NKK, Shibaura, and Ishikawajima revived or inaugurated retirement funds, very likely in response to the debate over and threat of a law. Finally, the law indirectly pressured companies to change the status of long-term "temporary" employees. Officials dealing with labor issues disapproved of the practice of employing a buffer group of expendable, poorly compensated "temporaries." Article 5 of the law stipulated that all workers with over 6 months' tenure, no matter what the form of their contract, receive full retirement benefits.[4] This eliminated one attraction of placing workers in the temporary category: the ability to save money by excluding them from non-wage benefits. The law forced Uraga Dock Company to decide whether "to fire these workers or elevate them to regular status."[5]

The evolution and impact of this law anticipated that of many subsequent labor controls. Business pressure forced deletion of the most sensitive clause of the original draft, which would have guaranteed the right of all workers to their full share of the fund no matter what the reason for their leaving the company. The government could regulate treatment of workers only after respecting business wishes on a central issue. The law systematized and extended existing practices; it did not change them drastically.[6]

Informal government pressure was the second dimension to the rising state profile on labor matters in the 1930s. Despite the disappearance of labor unions from large enterprises, frequent strikes at smaller factories and a growing concern with national mobilization led government officials to reassess existing labor practices and exert pressure on particular enterprises over treatment of workers. At the Uraga Dock Company, bureaucrats intervened in several cases in 1936 and 1937, trying to raise the status of temporary workers. For example, an October 1936 memorandum from the director of the Yokohama factory to the company president began:

> Every day, about 180 workers are at work here, although only about 80 are officially regular workers. Therefore, there have been repeated inquiries from the prefectural authorities, and several days ago the Factory Director was ordered to appear [before the authorities] and give a report on the health-insurance qualifications of our workers.

Health insurance concerned the government because Uraga denied temporary workers this benefit. Raising the health-insurance issue was one way to pressure a company to offer regular status to temporary employees. In this case, Uraga agreed to give 30 of the temporary men regular contracts after 6 months, and the shipyard made regular workers of another 20 in May 1937, in response to the new Retirement Fund Law.[7]

By the mid-1930s, many interested observers and government officials responsible for labor problems were quite critical of standard business practice. Minami Iwao, a former labor manager at Sumitomo, wrote in 1936, after he joined the influential Cabinet

Research Bureau, that he and members of the Kyōchōkai agreed on the need for change in the present mode of labor management. He noted long hours, unstable wages, and the firing of workers in more mechanized factories as major problems.[8] In 1939, this attitude surfaced in a report of the Keihin Industrial Research Group on three labor disputes. In each case, rather than criticize the workers for striking, this report of a group by no means pro-labor criticized managers for not respecting workers and not paying sufficient attention to their needs. It called for "modern . . . scientific" labor management and criticized the "self-righteous, feudal outlook" of some managers.[9]

The Sanpō movement, which began in 1936, was potentially the most significant expression of this discontent (Sanpō is a contraction of *sangyō hōkoku,* literally "industrial service to the nation"). The several sources of the Sanpō movement included the far-right wing of the labor movement, centered on Ishikawajima's Jikyōkai, the Kyōchōkai, and elements in the Home and Welfare Ministries, especially the Home Ministry's Police Bureau. A sharp rise in disputes in small factories in 1936 and 1937 brought the movement to life. In the absence of unions or other worker organizations, dispute mediation was extremely difficult, for one rarely found two organized parties to the conflict. By 1937, a solution advocated by the right-wing labor movement and the Kyōchōkai, as well as many prefectural police departments, was the introduction of councils into all factories, to serve as forums for labor-management discussion and to prevent disputes. The Aichi Prefecture Police Department produced one of the most influential of these plans, calling for binding government arbitration in cases where the factory-level councils were unable to resolve a dispute. Such plans usually envisioned election of worker representatives and gave council decisions binding authority as well.

The lobbying of these groups led to creation of the Sanpō Federation (Sangyō Hōkoku Renmei), openly supported by the Home and Welfare Ministries, in July 1938. Ministry officials were prominent among the directors of the federation, although it was nominally independent and membership was voluntary. In

December 1940, this group was superseded by the Sanpō Association (Sangyō Hōkokukai), an official government organization under the jurisdiction of the Welfare Ministry. If the Sanpō system of factory councils had been enacted as conceived by its original advocates in nationalist organizations, the Kyōchōkai, and the government, it would have placed constraints on management authority within the enterprise. Business spokesmen were determined to resist any such encroachment, and, throughout the transition from movement to Federation to government-run Association, they were able to keep the Sanpō factory councils powerless.[10] Business protected its vital interests in the debate over the role of Sanpō, giving way in appearance more than in fact. Despite the Sanpō movement and substantial expansion of the informal government role, the impact of state initiatives in the 1930s on the shop floor was restricted primarily to the spread of retirement pay.

The brief reign of the bureaucrats then began, six years of rule by ordinance under the National Mobilization Law from 1939 to 1945. Led by the fledgling Welfare Ministry, the Japanese government issued a body of regulations concerning labor so unprecedented in number and scope that some scholars see in these regulations, broadly defined to include Sanpō, establishment of a "Japanese system" of labor relations and its spread throughout industry.[11]

The state issued regulations in rapid succession between 1939 and early 1942 to slow the rising rate of turnover among industrial labor. By this date, workers in heavy industry found it almost impossible legally to leave one employer for another, and possibly these regulations spread to both workers and managers the assumption that an employee would spend his career with one employer.

A somewhat more significant set of regulations focused on wages and company welfare.[12] Several of these tied day wages to age, and other orders encouraged the spread of family allowances. Exhortations accompanied the regulations. A continuous flow of books, pamphlets, and official statements encouraged managers to design wages to meet the livelihood or life-cycle needs of workers: wages should rise with age, the best single proxy for need;

income should meet minimum livelihood needs and should therefore be stable, ideally distributed in the form of a monthly salary;
incentive pay, subject to fluctuation and rate-cutting, should be
reduced or eliminated; family allowances should be provided. In
theory, such wage reform would encourage long-term employment
as well. If this combination of regulation and exhortation spread
the seniority wage system to much of Japanese industry, seniority
wages and permanent employment can be explained in part as
products of Japan's war experience.[13]

A harmonious worker-manager relationship has also been described as a wartime legacy derived from the Sanpō labor organization.[14] Although its creators conceived Sanpō as the antithesis
of labor unions, in two respects it may have encouraged the growth
of moderate company unions after World War II. The Sanpō factory discussion groups provided millions of workers in thousands
of companies their first experience at organized activity centered
on discussions of treatment, welfare facilities, and other labor
issues. This organizational experience and apparatus possibly provided a point of departure for unions organized after the war,
especially those formed with management support. Also, Sanpō
company units enrolled all employees as members, white and blue
collar, and in so doing might have encouraged postwar company
unions to include many white-collar employees in their ranks.
Further, a case has been made for significant Sanpō impact during
the war itself.[15] Respect for workers as servants of the nation performing valued tasks, and the call for equality and a better relationship between worker and staff, were parts of the Sanpō
ideology. To the extent these calls were heeded, a more harmonious, more egalitarian enterprise community perhaps emerged
under the stress of a war, which theoretically mobilized the entire
nation to cooperate and work together.

Japan's long, destructive war effort made severe demands upon
the economy and upon the nation's workers, and the effort to
produce the materials needed for the war proved in many respects
as futile as the attempt to win it in battle. Although the state
extended control over the economy and the labor force with

regulations intended to encourage efficient production and even reform the labor relationship, the varied demands of the war economy worked at cross-purposes. Regulations to hold down wages, and thus inflation, encouraged turnover in search of higher pay. Regulations to halt turnover led to a black market in labor where inflationary wages were paid. Sanpō rhetoric met a lukewarm reception. The immediate needs of war usually took precedence over the efforts of bureaucrats to change managerial behavior. Yet, there were very important exceptions. The wartime regulations were not all dead letters, and Sanpō not merely a propaganda organ. In a few crucial areas, government labor policy had an observable impact on the aspirations of workers, on management strategy, and on the structure of labor relations. It altered some existing practices fundamentally.

PERMANENT JOBS AND PERSISTENCY OF EMPLOYMENT

In a piecemeal series of regulations, the Japanese bureaucracy created a structure to recruit and train workers systematically, and retain them involuntarily, as "permanent" employees in the thousands of strategic factories producing for the war. In few respects could this state-enforced wartime "employment system" meet its avowed goals, and, in contrast to wage policy, it appears to have contributed relatively little to the postwar transformation of labor relations. Irrationality and futility were the defining features of the wartime manpower front.

The spirit of recruitment policy reached back to the 1920s, when some firms began to cultivate small groups of key skilled workers in company training or apprenticeship programs. In the early-to-mid 1930s, company-sponsored youth training schools spread further as a result of government pressure. Yet, the typical foremen and sub-foremen in heavy industry by 1940 were not the youths taken into a company upon school graduation some years earlier. A 1940 survey of 63,000 foremen and sub-foremen in large factories found that these men typically had been hired in mid-career, around age 30, by their present employer.[16] The "key workers" trained by a firm were not yet a vanguard of permanent employees, but the government sought to build on these private-sector training and recruitment policies in the face of tremendous demand for skilled labor. Regulations encouraged systematic recruitment of school graduates and required employers to train the youths. A revision of the Employment Agency Law in 1938 increased national control over recruitment. The Welfare Ministry gained jurisdiction over all employment agencies and emphasized the funneling of workers into strategic industries.[17] Two Technical Education Acts of March 1939 required many employers to establish worker-training programs. By the early 1940s, the government designated particular regions in which each enterprise could recruit a government-determined quota of new workers. Yokohama Dock sent its recruiters to Hokkaidō and Tōhoku in search of workers, going to the schools in the area to recruit graduates.[18]

The custom of recruiting through schools rather than relying entirely on personal connections encouraged the hiring of workers directly from middle or high schools. Regulations that forced companies to start or expand their training programs increased the well-established private sector responsibility for worker training, and companies since the war have continued to assume this burden. A document of August 1939 details the Uraga response to the education orders. The company set up a 3-year vocational training and moral education course to educate "key skilled workers" (*kikan shokkō*) at the Yokohama factory. It chose 20 workers from 121 applicants, all already employed by Uraga.[19]

In practice, however, the need to expand work forces rapidly, and to produce quickly and in quantity, served to negate the immediate impact of these regulations. Firms often quietly shortened or dispensed with training programs, especially for draftee workers. With orders in abundance, companies did not want to "waste" valuable manpower in the classroom. Ishikawajima was a particular offender in this regard.[20] Unprecedented demand for workers also hindered measures to insure systematic recruitment. Companies took their workers when, where, and however they could. Shibaura shareholder reports of 1938 and 1939 complained that an insufficient labor supply hindered operations, and the company told American investigators after the war that government labor policy had been insufficient to cope with the decrease in available skilled labor. The company therefore employed more women, students, and mid-career transfers. Its recruiters in the countryside wooed prospective workers with gifts.[21] Reports from the Yokohama and Uraga Dock Companies, NKK, and Shibaura, indicate that recruiting of new school graduates, regulated by government quota and carried out in distant prefectures, was a fierce struggle between competing employers. By 1942, maneuvering behind the scenes, bribes, and gifts were all common, but none of these companies could meet labor needs through hiring of school graduates alone.[22] Even so, school-graduate hiring and in-company training had been established in theory, and to some extent in practice, as proper procedure.

Labor turnover rose sharply after 1937, even in the large enterprises able to offer inducements to stay. The yearly separation rate among males in Osaka machine factories of over 50 employees reached 60 percent of the work force in 1939.[23] The expansion of old factories and construction of new ones led to a great influx of new workers, a sharp rise in the proportion in any given plant of men recently hired, and intense competition for skilled, experienced men. A survey of "several strategic industry plants" in 1939 revealed that 55.4 percent of the work force had been hired within one year. Only 30 percent had 5 years' tenure or more.

Beginning in 1939, therefore, the state promulgated a succession of ever broader, stricter turnover controls, as each new regulation in time proved ineffective. The Cabinet made its basic decision to take steps to limit turnover under the National Mobilization Law in June 1938 and enacted the first regulation in 1939.[24] Between 1939 and 1941, bureaucrats issued a scattered series of ordinances. Some enabled the government to register all workers, and others prevented unauthorized job-shifting. In December 1941, a comprehensive anti-turnover ordinance pulled together prior measures. It was finally enacted in January 1942, marking a new stage in government control of labor.

A simple rationale lay behind this fairly complex set of regulations. Bureaucratic spokesmen and high-level advisors in Prime Minister Konoe's brain trust, the Shōwa Kenkyūkai, prepared a lengthy discussion of labor policy in 1939 which outlined the reasons for labor controls. The group recommended identification of areas of labor shortage and a search for sources of labor surplus, the latter to be found in the agricultural and commercial sectors, peacetime industries, and among recent school graduates. The government was then carefully to distribute available labor to areas of greatest need, to insure that war goals were reached. Controls to prevent labor turnover would be a part of this policy. Also in the group's proposal was a call for control of wages to end imbalances among industries and to guarantee payment of a minimum livelihood wage. Without these latter wage reforms, the group felt, any turnover controls were likely to increase discontent, hurt efficiency, and encourage evasion. [25]

A Welfare Ministry bureaucrat offered a more concrete explanation of the first major regulation restricting labor mobility of April 1939. The ordinance, he explained, would end the loss to productivity caused by pirating of skilled workers and high mobility and would achieve the best possible distribution of labor. Employers were to obtain permission from the local Employment Agency office before hiring anyone, and, in the case of experienced people, permission would be granted only if the previous employer agreed. [26]

While this regulation meant increased paperwork for employers, and while it limited their ability to seek workers freely, they did not complain. The influential Kansai Industrial Federation (Kansai Sanren) even asked the government, in November 1939, to expand the existing turnover controls, as did its brother organization in the Tokyo area, Kantō Sanren, in 1941. [27] In an era of labor shortage, industrialists welcomed any effort aimed at slowing mobility and insuring an adequate labor supply.

The regulations unfolded gradually. Ordinances that required workers to register with the government were intended to allow centralized planning and control of worker distribution. A second set of regulations actually prohibited job changes without employer and government permission.

The first registration ordinance came in January 1939. Known as the National Registration System, it required only that individuals with certain specialized technical skills register with the government. In October 1940, the system expanded to require the registration of all workers, special skills or none. At the same time, a new National Youth Registration System forced all males aged 16 to 20, whether workers or not, to register with the government. In October 1941, this latter system broadened to require registration of all males aged 16 to 40 and unmarried females between 16 and 25. By 1944, it covered males 12 to 59 and unmarried females 12 to 39.[28] In bits and pieces, the government built a national manpower registration system.

A second, separate law of March 1941, effective that October, overlapped with the registration system and made it easier to keep track of and control turnover. This National Workbook Law required all technicians, factory workers, and miners to carry government-issued workbooks containing job histories, current status, and wage level. Each workbook was registered with the local Employment Agency. The law covered an estimated 6 million workers, roughly three-fourths of the national industrial work force.[29]

A set of restrictions on worker mobility evolved parallel to the registration network. In April 1939, the Employee Hiring Control Ordinance was issued. Under this regulation, workers who met certain conditions in 93 occupations in the heavy and chemical industries were not to change jobs without the permission of the local employment agency. It proved inadequate, and, in November 1940, a stricter Employee Turnover Prevention Ordinance superseded the hiring regulation. It covered male workers aged 14 to 60 employed in "all factories or mines engaged in military or related activities." All hiring of these workers required employment-agency approval, and workers who left their jobs without permission were in theory not allowed to work elsewhere for one year. The state used the Workbook Law of the following October 1941 to help enforce this last provision. Employers were to keep custody of each workbook and were not allowed to return it to any unauthorized leavers for one year after separation, which in theory prevented a man from presenting his workbook to a new employer.[30]

Given the demands of the war economy, the controls adopted struck government bureaucrats and managers in strategic industries as sensible and necessary. Workers viewed matters in a different light, and each new regulation consistently failed to slow turnover.

Following the first major anti-turnover regulation of April 1939, the intensity of turnover as measured in both separations and hirings fell somewhat through most of heavy industry, especially in machine and machine-tool manufacturing, but turnover once again began to rise in early 1940.[31] Speaking at a discussion of the turnover situation in August 1939, sponsored by the Keihin Industrial Research Group and attended by labor managers from Shibaura, Uraga, Ishikawajima, Hitachi, and over a dozen other firms, managers complained that, while turnover dropped sharply soon after the Hiring Ordinance was enacted, it later began to rise once more. Separations were noted to be especially frequent, and managers lamented their inability to keep track of job-switchers.[32]

The 1939 ordinances remained in effect but ineffective until late in 1940. A series of three discussions of wages and other labor issues took place in Kawasaki in October 1940, sponsored by the Kyōchōkai. Separate groups of workers, managers, and employment-agency officials spoke of the reasons for job-switching and detailed specific loopholes in the regulations and tactics used for evasion.

One worker from a steel mill claimed that, for every 10 men hired, another 10 left. Some returned to the countryside. Others were enticed by friends to better-paying jobs. This movement was illegal, as the April 1939 ordinance required such workers to leave a "work permission slip" (*dōi sho*) in the custody of any employer. For the worker to shift jobs, the employer had to surrender this slip to him. In fact, according to men at the discussion, many companies were so desperate they would hire anyone who would *show* the permission slip, even without surrendering it. This, of course, left the worker free to move to another job and pull the same trick. Employment-agency officials also complained that some workers forged these documents.[33]

Workers and managers alike offered several reasons for the persistence of illegal job-switching. Higher wages were naturally a major inducement. An official of one employment agency referred to a survey of 420 workers applying for job changes. One hundred twenty-two stated outright they were looking for higher wages, and many others indicated this indirectly. Workers, especially young ones, were seen to be very sensitive even to small increases in pay. A manager at a large machine factory noted discontent over unit-price cutting as a further wage-related cause of turnover.[34]

The unit-price problem touches upon another important reason for higher turnover. Workers were unable openly to express their discontent over rate cuts or unfair treatment. Unions no longer existed, and the Sanpō councils frowned, to say the least, on expressions of discontent. The Kyōchōkai moderator of these discussions observed that, in this situation, job-switching served as a substitute for disputes. Several workers agreed: While in normal times they would protest fluctuations in contract wages, quitting was now the only way to register a complaint.[35]

Observation of a counter-intuitive increase in movement from large to small factories suggests that segmentation into a dual labor market of high-paying big firms and low-paying small factories was less than absolute and varied with economic conditions. A manager of a machine shop employing only 250 said that many of his new workers came from larger companies, complaining that the "work there is boring." Another manager agreed. Workers left big places because "they didn't like the shop-floor atmosphere." Further, according to a manager of a large machine factory, tiny places were less restricted by the regulations and able to give rapid promotions and high wages in good times, thus attracting skilled workers from large companies.[36]

One employment-agency official criticized these mobile workers as selfish, for "they should work for more than money, to serve the nation," but not one discussant mentioned loyalty to the company as a force capable of slowing turnover.[37] Only one machinist, nostalgically and with dubious accuracy, lamented that, in the good old days, workers were committed to their jobs for the long haul, while "young workers these days have no such feelings."[38] The skilled worker emerges in these discussions as a man who switched jobs for higher wages or faster promotions, out of discontent with treatment, or simply out of boredom. With the labor market in his favor, he was in a position to be picky; another employment-agency official observed that, if a man did not like a factory, for whatever reason, he would move. His peers, his supervisors, and his government concurred in describing him as a man much like his Meiji predecessor. He had faith in his talent and ability to find work wherever he went, and he often still hoped one day to open his own small workshop.[39]

The more comprehensive Employee Turnover Prevention Ordinance of November 1940 was hardly more effective than earlier regulations in changing attitudes or behavior of the numerous skilled workers still ready and able to move if they desired. The government kept relevant statistics secret after 1940, so we must rely on qualitative and scattered quantitative evidence. A June 1941 review of the labor scene in the *Keihin Kōgyō* monthly report mentions continued turnover as a major problem, despite regulations. The report cites the case of one Yokohama area steel mill faced with 12-percent monthly turnover, mainly among experienced men, and it notes that 10 workers were leaving the mill for every 6 hired. Twenty to 30 percent of the turnover was reported to be illegal.[40] At a North Kyūshū factory, turnover in 1940 and 1941 remained "extremely high." It was reported impossible at times to be sure how many workers were really present, and there was a large gap between numbers on the work rolls and numbers reporting to work, despite the fact that the factory had a "thoroughgoing anti-turnover policy." Turnover was high among recent entrants and workers with long tenure, and loss of one-third of the work force in a year was common.[41] At Tōshiba, blocking labor turnover, especially the flow of workers toward small factories, was a major goal in 1940 and 1941. The company later admitted that its efforts were unsuccessful, and that productivity fell as a result.[42] At Yokohama Dock, also, anti-turnover regulations were not effective until late in 1941. The company could not stop a restless worker from quitting or moving to a smaller factory.[43]

The government was determined to control more effectively the movement and distribution of labor, and further regulations were inevitable. The Shōwa Kenkyūkai called for more comprehensive controls in early 1941. In August, the cabinet adopted an 8-point emergency labor policy, including the goal of better distribution of labor, and the Welfare Ministry drafted the Labor Turnover Control Ordinance in December 1941, effective from January 1942, to achieve this goal.[44] On paper, it closed the various loopholes in existing orders. All hiring, firing, or leaving, voluntary or not, initiated by the worker or by the company, would require permission of the head of one of the more than 500 offices of the National Employment Agency. In essence, the government legally froze all workers in place and took control of all new hiring, to be concentrated in strategic industries.

Labor managers at Ishikawajima and Yokohama Dock Company recall that, finally, with this very strict policy, labor turnover practically ceased.[45] One of the few bits of statistical evidence that speaks to this point, from the Yokohama Factory of the Uraga Dock Company, confirms this testimony. The company employed 293 workers and 74 staff personnel at this factory at the start of March 1943. During that month, it hired 2 workers, while not one was fired or left, and took on no new staff employees, although 2 were fired or left (a minuscule 6-percent yearly turnover rate). This is a sharp contrast to the yearly separation rate of 42 percent recorded among skilled workers at the same factory in 1939.[46]

Other evidence from 1942 and 1943, however, indicates that even this new regulation was not effective everywhere. A report prepared by the Uraga Dock Company concerning its main shipyard in Uraga, dated June 9, 1942, remarked:

Workers can generally be divided into two categories. 1. Workers who have been with the company for many years and, because they live in the area or have a close relationship to the company, are relatively moderate. However, they often tend to lack an inquisitive spirit and the ability to lead. 2. Workers who never stay more than 3 years, who move from place to place in search of higher wages, cannot be said to be absent. Of course, such workers are lacking in understanding of the war situation and just look for the best wages they can find in a situation of general labor shortage. The company wants to correct this problem and change their outlook, but difficulty in obtaining daily necessities and the inability to raise wages due to regulations, despite high prices, make it difficult to solve the problem.[47]

In May 1943, the Cabinet Research Bureau conducted an inspection of conditions at Kawasaki-area steelmakers and had this to say about labor administration at NKK:

Due to the labor shortage, we cannot say that the labor management situation at NKK is good. The worker separation rate is as high as 37.9 percent [not specified as a monthly or yearly rate]. This situation requires thorough measures on the part of the company. This cannot be solved merely through the guidance of the prefectural authorities or Sanpō, but requires activation of a labor inspection system as concentrated as that in military arsenals.[48]

Wartime manpower policy did not achieve its immediate goals. A shortage of industrial labor, especially skilled male workers, plagued the economy by 1937, and until 1943 it only intensified.[49] The war economy demanded great expansion of heavy and chemical industries, but the war itself led to the drafting of many of the skilled workers needed to man these factories, and efforts to cope with demand for both soldiers and workers radically changed the composition of the work force.[50] Factories replaced their drafted skilled men with unskilled recruits, student labor, draftee labor, Korean workers, women, prisoners, and prisoners of war. This was not a wise economic policy, as Jerome B. Cohen noted in 1949:

> Army insistence on the sanctity of the draft made impossible a reasonable exemption policy. With its dearth of skills, Japan should have been more lenient in its exemption of skilled workers than was the United States with its long mechanical tradition. The government tried to compensate for the Army policy and poured workers of every description into war plants, so that the actual numbers rose ... but this does not tell the story. Taking a coal miner with 8 years' experience [into the Army] and replacing him with a Korean farm hand and a 14-year-old student was not an efficient method of utilizing manpower. ... Skilled workers as a percentage of all productive workers declined from 34 percent in 1941 to 22 percent in 1945.[51]

The iron-and-steel industry had traditionally recruited its workers from among military reservists. These men were the first to be drafted, and the industry lost one-third of its skilled workers and foremen to the draft in 1942 alone.[52]

Neither did this regulatory effort have the long-range effect of promoting a pattern of school-graduate recruitment and career employment. The Army was likely to draft those few company-trained workers possibly seen by management as a loyal core of the labor force. Regulations that set regional recruiting quotas or prevented workers from switching jobs thus usually affected a pool of unskilled, inexperienced, and unenthusiastic labor. Mid-career draftees from peacetime jobs, women, and Koreans were unlikely to become career employees, even if kept at one company throughout the war. And, even when effective in retaining skilled men or male school graduates, the regulations apparently gave rise to frustration or resentment as much as they encouraged the notion that one ought to stay at one factory for an entire career. Labor managers at Yokohama Dock Company and Tōshiba recall that workers during the war by no means expected to spend their working lives with one company, and the 1943 report of high turnover at NKK suggests no tendency toward long-term employment.[53] Skilled workers here as elsewhere remained ready to shift jobs, even illegally, throughout World War II.

THE REGULATED WAGE

A barrage of rhetoric and regulation were the twin wartime sources of change in the nature of factory wages. As with manpower policy, the government initially spoke of controls solely in terms of macroeconomic policy and war strategy. Wage limits would aid the economy by controlling inflation; and, by regulating sectoral wage gaps, controls would funnel labor into areas of strategic importance. Then, in later years, the state went beyond such goals. In a major new departure, it consciously spoke of and used regulations as a microeconomic tool to improve industrial productivity and "reform" the labor relationship. Bureaucrats sought to shape a so-called livelihood wage, which in theory would meet the basic material needs of a worker and his family by rising automatically with age, seniority, and greater family responsibility. Of course, strategic military concerns were the ultimate justification for these steps, but the reasoning was one stage more complex than in the manpower case. Regulations were to end the inequality and insecurity of the prevailing wage system. This would improve morale and commitment within the factory. In the long run, productivity on behalf of the war effort would increase as a result.

The gap between the rhetoric of reform and the grim wartime reality of falling standards of living was immense. Japanese workers and consumers suffered more than their counterparts in other nations during the war. Havens compared workers in Japan, Germany, Britain, and the United States in 1939 and 1944, and the Japanese fared worst, earning a real wage of 33 percent less in the later year. The earnings of German workers fell only 2 percent, while those of workers in Britain and the United States rose 21 and 39 percent respectively. Cohen found that the real value of consumer spending in Japan declined from an index value of 100 in 1936–1937 to 78 in 1944, as compared to a drop to 85 in Germany and a rise to 122 in the United States. Odaka's study of Mitsubishi shipbuilding workers paints an even bleaker picture. Measured in 1934 yen, the average real income of these workers fell from 53.17 yen per month in 1939 to 15.48 yen in June

1946.[54] Nonetheless, some postwar scholars and former bureaucrats credit lasting change in the wage structure to the reforms. The vocabulary of reform persisted until the war's end as the justification for state intervention, and it requires serious attention.

The pet slogans of reform-minded officials and intellectuals were "appropriate" (*tekisei*) or "livelihood" (*seikatsu*) wages. These did not emerge suddenly and full-grown in the late 1930s. We have seen that, since World War I, the notion that individual wages ought to rise periodically had been accepted to some extent by managers, and even more fully by workers; this provided the point of departure for official displeasure with output pay and insistence upon wages growing over time to reflect changing worker needs. The more specific concept of the livelihood wage became a topic of intense debate among government bureaucrats, intellectuals, and labor managers as the actual wage controls evolved after 1938. In the context of this debate, the state could rationalize concrete steps such as the 1942 Essential Industries Ordinance in terms of reform as well as the demands of war.

One early advocate of the livelihood wage raised its voice in October 1938. The Keihin Industrial Research group, a reform-oriented private-sector organization, called for "wages to guarantee worker livelihoods" in its monthly publication. Because workers cooperate with the enterprise, the enterprise owed this to employees. The group continued its campaign in subsequent issues. Wada Ryūzō, head of the Labor Section at Shibaura, and an active member of the organization, wrote in 1939 that wages must guarantee the worker's livelihood. Output wages, therefore, should be distributed on the basis of the previous month's income instead of criteria involving skill evaluations. Editorials in May and July 1939 praised the Aichi Watch Company decision to abolish output wages and introduce a "family wage system" and criticized Keihin-region employers for continued use of output wages and reluctance to adopt such a truly "Japanese" system.[55]

A distinction between Japanese, livelihood, family-oriented wages, and Western, selfish, individualistic, skill-based output wages usually informed these and other similar statements.[56]

Officials in Keihin-area employment agencies echoed this theme in 1940 when they criticized the selfish spirit of individual gain still pervading the industrial world and called for wages designed to support a basic livelihood in place of prevailing wages rewarding skill. Livelihood wages were not only better for workers; they would also raise productivity by providing a decent, stable living. Skill-based wages only encouraged highly skilled, highly paid workers to work fewer days.[57] A 1940 survey of industry in Kyōtō concluded in a similar vein. "Output wages are imports of Euro-American style selfishness, encourage worship of money, destroy beautiful human feelings, and let hard-working youngsters get more money than older, tenured workers."[58] In the most extreme cases, the Japanese family system centered on the Imperial Household was invoked to condemn skill-based wages unrelated to family size and worker age.[59]

A less emotional critique with similar implications for policy came from Fujibayashi Keizō, an eminent professor at Keiō University. He complained that the "so-called beautiful custom of 'familism' has . . . merely been reflected in management ideology and not at all in concrete policy."[60] He argued that the labor problem in 1943 was low productivity and a lack of worker commitment to management goals; this manifested itself in turnover, absenteeism, and intentional restriction of production. Discontent with wage levels too low to sustain a worker and his family and anxiety over the future brought on these problems, and his solution was to insure a livelihood over the long run. Short-term measures such as incentive wages would fail, for they would only encourage slowdowns out of fear of unit-price cutting, and Sanpō exhortations to work hard were not sufficient. Fujibayashi's version of long-term livelihood wages included worker pensions, attention to education needs of worker families, health insurance, and an end to the insecurity brought on by the incentive- or output-wage system.[61]

Wada Ryūzō of Shibaura and his Keihin Research group were noteworthy as outspoken private-sector critics of existing wage practices, but they were still a minority in the business world.

Most of the attacks on incentive pay, and the calls for "livelihood wages" came from intellectuals such as Fujibayashi or government officials. The Japan Economic Federation (Nihon Keizai Renmei Kai), one of the two most powerful prewar business lobbies, spoke for its zaibatsu members in claiming that "fundamentally, payment for efficient work is indispensable for workers directly involved in production."[62] More specifically, Ōya Saburō, a wage specialist with the Sanki Kawasaki Engineering Company, stressed the benefits to be gained from skillful use of output wages: greater efficiency, less waste, higher profits, harder work, tighter supervision, better planning, "healthy" competition, and better accounting procedures. To those who argued that incentive wages made men slaves to money he replied frankly that people needed something to drive them, and money was the most effective source of motivation, certainly better than medals or certificates (often used by Sanpō). He believed monetary incentives were rooted too deeply in society simply to be dismissed.[63]

Out of this debate on the proper nature of wages in Japan, a consensus gradually emerged between 1939 and 1943. The mainstream representatives of the bureaucracy, big business, and the intellectual world came to agree in their official pronouncements on the need to combine livelihood and output wages, and they stressed the danger of over-reliance on either form of payment. Kōno Mitsu wrote for the Kyōchōkai in 1940 that wages must protect worker livelihoods, of course, but must also encourage efficient work.[64] Hirotsu Kyōsuke of the Shōwa Kenkyūkai likewise called in 1940 for wages that would ensure that basic needs were met, but he opposed the abolition of all incentive wages as a futile move likely to lower productivity, "as it did in Russia."[65] An "ideal wage structure" proposed for heavy industrial workers in 1940 by the Japan Industrial Association (Nihon Kōgyō Kyōkai) followed this advice; it included an age component, tenure component, career and rank component, and finally skill and efficiency components.[66] So, too, did the Central Price Council in its Wage Guidelines published in 1941 and 1943. "Wages should guarantee a minimum livelihood and encourage productivity," the

Council wrote in 1943. To this end, a base wage reflecting age, tenure, sex, and occupation should account for 70 percent of income. Additions should reward achievement or be given as allowances.[67] In 1944, wage expert Ōnishi Seiji agreed with the Central Price Council that roughly 70 percent of income should derive from a base wage offering enough money to keep workers at a subsistence level. This wage should reflect age, seniority, sex, family size, occupation, and location, with a range of wage levels given to workers in any given category to reward individual diligence, skill, and character. To make the base wage effective, raises in it had to be systematic and reflect these same criteria. Finally, to offer a fuller livelihood and also to stimulate production, Ōnishi was willing to grant an additional percentage of income in the form of incentive pay, so long as rate-cutting was prohibited. In addition, various allowances, especially a family allowance, could be paid.[68] Ōnishi was moved to support incentive wages to this extent because "the calls for abolition of output wages are fine and good, but can such a system meet production goals?" At the same time, he felt compelled to argue heatedly for a large base-wage component, linked to seniority:

> In Japan, there have been wage systems with base wages and yearly seniority increments. These systems, however, have been full of problems until now, and it is difficult to call the base-wage portion an amount that reflects long service. This would be the case if raises were regularly given out, but [this has not been so] due to irregularity of raises.[69]

These several model wages combining a livelihood base portion with an incentive addition call to mind the Yokohama Dock wage settlement of 1929. One advocate of "new wages with a livelihood and job component" explicitly recognized this similarity. Mori Kiichi also called for a base portion to guarantee a minimum standard of living and an incentive portion to stimulate productivity. The problem was the relative balance of the two. Mori cited the Yokohama Dock plan of 1929 as an early example of such a system, although he himself leaned toward a much higher proportion, 90 percent, derived from the base wage.[70]

Management's Japan Industrial Association, the government's Central Price Council, and several authoritative observers gradually accepted this definition of the mixed-livelihood wage in 1943 and 1944. In theory, this wage indeed resembled the Yokohama Dock plan of 1929, but the Yokosen wage was actually implemented. The advocates of the livelihood-wage reforms in 1944 were calling for essentially the same changes that had been proposed in 1939. This raises the possibility that the actual wage controls, which emerged in concert with the debate and theoretically brought several livelihood factors (age, seniority, location, and sex) into the wage calculus, brought little change in practice.

The incentive wage was a constant object of reformist attack, but the so-called "Western, selfish, skill-based" output wage in fact came to supply an ever greater portion of total income as the war progressed. Regulations did nothing to impede its use.

As the war began, the majority of heavy industrial enterprises used contract wages either exclusively or, more often, in combination with day wages, but the proportion of income derived from output pay varied tremendously from company to company, as it had for years.[71] A 1940 survey of 499 workers revealed that a mean of 81.2 percent of wages came from the base wage, the remainder from incentive wages or allowances.[72] Another survey, using 1941 to 1943 data, found that from one-third to one-half of income was paid on the basis of output, while Cohen's early postwar analysis concluded that wartime incentive wages "usually ranged from 20 to 200 percent [of the base wage]. As a rule, figures were between 40 and 70 percent."[73]

Whatever the proportional breakdown at a given firm in 1941, all available evidence shows a steady and substantial increase in output pay in the following years.[74] Odaka looked at four Mitsubishi enterprises, shipyards in Nagasaki, Shimonoseki, and Kōbe, and the Nagasaki Precision Machine Engineering Company. During the war, all four companies divided pay into base, incentive, and allowance components. Between 1937 and 1945, the proportion of income derived from the base wage fell sharply in each case, from roughly 70 to about 20 percent. Income earned in the form of both incentive pay and allowances rose correspondingly. Both these components moved from the 10- to 20-percent range in 1937 to the 30- to 50-percent range in 1945, with some variation among the four companies. [75]

At the Yokohama Dockyard, by this time also owned by Mitsubishi, a similar shift took place. The survival of monthly wage records allows close analysis of the change (Table 23). The incentive wage as a portion of total income rose slowly and steadily from about 20 percent in 1935 to a peak of 45 percent in late 1943, the last wartime year for which data survive. The greatest increase took place after 1940, when incentive wages still rarely exceeded one-fourth of income. If figures were available for 1944 and 1945, they would likely show a continued rise, for, in February 1944, Yokosen offered incentive wages to apprentices for the first time, even to those only in their second year of training. Finally, in June 1945, the company gave up the effort to encourage production through wage incentives, reportedly because bomb damage had made complex wage calculations impossible. Yokosen simply gave all workers fixed daily wages and various allowances. [76] The Yokohama documents may leave out the major cause of this change in policy just before war's end. Tōshiba also put all workers onto fixed monthly wages beginning in June 1945, because of *"strong requests from the military"* coupled with the difficulty of calculating wages under the chaos of the last days of the war. [77]

Less comprehensive data from the other Keihin factories show the surge in output payments to be a widespread trend. At NKK, the incentive portion was an extremely high 54 percent to begin with, and, after it rose further under intense pressure to increase output between 1936 and 1940, the shift was rather in the direction of greater allowance payments at the expense of both output pay and day wages. [78] But, at Ishikawajima, incentive wages rose from roughly 30 percent of average income for regular workers in 1929 to somewhere in the vicinity of 50 percent in 1943, while, at Uraga, incentive pay rose to 40 percent of the average worker's income by December 1944.

Table 23 Incentive Wages as a Proportion of Total Income
at Yokohama Dock Company, 1935–1945

Date	Average Worker Income	Incentive Wage Pro- portion %	Date	Average Worker Income	Incentive Wage Pro- portion %
11/1935	58.08 yen	19.80	10	54.47	20.23
12	59.39	21.56	11	54.45	20.51
1/1936	57.39	18.80	12	56.32	22.58
2	59.34	21.50	1/1939	53.23	18.12
3	54.52	20.20	2	55.98	22.38
4	53.66	21.26	3	54.40	20.22
5	52.29	18.60	4	54.93	22.02
6	53.38	20.76	5	54.37	21.04
7	52.56	19.60	6	56.50	23.27
8	52.67	20.25	7	56.26	23.21
9	53.21	21.01	8	56.36	23.38
10	52.60	20.00	9	57.09	24.41
11	53.42	21.32	10	56.91	23.82
12	54.94	22.58	11	57.46	24.59
1/1937	51.93	19.40	12	60.51	27.48
2	53.71	22.17	1/1940	41.48 yen	22.80
3	52.06	19.93	2	41.48	27.20
4	51.08	21.69	3	41.23	24.97
5	53.06	20.18	4	40.75	27.77
6	54.65	21.62	5	40.75	26.21
7	53.75	20.50	6	41.45	28.61
8	54.72	22.18	7	41.50	27.25
9	54.32	21.75	8	41.55	29.09
10	54.38	21.75	9	41.60	30.21
11	54.31	21.87	10	41.78	30.40
12	56.16	23.61	11	41.80	32.10
1/1938	53.41	19.67	12	42.45	35.43
2	55.50	21.64	1/1941	42.48	29.62
3	53.29	20.38	2	42.58	29.39
4	52.35	22.06	3	42.58	31.11
5	50.99	20.32	4	41.93	30.96
6	55.14	21.24	5	41.83	30.95
7	53.98	19.91	6	42.35	31.02
8	54.17	20.10	7	42.43	32.52
9	54.35	20.46	8	42.95	32.17

Date	Average Worker Income	Incentive Wage Proportion %	Date	Average Worker Income	Incentive Wage Proportion %
9	42.13	32.80	12	43.60	42.93
10	42.18	35.95	1/1943	43.65	36.47
11	42.23	32.97	2	43.65	41.70
12	42.95	35.70	3	43.63	42.45
1/1942	43.08	33.66	4	42.05	42.07
2	43.08	34.17	5	42.00	43.22
3	43.03	34.59	6	42.48	43.08
4	41.63	34.05	7	42.48	43.30
5	41.60	33.65	8	42.60	45.28
6	42.30	34.16	9	42.60	45.63
7	42.25	37.02	10	42.85	43.90
8	42.28	36.41	11	42.85	45.13
9	42.30	37.51	12	43.63	45.85
10	42.50	39.60			
11	42.55	37.70			

Source: Company Personnel Records

The explanation for the nearly universal turn to incentive wages is straightforward. As the war intensified, and as the quality and morale of the changing labor force declined, the need to motivate workers and uphold or raise production levels increased. Productivity was falling throughout the war, due to both lack of materials and lack of skilled labor. Steel output measured in tons per worker fell 60 percent between 1941 and 1944, primarily because of a shortage of skilled labor. Coal and aircraft production fell also. Tōshiba reports that, "despite government calls for motivation, and stimulants to production, the huge wartime labor force became less and less efficient."[79] Overall output per worker was low in Japan and fell more drastically than in other nations fighting the war.[80] Managers confronting this problem reached for the short-run solution; they offered more money for harder work through higher piece and job rates.[81] Given their view of workers as motivated above all by direct incentive payments, this is no surprise. The many pleas for livelihood wages and long-run wage stability as the way to raise production fell on deaf management ears.

In the final months of the war, pressure from supporters of the livelihood wage in the military apparently forced some enterprises to abandon output wages. Kaneko Yoshio, then of the Welfare Ministry, has written of a late wartime proposal to switch all employees to a monthly wage scale (as well as a single job hierarchy). The Mobilization Bureau of the Munitions Ministry developed such a plan in 1944, and the Welfare Ministry (headed at the time by General Koizumi Chikahiko, a doctor and former chief of the Army Medical Bureau) designed an even more radical version in 1945. Kaneko claims that neither plan was enacted, but the Tōshiba description of "military pressure" suggests that advocates of these changes nonetheless had some impact in the closing days of the war.[82] A shift to the use of monthly wages began with this pressure, although most companies continued to use incentive wages until the war ended. It continued in part due to union pressures afterward. This shift was not a management innovation. Tōshiba's director of the Welfare Section, Wada Ryūzō, had been calling publicly for livelihood wages since 1939, but he could not convince executives at his own company to accept his views until the military intervened in 1945.

While output wages took on greater weight despite regulations and criticism, government actions were truly important in the increasingly limited realm of day wages. Immediately prior to this era of wage controls, increases in the day wage were still inconsistent rewards over a man's career. A survey of 230 companies in 1937 revealed that only 57 (25 percent) raised day wages on a regular basis. The rest added allowances of one sort or another instead of raising day wages, when they felt the need to offer higher wages to attract labor. Shibaura issued several "extraordinary" (*rinji*) raises in 1937 and 1938, while Uraga added an "extraordinary" 14-sen-per-day allowance in 1938.[83] A manager in an electric-machine factory remarked in 1940 that "there is a tendency for workers entering the same year to be getting greatly different wages after two or three years, which is a problem for us."[84] And an official at a Keihin-area employment agency concurred in the same year: "Until now regular pay raises for adult workers have been very rare and often dead letters in practice. In reality pay has gone up through movement of workers from factory to factory."[85]

The great change brought about by wage controls was the spread to enterprises throughout heavy industry and much of the rest of the economy of the guaranteed semiannual or annual increase in the day wage, of clearly defined proportions and for all workers. Even if day wages constituted a shrinking portion of income, the significance of this change must not be underestimated. New expectations and assumptions about wages spread among workers and managers, and practices changed. The spread of guaranteed regular raises firmly established a systematic version of the so-called *nenkō* or seniority wage.

It took several years for this aspect of wage policy to come to the fore. Controls upon wages began in 1939, soon after the wage debate commenced, unfolding parallel to those placed upon the movement of labor. A Wage Control Ordinance, promulgated in March but not fleshed out with actual wage levels until August, aimed both to slow inflation by limiting wages and to slow turnover by adjusting the difference in wages offered by various employers. It only applied to starting wages and was limited to five strategic sectors of the economy, including heavy industry. It set upper wage levels only on wages paid to new workers, and prevented employers from raising pay of new people above these levels for the first 3 months after hiring. The regulation proved effective neither as an anti-inflation nor as an anti-turnover measure. By keeping wages in strategic industries low (starting limits were set at roughly 20 percent below prevailing levels in other industries), the government unwittingly accelerated the movement of workers into unregulated peacetime industries which offered higher pay. The 3-month limit combined with the exemptions for experienced workers and those in peacetime industries to vitiate the anti-inflation effect of the ordinance. To resolve this problem, the bureaucracy extended the order to all industries in July 1940.[86]

In October 1939, just two months after the details of the first wage ordinance were announced, a supplementary order froze *all wages* in a somewhat broader range of industries for one year. Again, the impact upon inflation and turnover was nil. This notorious "Wage Stop Order" indeed kept wages down, but prices continued to climb. The buying power of the workers fell, a flurry of disputes took place over wages, and job-switching into unregulated industries was stimulated further.[87]

Apparently little discouraged by the negligible impact of this first round of control, the Welfare Ministry promulgated a far more ambitious Revised Wage Control Ordinance in September 1940, roughly one year after issuing details for the first Wage Regulation. The first Wage Control Ordinance had focused solely on macroeconomic and strategic issues of inflation and turnover, but significantly different concerns prompted this revised order. It was the first concrete expression of the calls for reform as well as control, and its bureaucratic authors consciously designed it to guarantee workers a theoretically stable livelihood and thereby, they hoped, to raise productivity. It covered experienced workers as well as those newly hired. It set minimum as well as maximum wages, varying by sex, age, region, and industry. While the regulations thus guaranteed a minimum wage to each worker, and the minimum rose with age, the maximum limits applied only to the work force in the aggregate. Managers were free to pay individual workers, usually those with important skills or experience, more than the maximum, so long as the total quarterly wage bill of the firm did not exceed the total of maximum individual limits. Further, it was possible to exceed this limit with permission. The Ministry granted this measure of flexibility in deference to the managerial desire to keep factors of skill and experience as part of the wage calculus. As a result, wages paid to individuals did not precisely mirror the elaborate government wage scales based upon so-called livelihood factors of age, region, or sex; and, of course, firms still paid incentive wages of increasing importance. This ordinance forced Japanese managers to pay wages only loosely tied to age, and it did not explicitly touch upon seniority at all.[88]

Even so, the link between age and wages took on real significance during the war and immediately after. As the state forced mid-career people out of peacetime jobs and into heavy industrial factories, the new wage scales put the pay of these transferees well ahead of equally inexperienced but younger workers. Postwar unions took a cue from this regulatory effort and supported the use of age as an objective, predictable "livelihood" factor in calculating wages.

The state did not apply these regulations consistently throughout the war. By 1943, the government had concluded that existing wage controls were an obstacle to the top priority, stepped-up production, and a series of regulations softened the controls. The most important revision came in June 1943 when the maximum enterprise wage limits were eliminated. At the same time, in 1943, the bureaucracy officially endorsed the ideas that wages ought to meet worker livelihood needs and ought to correspond to age *and* tenure.[89]

The Welfare Ministry based this important 1943 regulation upon a wage-control formula it had worked out in late 1941 in an entirely separate regulation, the ordinance on Labor Management in Essential Industries enacted in February 1942. This regulation was arguably the most influential order concerning labor relations of the entire war.

The ordinance concerned itself with far more than wages. It declared that the primary obligation of both workers and managers in designated essential industries was to the state. No longer was the worker-manager relationship one of private contract between two parties. It gave company rules the force of law. It authorized the government to intervene extensively in the management of essential industries. A new corps of Welfare Ministry Labor Inspectors gained jurisdiction over all designated plants, with authority to issue orders concerning virtually any matter involving labor: hiring, firing, hours, punishments, rewards, bonuses, welfare facilities, hygiene, safety, disputes, and, of course, wages.[90] Some sort of government control previously affected most of these issues, but, by consolidating authority over all of them into a single system, the new regulation allowed both more extensive intervention and more flexible treatment of individual enterprises.

At the heart of the wage section of the ordinance was the principle that the state had an obligation to make sure wages were "appropriate," because employees now had a legal obligation to the state:

> Therefore, the existing system whereby wage regulations and rules regarding wage increases, the essence of the pay system, were left to the discretion of the employer is now changed to a system where prior approval of these rules is needed, their appropriateness is sought, and their content is made known to all employees. [91]

The ordinance required employers to compile written wage regulations and regulations for pay raises and submit these to the Welfare Ministry for approval. All subsequent changes in company rules also required approval, and the Ministry could order any changes deemed necessary. Wage regulations had to state starting and minimum levels for fixed day wages, minimum and guaranteed levels of pay where incentive systems were used, and methods of calculating unit prices or standard job times or rates. Most important, raise regulations had to specify the interval between raises, and the maximum, minimum, and average raises to be issued each time. [92]

The potential impact of the ordinance was far-reaching indeed. The government could mandate regular pay raises of clearly defined proportions and scope. In other words, it could force pay to rise with seniority. It could also require payments of various allowances. Furthermore, the change in general wage regulations of June 1943 authorized the extension of practices required in this Essential Industries Ordinance to the rest of industry. [93] The government was in a position to create a fairly rigid and nearly universal system of seniority wages.

The Welfare Ministry set to work promptly, collecting work and wage rules from about 2,000 enterprises and rewriting these to conform to model rules set forth in the ministry's "Guidelines for

Applying the Essential Industries Ordinance." The model wage rules stipulated that raises be given twice a year and that all workers be eligible. The only people excluded were those very recently hired, those absent without cause at a rate of 30 days or more for each 6 months, and those who had broken company rules. The new model rules also specified that the average yearly wage increase be at least 5 percent of the day wage and that individual increases fall within a range bounded by a minimum as well as a maximum figure.[94]

Business had no choice but to comply. Rules at the Mitsubishi shipyards in Nagasaki and Kōbe had long specified only the maximum allowed in each semiannual raise, and management had rigged the system to prevent all workers from receiving raises. Then, in June 1942, at the time of the first raises given at these yards after promulgation of the Essential Industries Ordinance, major changes appeared. All workers with over 6 months' tenure were made eligible for raises. The only exceptions were workers absent for an average of over 3 days per month. For the first time, Mitsubishi did not mention skill as a prerequisite to receiving a raise, although skill, character, diligence, and achievement were considered in setting the *amount* of the raise. Also for the first time, the company set minimum and standard amounts for the pay hike, together with the maximum. Although the government tolerated a considerable range, from a low of 2 sen a day to a maximum of 30 sen, the principle had been established in practice. No one who showed up to work was left out.[95]

Changes at the Yokohama Dock Company were almost identical. In the words of Yasue Masao, a labor manager at the time, "With the Essential Industries Ordinance we lost freedom in giving out raises. Previously, some workers were denied raises each time on purpose. Now everyone qualified for a raise each time around. The only exceptions were those with low attendance." This change strengthened the seniority bias of the wage structure decisively, he felt. "Before that, a talented mid-career worker could enter, rise quickly, and outdo a school-grad entrant."[96] Ōnishi's 1944 study of wages gives an example taken from another factory under the jurisdiction of the Essential Industries Ordinance. The regulations are identical to the model rules of the Welfare Ministry. Raises were to be given out twice a year, and the company set minimum, maximum, and average levels. Excepting frequent absentees, each worker qualified at least once, twice if his day wage was under 2.5 yen.[97]

To this extent, the Essential Industries Ordinance fulfilled its potential in practice. The Welfare Ministry forced Japanese businesses to rewrite their rules and offer regular wage hikes to almost all workers.

A remarkable proliferation of company welfare programs and all sorts of allowances, especially the family allowance, was due in part to similar bureaucratic intervention. Allowances and company welfare spread, due to a combination of government regulation and pressure exerted by the tight labor market, with a helping hand extended by advocates of reform in Sanpō and elsewhere. The Essential Industries Ordinance, in particular, played a significant role.

Many firms had adopted temporary rice allowances or extra wage allowances during World War I but discontinued them in the 1920s, and, for most of the 1930s, allowances were not a major part of the wage structure. A 1932 survey of large machine factories revealed that merely 5 of 290 factories offered any wage extra that could possibly be construed as a family allowance. Companies implemented a fair number of allowances between 1937 and 1940, in advance of regulations to require them, but many of these were "extraordinary" or "inflation" allowances of uncertain duration. The majority were offered only to white-collar employees.[98] Yet, by the end of the war, Cohen could summarize the "Japanese wage system" as a "queer mixture" of allowances, bonuses, regular day wages, and incentive pay:

> There were family allowances, commodity-price allowances, dwelling allowances, and allowances for leadership, special positions, night work, holiday work, regular attendance, first-class skill, second-class skill, overtime, seniority, and so forth.[99]

Ironically, the "family-allowance regulations" themselves never ordered companies to pay family allowances; these were a series of orders *permitting* their payment. The allowances began to spread only when the state exempted them from wage controls and so offered employers a simple way to give higher wages in what remained a competitive labor market, despite hiring and turnover regulations.

The first family-allowance ordinance, of February 1940, permitted employers to offer "temporary allowances" to workers with incomes of under 70 yen per month who had dependents under 14 years old. A mere 2 yen per household per month was the maximum. A notice from the Welfare Ministry in October 1940 broadened this quite limited regulation by authorizing private companies to give "family allowances" (*kazoku teate*) to workers with incomes of up to 150 yen per month. The allowance could offer up to 2 yen per dependent or 10 yen per household. Dependents included a worker's spouse, cohabiting parents over 60, children under 18, and other cohabiting handicapped or unemployed persons. In April 1941 and again that August, the Ministry raised the maximum limits and broadened the definition of dependent to include grandparents and grandchildren living with the worker.[100]

The initial response was less than enthusiastic. A mere 2.3 percent of all industrial workers were receiving the "temporary allowances" in June of 1940, several months after their authorization.[101] Only when a Welfare Ministry order of July 1941 exempted family allowances from the wage controls did they begin to spread rapidly.[102]

A combination of exhortation and continued regulation further encouraged the use of these allowances. Sanpō and related organizations spoke out strongly in support of the family allowance:

Labor management should not be a mere exchange relationship in Japan, where the family system is so important, but it should focus attention on the family and respect the family system both in the ideology of the "enterprise as one family" (*jigyō ikka*) and through family allowances.[103]

More important than exhortation was the Essential Industries Ordinance, actively used to promote allowances. Article 13 authorized the Welfare Ministry to issue orders to employers concerning allowances as well as wages. The model wage rules which guided ministry officials as they rewrote company rule books included this clause:

> Allowances are to be as follows: overtime pay, night-work pay, and vacation-work pay, perfect attendance, difficult job, and rank allowances, idle pay, vacation pay, a family allowance, an allowance to drafted workers, and one to workers participating in military assemblies.

These model rules set standard levels for each allowance, and the ministry in fact used its authority to force enterprises to offer them.[104]

Together these pressures made allowances an important part of a worker's income in heavy industry and elsewhere between 1940 and 1945. The wording of the family-allowance regulations implemented at the Keihin firms was identical to that used in the government regulations, evidence of the guiding hand behind their adoption. By 1941, the Yokohama Dock Company, Ishikawajima, Uraga, and Tōshiba all offered allowances of 2 yen per dependent per month, up to a 10-yen total, to workers with 160 yen or less in monthly income, exactly the limits set by the government. Dependents also included precisely those so labeled by the government, and all these companies raised the amounts and expanded the definition of dependent as the regulations changed.[105]

As the war came home to workers in the form of shortages, inflation, and fearful bombing, companies that could afford it went beyond the allowances required by law in an effort to raise attendance, morale, and productivity. Uraga offered a "shift allowance" of 130 percent of the day wage for daytime work and 200 percent for night work in April 1944. Also in 1944, it gave a "launching bonus" of 2 or 3 yen to each worker whenever a ship was completed. In August, a "tool allowance" of 5 yen per month was extended to all carpenters and wood-pattern workers using tools ranked at "20 points" or over who worked 20 days or more each month.[106]

The mix of forces that led to a proliferation of company welfare programs was slightly different. In the late 1930s, before regulations took center stage, the simple need to attract and retain workers led enterprises to expand their welfare offerings. Later, a clause in the Company Accounts Control Ordinance of October 1940 allowed expenditures on welfare benefits to exceed earlier limits set for health insurance, retirement pay, safety, and sanitary facilities. By this time, Sanpō was also actively working for the spread of such programs.[107]

The Essential Industries Ordinance played a minor part as well. It required all factories with over 1,000 employees to offer kitchen and dining facilities of certain minimum standards, create a nutrition committee, and employ the services of a nutritionist. It also forced these factories to maintain health clinics staffed by at least 3 nurses and 1 doctor. Factories that employed more than 200 women had to provide day-care facilities for their children. The ordinance also called on companies to provide exercise facilities. The impact of these orders was not as great as it had been on wages and allowances. The standards were low in some areas (2 attendants per 100 children in the day care centers!), and in others not much could be done with any sort of regulation. Nutritionists could not solve the problem of food shortages in the cities. In some cases, major firms already offered more than the law demanded.[108] Companies typically implemented or extended numerous welfare programs in the late 1930s and early 1940s to attract workers and, after 1940, to offer benefits not subject to control. Unlike new wage practices, they did not spread because of specific government demands, although Sanpō did encourage them.

Company housing was a major attraction for workers coming to live in the crowded, relatively expensive apartments and lodging houses surrounding factories in the region. Shibaura completed construction of a dorm housing 300 single workers in November 1938, and it set up a "housing union" the following year. A fund of 750,000 yen offered low-interest housing loans of 500 to 2,000 yen to employees with at least 5 years' seniority. Nippon Kōkan offered a similar loan program and built several hundred housing units for its workers. The air raids, of course, rendered the housing situation at both companies hopeless. Uraga was a bit more successful. By June 1941, the company had constructed housing for 1,000 workers of a 7,600-person work force, and had plans to complete units for another 2,400 by July.[109]

A brief look at Nippon Kōkan conveys a sense of the extensive array of welfare benefits implemented by 1941 at major Japanese manufacturers. The company boasted dormitories, a variety of training courses, family lectures, awards for school achievements of worker children, moral training, a military reservist association branch, athletic and hobby clubs, family outings, in-company radio broadcasts, a company hospital, a variety of savings programs (some involuntary), awards for healthy workers, compulsory yearly medical checkups, a safety council, commuter passes, a cooperative store, and a dining hall. Many of these programs were new, in particular the recreation activities.[110] Regulations and the labor market had together multiplied tremendously the use of allowances, special bonuses, and welfare benefits or facilities as tools of labor management.

The full impact of all the debate and regulations upon the thought and behavior of Japanese workers was not felt until after the war, but it was perhaps the most significant, if ironic, legacy of the bureaucratic era in labor relations. Concepts advanced during the war by bureaucrats and intellectuals close to the government did change the labor relationship, if not always precisely as intended.

Workers clearly agreed with criticism of output pay and calls for livelihood wages, although they were not in a position to influence management policy. Labor managers in heavy industry and outside observers repeatedly noted that workers receiving incentive pay or doing piece work purposely held back for fear that rapid production would bring a cut in the job rate or unit price.[111] A manager in a metal factory claimed at the 1940 Kyōchōkai discussion that workers really wanted long-term wage stability, not high wages over the short run. Participants in the worker discussion were unhappy with the insecurity of their wages. One watchmaker remarked, "I'd like the government to make regular raises legally obligatory. I've gotten only 2 pay raises in 11 years." A steel-worker echoed these sentiments. There were no rules for regular pay raises, except for trainees. He felt that pay did not necessarily get better with seniority.[112]

The few wartime disputes for which documentation survives tell a fascinating story. When workers were pushed to the point of drawing up petitions or demands, and occasionally striking, they adopted the vocabulary of the livelihood wage.

A petition signed by 171 workers at a plate-metal shop at Kawasaki Heavy Industries in 1942 complained about wages. After customary wartime assertions of patriotic loyalty, the petition requested financial relief, "to end the insecurity of our family lives." An incident involving similar demands took place at Hitachi's Tokyo (Kameido) factory in late 1942. A small group of workers pressed demands for wage hikes through their foremen representatives to the Sanpō Discussion Council. They wanted a 50-percent raise in output wages, fairer bonuses, an end to "unfair pay raises," a company guarantee to support worker livelihood, and preferential treatment of workers with seniority. When the demands were rejected, the workers decided to sabotage operations; they ruined several hundred units. Several arrests followed, and police accused two ringleaders as Communists.[113] Some of the demands were similar to those raised in disputes of earlier decades and need not be ascribed to wartime influences, but certainly the call for a livelihood guarantee, and perhaps also the demands for favoring of senior workers and fairer bonuses and raises, were influenced by the wartime discussion of these issues.

Workers at Tōshiba's former Shibaura factory, in June 1943, also raised demands reminiscent of the 1920s, against so-called dual wages (combined output and day wages). Here, too, the demands reflect awareness of the wartime regulations; they attempted to use them to worker advantage. Thirty-nine of the company's 70 crane operators signed a petition asking for a pay increase. After praising the war effort, the petition continued:

> The Welfare Ministry claims that a stable livelihood is necessary to insure a sufficient rise in productivity. If our livelihood is not guaranteed, we cannot fulfill our duty to the nation. The company has hitherto lamented its inability to grant raises in pay, due to wage controls, and we have been suffering tremendously as a result. Fortunately, reforms have been made recently in wage regulations, and we would like to take the opportunity to petition for the following, so that we may fulfill our duty to the nation as workers:
>
> (1) A pay raise of at least 30 percent, as in the case of the Shibaura Kōsaku Machine Company
> (2) Abolition of the individual [i.e. incentive] wage system left over from the days of company control by U.S. capital [General Electric]
> (3) Allowances to workers surrendering vacation days
> (4) Improved air-raid protection.[114]

The attempt to manipulate the ideology of the times failed. Management denied the demands, warned several leaders, and hushed up the incident before it became an official dispute. Police arrested one man as a Communist agitator.

Finally, in at least one case, workers in a non-strategic enterprise during the war directly appropriated the language of the Essential Industries Ordinance to demand wage reform. A group of workers at a lumber company in Fukui prefecture had formed a Technical Study Group some time prior to the dispute. Unhappy with low wages and the absence of raises, the workers submitted a set of demands for reform to the company in October 1943, after "thorough research into wages throughout the country." They called for a new set of wage rules *identical* to those mandated by the Essential Industries Ordinance. Raises were to be given twice a year to all workers employed for the previous 6 months, excepting only those absent over 30 times in that period, or over 60 times in the previous year. Their demands set forth minimum, standard, and maximum raise levels, and workers hoped to allow a smaller range of discretion to management than had been the case at Mitsubishi. They demanded a minimum raise of 10 sen a day.[115] The influence of the Essential Industries Ordinance went beyond the strategic factories to which it applied directly, stirring hopes and instigating worker demands for identical reforms elsewhere.

Contradictions riddled much of the effort to control wages by fiat during wartime. Keeping wages low encouraged turnover, moonlighting, rule-breaking, and low morale, so wage limitations worked against efforts to raise productivity. The livelihood wage concept also clashed directly with the desire of managers to offer short-term inducements to speed production. Viewed from the perspective of total income, seniority as a factor in heavy industry wages declined during the war; more and more income derived from incentive payments not usually linked to the day wage.

Yet, government regulations imposed fundamental changes in the wage structure on management, in a context of discontent with existing practice and widespread calls for reform. These changes were not often reversed after the war. Family allowances spread from a tiny handful of enterprises in 1937 to all of heavy industry, as did an array of other allowances and company welfare measures. In some cases, military pressure in the closing days of the war did bring an end to output wage payments and adoption of monthly wages. Finally, day wages changed decisively. Age entered the wage calculus for the first time. Most important, the principle of clearly defined raises for all workers at regular intervals became an established practice, no longer an ideal often violated.

Also, the workers themselves, to the limited extent that they took the lead and made demands, adopted the concept of the livelihood wage as their weapon and even turned the words of government wage regulations against employers reluctant to raise pay. In these actions was a portent of the labor defense of age- and seniority-linked wages and the demand for a "living wage" of the early postwar era.

EIGHT

Sanpō: Labor Organization without Unions

A broad coalition of bureaucrats, politicians, and intellectuals, together with some managers and a few groups of workers, enthusiastically supported the formation of the Sangyō Hōkoku Renmei (Sanpō) in July 1938. In the following months, a national Sanpō secretariat and the local police urged or coerced thousands of companies to set up their own Sanpō branches, usually staffed by a few men transferred from the labor or personnel division. The company branches were to sponsor a variety of activities, but the national organization initially placed highest priority on formation of Sanpō discussion groups at the factory and workshop level throughout Japan. These were supposed to solve a shifting mix of vexing problems. Before 1941, their central mission was to be promotion of harmony in the work place. The regular meetings of worker and staff representatives would discuss and resolve any potential problem before it became a contentious issue, and a spirit of industrial service to the nation would replace the prevailing selfish spirit of personal interest and work-place antagonism. Sanpō leaders also called for an end to some of the sharp and pervasive distinctions of status in the work place in this effort to build unity. All employees from the company president to the newest worker with a temporary contract were members of the organization. Sanpō rhetoric stressed the dignity of labor and the tremendous value of every employee's contribution, regardless of rank or status. In this spirit, the national secretariat trumpeted the slogan of the "enterprise as one family" (*jigyō ikka*).

As the Pacific War began, and the need to raise output took precedence over the desire to eliminate disputes, the early enthusiasm evaporated. The emphasis on harmony gave way to more practical concerns with attendance, efficiency, and productivity; Sanpō evolved from an organ to develop labor-management cooperation into a squad of morale-boosting cheerleaders calling for ever greater exertion and output. In propaganda terms, the "Imperial Work Ethic" (*Kōkoku Kinrōkan*) replaced the "enterprise family" as the leading Sanpō slogan, but the Sanpō councils did precious little to bring either harmony and equality of status, or greater morale, attendance, and productivity to Japanese factories. As with most of the manpower and wage regulations, the immediate fate of Sanpō offers a lesson in the pathology and contradictions of an authoritarian effort simultaneously to enact social reforms and exact tremendous sacrifice.[1]

THE SANPŌ ORGANIZATION IN THE WORK PLACE

The numerical growth of the Sanpō movement was impressive. Twelve thousand company units encompassing 2,530,000 workers had been formed by October 1939, barely one year after the Sanpō Federation was formed. By 1942, two years after the government-run Sanpō Association replaced the Federation, 87,000 company branches with 6 million members had been created.[2] The very spread and scope of this growth invites skepticism. What functions did these Sanpō organizations, often hastily formed under police pressure, actually perform? How active were the company or workshop discussion groups, and what impact did they have? As early as 1939, the Welfare Ministry criticized improper use of Sanpō groups as forums for airing discontent. According to a 1941 report, one metal-factory discussion group served mainly as a place where workers complained, asking for regular pay raises, livelihood wages, safe equipment, talented experienced foremen, and better welfare facilities.[3] On the other hand, complaints abounded that Sanpō units were moribund, especially after the government took charge in 1940.

Wada Ryūzō, chief of the Shibaura welfare section, was one manager who genuinely hoped to use the discussion councils to create trust between managers and workers. In 1939, he expressed this hope even as he hinted at an important obstacle to council success:

> Fear has repeatedly surfaced concerning how to respond when unresolvable conflicts of opinion emerge in the discussion councils. Basically, the issue is one of whether labor management is done well or not, whether workers trust the company or not. These groups ought, then, to be formed as a means to create this trust.[4]

His cause faced obstacles at both the national and plant level. National and regional business lobbyists successfully defeated the plans of reform-minded bureaucrats to let elected worker representatives serve on the discussion groups and authorize them to raise substantive issues of work conditions, hours, or wages.[5] Even when a manager such as Wada appeared willing to admit such important topics to the council agenda, the basic problem remained: Active participation of interested workers was necessary for the groups to function as he intended. From the early days of the Sanpō Federation, observers recognized this obvious fact. In its Basic Labor Policy statement of 1939, the Shōwa Kenkyūkai stressed the need for an organization that enjoyed worker support. "Without the conscious cooperation, from below, of the workers, [effective labor mobilization will be] impossible." Yet, as the Shōwa group may have realized in 1939, this statement embraced a contradiction. To insure effective mobilization, leadership of the Sanpō movement must remain firmly in bureaucratic hands, but worker, and even union, cooperation must be voluntary.[6] Or, as the Kyōchōkai stressed in 1941 in an ingenious rhetorical flourish, Sanpō must foster culture and a dedication to work through "human," not "mechanical," controls.[7] The Shōwa Kenkyūkai's second major work on labor, *Research on the New Labor Order,* also appeared in 1941 and echoed the same chorus.

Sanpō had somehow to stimulate the active cooperation of workers without letting the organization become an arena for conflict. The Shōwa group proposed an old idea unlikely to win managerial support: Let workers have some say in choosing representatives to the councils.[8]

Sanpō's bureaucratic leaders consistently decided to err on the side of safety, maintaining tight government and company control over Sanpō rather than risk encouraging active worker participation. Countless statements in 1939 and 1940 complained of the lack of vitality in the Sanpō structure, yet no major changes at the company level emerged. Hōsei Shichirō of the Shōwa Kenkyū-kai complained in December 1939 that the Sanpō organization was an empty shell. He too called for participation of elected worker representatives. Another observer described the local Sanpō units as inactive groups forced on companies by the local police and little understood by the workers. Nakajima Jinnosuke, also of the Shōwa group, detailed Sanpō's many failings in the summer of 1940. Most enterprise units were "open for business but on vacation" (*kaiten kyūgyō*). They were not autonomous and were usually forced on companies from above. They gave much time to ideological lectures and little to practical worker training. Managers used Sanpō to promote longer hours and more intensive labor and thereby aroused worker discontent. Finally, managers ostracized the Sanpō company units within the company. All real authority over labor remained in the hands of the existing personnel or labor departments.[9]

Observers offered various recommendations for stimulating worker enthusiasm as the war progressed, but the chorus of criticism repeated the same refrain. The Home Ministry's Police Bureau commented in 1942 that "much of the general membership views the organization merely as a group to facilitate rationing, and there are a good number of workers who ridicule the movement and are uncooperative." The report went on to describe the discussion councils as forums for complaint. The basic company units were "stagnant," the workers "indifferent." Unless Sanpō addressed bread-and-butter issues and dispensed with propaganda for which workers had no use, the movement was doomed to fail.[10] Fujibayashi Keizō commented in a similar vein in 1942. Labor policy was still controlled by company labor sections independent of Sanpō, workers were still treated with scorn, and Sanpō had yet to be "brought to life."[11]

By this time, the major thrust of Sanpō efforts had shifted from promoting harmony and cooperation toward encouraging production. This "increased-production movement" was always "about to get off the ground," but in fact it never did. As late as 1944, one critic noted once more that the Sanpō movement was too formalistic, imposed from the top down without involving the workers directly. Once again, a call was issued for concrete Sanpō actions to support the livelihood of its members instead of campaigns built on empty slogans.[12]

Perhaps these critics protested too much. They were bureaucrats or intellectuals who supported Sanpō in theory and maintained a vested interest in its continued existence. As civilian ministries fought with the military for a share of the budget, to claim that current efforts were succeeding, while military efforts clearly were not, was an unwise strategy for defending bureaucratic turf. By highlighting or even exaggerating labor problems, these men could justify continued support for Sanpō, the theoretical solution. The few councils that did function actively were reported to be in heavy industry, so that an inquiry into the fate of Sanpō in Keihin factories offers a reasonable test of this possibility.[13]

If any Sanpō council ought to have been an active force promoting trust, cooperation, and workplace harmony, it was the Ishikawajima version. The Jikyōkai union provided whatever worker excitement or leadership there had been during the years leading up to Sanpō's formation. In July 1938, Ishikawajima formed the first company Sanpō unit in the nation, and, in August 1941, Machida Tatsujirō of the Kyōchōkai praised the Ishikawajima Jikyōkai as one of the major inspirations of the Sanpō movement.[14]

Yet, the Sanpō organization at Ishikawajima experienced limited success. The Keihin Industrial Report of September 1938 notes

that, while the precocious Sanpō unit at Ishikawajima ought to
have exerted local impact, other Tsukishima manufacturing enterprises were, in fact, either indifferent to Sanpō or unaware of it.
The island's second largest factory, Ishii Ironworks, showed no
interest at all in forming a Sanpō branch. Even nearby labor
managers seemed unaware of Sanpō and the Ishikawajima example.[15]

Meetings of the company-wide Factory Discussion Council at
Ishikawajima took up a narrow range of innocuous topics. In each
case, staff and worker councils met separately. The worker agenda
for the second meeting, August 5, 1941, included a talk on the
Nogi lecture series and the Nogi spirit, a description of the new
Discussion Center, and discussion of vacation days, possible supply of breakfast after all-night work, safety, work cards, the need
for discipline, and retirement policy. The third meeting, held on
December 26 and 27, 1941, examined establishment of an Efficiency Promotion Council, a petition to raise allowances for work-
related travel, and the levels of condolence gifts offered to survivors
of deceased workers.[16] These were not issues likely to raise expectations that important matters could be broached, let alone settled,
at factory council meetings.

The workshop councils were the Sanpō organs farthest removed
from central bureaucratic control. Documents surviving for
Ishikawajima describe the alternation of these groups between
moribund periods and times when more active councils heard complaints but offered no mechanism for their satisfaction.

The company's Sanpō Newsletter describes two "model" workshop meetings in the April 20, 1941 issue. The "very active"
crane-shop council convened its monthly meeting on April 1, the
chairman distributed minutes of the previous meeting, and he led a
"thorough" discussion of means to resolve several outstanding
problems: conservation of materials, recycling, safety, and fire
prevention. Another active council, in the casting shop, met on
April 4. Discussion began with a problem; few of the decisions
of the previous meeting had yet been acted upon. However, an
"amicable" review of several of these followed: gas leaks and

countermeasures, the leaking workshop roof and lack of buckets, and poor lighting.[17]

The June meetings in the machine shop were a bit more substantive. Shop supervisor Satō urged workers to speak their minds frankly. The major issue raised in May had been a request for 1 day each month on which workers would return home early, because full days off had been reduced to 3 per month. The matter was "fully discussed from the point of view of how to cope with a fuller work load and home life without going home early." In June, the issue arose again, and Satō pledged understanding for those who could not always work overtime and had to go home early on occasion. The men raised several other gripes. They criticized company food, formed a committee to investigate the matter, and issued a call for superiors to respect their subordinates so as to motivate them.[18] At least as reported in the newsletter, this council discussed issues of some importance to workers, although solutions took the form of exhortation rather than action.

Finally, the metal-frame shop which met that same June dealt with a more serious problem in similar exhortatory fashion. Quarreling among work groups over access to raw materials had become a major drag on production. The issue mattered greatly because work groups that obtained materials had more work and higher output pay. The workshop supervisors proposed reorganizing the work process so that the entire shop was responsible for every project, and idle workers were shifted to help busier groups. Workers objected that, if foremen moved people around to keep everyone busy, they would force less experienced workers upon some groups and adversely affect the group's output wage. The chairman could only reply that the present crisis was no time for pursuit of individual profit.[19]

An item in the April 1942 newsletter sums up the problems faced by workshop councils with surprising candor. In their factory council incarnation, the Ishikawajima councils had predated Sanpō by a full decade, but, after several years in operation, the earlier groups had declined in vitality "as most organizations tend to do." The Sanpō movement had brought new life to workshop councils, but then once again most of the councils became rather inactive, because shop-floor proposals were often not acted upon to the satisfaction of workers. After noting that the company had placed new leaders in most councils and had promised to do better in the future, the report concluded:

> There has been and still is a tendency to misunderstand the true role of these councils, treat them merely as places for making requests or demands, and lose interest when the demands are not acted upon immediately. Old ideas have not been rooted out sufficiently. . . . The real role of these councils is not to present demands or requests but to settle any problems in the council through discussion. Then the company will no longer be someone else's company, the workshop no longer just a place to work. [20]

Despite this rousing appeal, neither Sanpō nor managers had persuaded Ishikawajima workers that the company was theirs. To the contrary, management attempted to motivate workers by stressing an obligation to country, *not* company:

> We are not working for the company, but for the nation. We are not working for shareholder profit, but for the nation. . . . The old American-British-Jewish idea of labor as a commodity, of work for the sake of money, must be discarded. . . . A worker of the New Asian Order raises his hammer for the nation, not for money or for the company. [21]

Even at this company, which gave birth to a union movement stressing the fusion of labor and capital interests and played an active role in the formation of Sanpō itself, the factory and workshop councils were not seen to have built trust between worker and supervisor. Sanpō probably encouraged patriotism; it did not foster loyalty to the enterprise.

Councils at other Keihin factories were equally ineffective. They dealt with unimportant problems. The Yokohama Dock Company typically raised subjects such as improving attendance or enforcing work hours at the meetings. Workers brought up issues such as supply of uniforms, entertainment or athletic facilities, erection of a dining hall, or factory safety. The company appointed all council members, a change from the pre-Sanpō era when workers had elected representatives to the factory council. Meetings were formal, almost ritual affairs with agendas and resolutions rigidly set in advance. Workshop meetings did take up one significant issue, the level of incentive pay offered in each shop. Foremen were concerned that their work groups or workshops receive incentive pay in line with other shops, and the meetings addressed and reportedly redressed discontent over imbalances.[22]

Another sign of Sanpō's weakness was that companies such as Tōshiba and Uraga Dock handled most of their important labor issues outside the Sanpō framework. In 1938, Shibaura expanded its labor section, renamed the welfare section, and gave it a larger staff and a broader set of responsibilities for labor management, work safety, insurance, and personnel decisions. Plans were proceeding concurrently for the establishment of the Shibaura Sanpō organization, but, despite Wada Ryūzō's enthusiasm, top management wanted to isolate Sanpō from crucial decisions of labor management.[23]

At Uraga, too, Sanpō betrayed the hopes of its official founders. According to the 1938 bylaws of the Uraga Dock Company Sanpō organization, typical in their tone and content, the organization aimed to "harmonize the wills" of all employees and promote the success of the enterprise, the welfare of the workers, and the growth of industry. Discussion councils would deal with efficiency, treatment of workers, welfare programs, and mutual aid. Sanpō would also join in cultural, educational, and recreational activities. The results would be labor-capital unity, patriotic service, and greater productivity. Yet, from the outset, the enthusiasm expressed in these Uraga bylaws was not shared widely. Only 300 of 3,619 workers attended the opening ceremony of October 12, 1938. Uraga did not form workshop discussion groups until three years later, in October 1941.[24] And, in subsequent years, the company ignored the organization when it addressed those very problems most appropriate for Sanpō consideration. In mid-1942, a company report discussed young workers hired just out of school who had been squandering their wages and misbehaving.

The report recommended "careful surveillance" of the workers but did not call for Sanpō action.[25] The problem continued as young conscript laborers entered the yard in 1943. In December, several division chiefs held a meeting with these draftees, outside the Sanpō council structure, to discuss their complaints regarding poor treatment by foremen and labor section personnel, excessive all-night work, haphazard instruction, and dirty toilets.[26] By late 1944, several months of 24-hour operation on two 12-hour shifts had exhausted workers and reduced efficiency. The company decided to take most of the workers off the ineffective night shift, require those still working nights to remain for the next morning's assembly to "prevent carelessness due to inadequate supervision," and "put discussion councils to greater use to harmonize the relations of superior and subordinate."[27] Only in this last case did Sanpō provide one part of the attempt to solve the problem, but the company had already given up hope of improving night work performance.

To the end, the bureaucratic and managerial leadership of Sanpō was unable to resolve the basic contradiction between the need to motivate worker participation and the fear of surrendering any real authority or autonomy to workers.[28] The critics of Sanpō were correct. Many councils existed on paper only, meeting irregularly or often just once for an opening ceremony to satisfy police demands. Many workshop groups were never formed. Managers fearful of confronting workers directly would cancel meetings if it appeared that difficult demands were to be raised. Even the workshop councils, supervised less tightly than the factory groups, were ineffective because workers were afraid to speak their minds in meetings led by their immediate superiors. Almost the only issues raised by management concerned hard work, moral education, discipline, and productivity. Workers either regarded the council meetings as occasions for making complaints and demands over conditions or else showed no interest in the meetings at all when their earlier complaints were ignored. Their apathy was understandable. As a manager at the NKK Tsurumi Shipyard remarked in 1941, many workers left home at 6 a.m., commuted for an hour, and worked twelve hours at double the normal pace due to the labor shortage. Returning home by 8 p.m., they had energy only to sleep, and neither time nor interest in morale-boosting activity.[29]

In addition to running the ineffective councils, most of the Sanpō units at major firms took some responsibility for company welfare, so that the Sanpō organizations were not completely empty shells. The promotion of company welfare programs was probably the major short-term accomplishment of Sanpō. At Ishikawajima, Sanpō sponsored and ran an impressive list of activities: savings programs, a military support corps, an athletic section sponsoring various team and individual sports, a haiku club, and other cultural groups, such as a calligraphy circle, a housing section, health insurance, hygiene, safety, and mutual-aid groups, a consumer cooperative, an education section, and a discussion center to which workers could bring work, family, or legal problems.[30] In addition, it published a monthly "Sanpō Newsletter," our major source of information on Sanpō activities at Ishikawajima. Some of these were existing programs merely shifted to Sanpō control, but others, especially the extensive sports and cultural activities, were new. At Uraga, too, Sanpō was most active in sponsoring new entertainment programs, such as movies, plays, lectures, and a magazine. At Tōshiba, the main Sanpō effort went into "cultural activities," including athletics, exercise, spiritual training, reading circles, zen meditation, flower arranging, and sewing classes. At both companies, the labor or welfare sections retained control over more expensive and substantive programs, such as housing, technical training, and an expanded hospital at Uraga.[31]

Sanpō activity was only one of a broader set of government and economic pressures responsible for the proliferation of welfare and club activities, and many of these programs may well have spread without Sanpō. An item from Ishikawajima's Sanpō Newsletter shows that much of the new "activity" took place in name only. The reporter praised the tennis club formed in the spring of 1941. He was surprised that it had actually been functioning for two full months. "There are so many Sanpō clubs that just announce their formation and then merrily go along for months without really doing anything, 'open for business, but on vacation.'"[32]

STATUS, MORALE, AND SANPŌ

No less than the ineffectual Sanpō organizational apparatus, the frequent Sanpō calls for equality of treatment, greater morale, and more intensive labor created a gap between a rhetoric of reform and an unchanging reality. Statistics do indicate a slight rise in blue-collar pay relative to that of white-collar staff, but the status and respect accorded laborers within the company changed hardly at all.[33]

The worker view of his social status in the early days of the war is reflected in the 1940 Kyōchōkai discussion involving several workers from the Kawasaki area. Participants were asked, "Do you want your children to be workers?" An electrical worker replied: "Anything but. Preferably a bureaucrat or something like that." A machinist answered that, even though his income exceeded that of a university-trained technician, "status, after all, is status, and I want to give my children a proper education." Employment-agency officials spoke of the need to end the lack of respect for workers. The workers agreed that Sanpō should address and redress the damaging notion that one became a worker only if nothing else was available, and should encourage pride in being a worker, but all discussants felt attitudes toward them unchanged despite much recent talk on the subject.[34]

The Shōwa Kenkyūkai wrote in 1941 on the need to trust and respect workers, to allow Sanpō to have a real voice in factory affairs, and to give workers an active role in the organization. If workers were trusted and respected, they would respond in kind.[35] Government observers of the factory scene consistently lamented the absence of these attitudes. The Home Ministry's review of labor relations in 1941 complained that employers lacked respect for conscripted laborers and viewed labor problems as less important than material procurement or financial matters. Staff workers still tended to look down on workers. In sum:

> Although managers pay lip service to the notion of the enterprise as a family (*jigyō ikka*), in actuality their treatment of workers and staff is fundamentally different. The former are taken care of by labor managers, the latter by personnel managers. The concept governing labor management is that, if the enterprise is a family, the staff are family members and the workers are family servants.[36]

In the closing days of the war, official observers only echoed the same refrain. Minami Iwao, now Sanpō's Kantō Regional Director, asked in 1944 how a movement to unite all in the factory could succeed if its leaders remained scornful of workers. He issued yet another call to respect workers as people with important technical, economic, and organizational ties to the enterprise. Technology should be developed to help people, not oppress them. Wages should be adequate and the organization, too, must not abuse its lower-ranked members. He recommended creation of a single personnel office to take care of workers and staff together and help build a relationship of trust and mutual good will.[37]

Although the Munitions and Welfare Ministries in the closing days of the war drafted plans to integrate staff and workers in each firm into a single hierarchy of job and status ranking, these plans died on the shelf. All available evidence from the shop floor indicates that discriminatory treatment of workers, viewed by management as outsiders, remained the rule. Semiannual bonuses to workers increased somewhat during the war relative to staff bonuses. A survey of 22 heavy industrial firms in Kanagawa in 1939 found worker bonuses to be about 10 percent of office staff bonuses. This was an improvement over the NKK situation several years earlier, where worker bonuses reached a mere 3 percent of those given to office staff, but the gap was still large.[38]

A 1942 survey of a North Kyūshū factory concluded that, despite all the recent talk about respect for labor, "the scorn for work and workers still remains a deeply rooted social concept." Partly as a result, "selfish individualism remains at the root of the worker's world view, or has increased under recent stresses." The author blamed the passive Sanpō organization for much of this state of affairs.[39]

The war and Sanpō brought little change to Nippon Kōkan:

> During the war, the gap between white and blue collar was as wide as ever. Until the very end of the war, the difference in status was great. Sanpō had an ideology of winning the war through cooperation, but this had no impact on actual status differences or treatment. But, after the war ended, by 1947 changes had come as a result of the labor-union stress on equality of worker and staff.[40]

The fate of one labor manager, Kiyomizu, who tried to change the status quo at NKK, offers instructive support of this statement. Kiyomizu was reported to be a progressive manager who insisted on fairness in dealing with labor, better treatment of both workers and staff, and an end to the image of NKK as a company where workers traded their lives for their wages. He was also active in the Kyōchōkai and the region's Sanpō movement. Suddenly, in April 1938, just as the plans for launching the Sanpō Federation were coming together, NKK transferred Kiyomizu to a post at the company hospital. *Keihin kōgyō* commented that NKK did not understand the need to grant prestige and independence to the labor-management staff in the personnel department. It concluded that "this is a regressive attempt to control the factory through the executive board."[41]

Labor managers at both Ishikawajima and the Yokohama Dock Company, when asked to describe the changes that took place in the worker-staff relationship during the war, unanimously denied that changes occurred. Kanai Tatsuo of Ishikawajima recalled:

> While there was talk of unity, through Sanpō and elsewhere, it was all very formal, nominal. In reality, the worker-staff gap remained and remained great, even at the height of the war. After the war, for the first time, the situation changed. During the war, the entrances to the company, uniforms, use of time clocks all were and remained different. There was discrimination on every level. It didn't shrink a bit, despite Sanpō. Bonuses differed greatly. Wages for workers were paid by the day, for staff as a monthly salary.[42]

Yasuo Masao of Yokosen echoed this view. Sanpō did little to change the fundamental division at the Dock Company between staff and workers. Until after the war, the Dock Company maintained separate entrances, administered body checks at the gate to workers only, and offered very different bonuses and pay raises. Workers were paid by the day, staff by the month.[43]

Unusually detailed evidence from the Uraga Dock Company details the continued discrimination there. The company gave staff members 6- to 10-day paid vacations each year and yearly medical check-ups, and denied both to workers. In 1940, it set send-off allowances for drafted employees at 55 yen for workers and 80 or 90 yen for staff. Bonuses passed out upon launching of each ship were generally 4 yen for staff and 2 yen for workers, even in 1944. Compensation for workers killed by air raids or in military service was less than for staff. The same held true for allowances initiated in 1944 for working under dangerous conditions: 2 yen per month to workers, 3 yen to staff. The single exception was the family allowance, identical for all, but of course the government had ordered this under the Essential Industries Ordinance. In cases where company discretion prevailed, the difference in treatment of white- and blue-collar employees was thoroughgoing and purposeful.[44]

The talk about better treatment naturally struck a sympathetic chord with workers who had been interested in these issues for decades. The vast outpouring of these sentiments came after 1945, but, during the last years of the war, workers took direct action to end discriminatory treatment in a few cases. At Sumitomo Chemical's Osaka plant in 1944, workers demanded and won equal retirement and severance pay after a 2-day strike. Also in 1944, Kanebō workers struck for one-half day over a rumor of imbalances in distribution of rations to staff and workers.[45] But, on the whole, the desire to end discrimination did not lead to action until workers had the power to take matters into their own hands after the war.

Official exhortations to respect workers and treat them on a par with staff confronted a managerial view of workers as second-class citizens, and the exhortations catalyzed very little change. The enterprise-as-family analogy continued to approximate reality only when it recognized workers to be family servants, not members. Wartime policies were helpless to prevent the deterioration of whatever sense of community had existed between managers and workers in the factory. Skilled workers in leadership positions were drafted, attendance fell, and morale sagged. Finally, disputes still took place, even though no organized framework existed to encourage, exploit, or unite sporadic instances of resistance.

The behavior of Japan's workers during the war does not support the myth that the Japanese have historically been compulsive hard workers, either because of a tradition of intensive rice cultivation, a Confucian ethic, or corporate loyalty. Cohen painted the broad picture from the perspective of the economy as a whole. Japanese authorities were unable to extend work beyond 11 or 12 hours a day in 1941 because "workers simply took more days off." The average number of days worked per month in all industries in May 1944, for example, was surprisingly low, ranging from 22.7 days in shipbuilding to 24 days in the metal industry. In effect a 5-day work week, this was well below the attendance for 1935 when 21 men at NKK and one other Kawasaki steelmaker averaged 26.6 days per month over a 3-month period (Tables 20, 21). Furthermore, the 1935 figures cover the summer months, when intense heat was likely to lower attendance. Cohen concluded that absenteeism was a serious problem from before the time of, and unrelated to, the air raids. He uncovered one case where draftees and skilled workers alike went home rather than work when the only chore available was clean-up of debris.[46]

At Keihin factories, attendance during the war was indeed poor, and it worsened dramatically late in the war. In May 1940, the Kanagawa Factory Association newspaper noted that absenteeism ranged from 15 to 22 percent in Kanagawa factories and throughout the nation. The report ascribed this to discontent with wages and working conditions and noted that "many 'absent' workers have actually left their jobs to work at other factories."[47] This same observer later wrote of a 1941 survey where 5 to 9 percent of the workers at 11 factories had been absent for over 2 consecutive weeks.[48] Itō Nobuo of the Yokohama Dock Company reported in his memoirs that 20 percent absenteeism was common during the war. As earlier, attendance fell on Mondays and on the day after payday, but, beginning in 1941, attendance at the Dockyard also began a steady overall decline.[49] Attendance at Ishikawajima stood at a similar low level, 83.6 percent at the main Tsukishima factory, 81.5 percent at the Fukagawa auto plant. These two factories classified 5 and 3.6 percent of their workers as "long-term absentees," a euphemism for illegal job-switchers or escapees. Another 1943 report on material and personnel problems described attendance at Ishikawajima as worsening; on average, only 80 percent of the force came to work. Perhaps due to better pay, status, and work conditions, the staff commitment was substantially higher, with attendance ranging from 89 to 91 percent.[50]

Just after the war, occupation authorities compiled the most complete attendance data available. The many Tōshiba factories, including the old Shibaura Engineering Works plant in Tsurumi, faced steadily falling attendance soon after the China War began. Monthly absenteeism at the Shibaura plant, for males only, rose from around 5 percent between 1935 and 1937 to 9 percent by 1939, and then gradually increased to over 20 percent by 1943, before peaking at well over 50 percent in 1945. Figures for other plants were similar (Table 24). Absenteeism at factories throughout Japan reached daily or monthly averages of 20 percent even before the air raids forced workers to flee the cities.

Declining morale paralleled the drop in attendance. The inexorable tightening of the net of controls thrown over Japanese workers was a major cause. In 1939, the *Keihin kōgyō* observed much discontent with the controls among workers, and occasional emotional confrontations with management. One particular point of contention was employer refusal to grant the "permission slip" necessary to workers wishing to change jobs.[51] The Kyōchōkai review of labor relations in 1939 noted many minor disputes, in particular due to irritation at the need for permission to change

Table 24 Absenteeism at Various Tōshiba Factories, 1935–1945

1. Tsurumi Engineering Works: All Male Employees[a], June Each Year

Date	Percent Absent	Number Employed
1935	5.0	3,277
1936	5.2	2,928
1937	5.8	4,579
1938	7.5	5,513
1939	9.1	5,912
1940	14.8	5,109
1941	15.1	6,330
1942	17.2	6,712
1943	22.3	6,496
1944	21.1	4,975
1945	51.0	3,912

2. Tsukagoshi Factory, Males, Blue Collar, Yearly Average

Date	Percent Absent	Number Employed
1937	6.0	13
1938	10.0	214
1939	14.0	257
1940	18.0	299
1941	21.0	347
1942	25.5	483
1943	31.0	561
1944	38.8	791
1945 (April)	34.6	151

3. Komukai Works, All Male and Female Employees, June Each Year

Date	Percent Absent	Number Employed
1939	8.0	1,474
1940	8.2	1,625
1941	9.3	2,150
1942	9.2	3,003
1943	15.2	3,838
1944	22.7	6,673
1945	66.4	3,230

4. *Ōmiyachō Works, All Male and Female Employees, June Each Year*

Date	Percent Absent	Number Employed
1940	7.9	585
1941	8.5	606
1942	9.2	960
1943	9.4	1,262
1944	52.01	3,054
1945	57.81	3,584

5. *Yanagimachi Works, All Male and Female Employees, December Each Year*

Date	Percent Absent	Number Employed
1936	7.1	772
1937	7.6	1,488
1938	8.0	3,664
1939	7.7	4,836
1940	8.5	5,033
1941	8.2	5,153
1942	11.3	5,290
1943	18.8	4,307
1944	25.5	5,380
1945	31.6	4,462

Source: United States Strategic Bombing Survey in Japan, "Report on the Shibaura Engineering Works."

Note: [a]Roughly 80% of employees were blue-collar workers

jobs. Kanagawa prefecture officials counted 400 to 500 such small incidents in 1939, in addition to numerous cases where workers, feeling trapped, went on slowdowns, worked less efficiently, or just did not show up.[52] The Kyōchōkai Labor Yearbook for 1940 also took note of the adverse impact of controls, by this time affecting far more workers. Violations were reported to be on the rise.[53] The Home Ministry survey of labor conditions in 1941 found:

The impact of the controls seems to be considerable. They can create a feeling of oppression, of government high-handedness, leading to discontents, complaints, work-place tensions, lower morale and productivity. For instance, many workers reacted to the labor mobility restrictions with the complaint "We've been nailed to our workplace." This led to organized and unorganized slowdowns and lower efficiency.[54]

The wage controls brought a similar response. Some workers reportedly complained of forced sacrifices for the sake of capitalists. According to the Home Ministry in 1941, wage controls hurt morale and productivity, increased illegal mobility in search of higher wages, and led to more pirating.[55]

The use of conscript labor was another side to the morale problem. The controls affected young draftees most directly, and they were among the most resentful. The difficulty of disciplining draftees, integrating them with the existing work force, and motivating them are recurrent themes in reports on wartime labor. *Keihin kōgyō* claimed in 1941 that their integration into the regular labor force was not proceeding well.[56] The Home Ministry report on labor of 1942 discussed the draftee problem at length. It described discontent with wages, food, treatment, and facilities, and trouble with absenteeism, delinquency, moonlighting, deliberately shoddy work, and even group violence.[57]

One such flare-up took place at Uraga in retaliation for the beating of a drafted worker by his dorm supervisor. Antagonism between local boys and draftees from northern Japan was a background cause of the incident. A total of 9,423 youths were enrolled at Uraga as labor draftees in December 1944. The military had "redrafted" a full 17 percent, and, of the remaining 6,881, a strong 20 percent (1,392) were registered as absent for over 2 weeks. This is all the more striking when compared to the 7.7 percent total of long-term absentees among experienced non-draft labor.[58] Uraga was unsuccessful in motivating a large minority of its draftee labor force simply to report to the yard, let alone work effectively.

One symptom of the morale problem which went beyond absenteeism but fell short of the labor dispute was so-called "sabotage" (in Japanese, *sabotāju*). As used in Japanese, the word usually does not include the destruction of equipment or concerted obstruction of work. It refers to small-scale slowdowns, isolated incidents of foot-dragging, and production of defective goods by individuals. The workers who one day refused to help out with the cleanup of debris would be guilty of *sabotāju* as defined in Japanese.[59]

Officials reported numerous such cases throughout the war, especially in 1942 and after. In 1939, the Kyōchōkai observed that workers who feared retribution would stop short of initiating a dispute and loaf or engage in *sabotāju*. The Kyōchōkai also reported that, in 1940, the proportion of defective goods reached or exceeded 60 percent of output in some factories, and a writer for the Shōwa Kenkyūkai noted in a similar vein that an atmosphere of sullen discontent was evident in Keihin-area enterprises where *sabotāju* affected 30 percent of all products in some cases and was poisoning the atmosphere.[60]

Precise measurement of this type of behavior is impossible, but frequent references to the problem indicate that it remained a common way for workers to express frustration when denied any meaningful, organized outlet for discontent. Both the Kyōchōkai and the Home Ministry stated that incidents of *sabotāju* as well as absenteeism and "escape" had increased in 1941, although actual labor disputes had declined. With organized dispute action nearly impossible, the Home Ministry concluded that *sabotāju* activities were "disputes of a different color."[61]

This Home Ministry report listed 8 types of common non-dispute resistance, ranging from tardiness, early quitting, absenteeism and escapes, to illegal job-switching, moonlighting, workplace foot-dragging, delinquency at work, and group violence against management. While the far more oppressed Korean or Chinese laborers carried out most of the violence, some Japanese were also involved, including workers at the huge Mitsubishi Aircraft plant in Nagoya, as well as those at a strategic factory in Tokyo.[62]

The state discontinued comprehensive yearly labor surveys after 1942, but, through the pages of the monthly Special Police Report (*Tokkō geppō*), one senses the range and extent of *sabotāju* and related activities late in the war. The 16 issues of the Report issued between January 1943 and April 1944 reported 25 specific incidents and referred separately to a general rise in strikes

and sabotage, in both the Japanese and English senses, beginning
in late 1942.[63] The more serious incidents involving workers in
heavy industry included the destruction of 1,422 units at Hitachi's
Kameido plant in Tokyo by 13 workers upset over treatment, repeated destruction of equipment at the Hatohama Dock Company
in Ehime prefecture in response to foreman violence and unfair
rationing, a refusal to work overtime by a handful of workers at
the Amagasaki Dock Company in Osaka upset at a reduction in
overtime pay, which resulted in violence toward the guard who
ordered them to work, a brawl at a regional subsidiary of Shibaura
between rival groups of senior skilled workers and new skilled men
from Tokyo, and the destruction of a crane at Mitsui's Okayama
Shipyard by a worker angry at the high wages given less skilled
workers.[64]

These were all isolated incidents, even within the factories
where they occurred, not signs of coordinated resistance to management authority. In the context of falling attendance rates and
general resentment of labor controls and the labor draft, they are
but one manifestation of a wider problem with morale and discipline. Workers unable to feed themselves worked illegally on the
black market as day laborers or went back to relatives' farms where
they could at least eat.[65] Deprivation exacerbated work-place
tensions among those who still showed up, productivity fell, and
disputes occasionally erupted in spite of the substantial state
apparatus of control.

Labor disputes during the war ranged from strikes to quiet incidents resolved by police before a single demand was presented.
They reached a numerical low in 1941 but rose sharply in 1943
and 1944. That these disputes took place at all is significant,
given the lack of worker organization and the time, energy, and
resources devoted by companies, Sanpō, and the police to promoting harmony and preventing strikes.[66] Of equal importance
were the reasons for these disputes and the nature of their resolution. Wartime labor conflicts were sporadic, little-planned cases
of resistance to intolerable conditions, but they also had a wider
significance. They focused on critical issues of historic importance

to Japanese workers, which postwar labor would continue to address.

Consider first the statistical evidence. Table 25 enumerates the apparent sharp increase in the number of disputes toward the end of the war. The new category of "near disputes" (*mizen bōshi*) was added in 1943 to account for the tremendous rise in police involvement in labor mediation. When police learned of a situation in which the presentation of demands, a work slowdown, or a strike appeared likely, they would intervene before this dispute took place and impose a settlement.

The average size of all these incidents declined sharply during the war from peaks of 176 participants in 1937 and 203 in 1939 to a mere 33.5 in 1944. Furthermore, greater police attention surely led to the recording of incidents that would have escaped official notice in earlier years, so the statistical leap in the number of disputes in 1943 and 1944 probably exaggerates the labor problem. Certainly the final years of the war witnessed numerous small labor disputes, perhaps more than ever before, but these almost always involved only part of the work force at any factory.

The machine industry, broadly defined in the statistics to include almost all of heavy industry, was consistently the major source of unrest, topped only in 1940 by the mining sector, and Keihin factories were responsible for a large share of the total each year. Throughout the war, disputes arising from discontent with supervisors and their behavior were numerous, second in number only to actions demanding higher wages.[67] Outsiders mediated the great majority of these incidents. This usually meant the local police, and, toward the end of the war, they tended to favor the workers.[68] The Sanpō discussion councils, while designed originally to maintain work-place harmony, played almost no role in resolving these conflicts.[69]

One dispute that fits this pattern took place at the Uraga Dock Company in January 1940. Since August 1938, the company automatically had been deducting a portion of wages for deposit in national "Patriotic Savings Accounts." In January 1940, workers discovered that the company was improving its cash flow at

Table 25 Labor Disputes, 1937-1944

Year	Number of Actual Disputes (Strikes and Slowdowns)	"Near Disputes"[a]	Average Size (Participants)
1937	628		176
1938	262		70
1939	358		203
1940	271		121
1941	159		68
1942	174		54
1943	695	412	35
1944[b]	550	200	34

Sources: 1937-1942 from Naimushō, Keihokyoku, Shakai undō jōkyō (1942) pp. 538-539; 1943 from Tokkō geppō, 12/1943, p. 71; 1944 from Tokkō geppō, November/1944, p. 45.

Notes: [a]mizen bōshi in Japanese   [b]Through November, 1944

worker expense, systematically delaying deposit of their funds with the government; the money deducted in the fall of 1939 was still in the hands of the company several months later. The ship-builders held the labor section responsible. On January 19, work-ers suddenly put down their tools, and some men threw rocks through windows in the labor section. The police were dispatched, but the workers had more or less occupied the shipyard. The police finally took control and negotiated a solution in which the head of the labor section "voluntarily" resigned.[70]

In some cases, the wage issue converged with anger at the con-duct of superiors. Workers in the lathe shop of the Nagoya factory of Japan Rolling Stock Company were unhappy with low output wages in September 1943. Their foreman had promised to raise pay if and when productivity rose, but he later reneged. The Spe-cial Police intervened before a formal dispute occurred and imposed a settlement which favored the workers. It forced the company to raise the pay of experienced, skilled workers and change hourly wages to less variable day wages.[71]

After 1943, the Special Police Monthly Report ceased to dis-cuss individual disputes or near-disputes. The only surviving record of the 750 such incidents in 1944 is a tiny handful (34) of the many reports filed with the Home Ministry by prefectural authorities. Reports from Aichi prefecture (Nagoya) and Osaka survived in the greatest number. Unfortunately, no Tokyo-area reports are known to survive. Yet, even these few documents breathe life into the statistically typical pattern. [72]

Skilled workers at the Asahi Armaments Company of 1,665 employees were upset at the relatively low level of their pay compared to that of newly hired trainees. Choosing 5 representatives, they presented a demand for higher pay on July 28, 1944 which management "haughtily refused." They resubmitted demands for higher incentive allowances and a better management attitude. On July 31, the Aichi police entered the scene and determined that workers were indeed underpaid relative to those at other factories, and that staff did treat workers with scorn. While lecturing employees on the need to work hard, the police also told the company to mend its ways. That day, management announced a raise of 10 percent for men, 15 percent for women, promised restraint in the future, and pledged to open a Sanpō factory council meeting to discuss the issue. [73]

A similar dispute took place that month at a small Aichi metal-casting factory. Seven of the 50 employees were very upset because the company had adopted an incentive-pay system which gave factory workers up to 200 yen per month while keeping wages for those at jobs in the field, outside the factory, below 80 yen. Workers blamed the company for insincerity. On July 28, the Aichi police investigated and supported the worker accusation. They "requested" management to make improvements, and the firm immediately offered a 100-yen-per-month allowance to those working in the field. [74]

On September 1, 1944, the Aichi police again intervened, this time at the Ōe Airplane Parts Company. The head of the Labor Section had recently upset many of the 137 employees with his "dictatorial, abusive behavior." He had forced a group of workers to labor through the night with no meal and had beaten two men discovered taking unauthorized sick days to work at a nearby plant for more money. The police lectured the workers on the importance of giving their all for production and advised the company to take action against the Labor Section chief. He was transferred to a new post.[75]

Finally, the 461 workers at the Tōkai Electric Company had "made great efforts" to raise monthly production 23 percent between May and October 1944, after the factory was designated a military producer. These workers were unhappy that no changes in pay or treatment had rewarded their efforts. Once again the police arrived as a strike appeared imminent, declaring that management had failed to respond properly to worker efforts and instructing the company to make amends. It announced a raise of 20 to 30 percent.[76]

The scarcity of documented wartime disputes prevents a bold conclusion, but these cases do match the broad statistical picture quite well. Small-scale disputes were fairly common during the last years of the war, especially in urban heavy industry. Workers protested low wages, "unfair" wage structures, and poor treatment by their bosses. The Sanpō organization played no active role in these situations. Police involvement and sympathy increased, at least in part because concessions would quickly get everyone back to work, but, whatever its cause, police support put workers in a stronger bargaining position. While the lack of any organized base kept these disputes small and local, the workers who attempted them were generally successful during the final years of the war.

As a harmonious little society or large family of managers and workers, the enterprise community was more an ideal than a description of reality before the war began. Despite the rhetoric of the Sanpō movement and the creation of thousands of factory and workshop councils, this conception was at least equally unrealistic by the time the war drew to its disastrous close. Hyperbolic Sanpō exhortations and restrictive labor regulations did not inculcate in workers a sense of loyalty to the enterprise. Dispute actions decreased in number in 1941 and 1942, but workers reversed this in the next three years. Inflation, rationing, long hours, restricted freedom, and lower living standards took a serious toll. Workers in heavy industry during the war were often apathetic, prone to absenteeism and low morale, and occasionally hostile toward their employers.

If we are still impressed that a good many Japanese stayed on their jobs for so long despite truly miserable conditions, a patriotic (if uncritical) spirit and the will to survive are more effective explanations of this behavior than company loyalty. The cooperation of most workers was testimony to a belief that personal and national survival, not company glory, demanded sacrifice. The exhortations of businessmen surely reflect this perspective; their calls for diligent labor spoke primarily of service to the nation.

While Sanpō groped for a role during most of its existence, the organization did have a slight immediate effect, and it left a complex legacy. Sanpō, the government bureaucracy, and intellectuals all stressed the importance of livelihood wages, respect, and better treatment of workers. It is no surprise that workers regarded this rhetoric with favor and echoed it in occasional dispute activities. In certain respects, Sanpō ideology had much in common with the ideals expressed by more organized, assertive workers of earlier decades.

The success of numerous disputes in the last years of the war offered further support for these ideals in the form of police recognition that demands for better pay or more reasonable treatment were justified. The early postwar years of vigorous and often radical labor activity should be considered against this background. The changes brought by Sanpō and war regulations stimulated hope as well as discontent and reinforced ideas and practices, such as the regular pay raise, which labor unions would later defend. Isolated demands for livelihood wages and a "better management attitude" were of a different order of magnitude than the broad, industry-wide movements for livelihood wages or work-place democracy of just a few years later, but common themes can be found in the movements of the two eras. Postwar unionism did not emerge from a vacuum.

Neither did management strategy. Although themselves not very successful, the Sanpō factory councils offered one model to managers interested in promoting a cooperative and cooptable version of labor unionism confined to a single enterprise. They also left behind workers and staff members with some experience in running these groups. Factory councils of the 1920s, a bit more democratic in that members were often elected, provided a similar model for managers looking for ways to combat radicalism in postwar unions. These councils of the 1920s and of Sanpō comprised an important legacy for postwar management.

More generally, the entire bureaucratic experiment with labor controls set in motion a process of change. Some of this came during the war. Recruitment of school graduates became more systematic, allowances and welfare programs spread, and the seniority wage became a clearly defined part of the labor relationship. Much change, however, is found during the war itself only in the form of a blueprint for a potential future labor relationship, and the transition from blueprint to concrete structure was marked by difficult conflict.

Part Four

The Postwar Settlement

NINE

Japanese Labor Relations: The Worker Version

The link between war and revolution has been intimate in the twentieth century. In China and Southeast Asia, World War II acted as a solvent to established regimes. In Japan, the Americans preempted any revolution from within and would not tolerate a revolution from below, but the upheaval of the late 1940s and early 1950s was nonetheless profound. In the modern era, only the Restoration period rivals the postwar decade in the tempestuous nature and rapid pace of change. Yet, a remarkably persistent conservative political and social order emerged rapidly in the wake of this troubled period. Speaking of the two European postwar eras in this century, Charles Maier has observed that "stabilization is as challenging a historical problem as revolution," and, in Japan as well, the rapid consolidation of conservative stability in the 1950s demands careful explanation.[1]

Significant episodes in both the radical challenge to established authority and the ultimate achievement of conservative control took place in the factory. Industrial managers eventually fashioned a work-place order of considerable durability and adaptability. This settlement, whose outlines appear in rather clear form by the early 1950s, was a significant reconstitution of practices established in prewar factories, those developed during the war, and those imposed by an aggressive, often radical, labor movement after the war.

Considered in light of the tremendous gains labor achieved between 1945 and 1947, this settlement was clearly a triumph for management. In the first two years after the war, organized workers gained far more than even their maximum prewar demands, as they built upon the earlier desires for job security, wage security, and higher status within the firm and society. In this heady period of "production control," successful strikes, and rapid organizational gains, Japanese workers very nearly established a labor version of the Japanese employment system: guaranteed job security, an explicitly need-based, seniority wage, and a significant labor voice in the management of factory affairs.

Management in the late 1940s and early 1950s defeated radical labor and rejected the labor version of Japanese employment practices. The result was still a tremendous advance for workers when measured against the prewar or wartime systems described already. What emerged in the Japanese factory by the early 1950s was a fairly systematic and secure remaking of practices concerning jobs, wages, and status noteworthy for their selective and inconsistent application in earlier decades. The temperament of the reader will ultimately determine the stress upon gain or loss, as we trace the eventual triumph of the management version of Japanese labor relations. Most practices had prewar or wartime roots, but the occupation reforms and the demands of organized labor helped bring about most of the changes that resulted. Management responded to postwar labor with a fair degree of flexibility, incorporating prewar labor demands and wartime government pressure into a new employment system capable of satisfying or at least quieting organized workers.

The reforms of the American Occupation defined a new legal and political framework within which the events of the first postwar decade unfolded. The New Deal reformers who held sway during the period of initial post-surrender policy helped stimulate a labor offensive which far exceeded American expectations and brought major changes to both Japanese politics and labor relations within the enterprise. The mid-course shift in American policy likewise helped management regain the upper hand.

Initial United States policy was unequivocal in demanding legal support for labor unions for the first time in Japanese history. In September 1945, President Truman ordered that "encouragement shall be given and favor shown to the development of organizations in labor, industry, and agriculture, organized on a democratic basis." In October, MacArthur told the Japanese government to enact labor legislation to protect the rights of labor. Before the official Japanese government response two months later, workers responded on their own by organizing unions at an unprecedented pace. When the Diet approved a trade-union law in late December 1945, the number of union members in Japan was already approaching the prewar peak of 420,000. One year later, at the end of 1946, nearly 5 million workers were members of 17,266 labor unions.

The Labor Union Law guaranteed workers the right to organize, to bargain collectively, and to strike. It protected them against employer discrimination for union activity. These provisions were designed to encourage unions to protect their economic interests against their employers, and the Americans did not plan to encourage political unionism. Much to the displeasure of the occupation authorities (the Supreme Commander for the Allied Powers, or SCAP), labor unions quickly became involved in political battles and supported the Communist and Socialist Parties. Despite fairly successful efforts to tame these radical national unions, SCAP could not change the historically rooted, European-style habits of labor support for socialist politics. Full investigation of the complex political role of the labor movement goes beyond the bounds of this study, but we may note that, viewed from the factory, the ideological divisions among national union federations often appear less important than a concern with wage and job security common to workers in different unions.

Two further legal measures helped establish the very favorable early postwar framework for labor activities. The Labor Union Law had established a national Central Labor Relations Commission and regional commissions in each prefecture. The Labor Relations Adjustment Law of September 1946 clarified the role of these bodies, composed of labor, management, and "public" representatives. The commissions were designed to mediate in labor disputes, encouraging conciliation and voluntary arbitration. Either side could reject the advice of a commission. This law received its trial by fire in the major electric-power industry labor dispute of October 1946. The national Commission sided with the labor union, which had proposed a noteworthy new structure of "living wages," only to have management reject the Commission's mediation efforts. This dispute, a landmark in the history of Japanese wage practices, eventually ended with victory for the electrical power workers.

A Labor Standards Law, enacted in April 1947, was the final of the so-called "three fundamental labor laws" of the postwar era. It set minimum standards for hours, wages (to be established in separate legislation), insurance, injury compensation, and unemployment benefits. These were designed to protect non-union workers as well.

Even in the first year of the occupation, the Americans began to qualify their support for the activities of radical Japanese workers. In the spring of 1946, SCAP criticized Communist influence in the unions and denounced "disorderly minorities" accused of manipulating popular enthusiasm.[2] SCAP in particular condemned the "production-control" tactic, in which unions took over the factory and ran it without managers present. Between January and June 1946, 255 such incidents involving 157,000 workers took place. This was certainly the most radical form of activity ever undertaken by Japanese workers.[3] Workers at the shop floor who engaged in production control were, in fact, ahead of the political union organizers, since they challenged fundamental notions of private property and authority. In response, SCAP officials decided they had to "housebreak" the Japanese union movement. In February 1947, they prohibited a planned national general strike with political as well as economic goals.

By 1948 and 1949, the qualifications in SCAP support for labor resulted in legal changes designed to restrict the political activity of unions and limit their role in the public sector. SCAP also promoted anti-Communist "democratic cells" within major unions. In 1948, MacArthur proposed to a more than willing Japanese government that it revise the Labor Union Law to deny public-sector workers the right to strike, and new legislation late that year erected a system of dispute mediation for public-sector workers. The numerous and radical government employees, in the civil service and in national enterprises such as the railroads or tobacco monopoly, were thus placed under greater constraints than fellow workers in the private sector. This dealt a severe blow to the effort to build a united, nationwide, politically oriented labor movement. The new Ministry of Labor (established in September 1947) also followed SCAP directives, ostensibly designed to reduce union dependence on employers and encourage independent unions, by revising the Labor Union Law to prohibit most forms of company financial aid to unions. In practice, this served to weaken private-sector unions significantly, for free use of employer facilities for office space and meetings, on company time, was in many cases a sign not of company-union collusion, but of union strength in forcing employers to offer such benefits.[4] Finally, in 1950, SCAP and the Japanese government together engineered the Red Purge, in which 12,000 employees considered Communist Party members or sympathizers were ousted from their jobs and prohibited from union activity.

These steps to thwart radical, political union activities, and limit the rights of both public- and private-sector workers, helped bring about the revival of management authority and the ability to confront unions. But shifts in both Japanese and American economic policy were of even greater importance in tipping the balance of power back to management. Economic chaos and conditions of literal starvation for many workers, in a context of ineffective, inflationary government policy, were certainly the major direct cause of the surge of union activity of 1945 through 1947. Likewise, the harsh deflationary policies forced on the Japanese beginning in December 1948 provided management with the need and the opportunity to pursue a very hard line against the unions.

The dimensions of the economic crisis immediately after the

war are revealed starkly by a few simple statistics concerning prices, wages, and production. Inflation was far worse than even the World War I price explosion which brought on rice riots nationwide. The retail price of rice quintupled in 1946 and rose another 6 times in 1947: a 14-kilogram sack cost 5 yen in 1945, 28.2 yen in 1946, and 170 yen in 1947. In 1948, prices doubled again. Even the substantial wage hikes of 100 to 300 percent negotiated by unions in 1945 and 1946 could not keep pace with this inflation.

These prices made starvation an immediate fear even for a skilled worker. In March 1946, black-market rice cost 90 to 100 yen per *shō*, equivalent to 10 average servings. At this price, a family of 5 souls would spend 3,000 yen per month to buy each member just 2 servings of rice per day. The average monthly income of a Yokohama Dock Company worker in the spring of 1946, including overtime, was 1,914 yen.[5]

Yet, the Dock Company worker was fortunate to have a job. Production was at a standstill in many firms at war's end due to bombing destruction and lack of materials, and it dropped thereafter, barely rising in 1946 in response to determined pump-priming. Kanagawa prefecture counted 229,000 employed workers in August 1945, but, by October, 141,400 had lost their jobs. Overall employment stood at just 87,600, and the number of factories had declined from 1,465 to 1,392. Of these, only 826 were operating. The rest were closed, and 367 firms reported no definite plans to resume production.

The economic policies of the Shidehara and Yoshida governments of 1945 and 1946 were not helpful. Both men turned to red-ink fiscal policy to stimulate the moribund economy. Under Shidehara, the government paid out huge sums to big business for war equipment contracted for but not yet produced. Business did not respond with the expected productive investment, but rather used the payments to speculate by hoarding and reselling scarce raw materials whose value was skyrocketing with inflation. Prime Minister Yoshida and his Finance Minister, Ishibashi Tanzan, continued the controversial subsidies to firms in producer-goods industries, in the hope of stimulating economic activity.

The result was only further inflation and economic stagnation through the summer of 1946, and the threat of an even greater, total collapse of the economy by the next spring. But, when the government abandoned the policy of generous subsidies to business, production only declined still further, while inflation rose. Leading bureaucrats were predicting a total collapse of economic activity by March 1947. It was in this context that the Communist-led industrial union federation, Sanbetsu, organized the successful October offensive of 1946 for "living wages" and job security, and the Sanbetsu and Sōdōmei federations together planned for a national general strike in February 1947.

Yoshida and his successors, including Socialist Prime Minister Katayama Tetsu, had no choice but to turn to the bureaucracy and advocates of recovery through extensive state planning and control, striking some bargains with labor in the process. Under Prime Ministers Katayama and Ashida in 1947 and 1948, a new agency, the Economic Stabilization Board, directed the so-called Priority Production Plan. The Board regulated subsidy payments with greater care than before, focusing almost exclusively on the coal and steel industries. The theory was that, without coal, no recovery was possible, while the steel industry both used great amounts of coal and produced in large part for coal-mining industry use. These two interdependent industries were expected to lead the way to a general recovery. This policy enjoyed some success in 1947 and 1948, as coal production almost reached the official target levels. The Priority Production plan also drew the support of the moderate Sōdōmei wing of the labor movement, willing to cooperate and support capitalist reconstruction in exchange for respect for unionized workers and reasonable wages.[6]

Ironically, the economic policies of 1945-1946, focused exclusively on increasing production rather than controlling inflation, whether through war payments to business or subsidies to priority industries, provided a context which, together with SCAP encouragement, supported union demands and organizing efforts. The subsidies relieved some of the pressure to dismiss excess personnel, so that unions could in some cases defend jobs even as production remained stagnant. Likewise, subsidies and inflationary fiscal policies allowed firms to meet some of the wage demands raised by hungry and angry workers. Labor success in raising such demands in turn spurred more union growth and militance.

Furthermore, the institutions of capital and management were in disarray. The threat of the removal of capital equipment from heavy industrial plants, as reparations payment to Japan's wartime victims in Asia, hung over much of the economy. SCAP targeted portions of all the firms under study here for reparations removal.[7] While this threat loomed, capital investment in vital basic industries was not forthcoming. In addition, individual managers were under fire. The presidents and leading executives of NKK, Tōshiba, Ishikawajima, and Mitsubishi Heavy Industries were among those purged by SCAP in 1946 for their wartime activities.[8] In addition, unions commonly demanded the removal of executives whom they condemned as war criminals. Such economic and political uncertainty resulted in hesitancy, poor organization, and retreat in the face of labor demands.

Under the Priority Production policies of 1947 and 1948, championed by the self-proclaimed "reform" capitalists of the Dōyūkai, management regained some confidence. Also, the split between unions willing to cooperate, and those opposed to a capitalist reconstruction, placed an obstacle in front of unified labor actions, even within a single industry or a single firm. Within NKK, the union at the Kawasaki mill supported the moderate Sōdōmei, while the union at the Tsurumi mill supported the radical Sanbetsu federation, making joint action difficult.

Then, in December 1948, the draconian Dodge line, a plan to deal with inflation as the key to recovery, eliminated those economic conditions that had allowed unions even nominal success in wage or job struggles. Behind this policy was the broader strategic American decision, arrived at gradually between 1946 and 1949, to anchor its postwar Asian strategy around the recovery of a democratic, capitalist regime in Japan. The Americans decided that the inflation habit of its new ally had to be brought under control, even if the withdrawal symptoms were severe. Dodge prevailed upon the Japanese to slash government expenditures and balance the budget. He told fellow industrialists to eschew inflationary wage settlements. His policy severely curtailed demand, reduced income for many, and threw hundreds of thousands out of work, but it did slow inflation and pave the way to a recovery led by rapid, centrally orchestrated investment in heavy and chemical industries, and spurred for a time by the "godsend" of Korean War procurement orders issued to Japanese firms by the Americans.

In concert with the shift in SCAP and Japanese government labor policy, this new economic program placed labor at a decided disadvantage, for the obvious and rather attractive course for managers faced with the loss of direct subsidies or subsidized demand was to deny wage increases, cut wages, and fire thousands of workers. Much of the attraction lay in the opportunity to manipulate cutbacks so as to weaken union leadership wherever possible.

Recovery proceeded in fits and starts until 1955, when the high growth era began in earnest, but the contours of the new management version of Japanese labor relations emerged clearly in the early 1950s. The nightmare of shop-floor uprisings, where workers seized "production control," had long since ended, and the movement to build powerful industrial federations seeking to enforce a labor version of the employment system was overcome by 1949. The center of gravity in the labor movement became the enterprise union once again. With the support of the Japanese government and, until 1952, the Occupation forces as well, Japanese managers recovered their authority in the work place, renegotiated the early postwar labor contracts, destroyed many confrontation-minded unions, and made significant adjustments in wage and job policies. Organized labor remained important. The Sōhyō federation, founded in 1950, moved from its initial moderate, anti-Communist stance to mount a sustained political challenge to the government and to organize a nationwide system of wage bargaining. But, within the factories, management created a structure of great durability.

The rush hour of the unions transformed the social and economic relationships at the heart of life in the factory. As the balance of power tipped in the favor of organized labor, Japanese workers gained far better terms of membership within the firm and within society. They actively participated in critical decisions affecting work and wages. In the first two years after the war, simple survival was a major preoccupation for many, but workers nonetheless focused much energy on issues of status and the nature of their participation in the factory. They consolidated a labor presence by forming unions and demanding extremely favorable collective-bargaining contracts. In addition, they forced creation of powerful "management councils" which insured unions a voice in personnel and wage decisions, and they successfully called for reform in the rigid, discriminatory status hierarchy of the prewar and wartime factory. In total, this amounted to a basic remaking of the social and political structure of the enterprise.

Wages and jobs were naturally of paramount concern as well. Here, too, workers sat in the saddle as they sought to build upon and go beyond both the customary practices used to reward and favor senior, skilled men, and the wartime policies that had promised a living wage. The central thrust of the wage offensive was creation of a need-based, life-cycle wage structure. The October 1946 dispute of the electric-power workers was a peak of union success, and virtually all unions in the nation incorporated some version of this so-called Densan wage structure into subsequent demands. The unions also went beyond the paternal ideology of a management commitment to workers, as they demanded a contractual guarantee of job security. The 500,000 national-railway workers and the 40,000 employees of the Tōshiba company, in fact, won controversial promises of job security in 1946.

Managers eventually undermined, modified, or rejected outright all these achievements. At Tōshiba and JNR, they fired workers in 1949. In the electric power industry, they modified the wage structure and squashed the union. Throughout the nation, companies weakened the management councils and renegotiated contracts. Yet, some early postwar gains remained, as labor defended its achievements of greater security and respect, and fuller membership in society and the firm.

Retreating in the face of the aggressive and successful labor movement of 1945 and 1946, managers coined the slogan "recovery of management authority" (*keiei ken no fukkatsu*) to characterize their principal efforts over the several following years. This slogan was not an exaggerated rhetorical flourish. In the tumult of the immediate postwar months, unions in fact wrested significant control and authority from management.

The building of powerful unions was the first step. Despite the general impression one receives of disarray among business leaders, company managers made some attempts to head off the formation of unions in the very early days after surrender. One popular tactic was to manipulate the Sanpō organization. The Welfare Ministry ordered the Sanpō secretariat and regional offices to disband in September 1945, but it left the company units intact until early December. In the interim, companies sought to reorganize these into cooperative unions. This effort seldom worked as intended. To be sure, the leaders of the moderate Seamen's Union after the war were former Sanpō people, and the same was true of the leadership of the Tokyo Transport Union and the Yokohama Dock Company union. During wartime, these men had chosen to act within the prevailing institutional setting, but, even if the same men were later active in a postwar union, the meaning of their activity could be quite different. Several Yokosen activists sought their goals first in the setting of the Kōshinkai union in the 1920s and early 1930s, then through the factory council, later Sanpō, and finally the Yokohama local of the postwar Shipbuilders Union (Zenzōsen). But here and elsewhere such men successfully resisted the effort simply to convert docile and dependent Sanpō groups into unions. [9]

Some managers tried to anticipate union activity by establishing discussion councils or friendship groups, composed of worker and manager representatives and responsible for improving work conditions. These, too, were rarely sufficient to satisfy aroused laborers. In a clear bid to build on the remains of the Sanpō organization, Tōshiba organized a factory discussion council in November 1945 at the large Horikawa plant. All employees were to be members, and management appointed small committees in each section of the factory as the basic units of the council. Some workers objected. Four days later, 350 employees in the glass section (the factory manufactured light bulbs) joined to criticize the council and demand a 300-percent pay raise. The glass workers won this demand by November 27, and, riding the crest of victory, they united with workers throughout the plant to draw up factory-wide demands and found a factory-wide Horikawa Employees Union. This stimulated like actions at other company plants. By January, Tōshiba workers formed a company-wide federation of factory unions.[10]

Even when a firm appeared merely to be watching as its employees constructed a union unimpeded, activity behind the scenes very likely aimed toward control of the union. At Ishikawajima, the first union leaders in 1945 and 1946 were former leaders of both Sanpō and the notorious Jikyōkai of the 1930s. As a more radical clique with ties to the Communist Party ousted this group in 1946 and 1947, the company quietly directed Kanai Tatsuo of the personnel office to join the union and keep it from taking a sharp left turn. Elected union secretary, he was able to keep management abreast of developments within the union, but he could not and, at least by his own report, did not want to impose the will of the company on the union. An exasperated manager at one point in 1947 expressed his annoyance: "We went to all the trouble of getting you into the union, and what good has it done?"[11]

Just as managers turned to tactics and institutions used successfully against unions in the past, such as the Sanpō units, factory councils, or company "plants," unions relied on the experience of prewar activists in their rebuilding efforts. This was especially true of the Sōdōmei, the more moderate of the two major camps in the union movement to emerge by 1946. At the national level, prewar Sōdōmei leaders such as Nishio Suehiro led the reconstruction of a new Sōdōmei organization. Locally, prewar activists, again most often from the Sōdōmei, were also instrumental in pulling unions together at the company or factory level. In Keihin factories, such men helped form unions at the NKK Kawasaki mill, Asano Dock, Yokohama Dock, and a good many other factories. Through the fall of 1945 and winter of 1946, this was true even at factories whose unions went on to join the radical Sanbetsu camp by the summer of 1946.[12] The Sōdōmei had disbanded only five years earlier, so such continuities are not surprising. The Communist wing of the labor movement, squashed in 1928, lacked this numerous corps of experienced activists.

Organizations formed in factory units were the basic building blocks of the postwar unions. This was as true of unions organized autonomously by workers as it was of the abortive attempts of management to impose docile unions from above, and it is not a surprising development. There existed no effective prewar structure upon which to rebuild unions organized in craft or trade units. Prewar unions, weak or strong, were organized by factory or by enterprise and, most important, they all *acted* at the factory level. The postwar rush to unionize and present numerous demands focused on the factory union as well. Industrial federations came later.

The shipbuilders along the Keihin coast, from Ishikawajima, to Yokohama and Tsurumi, down to Uraga, all founded separate shipyard unions in late fall of 1945. Union leaders then began to work on building a regional, and finally a national, industrial federation. The result was the unaffiliated (that is, neither Sōdōmei nor Sanbetsu) All Japan Shipbuilding Workers Union (Zen Nihon Zōsen Rōdō Kumiai or Zenzōsen), founded in August 1946.[13] Labor at Tōshiba also built an unaffiliated federation on the base of factory units which sprouted independently of each other in late 1945 and initially made separate demands. By January 1946, most of these factory unions joined in a company-wide federation. This, in turn, joined and played a leading role in the Sanbetsu federation of electric-industry unions.

The steel pattern was a variation on both these themes. At NKK, workers at the various mills and shipyards of the sprawling firm organized first by factory or shipyard, as had the Tōshiba workers. Beyond this, the issue of broader affiliation produced a cacophony of conflicting claims. The company's Kawasaki and Tsurumi steel mills at first aligned with the Sōdōmei, while NKK's Tsurumi shipyard joined Zenzōsen. When the major national federation of steel unions joined Sanbetsu, in summer 1946, the Kawasaki union, with a tradition of prewar Sōdōmei activity, objected. It quit the federation and sought to build a competing moderate industrial union together with several unions at other mills, including Yahata. Yet, the nearby Tsurumi mill remained loyal to Sanbetsu. At the same time, the perceived need to present unified wage demands to management led to the formation of an enterprise-wide NKK union federation, similar to that formed at Tōshiba but far weaker. When this federation formed in November 1946, NKK presented to its workers the confusing spectacle of several independent factory, mill, or shipyard unions, aligned with a variety of opposed or unrelated industrial federations, including the shipbuilding Zenzōsen, the Sanbetsu steel federation, and the Sōdōmei steel federation, yet all joined together in an enterprise-wide union coalition.[14] For individual workers, the factory union was naturally the relevant, comprehensible unit of action. The ability to coordinate demands or strikes in an industry or even on the enterprise level did not emerge overnight from this situation.

The second noteworthy feature of workers in early postwar unions at the factory level was their tendency to form separate blue- and white-collar unions. Tōshiba was one exceptional case where all employees below the extremely high post of division chief (*buchō*) formed a single union from the start, at both the company and plant levels, and this exception may have its roots in the relatively muted forms of discrimination between worker and staff at Tōshiba during the war.[15] At most factories or shipyards, including Yokohama Dock, Uraga, Ishikawajima, and NKK, the blue-collar workers (*kōin*) organized unions first, with white-collar staff following suit several months later. At NKK's Kawasaki mill, initial talk of forming a single all-employee union was rejected by blue-collar workers, who felt they would be unable to cooperate with their supervisors. The wartime talk of unity among employees had not changed worker attitudes and company practices of discrimination at the steel mill.[16]

Workers were quick to use these infant unions. Beginning in early 1946, organized labor took several steps which together gave workers a fair claim to shared management authority in many cases. The production-control tactic was surely the most frightening for managers to witness. In hundreds of cases in early 1946, they saw their supposedly loyal employees lock out non-union personnel and run the plant themselves, until executives caved in to union demands. In 1946, production control was tactically wiser than a strike. Workers needed their wages desperately, and their unions did not have strike funds yet. Further, a shutdown would play into the hands of managers, who had, in any case, been hoarding materials and avoiding commencement of production. Anger at this "sabotage" provoked the use of production-control tactics.

One of the most dramatic and well publicized of these numerous events took place at NKK's Tsurumi steel mill, which produced sheet metal and steel plates. On December 26, NKK managers rejected the demand of the 1,250 employees for recognition of their union, higher wages, a pledge of no layoffs or firings without union consent, and union supervision of employee welfare facilities. The union responded by organizing a sophisticated production-control struggle, taking over the factory on January 11. Over a 2-week period, workers increased output from 18 to 19 tons per day and raised attendance 5 percent. The union was careful to follow the letter of the law as the workers themselves defined it. Matters requiring high-level authorization were settled in negotiations outside the plant between executives and the "production control committee," and payments made to the company were deposited in the company account. Yet, long-range troubles inevitably loomed. The union could not easily secure raw materials once the stock on hand was exhausted. In a dramatic negotiating session, 500 workers forced the issue by surrounding company headquarters in Tokyo. The outnumbered and physically intimidated executives granted all the initial demands.[17]

The production-control tactic asserted a labor claim to a limited form of "ownership" of the plant. In theory, it had revolutionary implications. In practice, production control fell short of a revolutionary movement. None of the leftist parties actively championed or sought to organize these widely scattered, grass-roots instances of workers' control into a broader movement to seize the means of production from capitalists, and, with rare exceptions, coordination between factories in complementary situations (a coal mine, a steel producer, and a consumer of processed steel, for example) was not within the capacity of these young, inexperienced unions. For a time, the political establishment was paralyzed in the face of production control. When the union at one coal mine accepted payments for coal in its own name during a production-control dispute, the company appealed to the government to outlaw this practice, but the Ministry of Commerce could only announce meekly that it had yet to determine whether such actions were legal. In the meantime, the union could keep the money! Finally, in June 1946, MacArthur condemned production control as an improper union tactic, and the Yoshida government led an effective crackdown on such disputes.[18]

While management and the government, with a little help from SCAP, overcame the challenge of production control, the unions remained determined to safeguard their interests by participating in management decisions. Workers sought to gain a voice through the traditional union tool of the collective-bargaining contract and also through the creation of management discussion councils (*keiei kyōgikai*). Negotiations over contracts were often prolonged and bitter, but, until 1947, unions almost invariably won agreements quite close to their initial demands, and these contracts varied little from place to place, despite ties to different national federations. By June 1946, 17 percent of unions in Kanagawa had won contracts, and the pace picked up thereafter, as labor concern with production control gave way to an effort to consolidate and broaden newly gained union power. The second half of 1946 witnessed a rash of contract disputes, and the issue reached a peak of intensity.

Unions concluded most of these contracts at the factory or enterprise level, a reflection of both the central place of factory unions in the Japanese labor movement and the determination of managers to maintain this situation. Leaders of the national federations did stress the importance of industry-wide agreements as the first step in going beyond the factory to build powerful industrial unions; by summer 1946, industry-wide agreements became a priority, especially for the Sanbetsu Congress. Yet, with a few notable exceptions in the electric-power, printing, and machine industries, labor fell short of this critical objective. Contracts were generally written at the enterprise level, as managers dearly wished to do, although the goal of industrial unionism was not abandoned.[19]

Invariably, these contracts bound management to consult and gain the consent of the union in virtually all matters related to personnel policy and wages, without setting out detailed rules for particular cases. NKK's Tsurumi steel union in the Sanbetsu camp won such a clause in early 1947. Management would have to gain union consent (*dōi*) for all job transfers and layoffs. At the Kawasaki mill, in a contract won by the Sōdōmei union there in October 1946, managers were also bound to "consult and gain approval" (*kyōgi kettei*) from the union for all firings, hirings, transfers, punishments, rewards, and changes in the work rules. The Tōshiba union had gained similar control even earlier, in May 1946; no actions would take place in personnel and wage matters without union consent.[20]

The management discussion councils, usually created and given substantial powers by these contracts, surely contained pitfalls for labor, even as they attracted widespread union support. Properly manipulated, they could serve to coopt independent unions, as had the factory councils of the interwar era. In the early postwar days, most unions were powerful enough to prevent this. Fully two-thirds of the collective contracts concluded by mid-1946 provided for councils, and these bodies had considerable authority.[21]

The Tōshiba management discussion council was typical. Twenty voting members constituted the council, 10 chosen by the union and 10 by the company. In addition, the company president was the non-voting chairman. The council could discuss wages, labor conditions, welfare facilities, and the "democratic organization and management" of the firm. Council bylaws *bound* both union and company to implement all council decisions in good faith.[22]

While more than advisory bodies, few councils were consistently effective decision-making entities. With equal union and management representation, and with no set of rules or precedents to guide behavior in wage and job decisions, they could function smoothly only so long as no major differences arose. In major disputes, at Tōshiba and elsewhere, the councils invariably declared their inability to reach agreement, and the two sides moved to collective bargaining and perhaps a strike. In the supercharged atmosphere of the late 1940s, with unions determined to defend jobs at all costs, and managers desperate to cut payrolls, open conflict and a test of strength, not discussion, resolved most issues.

Even so, these councils were important. They met frequently and debated vigorously. For the first time in their lives, Japanese workers sat down with their employers as recognized equals and discussed matters of vital concern: jobs, wages, plans to expand or shut down plants. Minutes of the deliberations of several of these councils survive, and they convey dramatically the tone of a newly egalitarian discourse. Workers dispensed with polite forms, raised their voices, and expressed their anger directly. Quick-witted, sharp-tongued union leaders humiliated and confounded inarticulate managers. The relationship between workers and managers, employee and employer, had changed dramatically.[23]

This new tone and substance of the labor relationship brought about the creation of a more egalitarian social and economic order in the factory than had existed ever in the past. The actual changes were of varied significance. Some were symbolic and others affected pay envelopes. Workers did not gain all they sought, and no harmonious paradise resulted, but the workers, led by their new unions, were certainly the chief force pushing for most changes.

As the war ended, the gap between worker and staff (*kōin* and *shain*) was still forbidding. Yet, official wartime rhetoric had told workers they were valued servants of the nation, whose contributions ranked in importance with those of owners and executives, and, in their unrealized plans for reform, the military and civilian bureaucrats had sought to join workers and staff into a single hierarchy. Management ideology, too, had always invoked the image of firm as family. In the early postwar days, workers sought to eliminate detested forms of status discrimination and close the gap between rhetoric and reality, between their own sense of their worth and the low status and treatment offered by the company.

"Unity of worker and staff" and "abolition of the status system" were the two great slogans of this movement. During the first postwar year, labor made substantial gains. The initially separate staff and worker unions merged at NKK, Uraga Dock and Ishikawajima. Labor leaders considered these unified unions both a means to attain uniform treatment of all employees, and an important sign that a new equality was emerging in the workplace. The petty signs of discrimination (removal of which was cheap, if not in fact cost-effective as it raised morale) went first. No longer was the privilege of sewing the company trademark, NKK, on to a uniform reserved for staff alone. Gone too were the separate dining halls and separate gates. [24]

A bit more controversial was the abolition of the actual categories of worker and staff as symbolic and functional entities. The NKK union proposed a new ranking plan in spring of 1946, but the complex legacy of envy and distrust raised controversy, not only between union and company, but within the union itself. Some union members demanded that workers be raised to the "staff" category (*shain*), but others supported the conversion of all to a neutral term, employee (*jūgyōin*). The latter resolution prevailed in the settlement reached with the company in 1948. Negotiations followed a similar course throughout the nation;

designations of worker and staff gave way to the employee appellation in most cases by 1947 or 1948.[25] The result was not the end to all hierarchy but the joining of all employees into a *single* rank system. New, purportedly functional classification ladders, typically climbing through apprentice, operative, foreman, supervisor, section chief, to division chief, were adopted, often in the face of union resistance to a perceived reconstitution of the old status order. Such fears had foundation; factors such as educational background still limited how high most operatives could hope to climb. But in theory, at least, all employees in the firm were ranked on a single ladder for the first time.

Building on this new equality, anchored in the all-employee unions, workers sought several more substantive reforms. A unified company-wide pay scale, offering monthly wages and uniform bonuses to all employees, and uniform policies concerning promotions and pay raises, were the critical and often most difficult achievements. Many unions did gain these reforms, together with the new classification and ranking systems. Some workers raised voices for change in this direction even in 1945. That December, for example, the new union at the Mitsubishi Shipyard in Nagasaki demanded and gained an end to discriminatory badges and insignia, the inauguration of equal paid vacations for workers and staff, and equal semiannual bonuses.[26] Final resolution of substantive status issues usually took two or three years, but, in 1947 and 1948, many unions, including NKK, gained some version of a unified pay system, with monthly wages for workers, and equal bonuses.[27]

The remaking of the enterprise community was a process, not a finite event. By 1948, workers had gained much power through their unions and their contractual right to a voice in company decisions; they had gone considerable distance in reforming the decades-old status system, but the process was never complete. As the initiative shifted back to management in the era of the reverse course and rationalization, these gains would be challenged.

BEYOND THE SENIORITY WAGE: UNIONS AND WAGES

During World War II, the need to pay workers at least a minimum living wage gained official sanction and, for the first time in Japanese history, the government actually intervened with a complex set of wage controls, in part designed to establish such a wage. These controls failed. They were not consistent in conception or application; they could not prevent the spread of incentive payments, and the collapse of the war economy rendered any attempt to protect living standards during the war futile. Even so, the principle of regular raises for all, regardless of skill or performance, was forced upon management, and the spread of a tangled web of allowances for food, commuting, attendance, or family size also hinted at a wage structure focused on the need of the worker, rather than his skill or productivity.

The wage controls continued in effect, but ineffective, for over a year after the war. As had the wartime Japanese regime, SCAP saw them as possibly useful in controlling wages and prices, a sign perhaps of the universality of the bureaucratic temperament, but more likely a result of the trend toward state intervention in economic policy stimulated on both sides by the demands of war.[28] Wage controls never completely disappeared. The state continued to play a regulatory role when the cumbersome wartime controls eventually gave way to a legally established minimum wage, but the demands of labor were far more significant than the minimum wage in shaping the postwar wage structure and setting wage levels.

By late 1946, the labor movement had moved well beyond the ideal version of the livelihood wage supported by the Welfare Ministry in wartime. The victory of the strong electric-power union (Densan) in December brought labor several giant steps down the path of a livelihood, need-based wage. Further advances initially proved difficult, and, as managers regained confidence, labor indeed retreated some from the so-called Densan wage structure. Significant labor defeats in the late 1940s and early 1950s allowed management to regain much flexibility in calculating wages, and companies reestablished the link between the firm's ability to pay and the size of a wage increase. Yet, the gains were sufficient to insure the retention of a wage structure which, in fact, tied income significantly to individual needs as they varied over a worker's career.

The story of early postwar wages is, in large measure, the struggle for a need-based, living wage. Demands for system and stability were also part of this story, as labor continued to support regular pay hikes, fairly distributed, the security of monthly wages, large bonuses, and reduced reliance on individual output payments.

For roughly the first year after the war, wage disputes focused on extraordinary allowances rather than the two components of "base wage" and output pay, which had accounted for most of the prewar wage package. As during the war, wage controls limited the base wage, and the huge pay raises needed to even begin to cope with inflation were granted in the form of all sorts of allowances: "food allowances," "price allowances," "extra allowances," "special allowances," and so forth. As a result, in the typical industrial wage, as calculated in a national survey of December 1946, only 17 and 21 percent of wages derived from the base and output portions, respectively. The remaining 62 percent came in the form of these so-called livelihood allowances.[29] As the composition of wages shifted, the nominal level of pay also rose; workers faced with the doubling of some prices in the worst months demanded and gained 100-, 200-, or even 500-percent wage hikes. At Uraga Dock, ceaseless negotiating between union and management resulted in at least 4 pay raises between September 1945 and December 1946. Average monthly income rose from 128 yen to 1,476 yen during this period. The company also adjusted the wage structure each time it granted a raise, creating new "attendance," "dependent," "ration," "temporary," and "price" allowances. Naturally enough, the portion derived from the base wage dropped from 50 percent of income in August to less than 20 percent a year later, and the total allowance portion rose accordingly.[30]

Neither managers nor workers were happy with this bewildering new pay structure. Although workers preferred allowances (in theory responding to specific needs) to fluctuating output pay, they feared it would prove easier to discontinue an allowance than to lower the basic wage rate. They sought to incorporate the allowances into a higher base wage. Managers, too, favored a larger base-wage portion, far easier to calculate and control than a half dozen or more allowances. Once controls on the base wage were lifted, workers and managers both sought to restore the base wage to the center of the wage structure. The conflict came over the criteria to be used in its calculation. The major confrontation took place during the Densan dispute, the centerpiece of the Sanbetsu Congress's "October offensive" of 1946.

The decision to abolish most wartime wage controls in September helped the electric-power workers press their case, although the union had been preparing its demands for several months, and the demand for need-based wages can be found elsewhere in the months preceding the Densan dispute. In June, the Tōshiba workers, who also played a central role in the Sanbetsu October offensive, pushed for a wage derived from their calculation of an "ideal family budget," a sum sufficient to provide the necessary calories to an average worker and his family. The union decided a monthly wage of 377 yen per person (including dependants) was needed to allow each worker and dependant a bare minimum of 1,741 calories per day. The pay raise gained by July fell well short of this. It remained for the Densan workers to sustain a more spirited defense of a similar concept that fall.

The electric-power workers were well situated to lead the drive for a new wage structure. The endeavors of the wartime economic bureaucrats had focused on electric power. In a controversial prelude to more general efforts at total mobilization, the government nationalized the electric-power-generating industry in 1936. It further created a nationwide network of 9 regional power distribution companies in 1942. Nationalization engendered in the workers simultaneously a distaste for bureaucratic control and a sense of common purpose among men performing skilled tasks in isolated but interconnected locations throughout the nation. In addition, the high level of education necessary for blue-collar operatives in this industry resulted in a relatively small gap in education and sentiment between these men and their supervisors. Finally, the constant dealings with the bureaucracy and the relevance of central political decisions to the fate of the industry created a politically concerned corps of union members. In a 1947 poll, 57 percent of the employees supported the Socialist Party and 13 percent supported the Communists.[31]

These workers were able to build a powerful union. They first formed separate unions in the 10 component companies of the system (9 regional distributors and the central Japan Electric Power Generating Corporation) during the fall and winter of 1945 to 1946, and then moved toward a national federation by the early spring. While the federation was a loose coalition of 10 unions sending representatives to a central committee, rather than a tightly structured industrial union, it nonetheless joined the Sanbetsu Congress at its inception in August 1946 and emerged as a critical element of the left-wing union movement.[32] Three months of lively discussion within the several electric-power unions produced the historic agenda for the October offensive. On September 10, the union federation presented 3 demands to management for a minimum wage, a new system of retirement and severance pay, and the end to bureaucratic control of the industry. The wage demand is remembered as the heart of the Densan program. It called for a fixed minimum wage based on the cost of living, adjusted to reflect regional variation, additional pay to reward ability, seniority, and attendance, the elimination of imbalances based on rank or educational background, and a commitment to adjust wages in the future to reflect price changes. As Figure 4 reveals, the detailed structure called for by the union reestablished the base wage as the major source of income. Most important, the base wage was calculated explicitly in accordance with need. Two-thirds comprised a "livelihood guarantee" based wholly on an individual's age and family size. The remainder derived from an "ability" portion (about 25 percent) and a seniority portion (roughly 5 percent).

It took the Densan workers just over 2 months to win virtually

Figure 4 The Average Densan "Livelihood" Wage, January 1947
(all percents are proportions of total income)

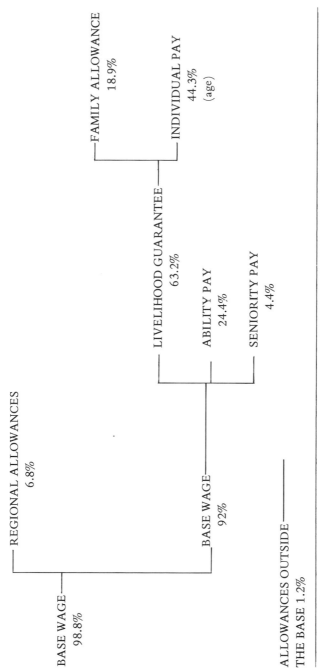

BASE WAGE
98.8%

REGIONAL ALLOWANCES
6.8%

BASE WAGE
92%

LIVELIHOOD GUARANTEE
63.2%

ABILITY PAY
24.4%

SENIORITY PAY
4.4%

FAMILY ALLOWANCE
18.9%

INDIVIDUAL PAY
44.3%
(age)

ALLOWANCES OUTSIDE
THE BASE 1.2%

Source: Keieishi, pp. 223–225

their entire program. The strike attracted wide attention for at least two reasons. It was the first dispute mediated under the new Labor Relations Adjustment Law and was thus a test case for the postwar structure of dispute mediation. The workers skillfully manipulated the equivalent of a strike, the power blackout, to apply pressure *during* the negotiations. This is a point worth noting. Prewar unions could not legally negotiate. Disputes were all-or-nothing affairs. After the war, unions and strikes reemerged simultaneously with a new framework for settling disputes. Japanese unions from 1946 until the present have viewed striking not as the last resort after the failure of bargaining but as an extension of diplomacy, a pressure tactic to be employed for short periods during negotiations to strengthen the hand of union representatives at the bargaining table.[33] The electric-power workers applied this pressure effectively, with a 5-minute "show-of-strength" blackout on October 18 while negotiations were stalemated, the threat of further, selective power shutdowns aimed at major factories, and finally, in late November, the decisive threat of a prolonged nationwide shutdown.

The defensive and indecisive management posture was a second noteworthy feature of the Densan dispute. Union leaders successfully pushed executives from the power companies to form a joint management body to negotiate on behalf of the entire industry; the companies could not divide and conquer by confining the issue to negotiations at the enterprise level. Both labor and third-party mediators criticized poor management preparation. The firms came to the negotiating table without a clear position, indeed with no clear awareness of the nature of the demands already submitted, and the union representatives ridiculed them in the early bargaining sessions.[34]

On November 30, 1946, the government and power industry agreed to implement the Densan wage structure as demanded by the union. Most unions at this time were too preoccupied with winning simple pay raises in a struggle for sheer survival to focus on long-run strategy. In this context, the Densan workers' achievement was considerable. This was a mode of payment based on a social rationality, the logic of labor more than of capital; it specified pay according to need with only slight attention paid to attendance and a company evaluation of ability. It was the labor version of the aborted bureaucratic plans for a livelihood wage conceived in the Welfare Ministry during the war. This link between wartime state planning and the union program was direct. The union's wage committee that designed the Densan structure drew upon the wartime experience of union supporters in the personnel sections of the power companies. These men saw a chance to give substance to the largely empty promise of wage regulations based on age and seniority, which they had helped implement on the company level, or to wartime research into the caloric intake needs of workers.[35] The Densan wage was a crisp, elegant structure, standing in sharp contrast to the cumbersome systems in use throughout the nation. It very quickly became a model for the demands of unions all over Japan, regardless of affiliation or ideology.

Before the Densan struggle was over, the Tōshiba union had gained a similar, although significantly less explicit, commitment to a "minimum wage based upon the cost of living," to be worked out in meetings of the management discussion council. During 1947, the air was full of such plans: wages based on calorie counts, on cost-of-living surveys, on price indices. By June 1947, the Kanagawa Prefectural Economic Recovery Council, which included representatives of Sanbetsu, Sōdōmei, and management, officially committed the prefecture to promoting "a rational wage system with a minimum wage based on the cost of living."[36] But the experiences of the region's steel and shipbuilding unions prove that commitments were easier made than implemented. Full adoption of Densan-style wage structures elsewhere was rare.

The Sōdōmei union at the NKK Kawasaki mill fought for a Densan-type wage for over a year, beginning in early 1947, just after the electric-power settlement. The union sought to scrap most allowances and incorporate them into an enlarged base wage. Management agreed in principle, but the composition of the base wage was the controversial issue here too. The union hoped to peg it almost entirely to family size and age, with a slight variable portion tied to job class. This was essentially the Densan pattern, although the NKK union from the outset was willing to countenance an incentive portion, in addition to this base wage. The settlement reached in March 1948 was a compromise. In addition to age (and in place of family size), management insisted upon the inclusion of seniority and an ability rating as factors in calculating the base wage. To some extent the union retreated from the initial insistence on a living wage based on need; all the same, the result was a wage closely linked, in its major component, to objective characteristics of age and seniority that were likely to rise with need.[37]

The shipbuilders in Zenzōsen did not fare so well. They too demanded a wage close to the Densan type in March 1947, just after MacArthur forbad the general strike. The national federation set out model demands, but negotiations took place separately at each company. All the member unions initially proposed the Zenzōsen model, in which the base wage was to consist of livelihood and ability portions, the average level was to slide with changes in a price index, and the livelihood portion was to reflect age alone. By the end of 1947, their failure was clear. The companies would agree only to an average (not minimum) wage for a typical worker, 35 years old with two children. Management insisted on and retained a free hand in distributing wages around the average, using criteria including rank and seniority to determine individual levels.[38]

Considered in historical perspective, the negotiations and disputes in the wake of the Densan victory established significant precedents even as they failed to attain wages modeled precisely upon the electric-power settlement. During countless meetings of management councils and frequent collective bargaining sessions, unions and companies drew a new bottom line, acceptable to both sides. First, the base wage, now usually calculated as a monthly payment and more secure than either revocable allowances or fluctuating output pay, would comprise the major portion of worker income. The average weight of the base portion quickly increased from a low of 17 percent of income in 1946, to 39 percent in 1948, to nearly 70 percent in 1949, and it rose gradually thereafter.[39] Second, the regular raise, written into company rule books during the war, would remain regular, as unions bargained each year over the level of this increment, now truly a "seniority pay raise." In 1946 or 1947, the significance of these regular raises, granted yearly or twice a year and usually good for a 5- to 10-per-cent hike, paled in the face of inflation and demands for 100- or 200-percent raises in the base wage. Yet, companies still gave out the regular seniority raise each year, in addition to the larger cost-of-living settlements, only now they discussed the matter with unions. Thus, the Tōshiba union, in January 1946, in its first company-wide demands, called for a 500-percent pay hike *and* a guarantee that "the rate of each periodic pay increase shall exceed 10 percent on average." The union continued to press for and gain at least this raise in following years.[40] The NKK Kawasaki union tried to go further, demanding that regular raises henceforth come twice a year (instead of annually) in 1947. Apparently this was denied.[41]

Finally, age, need, standards of living, prices, and inflation would now influence directly the setting of wages. Unions could not reject outright the traditional prewar management standards of ability and diligence; they did restrict their application considerably between 1946 and 1948. And standards seen as a legitimate basis for wage determination by both sides, especially seniority and experience, continued to play a major role, now within a framework set by negotiations, rather than through arbitrary management judgments. The mechanism by which these factors, old and new, would combine to set wages emerged during the labor offensive of 1946–1947. It came to be called the "base up" (*bāsu appu*). Unions did not win the minimum, livelihood, age-based wages of Densan; they did bargain to increase the level of the average "base wage," in its simplest form the total base-wage bill of a firm divided by total employees. They assumed that reasonably just distribution around this average, in accordance with age, seniority, and ability, would result in an approximation of the living wage they sought. Again, we find a wartime derivation for this practice, for the Welfare Ministry initially adopted the "base-wage" calculation as a means to control (actually limit) labor costs during the war. Rather than worry about controlling individual wages, they had asked companies to calculate the "average base" according to the Ministry's formula and had then placed limits on it. [42]

In the chaotic years of triple-digit inflation, unions called for a new round of "base-wage" negotiations as soon as they achieved a previous level. Between 1945 and 1948, the unions at Ishikawa-jima, Uraga, and Yokosen negotiated 7, 9, and 11 pay raises respectively. [43] Only after inflation subsided did the more familiar contemporary practice of annual "base-up" negotiations emerge. Before this could happen, however, unions would face a final management effort in the early 1950s to reject the base-up concept and restrict all increases in pay merely to the regular raise, making no additional allowances for inflation.

Piecework and incentive-pay schemes of all sorts flourished in prewar and even more so in wartime Japan. In addition to objective standards for the "livelihood" base wage, and higher levels of base pay, postwar unions also sought to prevent the return of insecure incentive pay. In this effort they enjoyed a measure of success. At some companies, the category of output or incentive pay vanished entirely for a time. This was true of both Tōshiba and Yokosen, where managers had abandoned their longstanding commitment to incentive pay in the summer of 1945. At Tōshiba, a new form of pay-by-result did not return for two years. The firm only used a base wage and various allowances to calculate wages. At Yokohama, the incentive-pay category remained, but its character changed. Since the company was hardly producing, it could not reasonably calculate this portion on the basis of output. The yard abolished the "output factor" in setting output-pay levels, and each worker received a sum reflecting attendance and a job classification. And, in cases where managers persisted in offering an output-based wage portion, the unions were often able to win a guaranteed minimum level, something they had sought but seldom achieved before the war. The Ishikawajima union in 1946 successfully demanded that the firm's "efficiency payment" (*nōritsu kyū*) be a guaranteed minimum of 50 percent of the base wage.[44] Japan's major business newspaper, the *Nihon keizai shimbun*, was thus led to observe, in August 1946, that, as the result of both union pressure and the dismal business prospects of many firms, "during this period [winter 1946], the Japanese wage structure, which had efficiency wages (*nōritsu chingin*) as its basic principle, collapsed, and a so-called living-wage structure emerged.[45]

By 1947, it became clear that the concept of output pay was down but not out. Managers nationwide began to push for renewed links between production and wages. This drive coincided with the broader retreat of radical labor, and managers often succeeded in reestablishing the output link. In 1947 and 1948, the shipbuilding unions in the Zenzōsen federation found themselves on the defensive, as managers were able to increase the weight given to efficiency payments and, in some cases, reintroduce individual output factors into the calculation.[46] At Tōshiba, also, in mid-1947, the company introduced "production incentive payments" amounting to 36 percent of total income in the average case. Managers were determined to relate pay to the total output of the firm, and, through continued negotiations with the union, they gradually increased this incentive portion to half the average wage in early 1949.[47]

Two crucial factors distinguish the widespread production-incentive systems of the late 1940s from the incentive pay of the prewar and war years. First, the connection between individual productivity and the level of output pay was usually indirect after the war, so the issue of rate-setting or rate-cutting was less significant to workers. In most firms, including Tōshiba and NKK, production quotas were set at the factory level, unlike the individual or small group quotas common before the war. The issue here for managers was less to speed up the exertions of individual workers than to establish a link between the total output of the firm and the total company wage bill. This would keep total wages in line with a firm's income and ability to pay. The output premium for the entire factory or company would depend upon total output, but, in distributing this to individuals, the company usually calculated the production incentive on the basis of attendance or simply gave it out in direct proportion to the base wage. The more indirect and secure these payments became for individuals, the less antagonism they aroused.

Individual performance occasionally did enter the output calculation. At Yokohama Dock, beginning in February 1947, a periodic grading of each worker was used to help determine his share of the total output premium. A class 9 grading was given to the average skilled worker. Supervisor evaluation could raise or lower this by 4 grades, and each grade would raise or lower the output payment 10 percent. In this case, the second important new feature of incentive wages in the postwar era served to restrict the potential for abuse: Unions played a role in the design and implementation of incentive or output wages. The Yokohama system was devised by the Management Discussion Council, and the union retained a voice in setting both standard grade levels and the high and low grades possible for individual workers.[48] At Uraga, the company agreed to allow a special labor-management committee to oversee implementation of a new system of output pay introduced in March 1947, and, at NKK, the Kawasaki union demanded a more secure version of the incentive wage when a drop in output in September 1947 threatened to eliminate entirely the output wage introduced just six months earlier. A compromise of June 1948 guaranteed half the output pay, regardless of actual production levels.[49]

Unions did back-pedal considerably on the issue of output pay after 1947. Under pressure of the deflationary policies of late 1949, companies including NKK squeezed individual pay envelopes by manipulating factory quotas, but, on the whole, this issue had been defused. Pay by result was no longer the unstable reward that had provoked such bitter complaints from Shibaura workers in the 1920s and even during the war.

The bonus ranks with the base and incentive wages as an element of Japanese wage practice transformed by the presence of labor unions. Beginning in 1946, unions without exception began to bargain each June and December over the size of the "bonus" payment. In the context of ongoing, concurrent struggles for a livelihood base wage, unions came to define the bonus as part of the management obligation to guarantee a secure livelihood. Changes in the bonus present a microcosmic summary of the whole spectrum of changes that came to early postwar labor relations. Unions and managers established bonus levels through the Management Councils or collective bargaining. Workers no longer received a tiny fraction of the staff amount; all employees took home either a uniform sum or a uniform multiple of their monthly base wage. Managers were no longer free to discontinue or reduce the bonus during bad times; indeed they had a special obligation to help workers in such periods, according to the unions. The bonus was no longer a revocable form of profit-sharing. But, finally, the new definition of a bonus as part of a livelihood wage was not engraved in stone. Labor would have to defend its definition during the management revival to come.

For about two years, the labor movement made substantial progress in imposing on management its version of a Japanese style wage. The labor ideal was a more or less pure "livelihood" wage, calculated and paid in accord with need. Unions sought livable minimum levels for workers of entry-level age, and they tried to insure continued living wages by insisting on the priority of age, seniority, and family size in subsequent raises. They sought to reduce or eliminate the significance of output pay, and make those portions remaining as secure as possible (and thus not very effective as incentives). They also narrowed the gap in compensation for white- and blue-collar work, by negotiating for uniform bonuses and monthly wages for all employees, as well as a unified structure of base wages for all.

Seniority as part of the wage calculus remained. As they had since the 1920s, wages remained a function not of the skills a man brought to the job, but of a complex variety of factors depending in some measure on rank and tenure in the enterprise. The great postwar change was the inclusion of a labor voice in defining these factors, and, because of labor demands, for the first time a man's economic needs as a member of society entered the wage equation.

The Densan wage was the least equivocal example. The union dubbed it a "socialist wage," for it varied according to need, according to the "logic of labor and not of capital." Even seniority was less important than age and family size in the Densan case. Such unqualified triumphs were few, and labor was to retreat a good bit by the mid-1950s, but many of the practices associated with the livelihood wage would prove durable.

DEMANDING PERMANENT JOBS: THE IMPOSSIBLE DREAM

Job security in short order naturally emerged as a union goal every bit as important as wage security. It remained far more elusive. The security implied in the management ideology of paternal care had been a fair-weather promise before the war, and it remained so in 1945. As economic activity plunged at war's end, companies quickly turned to mass dismissals.

Millions lost their jobs. No firm could long maintain its swollen wartime force with the economy operating at 20 to 30 percent of wartime levels. In this context, the decision of several major unions to place their new and untested strength on the line in defense of jobs defies the "rational" explanation of an observer accustomed to the workings of the North American or Western European labor market. Why did unions not take a more realistic, attainable position and seek to define a framework, based perhaps on seniority, for the orderly layoff and eventual rehiring of workers? How could the Tōshiba union possibly expect to defend 35,000 jobs (compared to a wartime peak of 42,000), when 40 percent of the plant was damaged by bombing, the firm's considerable foreign assets were frozen, and monthly wages totaled 70 percent of the value of goods produced?[50]

Characteristics of union organization and wage determination with historical roots influenced union behavior. For an individual whose pay was linked in some measure to his seniority and status with a firm, firing not only took away a job, but it condemned him to lower wages with his next employer. He could not take his seniority and rank with him. For unions that limited membership to employees in a factory, and had not yet built inclusive national federations, loss of a job meant loss of a union member. An "unemployed member" of the Tōshiba Employees Union was a contradiction in terms. Fear of starvation completes the explanation for this behavior. Japan lacked an effective public-welfare system, and, in 1945 or 1946, the threat of unemployment was literally a threat to survival. Furthermore, many workers believed, with good reason, that executives had chosen to "sabotage" recovery and limit production so as to hoard valuable raw materials. Corollary to this belief was the conviction that layoffs were unnecessary. Work could be had if managers would stop hoarding and start producing. The production-control tactic derived from such logic, as did the decision to resist firings. In addition, there were no rules for layoff and rehiring; firing was an all-or-nothing affair, an attack on the individual's present livelihood, his future earning power, and the union organization.

One precocious group of workers at the NKK Tsurumi shipyard even resisted the first wave of firings just after the surrender, before a union had been formed. In October 1945, 4 out of a group of 524 workers dismissed at Tsurumi decided to protest. Experienced prewar labor activists seeking to rebuild the union movement quickly found these men and helped them form a struggle group and, in short order, a union preparation committee. Before a threatened strike could materialize, the surprised company revoked the firing order.[51] But, more often in the immediate post-surrender months, managers could and did dismiss their workers, especially draftee labor and recent wartime recruits. Scholars estimate that 4.1 million people lost their jobs between August and October 1945, at which time the number of unemployed, including returned soldiers, stood at roughly 13 million by one estimate.[52]

Dismissals did not cease with the formation and growth of unions in the following months, but the fear of provoking labor did lead to some hesitance. As 1946 wore on, a good many firms still felt themselves saddled with far too many workers. The unions, for their part, were gaining confidence and had come to believe that management sabotage was the enemy. A showdown over jobs was inevitable. The two showcase job disputes of 1946 were those of the railway workers in the public sector and the Tōshiba union in private industry.

The bureaucratic managers of the Japan National Railways (JNR) announced in July 1946 their long-range intention to dismiss 130,000 of their 540,000 employees, with 72,000 firings to come immediately. But, when the railway union appeared truly capable of stopping the trains in a national railway strike called for September 15, the Railway Bureau revoked the firing order in a dramatic last-minute announcement on September 14.

The Tōshiba union sought to follow up on this sucess and win for private industry the same promise of "full employment" (no firings) attained by JNR workers. When the Yoshida Government finally announced an end to government war payments in August, the union realized dismissals were inevitable. The company had not laid off any workers since the war ended, relying on attrition to reduce the work force from 43,000 to 32,000, and hoping to convert successfully and quickly to peacetime production of essential consumer goods. So long as the government payments flowed in, Tōshiba could handle its 1.3-billion-yen debt and maintain its work force. But, at the August 14 meeting of the Management Discussion Council, the company announced that, in view of the end to war payments, it had no choice but to reduce the force. No numbers or dates were announced, and the union sought to preempt management by building a strike organization and flexing its muscles. It called for a 24-hour strike on August 20, effectively carried out by 17,000 of the 32,000 employees, and it led a well-publicized demonstration of 2,000 workers in front of the Imperial Palace in late August.

Tōshiba still had not announced any specific dismissals by mid-September, and the Management Discussion Council was deadlocked. On September 14, the union declared its intention to strike on October 1 for 3 simple demands: a vow of no firings, a minimum livelihood wage, and formation of a democratic recovery council at the company. Management refused, and a 55-day strike began. The union held together. Over 90 percent of the workers honored the strike. Mediation efforts progressed slowly, while, outside the factory, union activity and local support were reminiscent of the community-based disputes of twenty-five years earlier, just after World War I. On November 26, the Tōshiba union gained a settlement close to its initial demands. Management pledged that

> the company and employees will give their utmost efforts to actively raise production, and the company will absolutely not fire anyone for reasons such as "rationalization." The company will absolutely not fire any union members because they are union members, unless they have broken company regulations. The company will consult with the union concerning the firing of any workers with poor attendance, or any workers who fail to carry out duties, or who violate company rules.[53]

Tōshiba was the most important but not the only union at a private firm to demand such a "no-dismissal" vow. The Sanbetsu Congress pushed for these same 3 promises through other affiliated unions. In Kanagawa, 12 other unions, with about 6,500 members, raised similar demands in the fall of 1946, and most gained some form of a pledge not to dismiss workers in the near future.[54]

At Tōshiba, at JNR, and at many smaller factories, the labor movement tried to lay the permanent job as one cornerstone in its remaking of the Japanese structure of labor relations. On the surface, the unions had succeeded, but "no firing" promises were only as strong as the unions that enforced them. Without recovery and expanded production, jobs were not safe, and recovery did not come soon. What actually followed the pledge not to fire, at Tōshiba, JNR, and throughout the country, was a cold war on the job front. Managers were constrained from reducing personnel as they wished, for a time. Any assessment of managerial behavior in Japan since the war must to some extent credit the experience of these years with generating the commonly cited reluctance to fire. But, in 1946, such reluctance was certainly not yet greater than the determination eventually to reduce work forces and break the union hold on jobs. The basic tensions remained, and the decisive showdown at Tōshiba and in most of Japan came three years later, in a climate far less favorable to labor.

A desire for more than simple wage and job security links together all aspects of the labor offensive of these years. Workers sought what had been denied them for decades: a measure of equality as citizens and as employees. This equality had an economic dimension, of course, expressed in demands for a living wage on a par with staff employees as well as demands for secure jobs. It also had political and symbolic dimensions, seen in demands for participation in management discussion councils and for reform of the status system. The desire for respect, so much a part of worker ideology since the turn of the twentieth century, was present and powerful in 1946 and 1947. While unions gained support and strength to the extent they helped members realize these desires, the value placed upon membership in society's mainstream (the middle class) and higher status in the firm was not conducive to a sustained, class-conscious movement. In the following years, a combination of timely management concession, hard-nosed bargaining, and union-busting was sufficient to divide the labor movement, isolate its radical wing, and reconstruct a powerful capitalist economy built upon a remodeled, management version of Japanese labor relations.

TEN

The Management Revision

The third year of American occupation marked a shift in the political and economic climate; new winds blew, conducive to a management revival. Reform of the Labor Union Law together with the stringent economic policies of the Dodge line provided an opportunity and a stimulus to managers unhappy with events since 1945; from 1949 to 1953 a period of bitter conflict resulted. Three issues dominated these fierce, occasionally violent struggles. Most important by far, managers sought to retake control of the work place. This involved revising collective contracts, reforming the labor-management discussion councils, and breaking the back of radical unions. Once successful, managers could turn to the crucial issues of pay and jobs. In wage negotiations they denied any obligation to grant yearly pay raises sufficient to maintain or raise standards of living. Finally, companies retreated from their promises, extended in times of weakness to gain temporary peace, not to dismiss large numbers of workers. By the end of the first postwar decade, big business in Japan had won major battles on all three fronts. The labor relationship further evolved in a context of domination by management, and the intensity of conflict subsided. The so-called Japanese employment system "discovered" by James Abegglen at about this time had finally assumed its contemporary guise. The union presence insured a system far more predictable and favorable to workers than that of the interwar or war years, but the management revival sharply distinguished this from its early postwar incarnation.

RETAKING CONTROL

The absence of any national association of employers was one clear indication of the disarray of the capitalist elite just after the war. From 1930 to 1942, the National Federation of Industrial Organizations (Zensanren) served as an effective "peak organization" pressing its version of the business interest on labor issues upon the government. Zensanren dissolved under official pressure during the war, but the challenge posed by government intervention in wartime did not approach that of the labor movement after the war. Employers in postwar Japan acutely felt the need to reorganize. In the winter of 1946, sentiment favoring creation of a national organization to deal with labor began to build among leading capitalists in the Japan Industrial Club. SCAP saw the matter differently. Still strongly committed to standing the labor movement firmly on two feet, the Americans rejected as premature a business proposal to found a remodeled version of Zensanren. Management had to content itself with creation of the Kantō Managers Association, formed in 1946 as a nominally regional group, but strategically placed in the Kantō region, the center of political action and an area of great prewar Zensanren strength.

The Americans changed their approach here as elsewhere in 1947, and they gave their blessing to the rebuilding of an employers' organization. In August, the Kantō group became a loose national federation of management organizations, and this in turn evolved into the still powerful Federation of Japanese Employers' Associations (Nikkeiren) in August 1948. The organization was built of 9 regional and 23 industrial associations representing virtually all Japan's major enterprises.[1] From the start, Nikkeiren and its predecessor groups recognized in principle the right of labor to organize, but they consistently sought to restrict the power and scope of unions. Nikkeiren emerged as the coordinator of a management agenda for reform of labor relations.

A series of Nikkeiren and government statements in 1948 and 1949 launched the offensive to regain control of the enterprise. The management discussion councils naturally came under attack. By June 1948, 44 percent (15,055) of all unions were participating in such councils, and 80 percent of all collective contracts spelled out terms for their operation. The great majority had substantial decision-making powers. They took up personnel issues and discussed production plans, disposition of company assets, and the overall direction of the firm. Nikkeiren issued a strong paper "On Securing Management Authority" (*keieiken*) in May 1948. The group criticized the "excessive" powers granted management discussion councils; labor had gained an unacceptable degree of "management authority" over the personnel and even the financial decisions of the firm. Renegotiation of collective bargaining contracts was a prerequisite to reforming the councils, for the contracts gave the councils as well as the unions their considerable power. The government soon offered its support in a December 1948 "notice" (*tsūchō*) on Democratic Labor Relations which pointed out the "excesses" of existing contracts, encouraged their renegotiation, and called for greater management authority and limits on the scope of union activity. Subsequent Nikkeiren statements elaborated on the management stance. In September 1949, the group issued a call to "Establish New Labor Relations." Its theme was the need to reestablish management authority and work-place hierarchy.[2]

The slogans were now in place. It remained for managers of individual companies to give them substance. As the Nikkeiren policy merely echoed and reinforced existing sentiments in firms nationwide, a well-coordinated response was forthcoming. The revised Labor Union Law of late 1948 strengthened the hand of managers. Although changes ostensibly were made to encourage union openness and independence, they in fact put unions on the defensive. Full-time union officials could no longer take salaries from the company, and the separate youth and women's groups, a source of radical energy in most unions, were forced to disband as "discriminatory" organizations.[3] Unions naturally defended the privileges won in 1946 or 1947; the struggle over all these issues often lasted several years and only subsided with the Red Purge and the replacement of radical unions by cooperative "second unions."

The battle was joined throughout the Keihin region and the nation in the spring and summer of 1949. At Tōshiba, at the ship-building firms, and at NKK, management uniformly proposed contract revisions and announced its intention to abandon the previous contracts when they expired. The unions rejected the new contracts with equal unanimity, but the outlook for labor was discouraging. One early defeat came at the Mitsubishi shipyard in Nagasaki. By December 1949, the union there signed a new contract which converted the management council from a decision-making to an advisory body and restricted union activities within the shipyard. Unions at the Keihin shipyards and steel mills and at Tōshiba did not capitulate so readily, and the so-called "no-contract era" (*mukyōyaku jidai*) of 2 to 4 years' duration began at these and other firms.

The settlements eventually reached were no better than at Nagasaki. At NKK, workers at the Tsurumi mill with its Sanbetsu connection fared no better than those at the Kawasaki mill with its Sōdōmei ties. By 1951, both unions had joined a new steel-union federation within Sōhyō, a national federation which emerged out of the 1949–1950 destruction of Sanbetsu. While Sōhyō led a "Labor Contract Movement" in 1952 against unfavorable new contracts, it enjoyed little success.[4] The Kawasaki union settled in June 1951, accepting an emasculated management council, and the Tsurumi workers gave way in late 1952. The Tsurumi settlement is well documented, and the contrast with the 1947 contract, concluded on union terms, neatly summarizes the transition of these years. The 1947 contract guaranteed freedom to take part in union activities on company time and to use company facilities. It required that union officials be treated no differently from other workers in matters of pay and promotion. It bound management to obtain union agreement (*gōi*) for all firings and job shifts. The 1952 contract outlawed political activity on company property, limited the number of full-time union officials, and ended the policy of company wage payments to union officials. Only reduced wages would be paid for recognized union activity on company time. The contract also limited the privilege of posting union announcements within the factory and replaced the clause requiring union "agreement" on personnel decisions with one pledging merely to consult the union on such matters. The management discussion council was replaced by a labor relations discussion council with limited powers and a narrower range of items to discuss. Finally, the contract established a mechanism to deal with worker grievances. The union of the 1950s was to respect management authority and function within a framework designed by the firm. The partnership in decision-making was ended, and a new partnership in consultation emerged, in which the union understood that management had the final word.[5]

The drive over several years to revise contracts and eliminate powerful management councils was linked intimately to the concurrent effort to destroy the Sanbetsu Congress and its constituent unions, nurture more cooperative unions at the enterprise level, and prevent these from building powerful industrial federations. The gradual destruction of the "old" Tōshiba union was one of the most notorious early examples. The attack on the union came during the decisive phase of the prolonged dispute over dismissals, covered in detail below. In a tactic typical of the era, managers quietly encouraged a group of moderate workers, unhappy with the intransigence and the Communist ties of the union, to form a new union (in some other cases called a second union). Tōshiba immediately concluded a contract with the new group and recognized it as the sole bargaining representative of the workers. These new unions, at Tōshiba and elsewhere, invariably established no links at first to Sanbetsu or other industrial federations. They later moved toward loose industrial federation with other moderate unions founded in similar circumstances. The "Red Purge" of the summer of 1950, launched by the Japanese government with SCAP approval, began in the public sector, but, by the fall, it reached private industry and struck an often decisive blow at "old unions" throughout the nation. Tōshiba fired 125 suspected Communists in the old union in October, and the new union issued a half-hearted denunciation in which it was quick to point out that it harbored no Communists. The old union was only able to organize a half-day strike in one of the plants where it retained support.

A complex triangular relationship ensued for a time, as management in fact bargained with the old union in plants where it was still powerful, all the while seeking to build up the new union. The two unions, fiercely antagonistic at first, eventually moved toward reconciliation, for the new union had to establish some legitimacy to win over a majority of employees, and it therefore took a reasonably hard line in some negotiations with the company. The old union, defensive and anxious to survive, seized on such hopeful signs to propose unified action and joint demands. Gradually the two unions moved closer to each other, and, in February 1951, a bit less than two years after the split, they formed a new, united Tōshiba Employees Union.[6]

With minor variations, similar stories unfolded at NKK, in the Keihin shipyards, and throughout Japan between 1949 and 1953. Sometimes the old union disappeared entirely or diminished to a small faction that never reconciled itself to the second union. In other cases, such as the Zenzōsen unions, the Red Purge and the election of new union leaders brought about a change in the character of an existing union without formation of a second union. The consequences for the Sanbetsu Congress were fatal; it finally dissolved in 1958 but was never again a powerful organization after 1950. In its place emerged Sōhyō (the General Council of Trade Unions of Japan) as the major national federation, and in the steel and electric industry new industrial federations (Tekkō rōren and Denki rōren) were formed within Sōhyō, drawing support from the new unions at NKK and Tōshiba.[7]

The fall of Sanbetsu was not simply a result of management pressure and the Red Purge. Within the national headquarters and at the local level, discontent with the sometimes heavy-handed Communist Party control of union policy provided both SCAP and company managers a corps of dissident union members willing to support new unions. The "democratic" movement emerged within Sanbetsu in 1948, at American instigation to be sure, but the movement gained momentum as it drew the allegiance of the Sanbetsu dissidents. These "democratic cells" (*mindō*) within Sanbetsu formed the core of the new unions or second unions of 1949 and after. Just as the Sanbetsu democratic cells were not simply pawns of SCAP, the new Sōhyō federation and its members did not become the apolitical, cooperative organizations the Americans and the conservative Japanese elite hoped for. Focusing on both wage demands, and the political issues of rearmament and the peace treaty, many new unions showed surprising signs of independence as early as 1952.[8] By 1953, industrial federations within and without Sōhyō were beginning to work together to coordinate wage demands, clearing a path to the joint spring offensives of the late 1950s and beyond.[9]

Managers between 1948 and the early 1950s retook the initiative in the labor relationship through contract disputes and a tough strategy of union-busting. Organized labor participation in, or control over, management decisions was now just a goal, no longer a reality. Unions remained a force to be respected in the 1950s, but they never transformed loose industry-wide coordination into actual bargaining at the industry level. The center of gravity in the union movement remained at the level of the individual firm. The beginnings of effective industrial organization in the electric-power industry and a few other cases in 1946 and 1947 indicate that workers in Japan were not by their very "Japanese" nature incapable of transcending allegiances to a firm; the early postwar enterprise unions were politically radical and confrontation-minded to a fault. The emergence and persistence of moderate enterprise unions was in large part the result of intense government and management pressure and manipulation of unions. Yet, the enterprise union would not have proved a durable structure if it had given back all the gains made in wage and job security. It protected sufficiently the benefits of "citizenship" in the firm and society to defuse the volatility of the early postwar labor relationship, even as managers vigorously reworked the wage and job settlements of 1945 to 1947.

THE WAGE SETTLEMENT

Buoyed by early signs of success and official support in the rewriting of contracts and retaking of "management authority," employers also sought to move away from the prevailing pattern of frequent, large pay increases and livelihood wages. On the national level, Nikkeiren took the lead on behalf of management. In position papers of April and September 1949, the group called for the elimination of livelihood wages paid without reference to the quality of an individual's labor. It suggested using job classifications to set wages in accord with the contribution of the worker, in imitation of American practice.[10] The job wage never caught on, except as an acceptably up-to-date nominal substitute for rank and seniority classifications, but the move away from the livelihood wage proceeded. From its birth in 1950, the new Sōhyō federation defended the livelihood wage against Nikkeiren reform proposals, and the organization gained prominence as the opponent of Nikkeiren on wage issues. The sparring of these two associations provided the context within which factory unions and managers fought the decisive battles over wage policies.

Even before Nikkeiren enshrined the concept in its "Three Wage Principles" of 1954, the goal of managers was to peg wage settlements to the profitability of the firm and gains in productivity rather than inflation and standards of living. Under the Dodge line in 1949, managers enjoyed fair success in this effort for the first time since war's end, for there was often literally no money to offer. Government credit sources dried up, and commercial banks would not lend to firms seen to be granting excessive wage settlements. One- or two-month deferrals of wage payment were common, and labor unions could only demand prompt payment of existing wages.[11] In 1949, large pay increases were out of the question; unions had their hands full preventing wage cuts. In shipbuilding, the Ishikawajima and Uraga unions both pushed for age-based minimum wages in the livelihood mold without success, while the NKK workers in Kawasaki failed to win any increases in their base wage. Managers here were following the spirit of the Nikkeiren paper of April 1949, which called for repudiation of the livelihood-wage concept.[12]

The boom of Korean War procurements of 1950 also brought renewed inflation, and a determination to push for higher wage settlements. As before, most unions phrased their demands in terms of livelihood need and called for substantial increases in the base wage. More radical groups such as the old Tōshiba union demanded a pay increase of a fixed amount across the board, rather than a percentage increase. This would give the younger, lower-paid workers a proportionally larger increase and, in effect, raise the minimum pay level. Managers were usually able to reject such demands and link some of the wage increase to increased output. NKK managers accepted a union call for a 2,000-yen average pay hike, but incorporated only 400 yen into the base wage. They offered the remainder as a factory-wide incentive portion, payable when output reached a minimum level.[13]

A standard pattern in the timing and organization of wage bargaining was beginning to emerge out of such give and take. During the first three postwar years, inflation had been so great that wage disputes followed one another in a rush; 2 or 3 increases at a plant in less than a year were common. In 1949 and 1950, the issue of dismissals and the defense of jobs took precedence over wages, and the new pattern was not readily visible. But, beginning around 1950, most unions organized just one annual base-wage offensive, usually in spring. This was true of the shipbuilding unions, of NKK, and of Tōshiba in 1950 and each year thereafter. Furthermore, the industrial federations within Sōhyō, such as steel or electric manufacturing, or even those outside it, such as Zenzōsen, started actively coordinating the demands of its member unions. The leaders hoped to revive the momentum toward industry-wide wage bargaining which had stalled after 1947. While these hopes went unrealized, union experience with the yearly wage offensive gradually led to more sophisticated, better coordinated spring bargaining seasons. In 1953, 6 major industrial federations (metal, electric, steel, shipbuilding, automobiles, and electric wire) initiated talks aimed at building a coordinated, multi-industry wage offensive.[14]

Of equal significance was the emergence of a predictable pattern in the content and dynamics of wage negotiations. Beginning in the 1950s, a regular pattern of yearly bargaining invariably produced some mixture of the so-called "base-up" and the regular raise. The measure of victory in wage confrontations of the early 1950s was the mix between these two distinct forms of pay increase. A "base-up" was a raise in the total wage commitment of a firm. It raised the level of the entering wage as well as all other wages, one of the major attractions for unions seeking to improve wages for the younger, often radical members. It lifted the total wage *structure*. A regular raise (*teiki shōkyū*) was usually smaller. It increased a firm's wage bill only slightly, if at all. In a regular raise, the pay of each *individual* went up by an agreed proportion (with some variations for evaluation of performance), but the entire structure remained at the same level. A firm would not pay any more than before if retirees and newly hired were in proper balance. Considered in graphic terms, the base-up "lifted" the wage curve, increasing the area underneath it (the wage cost), whereas the regular raise only moved individuals along the curve, leaving the wage curve untouched and the cost to the firm unchanged.

Clearly a large base-up settlement plus a regular raise was the labor goal; managers naturally favored the regular raise by itself. A base-up had "livelihood" overtones that the regular raise did not. The great irony of course is that, for prewar workers, a *guaranteed* yearly pay hike, that is, the regular raise, was an ideal demanded but seldom gained. Systematic base-up settlements had been out of the question. The management custom had been to offer selective, inconsistent pay hikes; workers had sought a universal regular raise. Now the prewar labor "maximum" was the minimum settlement acceptable to a union. Indeed, for a union to gain only a regular raise was to admit defeat. Such defeats were not uncommon in the 1950s, but even a defeat was an advance over the situation ten or fifteen years earlier. Since experienced workers could recall those days, a historical perspective helps explain their acceptance of such "defeats."

Nikkeiren and Sōhyō locked horns over the theoretical issues in a war of words from 1952 to 1954; managers and unions fought over the details in a series of bitter disputes at the company level. Sōhyō set out to win an explicit livelihood wage with its bold wage platform, prepared to coincide with the spring wage negotiations of 1952. It rejected the Consumer Price Index as a guideline in formulating wage demands and offered its own calculation of a minimum cost of living as a more accurate reflection of the consumption patterns and needs of workers. Sōhyō urged its unions to demand an average of 25,000 yen per month. This was the wage derived from the new calculation, dubbed the "market-basket formula."[15]

Nikkeiren issued a series of opinions between 1952 and 1954 as it coordinated resistance to the market-basket approach. In June 1953, the management lobby produced a "Basic Wage Opinion": Wages must reflect the business situation of a firm and the efficiency of workers. Nikkeiren reiterated this in February of 1954 with its famous "Three Wage Principles": 1. Wage settlements must reflect a firm's ability to pay. 2. They must be consistent with national economic needs. 3. They must support the growth of a strong private-enterprise system. More concretely, Nikkeiren called upon managers to offer regular raises rather than base-up settlements wherever possible.

The Nikkeiren position in fact ratified the detailed settlements already being worked out during these years; the management push for regular raises limited by the ability to pay began in 1950, and the Sōhyō market-basket formula was in large measure a reaction to it. The NKK steel union demanded a regular raise for the first time in 1950. Prior to this, demands for a hefty base-up took priority. The company had always offered the regular raise in addition, but this increase of roughly 5 percent did not draw major union attention until the base-up itself came under attack.

Each year thereafter, the Kawasaki union would demand both a base-up and a regular raise. In 1953, the union mobilized effectively, and it gained an average 8-percent base-up and 8-percent regular raise. In 1952 and 1954, it did not fare as well, and NKK workers had to accept a regular raise alone. This came to roughly a 10-percent raise each time.[16] At Tōshiba, beginning in 1952, the regular raise was also at the center of wage bargaining. The union obtained a 7.5-percent average regular raise that year, but in 1953 it settled for 6 percent. Of this, 2 percent was to be a fixed raise for all, the remaining 4 percent an average subject to individual evaluations. An even greater retreat came in 1954. Workers accepted a mere 4.7-percent raise, of which a nearly invisible 0.5 percent was to be fixed.[17] The shipbuilders also saw the previously separate base-up and regular raises consolidated into a single, usually lower regular raise between 1950 and 1954.

The Sōhyō market-basket-wage concept never took root in practice. The electric-power industry, targeted to lead the charge and build on the Densan achievement of six years earlier, in fact swallowed a revision in the Densan structure which gave greater weight to factors subject to company evaluation. The pay levels achieved by unions throughout Japan were far below the ideal levels derived with the market-basket formula. The shipbuilders federation, in 1954, decided their ideal market-basket monthly wage, for a man with a family of 3.5 people, should be 23,781 yen, but the individual unions settled in all cases for 18,000 to 19,000.[18] In the same year, the Tōshiba union demanded a 15-percent raise based on the market-basket model before accepting the 4.7-percent raise noted above.

These wage disputes of the early 1950s together resulted in a major victory for management. The logic of capital, a wage reflecting the ability to pay, prevailed over the logic of the labor movement, a wage according to need. The victory was not won easily. The years 1951 through 1953 are remembered as a time of especially intense confrontation in mines and auto factories, as well as in the firms studied here, and wages were often at issue. Unions invariably resisted when a firm suddenly announced it would grant

only a small regular raise instead of the substantial base-up of previous years. Even the shipbuilding workers, considerably less
radical throughout the postwar era than either Tōshiba employees or the men at NKK's Tsurumi mill, rose to offer a stiff challenge when management announced suspension of the base increase.
Ishikawajima workers called strikes in 1951, 1952, and 1953; they
were able to win small increases in the wage base as well as regular
raises each time. Only in 1954 did managers succeed in suspending
the base-up entirely. The Yokosen shipbuilders acted with similar
determination.[19] The shipbuilding unions used these strikes to
wring concessions while bargaining took place, but, whereas Densan workers using similar tactics in 1946 were able to move in step
throughout the electric-power industry, few industrial federations
of the 1950s could prevent a weak member union from reaching a
quick settlement, even while further strikes were planned. This
happened quite often in the steel industry; the NKK Kawasaki
union more than once found itself out on a limb after the Yahata
or Fuji ironworkers had climbed back and settled. At this point
they were vulnerable to the company admonition that a strike
would only benefit their competitors and hurt the long-run interests of both labor and management at NKK.[20]

Managers also made gains in many of these same disputes in
their fight to return efficiency to the heart of the wage calculus
and reduce the importance of factors such as age or family size.
The average amount of a pay increase, whether determined by a
base-up or regular raise, was always one important issue in wage
negotiations. The factors used in setting individual pay raises
above or below the average was another. Unions defended the
need principle at the individual level by calling for "objective"
criteria, especially age and family size, as the basis for setting
raises. They sought to limit the use of performance evaluations
carried out by supervisors and restrict the variation in the average pay hike resulting from high or low performance ratings. The
guidelines issued by Zenzōsen in 1954 called on its member
unions to reject the use of a "grading factor" (*seiseki keisū*) in
distribution of wage hikes. Tōshiba workers, in 1955, sought to

revise the standards used in giving out the regular raise, and the NKK union tried to skew the distribution of wage hikes in favor of lower-paid, younger, entry-level workers.[21] One common tactic supported by Sōhyō was to call for a guaranteed minimum in the pay increase, either an amount or a percent, with an additional portion to be added in accord with subjective evaluation but to deviate little from an average decided in advance. Unions dubbed this the "fixed-raise-plus-alpha" formula, and it fared better than the market-basket wage.

Managers, on the other hand, especially those with prewar experience, longed for the days when their discretion alone had determined who would receive pay hikes, who would not, and how far above or below the average these would be. Yasue Masao of the Yokosen personnel office maintained this attitude even in 1980 as he criticized both wartime regulations and the postwar unions for transforming a rational system of selective raises, carefully tailored to motivate the workers, into a rigid, irrational system marked by "excessive egalitarianism" (*akubyōdō*), in which everyone took home a pay raise, deserving or not.[22]

In fact, the outcome of the disputes between men like Yasue and the unions was not so rigid or irrational as he claims; performance as a criterion slowly crept back into wage calculations. By the early 1950s, well over 90 percent of major Japanese firms used factors such as ability ratings, job classification, attendance, or supervisor evaluations, *in addition to* the Densan-type, livelihood factors of age and family size, in setting the base wage and giving out raises. Most often a part of the yearly pay raise would be "automatic" or objective, linked directly to age and seniority, and the remainder would depend upon an evaluation that took ability, attendance, and performance into account.[23] In the evolution of this system, more subjective than that found in 1945 to 1947, but more objective than anything of prewar vintage, seniority emerged as a factor acceptable to both sides. Managers preferred it to age or family size, for it usually bore some relation to efficiency. Workers preferred it to potentially arbitrary evaluations, for it was objective and predictable.

Principles of efficiency versus need were also at stake in disputes over bonuses and output pay during the management revival of the early 1950s. Nikkeiren, in 1950, declared that bonuses were fundamentally distinct from wages. They were passed out at management discretion; they should not be subject to collective bargaining. Further, they should be linked to increased productivity and efficiency.[24] Here Nikkeiren and company managers were less successful than they had been with the regular raise. Labor defended its interest successfully. One suspects, indeed, that managers gave way on the bonus issue in order to concentrate all efforts on the concurrent disputes over raising the wage base and granting regular raises. Simultaneous union victories on bonuses and defeats on the "base-up" are found in several cases. For unions, a healthy bonus softened the pain of defeat; for the company, this was a less expensive battle to lose. Commonly, a union unable to win its spring base-up demand would announce the "conversion" of that effort into a June "bonus struggle" and carry on vigorously.

Despite Nikkeiren's stand, the bonus remained an issue for collective bargaining. Major unions applied consistent pressure to gain semiannual bonuses with little reference to economic conditions. Shipbuilding workers at the Keihin yards threatened and carried out strikes almost each year between 1950 and 1955 over bonuses. They usually gained an average semiannual bonus of 1 month's pay; and these 2 extra months' pay each year became a normal part of the system as far as workers were concerned. Companies seldom could reduce the standard, expected levels.[25] As the years passed, bonuses took on a life of their own. Banks came to structure housing loans to include a large "bonus-time" repayment twice a year, as well as a monthly installment. The same institutions lending money to a corporation thus had an interest in continued bonus payments to the workers. Unions also gained some voice in the distribution of bonuses around the average, usually by negotiating for a formula in which objective factors, such as individual base wage and family size, determined the size of the bonus rather than subjective merit evaluations.[26]

Production quotas and incentive pay remained part of the wage envelope in the late 1940s and early 1950s, but, despite the emphasis placed by Nikkeiren on linking wages to efficiency, the importance of output pay slowly decreased. It accounted for 20 percent of manufacturing sector wages in 1950 but only 13.5 percent in 1955, and a mere 6 percent by 1965.[27] Managers did not lose interest in output and productivity during these years. Rather, continued evolution of industrial technology toward more complex processes less amenable to rate setting, and continued pressure from labor, led to emphasis on long-term evaluations in fixing the level of a pay raise and the pace of promotion as a superior way to motivate labor. In the early 1950s, managers set rates of output pay and determined the mode of distribution through bargaining with the unions, as they had done since the war ended, and labor consistently sought increased rates, guaranteed minima, and distribution in accord with the same objective factors used for bonuses. A "production-incentive" payment which varied only as the base wage varied (so long as the minimum quota was met) was not much of a direct stimulus to efficient labor. At Tōshiba, for example, the production incentive wage, so called, of the early 1950s was distributed solely in accord with attendance and the size of the base wage.[28] Rather than rely on such dubious direct incentives, managers gradually turned to the indirect incentive of periodic evaluations. The great emphasis managers placed on their freedom to use such evaluations in setting the regular raise for an individual was part of this long-term transition, not unlike the substitution of term-paper and final-exam grades for daily quizzes and weekly grades as tools to motivate students.

By the mid-1950s, wage bargaining in Japan followed the same basic pattern it has ever since, as unions and managers at the national, industry, and company levels wrangled once a year over the average amount and the distribution of the regular raise and, usually, an increase in the wage base as well. As this pattern emerged in the early 1950s, an important shift away from the livelihood wage took place. Pay raises fell far short of union demands; firms were well able to afford them, for rapid investment in new equipment resulted in substantial increases in productivity. The ratio of manufacturing output to hours of labor increased far more rapidly than did wages between 1950 and 1955. Productivity nationwide rose 150 percent during this period.[29] Closer to home, productivity nearly doubled at the NKK mill in Kawasaki, which turned out 88 tons of steel per worker in 1950 and 164 tons in 1955.[30] Wages invariably lagged behind such gains in output; Nikkeiren successfully affirmed the principle that wage hikes not exceed a firm's capacity to pay. At the same time, workers in these plants could look back and conclude they had gained. Their wages easily grew faster than inflation, even as they lost to productivity. Nominal wages almost doubled, and real wages increased by roughly one-third in the manufacturing sector during these years.[31] This was recovery on management terms to be sure, but the workers shared some of the growing pie even as the labor movement retreated.

The settlement of the 1950s was more complex than terms such as *management victory* or *labor defeat* convey. We can determine winners and losers only in specific disputes of limited duration. What finally emerged by the end of the first postwar decade was an amalgam; the Japanese wage system discovered by Abegglen and studied by his successors in truth is a management revision built out of three distinct prior incarnations of Japanese wage practice: a prewar version dominated by management, a wartime government version, and an early postwar labor version.

The entry wage is set by age, sex, and education background. Unions negotiate to establish minimum levels for each category. As a result, a 25-year-old with no experience will start out earning substantially more than an equally inexperienced 18-year-old of the same sex and education, even if the two work side by side on identical tasks. The importance of age has roots in three of the historical versions of wage practice. In the prewar era, many factories used age to set starting wages for their inexperienced teenage trainees. During the war, the government forced all companies to adopt elaborate age-based scales for the entry wage which covered adult workers as well, for the labor draft brought inexperienced adults to many plants. After the war, unions stepped in to negotiate for the continued use of these scales and seek higher minimum levels for young workers.

The practices used to determine subsequent raises have equally diverse roots in the past. The judgment of foremen and supervisors and the changing fortunes of the firm were usually the sole criteria in the prewar era. This is no longer true. Objective standards and regularity entered the picture due to wartime regulations and the efforts of postwar unions. The collective-bargaining contract concluded in 1952 at the Tsurumi mill at NKK was typical in its codification of this pay-raise system. It bound the company to announce regular raises on March 1 each year. Amounts and distribution were to be decided through discussion with the union.[32] In the late 1960s, Dore found the same system at Hitachi. A contractual agreement set a floor on the yearly raise given to each employee, and it set boundaries on the wage gap allowed between employees of the same age due to variations in their yearly raises.[33] In this system, the prewar practice of evaluation by foremen did not disappear. It was transformed into the ostensibly more modern postwar practice of the merit evaluation. The union set limits on the impact of these evaluations, but the cumulative effect on wages of high or low ratings can still be substantial, and workers reportedly care a great deal about them.[34]

Management discretion and union participation, subjective judgment and objective standards, are thus joined in a structure composed of heterogeneous elements reaching back through several distinct past eras. The common ground shared by the various elements is their link, implicit or explicit, to seniority, at once a rough proxy for both need and ability. Seniority, therefore, is likely to endure as a factor in the wage equation, because workers and managers, for reasons not always the same, find it an effective and useful measure of the value of labor.

The most important change over the long run, from prewar, through wartime, to postwar practice, was the shift from an arbitrary, customary wage system to one of greater regularity and, at times, rigidity. Considered from the management perspective, the early 1950s witnessed a significant move away from the rigidity of the livelihood wage imposed by labor just after the war. Unions and many workers see the matter differently. To them some of the insecurity and potential for abuse of power, inherent in prewar wage practice, returned in the early 1950s. Yet, an important degree of regularity remains. Because unions continue to play a role, there is "order in the distribution of rewards."[35] This order is subject to change as basic tensions between goals of management and union remain. The major modification to have taken place since the 1950s has been a gradual flattening of the seniority wage curve. In 1954, wages for employees aged 40 to 50 in medium and large firms were double those of 20- to 24-year-olds. Two decades of relatively larger raises for the younger workers meant that, by 1975, the pay of the older group was only 1.6 times that of the young workers.[36] In the early years, it was the union, with many young members, that often pushed for this change, but this trend is now likely to continue for a different reason. As the work force ages rapidly, unions are pushing to extend the retirement age, and managers are seeking to lower their total wage bills by slowing the pace of raises for older employees. One trade-off made in collective bargaining in several prominent cases in the late 1970s was to raise the retirement age in exchange for reduction or elimination of regular raises for the senior employees. Whatever the outcome of continued negotiations, whether managers gain greater discretion over pay raises or unions win more rigid standards, pay is likely to attach not to a job but to individual attributes of age and experience. Even if managers deny that they in principle pay livelihood wages, income in fact will rise in rough correspondence to need for most of a man's career.

A final observation on wages in Japan is pertinent here. Observers approaching the contemporary Japanese wage scene unaware of or uninterested in the historical context inevitably talk of a managerial effort to abandon traditional, irrational seniority wages in favor of more modern formulae which will give proper reward to skill and efficiency. One noted Japanese scholar writing in 1972 observed that on the occasion of the regular or annual wage increase, the employers use some type of personal evaluation plan, so that they gradually are coming to employ modern techniques to overcome irrationality in methods of wage determination.[37]

The reader aware of the historical record may be forgiven an ironic smile. In their reliance on personal evaluations, these "modern" managers are no different from their "traditional" predecessors in the 1950s and in the prewar era. Such "traditional" wages were never irrational, if irrationality implies a failure to provide incentives or a lack of concern with efficiency or evaluating workers.

Tradition and modernity are slippery notions. They are not helpful markers of the start, the finish, or major points along the way, in the history of labor relations in Japan. The modern concern with efficiency and output was always manifest in the wage policy of managers. Only the methods to safeguard this concern underwent change. The concern with security was of similar prominence in the action of workers. It did not change, but the means employed to gain it became more effective. The historical journey took managers and workers not from traditional to modern but from arbitrary to regulated wage practice, passing along the way through eras of government regulation and labor domination.

THE JOB SETTLEMENT

The promises of job security wrested from some firms at the height of labor power rested on a shaky foundation of union pressures which collapsed in 1949. The third front in the management offensive of 1949 to 1954 was the "consolidation drive" (*kigyō seibi*) to first dismiss excess personnel and then maintain lean work forces, as a recovery premised on capital investment and higher productivity gained momentum. The battles on this front were fiercer and more prolonged than any in Japanese labor history. Disputes dragged on for months, and labor-movement sympathizers and historians refer to several of these simply by their duration: the 113-day Miike coal strike, the 173-day Japan Steel struggle, or the 77-day Amagasaki Steel strike. With recovery in subsequent years, the need to fire receded but never disappeared. A degree of job security emerged in most industries by the late 1950s, to be sure, but the permanent-employment label still misleads more often than it informs, whether applied to the immediate postwar decade or the years thereafter.

In postwar Japan, job security for regular workers has been threatened first when depression or recession raised the problem of "excess" employees. Also, plant modernization and technological innovation even in expanding, profitable industries has eliminated jobs and brought pressure to fire. Constant scrapping and building of plants made certain skills and job categories obsolete even as it created new ones. Between 1949 and 1951, Japanese workers quite evidently faced the former problem. In the early 1950s and to some extent ever since, the technological pressure on jobs has been a factor in a wide variety of industries. The response of managers to this pressure in the high-growth era and beyond was shaped by their experience in the first postwar decade.

If economic collapse made the defense of jobs difficult in 1946, the combination of the Dodge line and a new management determination to take on unions made it nearly impossible in 1949 and 1950. Shipbuilding workers in the Zenzōsen federation tried to elicit renewed "no-dismissal" promises as layoffs appeared certain under the Dodge line, but these pleas for a policy of no layoffs for one year were not heeded. Management typically responded, as at Ishikawajima, with a pledge to avoid firings and to consult the unions, but, when the consultation came, it focused only on timing and choice of the victims. None of the shipbuilding unions could prevent dismissals. As in the Depression, they could only bargain for higher severance-pay settlements or save face by seeking voluntary leavers, rather than reduce the number fired outright.[38]

Workers at Tōshiba were no better able to prevent dismissals in 1949, and management success here had widespread impact. Just as the successful defense of jobs at Tōshiba in 1946 discouraged other firms facing strong unions from undertaking dismissals, the firing of 20 percent of the Tōshiba work force in 1949 gave a green light of sorts to firms nationwide. The union knew that dismissals were inevitable for nearly a year before they actually came, but it was unable to organize effectively to counter the carefully planned company strategy. The Tōshiba story from 1946 to 1949 is the national story of Japanese labor and management writ small.

Managers at Tōshiba had been looking for ways to trim the work force ever since the war ended. In a frank letter to shareholders written to explain the issues at stake in the 1949 dispute, the company claimed that it had carried an excessive payroll between 1946 and 1948 out of "consideration for workers and their families," relying only on attrition and transfers to reduce the work force as much as possible. Part of this "consideration" of course was Tōshiba's assessment of the power of the union, known for its ingenious tactics. As the company went on to explain, the new economic policies of December 1948 changed the relevant considerations. Banks lending to the firm were now insisting that it shut down the many small, scattered, money-losing plants located in rural areas during the evacuation phase of the war. This was a condition for a much-needed loan of 600 million yen. The Dodge policies directed banks not to lend money to companies operating consistently in the red, and the cutbacks in the national budget mandated by Dodge sharply reduced government and electric-power industry procurement, both major sources of demand for Tōshiba products. The report concluded that the company had no choice but to undertake "thoroughgoing rationalization."[39]

One can imagine that the shareholders, who had not seen a dividend check since April 1945 (and would not until March 1951), needed little convincing of the need for dismissals. The workers were less agreeable, but they faced a united set of powerful institutions; the Japanese government, SCAP, Nikkeiren, and the major banks all understood that confrontations with labor were inevitable under the Dodge line, and they were pleased to help Tōshiba and many others take on the unions in such a favorable context. Management moved cleverly and was able to play on the fear of losing a job to split the union. Rather than notify the union or the workers of those to be fired, management first sent notes to those it intended to keep, informing them that their future at Tōshiba was secure and asking their cooperation in rebuilding the firm. Managers also timed the announcement of the long-expected dismissals to coincide with a scheduled 6-month repair job of deteriorating but critically important machinery at the main Horikawa factory, a union stronghold. This insured that the anticipated strike at Horikawa would have only limited impact on production.

On July 5, 1949, Tōshiba announced its plan to fire 4,581 of the 22,207 employees at its 16 major plants. It offered fired workers from 3 to 6 months' extra severance pay. The union carried out a series of short strikes designed to build momentum toward a longer stoppage, and it also used the innovative "couple" (*abekku*) tactic: A union member accompanied a sympathetic non-union plant supervisor or section chief to the bargaining table to argue together that "X workshop can't afford to fire any one." Despite such organizing from the bottom up, the union literally fell apart in the face of the dismissals. "Outside activists" from JNR and other unions reportedly intruded and spoke at a controversial meeting of the Horikawa plant union on July 14 called to discuss the union response. Dissidents active in the democratic cell movement there seized on this violation of union autonomy and called for a new, independent Horikawa union. By July 16, the issue had spilled over into other plants. Voices were raised for new, non-Communist unions throughout the enterprise. By November, the new Tōshiba union federation had been formed and the old union gave up its fight, formally accepting the dismissals originally announced.[40]

The Tōshiba drama was reenacted throughout Japan. The national railway, also unable to fire employees as it wished in 1946, due to union resistance, finally dismissed 100,000 workers in two layoffs beginning in the summer of 1949. As at Tōshiba, Communists and Sanbetsu leaders were signaled out for dismissal, and the union suffered a major defeat. In Kanagawa, several other prominent employers dismissed comparable proportions of their work forces soon after the Tōshiba announcement. In October, Nissan fired 23 percent of 8,700 and Isuzu fired 26 percent of 5,500 workers. About half these men were employed in Kanagawa near the main Tōshiba factories. The auto-workers contested the dismissals for two months, with no success. Finally, in the spring of 1950, the giant Hitachi firm, Tōshiba's major domestic competitor, fired 5,555 of its 31,500 employees; here too the union collapsed under the weight of this blow.[41]

The union movement lost every major battle in 1949 and 1950, but the disputes which invariably accompanied mass dismissals did have an impact on management strategy and the labor relationship. In the recovery that began in 1950, unions continued to place defense of jobs high on their list of priorities, and managers began to choose labor peace over dismissals. Through a process of continual negotiations and disputes over both dismissals and transfers of idle workers, the two sides thrashed out a set of rules concerning job security which has been critical to Japanese industrial policy and labor relations ever since. Unions defined their role as protecting jobs *in general* within a firm; managers responded by modernizing and expanding with the workers on hand, rather than firing those with obsolete skills and hiring cheaper, younger workers, even if this meant retraining the expensive adults. They also responded in the 1950s and 1960s by hiring temporary employees in expansionary periods to serve as a buffer protecting the jobs of regular union members who would not tolerate layoffs.

Union behavior had historical roots. We have seen that unions in Japan have never been craft or trade organizations. They were not committed to protecting particular occupations under attack by automation, but came of age, even in the early twentieth century, in a context of constant technological modernization. They had always sought not to protect a craft but to defend jobs at a firm. The union at Yokosen in the 1950s feared layoffs and behaved much as its predecessor had in the 1920s, with somewhat greater success.

A corollary point can be made concerning management. Their decisions were made with reference to very recent history, and they also echoed strategies of the more distant past. The decisions of the 1950s and 1960s to retrain rather than fire and hire were taken under some pressure from the labor movement, with memories of the 1949 struggles still fresh. These decisions usually represented a careful weighing of the costs and benefits of alternative labor-management strategies. Assessment of a union's power and its likely response was critical. Ideological commitments to the role of the paternal, traditional, benevolent employer appear secondary. Thus, managers at Yokosen moved with care in dealing with idle or excess workers in both the 1920s and 1950s, but their calculations of union power led to different policies. In 1927, the "secondary skill" plan would have shifted men to relatively unfamiliar tasks rather than firing and rehiring, but Yokosen never fully implemented it. In the 1920s, this company often fired idle workers, but, in the 1950s, they would transfer the excess labor within the firm or the Mitsubishi group.

Both steel and shipbuilding furnish examples of the working out of this job settlement. Output rose dramatically in both industries in the 1950s, but the rapid import of technology allowed major firms to maintain a level work force or even reduce the number of employees. Recovery did not necessarily expand job opportunities. Total employment in shipbuilding actually fell between 1952 and 1963 from 97,000 to 95,000 production workers, while output more than doubled. Employment at the NKK Kawasaki mill dipped from 13,404 regular workers in 1950 to 13,119 in 1955, despite an increase in output from 1.2 to 2.15 million tons of steel per year.[42] Productivity, rationalization, and lean work forces were the watchwords for managers superintending the recovery of the 1950s; jobs were by no means safe.

When NKK streamlined operations in 1953 at its Kawasaki mill by abolishing the position of maintenance worker in each section and giving new maintenance responsibilities to the machine-tooling workers, the union was on guard. But, rather than protest the loss of the maintenance posts, it sought a promise that these workers would be reassigned and guaranteed no loss in pay at the new jobs. Management went along, shifting the former maintenance people to the ingot factory at the mill.[43] Such issues arose often at NKK. Union leaders and managers met in the discussion council, less powerful than in 1945 but still functioning, and they worked out the terms in each case. Gradually, the practice of more or less automatic transfers and the avoidance of layoffs evolved. A parallel case at Yokosen involved the problem of idle workers during a slump in the summer of 1953 and again in 1954. Many shipbuilders chose to string along with the idle workers, either ordering week- or month-long vacations, cutting hours, or closing down one day a week, all without pay. If preferable to dismissal, idling at roughly 60 percent of normal income was still unacceptable to Yokosen workers. In 1953, the union sought and gained the transfer of 101 workers to a nearby subsidiary as an alternative to the idle plan. In 1954, it went to court protesting the idle plan of that summer, and management abandoned it and resumed full pay after a 5-week dispute.[44]

At both NKK and Yokosen, the union acted to keep workers employed at the firm in some capacity (and in the union), and managers acquiesced. The Tōshiba union in 1954 tried to do better, for a transfer settlement could entail considerable sacrifice for the individual forced to move to "save" a job as a result of a union-company agreement.[45] The company announced a plan in late 1953 to close its tiny factory in Kōfu, well outside Tokyo. The plant made components used at the Horikawa factory in Yokohama, and Tōshiba wanted to move the entire operation, and the workers, to the Horikawa plant. The union agreed this would be a far more efficient arrangement, but it sought to keep these workers at Kōfu, *and* generate new jobs at Horikawa, with a proposal to retool the Kōfu plant to manufacture a different product while hiring new people at Horikawa to produce the former Kōfu products. Management refused. It would transfer those willing to make the move, but it would not keep the old plant open. When a threatened strike failed to materialize, the union had no choice but to accept the company plan and bargain over terms of separation for those unable or unwilling to move. Thirty-eight workers accepted transfer offers, and 12 left Tōshiba.[46]

This case clarifies the limits to job security in the 1950s and beyond. Unions could defend regular jobs within a firm, but they could not, and still can not, intervene over specific jobs at specific factories. These two goals may be mutually exclusive in a capitalist economy. One is hard-pressed to conceive of a profitable firm which is unable to either transfer *or* dismiss "excess" workers. If a union has power to prevent job transfers (as many American unions do), it is unlikely to be able to prevent dismissals. It will, instead, seek to set rules for the rehiring (by seniority) of employees in the particular job category. [47]

By the mid-1950s, a settlement of the job issue was in place. Yamamoto Kiyoshi documents one enlightening example in which managers of a petrochemical firm spent a greal deal of money in following the unwritten rules of this settlement. The unnamed firm, the largest of its kind in Japan, constructed a new, highly automated plant in the Keihin area in the late 1950s. It began operations in August 1960 with 602 employees. The interesting fact is that only 30 percent of the 402 blue-collar employees were newly hired. The company transferred the remaining 70 percent at considerable expense from as far away as Kyūshū (35 percent), Hokkaidō (10 percent), and Chūgoku (20 percent). Yamamoto asks why management transferred workers, most of whom needed retraining, rather than hiring and training new people locally. Of course, one would expect a corps of experienced supervisors and foremen to be transferred, and all the foremen were in fact transfers, but this experienced corps certainly could be far less than 70 percent of the work force. The cost of this choice at first glance was tremendous (Table 26). Over 5 years the firm spent nearly three-quarters of a billion yen (over 2 million 1960 dollars) more by transferring than by hiring cheaper, inexperienced labor from the Keihin area.

The answer is found in the hidden cost of firing which the company avoided by the transfers. The director of the new factory remarked:

> By transferring, we use older, more expensive workers at the new factory [and still must retrain them]. It would be more rational to have these excess people quit. But we don't want to fire them and cause

a dispute with the union, so we decided to use and retrain these people.

The head of the personnel section at the Kyūshū factory added, "As you can see from what happened at Miike coal mines [several prolonged strikes over dismissals], if we fired them, we wouldn't get off with just a 2- or 3-month dispute."

Table 26 Hypothetical Cost of Transferring vs. Firing and
Rehiring, Japanese Petrochemical Plant, late 1950s

Item	Cost in yen
a. Number transferred	343 people
b. Yearly income (average) per transferee	469,560
c. Yearly income (average) of new hiree	215,400
d. Difference of hiring new people or transfers (b–c)	254,160
e. Average retirement/severance pay if all transferees had been fired instead	234,300
f. Five year difference in total labor cost (a·d·5)	435,884,400
g. Total transfer and moving costs (a·20,000 yen per person)	68,600,000
h. Cost of building new dorms for transfers (a·900,000 yen per unit)	308,700,000
i. Cost of retirement payouts if transferees are fired (a·e)	80,364,900
j. Five year cost of transfers to company (f+g+h)–i	732,282,000
k. Yearly sales of the company	20,406,430,000
l. Daily sales (k/365)	55,910,000
m. Daily gross profit (l·20.7% profit rate)	11,500,000
n. # of days of lost profit equivalent to cost of the transfers	63.7 days

Source: Yamamoto Kiyoshi, Nihon rōdō shijo no kōzō, pp. 268–269.

The rationality of managers in this case included an assessment of the cost of the dispute likely to occur if they fired the workers no longer needed in Hokkaido, Kyūshū, and Chūgoku instead of transferring them. The yen cost of the transfers was roughly equivalent to the anticipated cost, in lost profit, of a 2-month work stoppage. If such a dispute were probable, then the transfers were not an expensive choice, especially if one considers other likely costs of a dispute: negative publicity, lower morale, and loss of orders to competitors during a shutdown.[48] And prolonged disputes over firing were common. Table 29 indicates that roughly half the job-related disputes (in years for which data are available) lasted for more than 1 month, in contrast to the much smaller proportion of prolonged disputes over other issues. These chemical-industry managers were not making decisions based on unrealistic fears. The likelihood that workers would resist made job dismissals an unattractive, even irrational, choice in the Japanese context.

Observers and participants have been tempted to describe this pattern of employment with adjectives such as *permanent* or *lifetime*. There is a kernel of truth in such usage, but no more. To be sure, managers at NKK, Tōshiba, Yokosen, and this petrochemical firm all chose transfers over firing and rehiring, when the issue arose. In addition, much of the blue-collar work force in large firms since the 1950s has been hired right out of school, without exerience, in the expectation and hope that the investment in worker training would pay off through long, effective service to the firm. Such school-grad hiring was a small part of the picture in the 1920s and 1930s, and the government sought to reinforce it with regulations during the war, to little effect. Only with recovery did this practice take on major statistical significance (refer to Table 8). A phrase was coined to describe it: "regular hiring" (*teiki saiyō*), a parallel construction to the term "regular raise" (*teiki shōkyū*). Expanding, modernizing companies hired inexperienced young workers, willing to learn; transfers alone could not usually man an entire new plant, and the supply of experienced adults contracted as economic growth gained momentum. Managers hoping to recoup their investment in training these workers had good reason to stress the mutual commitment of firm and employee on every possible occasion, including discussions with Western sociologists. They had motive, even, to invent the notion of a loyal "permanent commitment" among workers as part of the elusive good old days, part of a spirit now in jeopardy. Unions anxious to prove their strength and attract support had their own reasons to boast about their struggles to guarantee job security. This combination of expectations, ideology, and rhetoric from both sides conspired to create the myth of the permanent job, past and present.

In fact, the behavior of workers and companies after hiring describes a far different historic and contemporary reality. Only a minority of blue-collar workers in the postwar era actually signed on for the long haul of 10 or even 5 years. We saw that roughly 15 to 25 percent of Uraga and NKK workers hired in the early 1920s remained at their jobs for such periods; less than 10 percent of Shibaura hirees spent careers at the Engineering Works between 1904 and 1938. The commitment of postwar labor was more substantial, probably because better conditions moved fewer to quit and unions allowed fewer to be fired. But it was not "permanent." Consider the data from Ishikawajima Harima Heavy Industries (IHI, the descendant of the Ishikawajima Shipyard), the Mitsubishi Heavy Industries' Yokohama Factory (formerly Yokohama Dock Company), and Tōshiba Electronics, covering various periods between 1955 and 1980 (Table 27). Within 6 or 7 years of hiring, about one-half of those hired had left each company. The rate of separation rises to over 60 percent after 10 years at Mitsubishi and in the middle-school cases at Tōshiba. These data, which include only those hired directly out of high or middle school as regular workers, cover cohorts that experienced the labor shortage of the booming 1960s as well as groups hired on the eve of the severe shipbuilding depression of the mid-to-late 1970s. In 3 of the 4 blue-collar cases, the attrition rates are quite similar. Only Tōshiba's high-school recruits appear more settled. The company's university graduates are in another league entirely. Forty-one of the 44 members of the "class of 1955" were still at the company 25 years later; the term *permanent employment* seems fair enough only when applied to managers themselves.

The *lifetime* and *permanent* labels do not describe with accuracy the employment experience of a majority of blue-collar workers hired from the 1950s to the 1970s by these heavy industrial giants. One could call the glass half full and stress that about 40 percent of the Mitsubishi workers hired in 1968 remained at the company 12 years later and similar numbers of Tōshiba workers stayed for 20 years, but data from the United States suggest that Japanese workers are just slightly more settled than their American counterparts. Unfortunately, no precisely comparable cohort data are available for American companies, but, in his searching comparison of American and Japanese labor relations, Koike Kazuo presents some useful aggregate data for 1966 and 1967. These show that far more American than Japanese workers had less than a single year of tenure with a given employer. To this extent, the American work force included a larger proportion of job-switchers. Also, a somewhat higher percentage of Japanese than American workers had from 1 to 15 years of tenure; proportionately more Japanese had what can be labeled fairly long tenure with one employer. At the same time, a *greater* proportion of all American workers had more than 15 years' tenure at one enterprise, 23 versus 17 percent.[49] The Japanese blue-collar experience in the 1960s and 1970s can best be called one of relatively long-term employment. In addition, given the apparently greater investment of Japanese firms in training of young men expected to be long-term employees, a Japanese manager would view an attrition rate of 50 percent over 5 years as more serious than an American executive.

Finally, and of equal importance, job security in this system is not absolute, even for those who choose to stay. In the chemical company transfers, Yamamoto finds two critical factors present in his case that were not always present elsewhere, and at other firms managers behaved differently. First, managers perceived the union to have power to inflict costly damage. The company needed the productive capacity of the factories from which transfers were made, and it feared a strike. Had these old plants been scheduled for closing as in the Tōshiba dispute at Kōfu in 1954, the threat of a strike would have been less of a deterrent to dismissals. Second, the new plant was large enough to absorb the excess workers. In some cases of labor-saving innovations, this was not so. In 1957, two other major chemical firms fired 356 and 339 workers, respectively, in similar cases of plant modernization.[50] They were

Table 27 Persistency of Employment, Blue-Collar Males,
          1955–1980

a) Mitsubishi Heavy Industries Yokohama Shipyard, High School Grads

Year Hired	No. Hired	Tenure in 1980	No. Remaining in 1980	Percent Remaining
1968	27	12	10	37.0
1969	146	11	55	37.7
1970	197	10	82	41.6
1971	329	9	117	35.6
1972	332	8	141	42.5
1973	171	7	86	50.3
1974	166	6	88	53.0
1975	174	5	100	57.5
Totals	1,542		679	44.4

b) Ishikawajima Harima Heavy Industries, High School Grads

Year Hired	No. Hired	Tenure in 1975	No. Remaining in 1975	Percent Remaining
1968	1,107	7	550	49.7
1969	1,090	6	640	58.7
1970	1,327	5	773	58.3
1971	1,247	4	798	64.0
1972	960	3	745	77.6
1973	173	2	137	79.2
1974	714	1	672	94.1
Totals	6,618		4,315	68.8

c) Tōshiba Electronics, High and Middle School Grads, and University Grads

Year Hired	No. Hired	Tenure in 1980 (Sept. 1)	No. Remaining in 1980	Percent Remaining
Middle School Grads				
1957	290	23	135	46.6
1958	309	22	139	45.0
1959	328	21	130	39.6
1960	409	20	170	41.6
1961	614	19	253	41.2
1962	1,418	18	417	29.4
1963	937	17	316	33.7
1964	1,102	16	394	35.8

Year Hired	No. Hired	Tenure in 1980 (Sept. 1)	No. Remaining in 1980	Percent Remaining
1965	917	15	308	33.6
1966	568	14	201	35.4
1967	891	13	281	31.5
1968	1,025	12	304	29.7
1969	713	11	242	33.9
1970	678	10	243	35.8
1971	141	9	61	43.3
1972	27	8	19	70.4
1973	90	7	47	52.2
1974	136	6	66	48.5
Totals	10,593		3,726	35.2
High School Grads (Skilled)				
1964	178	15	117	65.7
1966	105	14	70	66.7
1967	548	13	321	58.8
1968	1,045	12	572	54.7
1969	1,373	11	776	56.5
1970	1,897	10	1,049	55.3
1971	768	9	514	66.9
1972	287	8	181	63.1
1973	1,038	7	606	58.4
1974	746	6	538	72.1
1975	340	5	288	84.7
1976	47	4	40	85.1
1977	298	3	272	91.9
1978	115	2	107	93.0
1979	130	1	125	96.2
Totals	8,915		5,578	71.3
College Grads (White collar)				
1955	44	25	41	93.2

Sources: Company personnel records

not unique. Tables 28 and 29 document the numerous cases where dismissals led to labor disputes between 1946 and the early 1960s. While many of these were in the beleaguered mining sector, several came in expanding industries when a firm elected not to transfer men when it closed one outmoded plant and expanded elsewhere.

The job settlement which in fact emerged in the 1950s and 1960s rests on a balance, in tension, between managers and unions. It is an implicit settlement; no contracts spell out job guarantees. The employment pattern is a set of tendencies, not inviolate rules. Where unions have been strong and industries growing, the regular workers have attained something approaching a guaranteed job. They retain the right to quit, and the majority of those hired exercise it at least once in a career. And they affirm the right to remain if they choose.[51] Table 28 suggests that, in the largest firms, economic conditions and union pressure finally combined to defend jobs effectively in this system in the 1960s. We cannot precisely weigh these two factors. Certainly, high growth would have reduced the pressure on jobs, even without unions or disputes. But the petrochemical and other examples show that dismissals could be an attractive option even in a growing firm, in the absence of union pressure. Surely, the fact that dismissal disputes were often lengthy and difficult to settle helped convince managers of big firms to avoid dismissals almost without exception by the 1960s (Table 29).

In exchange for this degree of job security, unions continued to allow managers near total control over transfers and job definitions, a tremendous gain for business in an era of continuous technological innovation. Managers also retained leverage at the margins of the system in the 1950s. Some workers were still not full members; temporary employees and subcontractors did not enjoy the secure jobs and steadily rising pay of the regular men in the large factories.

The prominence of temporary workers in the Japanese settlement of the 1950s suggests that the group of full members made gains only at the expense of people on the margins. Is the emergence and persistence of a sizeable pool of underprivileged workers thus inevitable in a capitalist society? If the question had been posed in 1900 or 1930, we may well have answered yes and placed the entire Japanese blue-collar work force, with the possible exception of foremen, into the marginal group of second-class citizens. But the place of regular blue-collar men did change after 1945. Further change in the status of those left outside the system of the 1950s was to be an issue in future years, and the question of who will be how secure in his or her membership in a company is still very much open and alive in Japan today.

Both men and women entirely outside of the big firms have continued to occupy a relatively insecure social and economic position. The overall rates of pay for workers in small (30 to 99 employees) and medium (100 to 499) firms respectively stood unchanged at about 70 and 80 percent of large-firm pay from 1950 to 1975. The seniority-wage curve in these smaller places has consistently been flatter than in the big firms, and jobs have been much less secure. These figures indicate very little change in the relatively low status and security of labor in the small- to medium-sized subcontractors which surround all huge Japanese companies.[52]

The case of marginal employees within the large firms is more complex. Use of so-called temporary workers reached a peak around 1960. In the great surges of growth after 1955, almost all large companies hired many of their new workers with low-paying, temporary contracts of from 3 months to 1 year, renewable at company discretion. Between 1959 and 1961, these temporary workers reached their peak, accounting for roughly 8 percent of all labor in manufacturing industry, and closer to 12 percent of manufacturing workers in firms of over 500. Over half of all workers hired during the Jimmu boom of 1956 signed on with temporary contracts. In some industries, the proportion was far higher. Electrical-machinery firms hired over 90 percent of their new people as temporaries in 1956, and, in late 1961 at Tōshiba, about 19,000 people, one-third of the work force, were temporaries. The plight of such men and women in factories nationwide, paid barely half the wage of their average regular counterparts, denied benefits, and, of course, easily fired, began to receive widespread attention in the late 1950s.[53]

For almost a decade, until reliance on temporaries began to

Table 28 Labor Disputes Over Job Dismissals, 1946–1982

Year	Total Disputes[a] Over Dismissals	Number (%) in Large Firms (over 5,000 employed)	
1946	183	Data	
1947	113		
1948	179		
1949	347	not	
1950	259		
1951	102		
1952	141		
1953	127	Available	
1954	203	5	(2.5)
1955	191	21	(11.0)
1956	162	19	(11.7)
1957	162	14	(8.6)
1958	218	10	(4.6)
1959	144	14	(9.7)
1960	93	5	(5.4)
1961	117	3	(2.6)
1962	137	8	(5.8)
1963	93	6	(6.5)
1964	111	8	(7.2)
1965	137	4	(2.9)
1966	147	4	(2.7)
1967	113	1	
1968	110	1	
1969	86	1	
1970	106	1	
1971	105	1	
1972	135	3	(2.2)
1973	73	0	
1974	124	1	
1975	135	3	(2.2)
1976	121	0	
1977	126	2	(1.6)
1978	128	1	
1979	91	4	(4.3)
1980	109	2	(1.8)
1981	107	1	
1982	129	3	(2.3)

Source: Rōdōshō, Rōdō sōgi tōkei chōsa nempōkoku, for relevant years.

Note: [a] Dispute includes action short of a strike, such as slowdown.

Table 29 Duration of Labor Disputes, 1962–1963, 1976–1982

Year	Total Resolved Disputes over Dismissals	Number (%) of Prolonged Dismissal Disputes (over 31 days)		Total Resolved Disputes	% of All Disputes that were Prolonged
1962	135	54	(40.0)	1,667	20.5
1963	92	38	(41.3)	1,383	19.5
—	—	—		—	—
1976	108	64	(59.2)	7,895	26.0
1977	102	58	(56.9)	5,945	19.5
1978	114	58	(50.9)	5,324	20.2
1979	77	46	(59.7)	3,912	15.4
1980	99	47	(47.5)	4,253	16.8
1981	91	49	(53.9)	7,545	8.1
1982	102	57	(55.9)	7,310	8.3

Source: Same as Table 28.

Note: Data on length of disputes by issue were only compiled in these years.

decrease in the early 1960s, managers saved considerable sums on labor costs while they increased work forces and output. At Tōshiba in 1956, an average "temporary" cost the company roughly 6,000 yen less per month than an average regular worker. The 5,377 temporaries on the payroll saved the firm a total of 32 million yen per month, roughly 13 percent of profits each month in the second half of the year. The destruction of powerful "first unions" in major firms throughout the nation and their replacement by cooperative and weaker "second unions" made possible similar savings nationwide. The early Tōshiba union was typical in holding veto power over all personnel decisions; had it survived, this union would not have allowed the hiring of temporaries. This would have slightly weakened the balance sheet, but it would not have brought on corporate failure; a strong union could have required that all these people gain regular wages, and it appears the company would still have turned a profit.[54]

Beginning around 1960, two forces intervened to reduce gradually the ranks of the temporaries. First, some temporary workers organized and sought to convert their contracts to regular ones.[55] The issue arose quite early at NKK, in 1951, when 1,066 workers, 7 percent of the force, were temporaries. These NKK workers formed their own union with some support from the regular group. By 1955, the temporary union had reached an agreement on the upgrading of more than 960 workers, 31 percent of all temporaries hired in this period. Over half the others either left or were fired, and the number of temporaries gradually declined. In 1962, the company abandoned the category of temporary worker, in the words of the union history, "due to changes in the social situation." At Tōshiba, the company refused even to discuss the temporary issue with the union for several years, but, beginning in 1959, bargaining did take place each year over the number of temporaries to be upgraded to regular status. The company agreed to convert over 8,000 workers between 1960 and 1963. Nationwide, roughly one-fourth of the temporary workers in Japan were promoted to regular status each year between 1960 and 1962, and the total was closer to one-third in 1963 and 1964.[56]

The unions of the 1950s had not been able to prevent the hiring of temporaries in the first place, and later demands for improved status for the temporaries affected only the timing and extent of promotions. Reinforcing any union pressures was a second, more important force: a long-term change in the labor market from a condition of chronic oversupply to a severe labor shortage by the late 1960s. As NKK was eliminating the temporary group in 1962, the Labor Ministry concluded that, except for new high-school or middle-school graduates, the pool of men able to enter heavy industrial work had dried up. New school grads had better options than signing a temporary contract, and, when companies upgraded many remaining temporaries (probably afraid of losing them to competitors more than cowed by union pressure), the proportion of temporaries in the work force as a whole declined. By the late 1960s, male temporaries had fallen to about 4 percent of all male employees in firms of more than 1,000 people; by the late 1970s, this figure stood at 1.6 percent (just 37,000 men). The figures for Tōshiba mirror this trend precisely (Table 30). In addition, temporary employment changed its meaning at many firms, where it came to be used as a trial period for a few new mid-career people, rather than as a ploy to maintain a buffer group of long-term but underpaid employees.[57]

The story of women temporaries was quite different, and it is far from closed today. The Labor Ministry report in 1962 noted that, in contrast to heavy industry's exhaustion of the supply of temporaries, light industry, including light electronics, still found a large supply of women willing to sign temporary contracts. This sex difference explains the relatively huge proportion of temporaries at Tōshiba and throughout the electronic industry. But Tōshiba did upgrade thousands of women to regular status, and, in both absolute numbers and as a percent of all women manufacturing workers in large firms, temporary females have declined since the 1950s, from levels as high as 100,000 and 12 percent of all women in some years to roughly 50,000 workers (about 9 percent) by 1978.[58]

Table 30 Temporary and Part-Time Employees at Tōshiba, 1958–1983

Date (March of each year)	Total Work Force	Temporary Workers (%) (a)	Part-time Workers (%) (b)	All Margin-al Workers (a+b)
1958	36,413	24		24.0
1959	39,726	29		29.0
1960	48,906	33		33.0
1961	54,902	31		31.0
1962	62,817	31		31.0
1963	62,010	17		17.0
1964	60,271	10		10.0
1965	61,730	4.9		4.9
1966	59,211	1.8	0.8	2.6
1967	62,672	6.0	3.9	9.9
1968	68,521	4.5	5.8	10.3
1969	72,140	3.7	4.6	8.3
1970	77,615	3.0	5.8	8.8
1971	74,711	0.4	1.0	1.4
1972	71,966	0.6	1.4	2.0
1973	74,800	2.2	3.6	5.8
1974	74,002	0.3	3.1	3.4
1975	68,030	—	0.4	0.4
1976	66,755	—	0.3	0.3
1977	64,781	—	0.8	0.8
1978	64,237	—	0.3	0.3
1979	63,235	—	0.7	0.7
1980	64,508	—		
1981	65,305	0.1	2.2	2.3
1982	66,679	0.2	2.6	2.8
1983	67,387	—	2.5	2.5

Source: Personnel Records held at Tōshiba Personnel Section

Note: — indicates less than 0.1%.

Temporary workers as a formal category of underpaid, under-privileged, insecure employment diminished substantially between the 1950s and 1970s, for men in particular. Has the marginal cushion for an enlarged community of full members thus lost its padding? Common wisdom answers no. Economist Nakamura Takafusa states plainly that, as major firms lost temporary male workers as their cushion in the 1960s, women workers (especially those married with children of at least school age) emerged to replace them.[59] At first glance, this conclusion seems unassailable. From the early 1960s through the 1980s, female employment rose far more rapidly than employment for males; by the late 1970s, women accounted for over half of new employment nationwide each year. In addition, a significant portion of these women served as "part-time" (*paato taimu*) employees, a formal category which only became common in the late 1960s. Indeed, the first official mention of "part-timer" hiring as a major phenomenon in the yearly Labor Ministry White Paper series comes in 1967, just two years after the last discussion of "temporary workers" as a major problem. The two categories overlap some, but they do not refer to precisely the same people. Some part-time workers are actually given contracts as regular workers. At the same time, over 95 percent of part-timers are women, unlike the temporaries, who have in the past included numerous men.[60] Despite these differences, one can certainly argue for their functional identity.

As workers called "temporary" began a numerical decline in the 1960s, women labeled "part-timer" increased even more rapidly. In one account, 2.6 million women, one-fifth of all female labor, were called part-time workers in 1980. This represented a quadrupling of part-timers since 1960. The number of firms hiring these women also rose dramatically, reaching 58 percent of all the companies surveyed in 1979. By the 1980s, the service sector employed over half these women, but part-timers were still numerous in manufacturing jobs. In 1970, 57 percent of the part-timers worked in manufacturing plants; in 1979, this figure stood at 37 percent of a larger group of part-timers.[61]

Why hire a part-time worker? The reason seems to have changed some over time. At the height of the labor shortage, in 1965, half the firms surveyed gave as their chief reason the scarcity of people willing to work full time, suggesting these women were not simply hired as a hedge against bad times. But 43 percent gave as reasons either the low cost of such people (12 percent) or the relative ease of firing them (30 percent). By 1979, the firms offering one or both of these latter reasons had reached 71 percent of all surveyed.[62]

Part-timers were, in fact, cheaper. Their hourly wages stood at roughly three-fourths those of full-time women, and women in general earned about 50 to 60 percent of the pay of men. Few part-timers received bonuses, retirement pay, or other "perks" of full membership. They also put in a rather long day, considering their nominal status. In 1980, they averaged 23 days a month, 32 hours per week. The government standard for part-time work was "under 35 hours per week," but over half the so-called part-timers in manufacturing in fact worked more than 36 hours weekly! These women were also more likely to be fired; their rate of "leaving due to company decision" was substantially higher than that of men.[63]

Can there be any doubt, then, that marginality is inherent in the postwar employment system, and that, by a combination of conscious managerial policy and long-term demographic and social change, the center of gravity of the marginal class shifted from "temporary" men and women to a growing group of "part-timers," almost all women? National statistics can be misleading. From the perspective of individual firms, the trade-off between temporaries and part-timers has been uneven. The Tōshiba case illustrates these ambiguities well (Table 30). After 1962, the temporary pool rapidly dried up, and, with the advent of part-timer hiring in the late 1960s, the firm indeed began to replace one group of second-class employees with another. But part-timers of this era, together with the remaining temporaries, never approached the proportion (or absolute number) of the temporaries of the first "income-doubling" boom, and, well before the oil shock, Tōshiba's marginal cushion was a scant 1 or 2 percent of the work force. The subsequent low figures reflect a hiring freeze in effect from 1975 to 1979, but, even with employment on the rise from 1979 to 1983, part-time employment remains insignificant.[64] These figures appear typical for large firms. In many industries, part-timers are most numerous in smaller companies, while temporaries previously had been found mainly in large factories. The electronics industry as a whole hired many temporaries in the 1950s and 1960s, and many part-timers later on, but the latter do not necessarily replace the former. Large factories in the electronic industry in the early 1980s had less padding in their work force than one or two decades earlier.

The behavior of firms faced with the need to cut back employment also suggests that the cushion was a good bit thinner by the late 1970s, despite the national increase in part-time employment. The Labor Ministry reported in 1972 that, "in contrast to recessionary periods in the 1950s when employment was reduced directly by the firing of temporary workers, in recent years, in part due to the decline in the number of temporaries, firings are relatively rare." A 1971 Ministry survey of firms who trimmed their forces that year lists 9 steps taken by one company or another. Less than 10 percent of the firms fired temporary workers. Hiring freezes and transfers of *regular* workers were far more common. In the oil-shock recession of 1975, the Ministry reported that seniority among women workers had increased in recent years and many were reluctant to leave their jobs; in some cases dismissals of part-timers or temporaries had proved difficult to carry out.[65]

For a complex of reasons tied to change in the labor market, and pressure from workers, organized or not, many large factories operated in the 1980s with a greater proportion of full members than a decade or two earlier. Common wisdom holds that remaining outsiders, in particular, part-time women with families, accept the low pay and insecurity of their jobs as an unavoidable trade-off for relatively flexible hours. This may change. The major federation of electrical-worker unions, Denki Rōren, found in 1978 that 60 percent of its female part-time members would prefer to work full time as regular employees. The attitudes of such people, still in the margin, foreshadow continued wrangling over their status.[66]

Clearly, the Japanese factory is home to a labor relationship distinct from that found in North America and Western Europe. If not a system of permanent employment and rigid seniority wages, even within the large firms alone, it demands a label nonetheless. It is, in Dore's phrase, an organization-oriented employment pattern.[67] It is built upon the premise of secure jobs and livelihood wages, *for full members only*. The wage is determined by attributes which inhere to membership in the firm, such as seniority, rank, and merit evaluations, with some attention to independent and objective attributes of the individual, such as age and family size. Skill as an independent attribute of the worker is largely irrelevant, as are proxies such as job category. Mediated by seniority, the connection between skill and pay is assumed to obtain sufficiently to satisfy workers and managers alike. Job security, likewise, is a function of membership and the ability of a union to defend those it defines as full members, a category that has broadened some since the 1950s. The centrality of membership in the organization is made clear by the consequences of losing or surrendering it. You leave the union when you leave the company, and you also lose the substantial company-specific element of your earning power.

This notion of membership is also central to an understanding of the process by which a more general stability came to Japan in the wake of the bitter conflict and upheaval of the postwar decade. The labor movement after World War II gained political rights, and workers used these to force their way into the firm and the society. The tactic of production control and the fears of pragmatic men, such as former Prime Minister Konoe and soon-to-be Prime Minister Yoshida, suggest that revolution was conceivable in 1945 and 1946.[68] First, the presence of SCAP and later a firm response by the Japanese government under Yoshida prevented a revolutionary movement from gaining momentum. Yet, radical steps such as the production takeovers had another aspect, linked to the consistent concern with membership. The Tsurumi workers who ran the steel mill for two weeks did so because managers were not seeking in good faith to resume production. Theirs was a conditional, not a categorical, denial of management authority; they took care to follow "legal" procedures as they defined them. Tsurumi workers were concerned with survival and with jobs. As the popularity of joint labor-management councils indicates, the thrust of the labor movement at the height of its power was to gain a share in directing the firm, to become leading actors in the organization, rather than to take it over entirely. The distinction is important. It contains the key to understanding the durability of the settlement that followed.

Workers did become part of the organization to a far greater extent than before or during World War II. Although managers rejected their program of control, participation, contractually secure jobs, and explicit livelihood wages, they conceded the status of "employee," the respect and security of a monthly wage, and the right to use all facilities to an expanding pool of workers. And they worked out an implicit system of job security and livelihood wages acceptable to most employees. From the perspective of the late twentieth century, this may look like a cheap set of concessions, largely symbolic, often imposed from above, and actually in management interest. But remember how different the situation had been in the 1930s and during the war. Think back to the scorn felt by Imaoka Junichi for the lazy shipbuilders at Uraga. And recall the fear of the Yokosen personnel managers at the sight of a tattooed laborer. In historical perspective, the postwar settlement emerges as a far-reaching transformation of the labor relationship. Managers could have staged a reactionary, rear-guard fight against the demand for membership. Probably because they recognized in 1945 and 1946 that such a fight would be hopeless, they did not mount a last stand in defense of the prewar or wartime order; instead they guided or sometimes shoved the desire for membership in directions amenable to their control. The result, by the 1950s, was new stability in a labor relationship which they dominated once again. Recovery and economic growth then brought many workers closer to their broader goal, membership in the middle class, formerly the domain of the salaried, white-collar man and his family. The worker, as employee, slowly gained a tentative foothold in the new middle class. As he consolidated it, the middle-class stability of Japan after 1960 took root.

Conclusion

Factory workers and corporate managers first appeared on the stage of Japanese history in the middle of the nineteenth century. For the following century they both confronted each other and compromised; in so doing they worked out the terms of their participation in factory life. Ironically enough, the social relations of industrial production most resembled those in the West at the outset. Several times since then, Japan's workers and managers have substantially reshaped the Japanese labor relationship, producing, by the 1950s, a social formation notably different from that in the West. If we divide this long process into stages, we see three major periods, each spanning several decades. These, in turn, must be divided into six important shorter phases (Table 31).

In the factories and shipyards built by the government between the 1850s and 1870s, and sold to private capitalists in the 1880s, workers and managers produced the first version of the Japanese labor relationship. This system of indirect managerial control over labor resembled arrangements found in early industrial societies in the West in several respects. Managers lacked experience in directing the labor of hundreds of men. In Japan, they relied on the prestige and expertise of the oyakata labor bosses, and Bill Haywood's comment applied to factories on both sides of the Pacific in 1900: "The manager's brains are under the worker's cap." Also, the first workers in Japan, as in the West, were unaccustomed

Table 31 The Japanese Factory in Historical Perspective: Stages of Development

1850	1a) Indirect Control	1850
1900	2a) Direct control asserted; Paternal ideology articulated.	1900
	2b) "Softer" paternal system reshaped to meet labor challenge —Japanese labor management practices emerging in customary form.	1917
1939	3a) Attempt at Bureaucratic Revision —attempt to impose more regular wage, job practices —Sanpō labor organization	1939
	3b) Labor Version —livelihood wage (age/seniority/family) —contractually guaranteed job —equal union participation	1945
	3c) Management Revision —seniority wage with important discretion —implicit job guarantee, for some —weak second unions	1947/1948

1850	1) Indirect Control —oyakata prominence —high mobility
1900	2) Direct Control —paternal ideology —authoritarian, capricious management practices
1939	3) Systematic, regulated labor relationship

to the discipline demanded by factory labor, and they were unwilling to commit themselves to a wage-earning career.

The advent of direct, *relatively* unfettered managerial control over labor marks off the second period in the history of labor relations, which extended from about 1900 to 1939. Managers took the lead in a major reshaping of the early, indirect pattern of labor-management relations around the turn of the century. They imposed a form of direct control of labor characterized by a few distinctive innovations and justified with increasingly self-conscious declarations of paternal care. Managers maintained direct, authoritarian control throughout the prewar era, but this system did not remain unchanged or unchallenged between 1900 and 1939. The years around the end of World War I constitute a watershed; the distribution of power in the work place shifted slightly, and managerial behavior changed. The twin shocks of the World War I boom and the rise of a labor movement rendered inadequate the early paternalistic mode of direct control; the late wartime confrontation of workers and managers, and the subsequent managerial response, reshaped the contours of factory life for a second time. In some particulars the interwar system that resulted prefigured the more recent Japanese pattern. The expectations of labor that a job be secure and wages reward seniority, and the expectation of management that employment involve a long-term commitment from the worker, took on significance in this era, even if expectations and actual practice were often incongruent.

The emergence of standardized, regulated patterns of labor management, in a context of relatively circumscribed managerial control, characterized the third long period in the history of labor relations, stretching from 1939 through the 1980s. This transformation of capricious customary practices into a reasonably secure and predictable set of institutions was a three-stage process in which the gap between expectations and practice narrowed. It spanned three remarkably different historical eras. The forces that changed managerial practice were government actions during World War II and labor-union actions immediately afterward. That state

policy and the worker offensive pushed managers in a similar direction for the sake of such fundamentally different causes, mobilization for war and defense of worker rights, is ironic; certainly
the impact of the unions after the war was less ambiguous and
more favorable to workers than that of the welfare bureaucrats
between 1939 and 1945. Finally, between the late 1940s and the
mid-1950s, managers took back the initiative, and one important
further resettlement of the labor relationship occurred, to endure
relatively unchanged for at least three decades.

Tensions among workers, managers, and the state are universal. Their unfolding in a particular historical context produced the
divergent Japanese pattern. The dialectic involved open confrontation on some occasions and a subtle series of actions and response
on others, but it was always central to the story. The historical
context included three features of particular note. The emergence
of a system of fairly unregulated capitalist enterprise in Japan was
of basic importance. It dictated constant managerial interest in
productivity and efficiency which shaped factory life and the
labor response in important ways. The imperatives of capitalist
development are not the same in all places at all times, however.
Japan's particular status as a medium-late developer led to some
of the more distinctive managerial departures. Third, the particular mix of preindustrial practices and ideas brought into the
new Meiji factory accounted for certain critical concerns of the
workers.

This last assertion, that preindustrial practices and ideas influenced the evolution of the labor relationship, brings an old debate
full circle. Some of the earliest works on labor relations in Japan
used the simple and misleading notion of the carry-over of feudal
values to explain subsequent institutional development. To deny
the explanatory power of this notion is by no means to deny all
connection between the Tokugawa past and the modern factory.
Preindustrial practices or values did not determine the course of
subsequent development, but a legacy from the past did influence
managers and workers as they defined the labor relationship. This

legacy embraced patterns of behavior and organization, as well as attitudes, but it drew only in part on a value system of the feudal era stressing obedience, loyalty, hard work, and paternalistic "beautiful customs."

The traveler and the oyakata brought their mobility and independence out of the artisan past and into the factory. The first skilled laborers were, in the main, independent men who gained experience and skill by traveling from job to job, and who saw this movement as central to a proper worker's career. A man improved himself by moving and polishing his skills. The corollary to this axiom of working-class life was that ultimately a skilled man could become his own boss. The single traveler could be reasonably sure of making a living as a wage earner wherever he went, but, as he grew older and married, he would seek to open his own small factory or become an oyakata boss before he tried to carve out a comfortable niche in a single firm. Even men who were indeed wage earners in large factories for most of their adult lives often aspired to eventual independence.[1] The rough independence of these men and their distaste for factory discipline created problems for large firms and for struggling young unions alike. Unable to control the laborers directly, managers ran their factories by relying on the knowledge and prominence of the oyakata. Indirect control was their first response to characteristics of the work force rooted in the past; in later years, economic growth led managers to experiment with a wide variety of policies designed to convince travelers to give up the wandering habit.

The tendency of Japanese workers to organize their unions in factory or workshop units is a second basic trait of the labor relationship with roots in the past. Craft organizations of the Tokugawa era were confined to urban centers, and the city-dwelling artisans were losing ground to rural producers when the industrial revolution came to Japan. With no tradition of effective guild networks to serve as a model, the travelers and oyakata of the Ironworkers Union, and their successors, organized by workshop and factory with hardly a second thought. From a Euro-American viewpoint, the limited scope of Tokugawa craft organization is a negative, peculiar, or "distorted" legacy, and Western scholars have tended to view the Japanese pattern of factory-based unions as a distortion of proper unionism. But it may well be that Europeans and North Americans, as early developers, were mavericks. Unless unusual preindustrial economic growth and manufacturing activity create a tradition of artisan craft organization transcending isolated urban centers, factory and workshop are surely natural points of departure for a labor movement in any country.[2] The Japanese tendency to organize by factory or workshop and not craft must be linked to the nature of Tokugawa artisan society before it is viewed as a reflection of a unique vertical social structure, a manifestation of a group-oriented value system, or the result of managerial manipulation of passive workers.

The past also influenced workers in their concerns for fair treatment and membership. These concerns were present in the early labor disputes of the nineteenth century. The workers who organized unions or who hastily formed "struggle groups" demanded more than better pay. In disputes over derogatory job titles or the absence of regular pay raises and bonuses, skilled locomotive engineers or machinists called for status and treatment closer to that of white-collar and technical employees. In the rhetoric of the Ironworkers Union or the speeches at an early "Labor Day," they demanded respect from society. Workers at the turn of the century were seldom able to win respect or concrete demands, but these aspirations remained and reemerged later in new contexts to influence the labor relationship.

This crucial notion of membership transcended the narrow bounds of the enterprise. Especially in the decades when the traveler pattern was common, the concern of workers with terms of membership in the firm was one part of a broader desire, rooted in the recent past, for membership in the mainstream of society. At least in the formal status order of Tokugawa society, artisans and merchants ranked a poor third and fourth behind samurai and peasants. After the Restoration, the capitalist successors to the Tokugawa merchants were eventually, if with no small difficulty, able to carve out a fairly respectable niche and justify their activities in terms of service to the nation. Factory laborers were less successful. Unlike aspiring young managers or technicians, they obtained nothing more than a rudimentary education. As the diploma of a technical school, high school, or university became the single most important credential conferring social status and respectability by the early twentieth century, the factory workers became perhaps a less respected group than the Tokugawa artisans had been. Certainly they felt themselves to be semi-outcasts, those left behind in "lower-class society." The very strong desire for respect, for "human" treatment, and ultimately for membership, whether in society or in a company, must be seen in this historical context. By viewing the matter this way, one can understand why the travelers who were active in the early Ironworkers Union would be interested in more respectable titles in a particular firm, and would rather fight than switch jobs. Even if the traveler was not thinking of a career at a single factory, he viewed his treatment while there as a matter of concern, linked to his respectability as a member of society.

The timing of Japanese industrialization and the emergence of a prominent model of bureaucratic organization together defined much of the context for the early managerial response to these workers. Even in the era of indirect control, managers saw turnover as a costly problem, and they took important steps to retain the most valuable skilled workers. The striking early sensitivity to this problem (not generally seen as a major cost in the United States until World War I) can be explained in large measure by Japan's place as a relatively late developer, for we may postulate a greater bottleneck in labor than in capital for a late developer, and a greater labor bottleneck for a late than an early developer.[3] Despite a large pool of unskilled rural migrants, skilled men were hard to find in Japan. The regular annual or semiannual pay raise, offered to some skilled men in both private and public firms in the nineteenth century, began as a device to retain them. The same thinking lay behind the more or less elaborate wage and promotion scales adopted by a very few innovative naval shipyards and private factories. But, if the scarcity of skilled men, a trait of the late developer, explains the need for some such policies, how do we explain the choice of these particular steps? Very likely, Japanese managers acted with an eye toward the nearby model of hierarchical salary and rank scales for officials in the increasingly prestigious and seemingly efficient bureaus and departments of the new Meiji Government.

In addition to a Tokugawa legacy and the particular timing of Japanese industrial growth, more general features of capitalist economic development also shaped the labor relationship in these early decades, and later as well. Long-term economic growth brought greater resources to the leading firms, and investment in new capital equipment in turn increased the value of skilled workers who seldom quit and who used expensive machinery efficiently. By about 1900, this process of accumulation had proceeded far enough to stimulate a major new departure, the first reshaping of the labor relationship. At varied moments in the interwar decade spanning the turn of the century, managers in the major heavy industrial firms began, with some success, to assert direct control over the work force and eliminate the oyakata. They usually converted independent labor bosses into foremen or replaced them with men willing to serve in a hierarchy of managerial control. The concurrent attempt to control the younger, unranked skilled workers more directly and impose stricter discipline upon them was less successful. The policies of direct control drew upon and developed a particular Japanese vocabulary of paternal care, but a major portion of the skilled men in heavy industry remained footloose and ill-disciplined, and significant numbers began to oppose managers. The challenge presented by these men eventually led to the second reshaping of the labor relationship.

Throughout the first half of the twentieth century, managers and workers continued to deal with each other in this multi-layered Japanese context of relatively late capitalist economic growth. The parties to the labor relationship themselves changed over time, and they changed in relation to each other, stimulating further internal changes. Less abstractly, workers developed more sophisticated ways of organizing and became stronger relative to managers. The latter responded with new policies and worked out a rough concensus concerning, for example, union-busting and factory councils in the 1920s. This, in turn, affected the labor movement. Management policies to control or discipline labor or to attract and keep skilled men often provoked an active worker response—a strike or a dispute. New policies or a changed management perspective would result, but future disputes could occur as soon as workers began to criticize the new status quo. Out of such give and take emerged first expectations and later practices concerning jobs and wages, in particular, that eventually became the core of a Japanese employment system.

This process can be described as a series of labor responses to management initiatives, or as the reverse. Ultimately, any new step was both response and initiative. The important new management policies of the nineteenth century, the incremental wage scale and the regular raise, were initiatives that established a framework for discussion and dispute over the following decades, even as they unfolded partly in response to worker behavior. Managers early in the twentieth century likewise responded to the independence of the Meiji worker and the need to profit from the use of expensive new machinery with a new system of labor control, offering special benefits to foremen, training some of their own workers, and developing the paternal ideology. Subsequent organized labor activity sought to extend these policies to a broader group of workers or transform capricious paternalism into systematic treatment.

The first two decades of the twentieth century witnessed the emergence of an energetic working-class movement in the growing industrial centers of Osaka, Kobe, Tokyo, and Yokohama which challenged part of the effort at more direct labor control. Organized labor in large factories rejected the newly articulated ideology of industrial paternalism, and workers showed scant enthusiasm for mutual-aid or educational programs designed to put this philosophy into practice. Talk of paternal care reinforced by limited material benefits was inadequate in the face of antagonistic workers, somewhat better organized and more aware of themselves as a class than in the nineteenth century.

The Japanese workers active in this movement continued to build organizations out of workshop or factory branches. Small, tightly knit work groups of from 5 to 20 individuals were the basic units of union and non-union labor activity. From around the time of the Russo-Japanese war, and especially in 1906 and 1907, workers built on the strength of workshop unity with some success and gradually growing sophistication, usually in the absence of unions, while foremen became less likely to side with workers and more apt to serve as mediators or company loyalists. During and after World War I, this non-union stream of labor activity in heavy industry began to merge with the better-known union movement of the Yūaikai. This coalescence was partly responsible for transforming the Yūaikai into the more combative Sōdōmei, and it gave birth to a host of other unions just after the war. The thought and behavior of impatient worker activists interested in disputes and concrete demands changed the union movement even as unions gave increased discipline and direction to the efforts of these workers. Even so, by 1921, well-organized, stable unions had only begun to harness the energy of workers.

The demands raised by both union and non-union workers reflected the multi-layered context. Workers absorbed ideas common to labor unions worldwide and mixed these with concerns derived from their particular heritage of values. After World War I ended in apparent victory for democracy and a new order in Russia, those most attuned to new ideas demanded the rights of labor, the living wage, the 8-hour day, and collective bargaining agreements. Some went further as Marxist thought grew in influence and popularity, calling for profit-sharing and an end to capitalist exploitation. Shibaura workers at the Tokyo factory supported the anarchism of their union leaders with enthusiasm in the early 1920s. The men at the Tsurumi plant also opposed capitalism as they fought for a Communist-Hyōgikai platform rejected by their Tokyo co-workers. Some workers assimilated radical programs well enough to make concrete demands over treatment which reflected these abstract ideological stands. Workers at Ishikawajima, Yokohama Dock, and elsewhere demanded that management return a guaranteed share of profits to workers in the early 1920s. At the same time, Japanese workers during World War I and just after made demands reminiscent of the 1890s for higher status or better treatment within the firm, reflecting particular Japanese conditions and consciousness. They sought regular raises, raises given equally to all workers, or bonuses approaching those granted to salaried, white-collar employees. Behind such demands was the continued desire for "human" treatment and fuller membership in both society and the enterprise. These two sets of ideas on occasion merged. In demands for worker election of foremen, raised in several disputes of this era, the new "democratic" notion of elections merged with the pre-union desire to insure fair treatment by superiors. And, in later decades, the persistent call for the worldwide labor goal of a living wage gained urgency from its resonance with the particular belief of Japanese workers that pay ought to rise with seniority and, by implication, need.

The more deeply rooted ideas were those focused on gaining equality of treatment and status within the system. They outlasted the prewar flowering of democratic and radical thought, bringing continued pressure upon managers and eventual change in practice. As in the nineteenth century, the notion of membership was at the heart of this Japanese bundle of ideas during World War I and after. Firms of the Meiji era apparently gave white-collar employees from top managers to some clerical workers wage benefits and a degree of job security and career opportunity that qualitatively distinguished their terms of membership in the organization from those of men and women in the factories.[4] In the twentieth century, companies very gradually extended some benefits of membership in the firm to factory workers. Labor-market and labor-movement forces were both at work here. In the nineteenth century, managers had already decided that the cost of turnover required some attempts to retain skilled workers, and the career-oriented wage scale and experiments with the periodic seniority raise first appeared. Once managers broke the ice, if not before, and offered benefits previously reserved to high-ranking staff to workers, both stated worker demands and unstated expectations created further pressure to enlarge the group of full members.

The combination of a more coherent and articulate ideological grounding for such demands, more sophisticated and cohesive organization, and the favorable economic conditions of 1916 through 1920 resulted in a period of unprecedented hostility and conflict. The first round in the clash of a vigorous but young working-class movement with the limited paternalism offered by heavy industrial managers went to the workers. Because a good part of the working-class offensive of those years attempted to gain respect and better treatment within the enterprise at the expense of forging industry-wide links, workers were vulnerable to efforts to divide and conquer or coopt them. Even so, they forced managers, bureaucrats, and politicians, their sleep troubled with nightmares of European-style turmoil, back to the drawing board between 1918 and 1921 to design a renovated, more cooperative version of paternalism. One small symbol of the resulting shift in management policy was the elimination of old-fashioned paternalistic vocabulary from the Uraga Dock Company Work Rules in 1921; pay was no longer "bestowed," merely "given." A bit more substantive were the plans for factory councils or company unions drawn up and implemented at Uraga, Shibaura, Yokohama Dock Company, and dozens of other firms.

Subtle tensions between workers and managers were as important as open disputes in reshaping the labor relationship. The fear of a strike or a union, or a desire to satisfy worker expectations before they were expressed as demands or even requests, could be as important as a strike in stimulating new policy. Policies that appear, at first glance, to have been unilateral management innovations often emerged against such a background. This was true of Shibaura's new labor management policies of 1915, prompted by the success of the Yūaikai at the Shibaura plant. Nippon Kōkan, in 1920, responded only to the *possibility* that inaction would lead to labor unrest when it reduced the work day from 12 to 10 hours, and the manager of the Kure Naval Yard acted in 1922 on the perception that inaction could encourage "dangerous ideas" when he implemented a pioneering system of seniority wages reflecting need, very similar to that adopted seven years later at Yokohama Dock.

By forcing managers to make symbolic and substantive changes and gaining a small measure of the respect they demanded, workers influenced the early shaping of a Japanese structure of labor relations. In these and other changes of World War I and its immediate aftermath, we can discern the formation of pieces of the so-called Japanese employment system. Under pressures from the wartime labor shortage and the labor movement, managers raised pay, implemented various bonuses and allowances, and resorted more regularly to the semiannual pay raise. Such incentives were sometimes defensive responses to worker demands, sometimes offered to keep skilled workers from switching jobs, and sometimes both. These scattered pieces did not form a coherent whole by 1921.

A major reshaping of the system of paternalism and direct control thus began in the early post-World War I years. It continued through the 1920s, as managers regained the initiative in their struggle with unions by holding off labor in the big shipyards in 1921. The working-class movement in large factories had not built a solid organizational foundation out of the more or less natural base of workshop or work-group units. Union leaders in the 1920s did organize a few strong factory unions, but they were unable to create industrial unions to join these units together effectively. Active unions were more often concerned with gaining company-specific demands and better terms of membership. Managers took advantage of this and, aided by government repression of left-wing unions and a decade of bad times, succeeded in fragmenting the union movement, diverting the energies of some workers into company-controlled factory councils, and eliminating union strength from almost all large factories by 1931. Small factories became the focus of organizing efforts and union growth by the mid-1920s, and the organized proportion of the work force declined after 1931.

Part of the managerial response to organized labor in the 1920s was a revised ideology stressing a cooperative version of paternalism.

Companies sought to blunt the edge of worker dissatisfaction with their status or treatment by calling for cooperation (*kyōchō*) and offering some forums for discussion between worker and manager representatives. These concessions only went as far as required by the effort to oust independent labor unions. Managers did not eliminate practices that separated workers from white-collar employees and humiliated them: separate entrances, toilets, and dining halls; body checks; punitive work rules; incentive wages; and job insecurity. Continued dissonance between even the new ideology and such practices resulted in continued demands for change, but workers were not powerful enough to win more than a few minor reforms.

Workers were on the defensive, but labor activities were important. A set of worker interests or expectations took shape clearly in pressures exerted for the spread or continuation of practices started earlier, and workers staked a claim to benefits which only became common when their power was far greater: regular seniority wage increases; a more limited use of incentive or output wages; guarantees of job security; and a recognition that workers were full members of the enterprise. Some of these policies, and a labor desire to make them more systematic, had been present earlier, but the hostile economic environment of the 1920s dulled the glamour of the traveler option and gave these demands a new urgency.

As workers articulated their interests, both the security of blue-collar jobs and the structure of day wages changed slightly. At the turn of the century, managers had been quick to fire as soon as business dipped slightly, and their response was equally rapid in the post-World War I slump. But labor activities in defense of jobs, in part perhaps stimulated by new management calls for a cooperative partnership, gradually changed matters on the level of policy as well as ideas. The value workers placed on membership goes a long way toward explaining the tenacity with which jobs were defended in the 1920s, when a cool appraisal of their weakness could have caused union leaders to avoid confrontations. In part due to this tenacity, the idea that workers ought to be treated like their superiors in the organization gradually took root. While more popular among workers than managers and never well translated into reality before the 1950s, this idea was nonetheless significant. The value placed on membership was expressed in early disputes, fed by management policy and the statement of a paternal ideology, and finally developed into an influential belief among workers that they had a right to be treated fairly and to "belong." Thus, although mass dismissals did take place during the Depression years of 1927–1932, managers carefully laid the groundwork for layoffs in most cases, negotiating with union or worker representatives over numbers to be fired and terms of separation. After a decade of struggles over job security, workers and, to some extent, managers both felt that to fire was to violate acceptable behavior and to break an unwritten compact.

Similarly, in the realm of wages, worker activity reflected and helped create expectations of regularity. When the periodic raise and the semiannual bonus first appeared, they were implemented solely at management convenience. In the 1920s, workers often called for the regular raise to no avail in labor disputes, and on occasion they affirmed the related notion that wages should be calculated with reference to a worker's needs. At least in the case of Yokohama Dock Company in 1929, workers gained such a wage.

The roots of post-World War II practices can be found in these expectations and practices concerning jobs and wages, as well as in calls for various forms of company welfare and experiments with factory councils. A combination of pressures from the labor market, tied in part to Japan's late-developer status, and pressures from the labor movement, pushed managers to adopt some of these policies by offering regular raises in times of expansion or moving slowly before firing in a depression. In addition, such managerial behavior resonated nicely with, and in turn reinforced, the paternal ideology. But the labor-movement pressure in the interwar decades proved to be weak; managers were free to ignore the dictates of a paternal ideology in the face of a more compelling logic of capital.

Because this countervailing business pressure was also at work, the history of labor relations between the world wars produced a complex of practices noteworthy for their inconsistency and insecurity. Taking a cue from German and American managers of this same era, numerous Japanese businessmen joined a so-called rationalization movement in the 1920s. At the firm level, this embraced a broad range of measures, from layoffs, wage cuts, and cutbacks in welfare programs to introduction of new incentive wage schemes or cuts in unit prices. The same business logic at work in Europe and the United States in the 1920s dictated policies that increased the insecurity of the worker's place in the company, in the belief that insecurity, not paternal care, would provoke efficient labor. Managers at NKK or Uraga, determined to raise productivity and survive in the face of severe international competition, suspended regular wage hikes and introduced unpopular incentive-wage schemes in the mid-1920s, and they and others eventually did dismiss thousands in the Depression at the end of the decade. As a result, the level of tension remained fairly high in the 1920s. Because worker membership in the enterprise was tenuous, the community or family metaphors so often used to describe the Japanese factory of this era are inappropriate. Because managers distrusted workers and saw them as ill-disciplined men in need of constant prodding, even the "paternal" label is misleading. A paternal father can be a stern, authoritarian figure, but he is expected to provide for his charges, and, most important, he expects his care to evoke reciprocal loyal obedience. Prewar managers did not rely on the paternal provision of care to secure efficient labor.[5] They sought to exact diligent work through incentive wages, strict rules, and unimpeded exercise of authority. This management attitude, together with the uncertain worker commitment to the enterprise (the two cannot be separated), set the tone of the labor relationship of the interwar years—a system of authoritarian labor control.

World War II initiated a process by which the bureaucracy and then labor unions transformed this system into a more secure and predictable set of practices and extended it to a larger portion of the work force than before. To some extent, wartime changes transcended the Japanese case. The Depression and then mobilization for war intensified state attention to social and economic planning and control in Europe and even the United States. Welfare Ministry bureaucrats in Japan were not alone in claiming that subjects or citizens called on to sacrifice for the state deserved a "living wage," if not for abstract principles of justice then simply to insure continued willingness to serve. Nor was the hollow ring to such claims, in the face of the reality of war, peculiar to Japan. But the existing system of labor relations was the point of departure for pragmatic bureaucrats who sought to control, or occasionally reform, society. Bureaucratic initiatives that focused on wages or the organization of labor sought to systematize and broaden customary and haphazard practices, such as the periodic pay increase or the use of factory councils.

The government limited management's authority to set the terms of work in 1942, imposing by fiat a wage system that guaranteed to all who showed up to work a yearly or semiannual pay raise and that made need, as reflected in age or family size, a mandatory part of the wage calculus. It gave the force of law to customary benefits expected by workers but not always offered by managers. This state sanction of livelihood wage principle and practice reaffirmed the justice or at least appropriateness of earlier labor demands. It stimulated worker expectations and demands both during and after the war.

The wartime state also sought to bring stability to the labor relationship and, later, to raise productivity, through the national network of Sanpō patriotic labor organizations. In some respects, the Sanpō movement, like wage policy, reinforced prior attitudes and expectations, restating calls for equality among all employees without using a democratic vocabulary. Sanpō ideology emphasized the need for equality in treatment of blue and white collar, and respect for the contribution of the laborer. Intellectuals associated with the Shōwa Kenkyūkai joined the chorus, and the Home Ministry complained in 1942 that managers paid only lip service to the notion of the enterprise as a family and that "treatment of workers and staff is fundamentally different."[6]

Most of these wartime policies had little immediate effect; they foreshadowed later changes more than they caused them. During the war, wage regulations did not bring stability to worker livelihoods, and Sanpō hardly changed the relationship of a wage laborer to the firm. Managers greatly increased their use of output pay and quietly resisted pressures for more egalitarian treatment of workers and staff. The gap between the status and treatment of blue- and white-collar employees remained wide, and low morale, rising absenteeism, and falling productivity were signs of continuing shop-floor tensions. A new wave of worker enthusiasm for democratizing (*minshuka*) the work place in the late 1940s in fact swept away many discriminatory practices and cleared a path leading to the reasonably egalitarian ideology and practices that treated the regular male worker and the white-collar office worker alike as "employees" by the 1960s.

A postwar employment system emerged out of a decade-long contest between unions and managers, refereed by a government generally unfriendly to organized labor. While much of the labor agenda, including demands for a living wage and job security, was of a piece with demands raised by workers the world over, a prewar and wartime heritage further shaped the particular constellation of demands raised by workers seeking to build a labor version of the Japanese employment system. Early postwar unions defined the living wage as payment based on need, and they hoped to use seniority, age, and family size as proxies for need. Seniority, of course, had been implicit in the calls for regular raises in the 1920s, as well as in bureaucratic policy during the war, and the bureaucracy had introduced the other factors during the war. These unions likewise defended jobs in the manner of their predecessors in the past, only now with more success. They refused to grant managers the right to dismiss anyone defined as a regular member, but the "second unions" of the 1950s left a good many workers outside this category. Unionized workers chose to place the emphasis on jobs within a company. Since the meaningful unit of union organization was the firm, they sought to defend jobs narrowly within a firm, rather than defend employment broadly within a craft or an industry. In similar fashion, the experiences of prewar and wartime labor shaped the postwar demands for a more egalitarian social relationship between workers and managers. As full members, the unionized workers claimed and gained a position on a single hierarchy of employees. This meant more complete access to welfare benefits and facilities than earlier, as well as payment of a monthly wage and bonus calculated on the same basis as that of managers, and some measure of participation in decision-making.

Managers viewed the gains made by workers at the height of early postwar union strength with distaste, if not alarm, and, between 1949 and 1955, they were able to make important adjustments to this postwar labor relationship. As in the interwar era, a logic of capital calling for efficient and productive use of labor led managers to seek to reinject an important element of insecurity into the labor relationship. By 1955, they had regained a significant degree of discretion in wage calculations and job decisions, and they had placed workers in a clearly subordinate position in any consultation that took place. But unions remained far stronger than in the interwar era, and this settlement left the regular workers in large firms with noteworthy gains. It gradually came to include many of the male temporary workers, although insecurity and low-status are still central features of factory life for the subcontractors and part-time women left outside the system. In a context of unprecedented economic growth, the settlement has proved remarkably enduring.

The history of labor relations in Japan involved conflict on several levels, although volatile class conflict was limited to the two postwar eras in the twentieth century. Concern with conflict does not deny Japanese culture or cultural values a place in this corner of Japanese history, but it does require that we use the notion of culture with care, together with attention to questions of power and conflict. At times, cultural values of consensus and loyalty within a group, such as the Yokosen shipbuilders in 1921, probably united it in conflict with others. We must not create a false dichotomy between culture and conflict; the two are not mutually exclusive but inseparable. Each takes on greater meaning when studied together with the other in a historical context. To simply credit cultural traditions centered upon an ethic of loyalty with a major role in the creation of an employment system is to lose sight of the dialectic by which history unfolds. Cultural values are not the same for all in the culture, and they change with history. They are interpreted and manipulated differently by different groups in a society. At times, they take on a class dimension. Managers spoke of beautiful customs to *avoid improving* conditions of work, while laborers demanded not only higher pay but better terms of membership when they *sought to improve* their situation. This working-class concern with and use of the "cultural" value of membership emerged out of a particular set of historical circumstances, shaped by the nature of Tokugawa society, the new Meiji order, and industrialization in a capitalist system. It in turn shaped the labor relationship.

Appendix
Notes
Bibliography
Index

Figure 5 Map of Tokyo-Yokohama (Keihin) Industrial Region, 1921

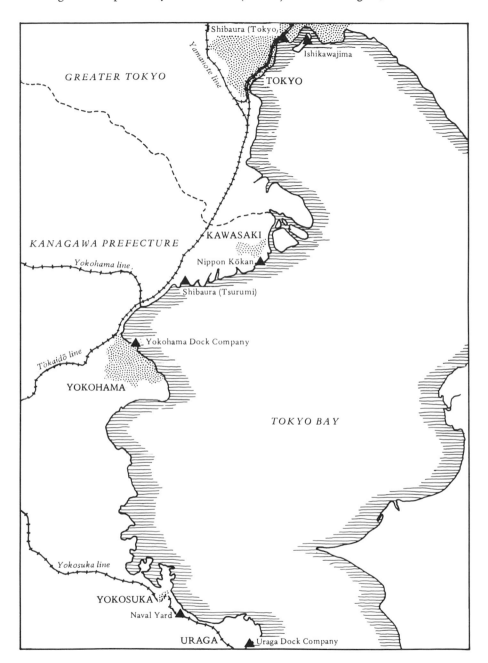

Source: *Kanagawa ken shi: shiryō hen*, Vol. 11 (Insert).

Appendix

Table A Production Indices, 1890–1945, Series One

Year	All Industrial Production	Machine Industry
1890	3.74	4.67
1891	3.50	3.79
1892	4.19	3.53
1893	4.44	5.01
1894	5.79	6.69
1895	6.57	7.70
1896	7.62	11.24
1897	7.82	11.86
1898	8.97	13.51
1899	10.34	8.31
1900	11.30	12.53
1901	12.59	11.52
1902	14.13	12.29
1903	15.04	14.43
1904	17.83	19.24
1905	21.79	27.78
1906	22.87	25.48
1907	26.44	28.73
1908	26.43	28.84
1909	27.49	24.61
1910	31.88	32.46
1911	35.65	40.77
1912	40.90	50.10
1913	44.02	47.68
1914	44.68	42.47
1915	48.64	39.93
1916	56.37	53.44
1917	65.18	68.83
1918	73.23	76.09
1919	79.02	83.15
1920	80.52	94.33
1921	79.51	76.43

Table A *(Continued)*

Year	All Industrial Production	Machine Industry
1922	92.71	106.89
1923	99.60	96.59
1924	107.75	118.07
1925	110.77	99.21
1926	127.38	132.76
1927	134.62	134.46
1928	147.44	155.63
1929	163.31	165.26
1930	158.38	133.60
1931	152.81	113.78
1932	167.71	133.38
1933	192.54	177.67
1934	213.33	206.86
1935	229.94	236.17
1936	245.35	255.38

Average production, 1921–1925, in each sector set at 100. For all industry, 100 equivalent to 1.787 billion yen. For machine industry, 100 equivalent to 330 million yen.

Production Indices, 1890–1945, Series Two

Year	All Industrial Production	Machine Industry
1934	89.6	84.9
1935	99.1	96.0
1936	110.6	118.8
1937	130.7	147.8
1938	143.7	192.7
1939	149.2	194.8
1940	149.3	208.7
1941	150.0	215.9
1942	144.8	234.1
1943	161.2	315.3
1944	182.1	463.3
1945	59.1	147.3

For series two, 100 is the average production in each sector in 1934–1936.

Source: NRUS X, 30–31.

Table B Bank of Japan's Tokyo Wholesale Price Indices, 1887–1944

Year	Old Index[a]	New Index[b]
1887	102	
1888	107	
1889	112	
1890	117	
1891	109	
1892	115	
1893	119	
1894	126	
1895	135	
1896	145	
1897	161	
1898	170	
1899	171	
1900	183	100.04
1901	175	95.97
1902	171	96.90
1903	183	103.09
1904	194	108.36
1905	213	116.36
1906	216	119.75
1907	233	129.29
1908	226	124.55
1909	215	118.76
1910	221	120.30
1911	229	124.70
1912	245	132.07
1913		132.32
1914		126.31
1915		127.76
1916		154.57
1917		194.50
1918		254.77
1919		311.98
1920		343.19
1921		265.09
1922		259.00
1923		263.48
1924		273.20
1925		267.84
1926		236.7
1928		226.1
1929		219.8
1930		181.0

Table B *(Continued)*
Bank of Japan's Tokyo Wholesale Price Indices, 1931–1945

Year	Old Index[a]	New Index[b]
1931		153.0
1932		161.1
1933		179.5
1934		177.6
1935		184.8
1936		197.2
1937		230.0
1938		257.4
1939		291.8
1940		332.2
1941		345.2
1942		361.7
1943		389.3
1944		451.7
1945		——

Source: NRUS X, 10–43.

Notes: [a]Old Index sets prices in January 1887 as 100 and surveys 40 commodities.

[b]New Index sets prices in October 1900 as 100 and surveys 56 commodities.

Table C (1) Strikes and Union Involvement in All Industry, 1897–1940

Year	Strikes	Strikers	Average Size	% Joining Strike at In- volved Factories	Union Involvement (%) % of Strikes	% of Strikers
1897	32	3,510	110			
1898	43	6,293	146			
1899	15	4,834	322			
1900	11	2,316	210			
1901	18	1,948	108			
1902	8	1,849	231			
1903	9	1,359	151			
1904	6	897	150			
1905	19	5,013	263			
1906	13	2,037	157			
1907	60	11,483	191			
1908	13	822	63			
1909	11	310	28			
1910	10	2,937	294			
1911	22	2,100	95			
1912	49	5,736	117			
1913	47	5,242	111			
1914	50	7,904	158			
1915	64	7,852	122			
1916	108	8,413	78			
1917	398	57,309	144			
1918	417	66,457	159			
1919	497	63,137	127			
1920	282	36,371	129			
1921	246	58,225	237			
1922	250	41,503	166	41	25	38
1923	270	36,259	134	47	39	52
1924	295	48,940	165	57	43	61
1925	270	32,472	120	45	60	81
1926	469	63,644	136	51	71	83
1927	346	43,669	126	—	67	83
1928	332	36,872	111	—	57	72
1929	494	60,084	121	—	61	81
1930	763	64,933	85	—	63	74
1931	864	54,515	63	54	70	69
1932	778	46,025	59	—	61	61
1933	525	35,880	68	—	48	47
1934	562	42,149	75	—	40	58
1935	531	31,853	60	39	43	52
1936	498	26,722	54	39	44	44
1937	530	53,429	101	44	38	52
1938	224	12,769	57	21	—	—
1939	290	20,640	71	24	—	—
1940	239	24,152	101	14	—	—

Table C (2) Strikes in Heavy Industry, 1914–1940

Year	Strikes	Strikers	Average Size	% Joining Strike at Involved Factories
1914	5	752	150	
1915	3	1,838	613	
1916	22	2,293	104	
1917	64	20,273	316	
1918	59	11,453	194	
1919	93	17,125	184	
1920	41	5,045	123	
1921	40	33,518	838	
1922	46	15,908	345	
1923	52	9,215	177	79
1924	68	9,583	141	57
1925	48	5,605	116	78
1926	74	10,101	137	60
1927	48	4,762	99	—
1928	55	4,142	75	—
1929	107	10,761	101	—
1930	182	7,351	40	—
1931	168	7,628	45	62
1932	100	3,349	33	—
1933	69	3,722	54	—
1934	69	3,746	54	—
1935	76	2,520	33	54
1936	71	2,701	38	40
1937	72	8,579	119	74
1938	35	1,419	41	9
1939	60	3,383	56	10
1940	42	11,974	285	16

Sources: 1897–1907 from *NRUS* X, 442.
1908–1913 from Hazama, *Rōmu kanri,* p. 61.
1914–1940, both 1 and 2, *NRUS* X, 446–467, 522.

Notes: C (1): Strikes include lockouts by management, 1897–1907, and dispute actions short of actual strikes, 1908–1913. 1914–1940 figures are for actual strikes only.

C (2): Actual strikes only. Heavy industry here refers to: Sum of two categories, "machine and metal-product manufacturing workers" (*kikai kinzoku hin seizō shokkō*) and "shipbuilders" (*zōsenkō*), for 1913–1923; and "machine and machine-tool manufacturing industry" (*kikai kigu seizō kōgyō*) for 1924–1940, including shipbuilders and metal workers.

Abbreviations used in Notes

KRUS   Kanagawa-ken, rōdō-bu rōsei-ka, ed., *Kanagawa-ken rōdō undō shi* (1966).

NRN   Ōhara shakai mondai kenkyū jo, *Nihon rōdō nenkan* (1920–1940).

NRUS   Rōdō undō shiryō iinkai, ed., *Nihon rōdō undō shiryō* (1959–1975).

Notes

INTRODUCTION

1. The best known descriptions of this system are: James Abegglen, *The Japanese Factory: Aspects of Its Social Organization*, and *Management and Worker: The Japanese Solution;* Robert Cole, *Japanese Blue Collar: The Changing Tradition*, and *Work, Mobility and Participation: A Comparative Study of American and Japanese Industry;* R. P. Dore, *British Factory-Japanese Factory.* W. Mark Fruin, "The Japanese Company Controversy," pp. 268–269, lists the work of scholars who have discussed the "Japanese Employment System." Dore, *British Factory-Japanese Factory,* Ch. 12, speaks of "the Japanese system," and in "More about Late Development," p. 139, he even adopts the acronym "JES."

2. Kazuo Koike, "Internal Labor Markets: Workers in Large Firms," in Taishiro Shirai, ed., *Contemporary Industrial Relations in Japan*, pp. 29–30, 38, and passim, is the only source I have seen that develops this theme in explicitly comparative fashion for contemporary Japan. He offers cross-national data on wages, length of service, and benefits to illustrate the similarity between Japanese blue-collar workers and white-collar employees in the West.

3. Koike Kazuo, *Shokuba no rōdō kumiai to sanka*, p. 6, offers a useful outline of these common perceptions of Japanese employment practices.

4. Early scholars in this field were most influenced by Ōkōchi Kazuo's prolific work in Japanese, which put forth this interpretation; see, for example, his *Nihon no rōdō kumiai*, pp. 9–10. Even Hazama's work reflects this view; see *Nihon rōmu kanri shi kenkyū*, p. 72. In English, Abegglen, *The Japanese Factory,* is best known for taking this perspective.

5. Kunio Odaka, *Toward Industrial Democracy*, pp. 1–3, concisely summarizes the "pre-modern-remnant" position and that of its critics.

6. Cole, "The Theory of Institutionalization: Permanent Employment and Tradition in Japan," pp. 46–70. Cole was apparently stimulated to write

this essay on the history of employment practices *after* conducting extensive research into contemporary labor relations, published in *Japanese Blue Collar*. Dore *adds* a chapter on "The Origins of the Japanese Employment System" to the end of *British Factory-Japanese Factory*. It would be unfair to call this an afterthought. It stimulated my own thinking on the topic tremendously, as did Cole's piece, but it does come after 374 pages on contemporary practices in Japanese and British factories and relies heavily on only two secondary works. Kōji Taira, *Economic Development and the Labor Market in Japan*, is one exception, an economist who has devoted almost an entire book to the history of labor relations and the labor market.

7. When I told Professor Hyōdō Tsutomu, my advisor at Tokyo University, at our first meeting that I planned to study the history of the Japanese employment system (*nihon koyō seido no rekishi*), he replied that the topic was fine but that, if I used that phrase with Japanese scholars, they would not understand what I meant. The common term for the topic, he said, was *rōshi kankei shi* (labor-management or labor-capital relations, depending on an important choice of characters). The difference is one of problem consciousness and not simply one of usage.

8. Cole, "Institutionalization," pp. 65, 53. Also see Cole, "The Late Developer Hypothesis: An Evaluation of its Relevance for Japanese Employment Practices," pp. 262–263, where he disagrees extensively with Dore but shares the view of management as the sole innovative force. Dore, *British Factory-Japanese Factory*, p. 401. In a more recent work on the subject, "Industrial Relations in Japan and Elsewhere," p. 369, one of his conclusions reflects a different perspective, closer to my own. "One is prompted [by awareness of the role of unions in Mexico] to look again at the early development of the *nenkō joretsu* system in Japan and to see what the unions have to do with it." Sydney Crawcour, "The Japanese Employment System," pp. 233–234, 240.

9. A few works do examine the bureaucratic role in the early years of industrialization. Unfortunately, they do not look at the government impact on labor practices in later years. Dore, *British Factory-Japanese Factory*, pp. 392–393, and "The Modernizer as a Special Case: Japanese Factory Legislation, 1882–1911." Byron K. Marshall, *Capitalism and Nationalism in Pre-war Japan*, Ch. 4.

10. See Magota Ryōhei, "Senji rōdō ron e no gimon," and Shōwa dōjinkai, ed., *Waga kuni chingin kōzō no shiteki kōsatsu*, p. 284. Magota indeed goes a good bit farther than I shall, below, in arguing that government actions were decisive.

11. John C. Pelzel has provided a fascinating, thought-provoking description

and analysis of the world of owners and artisans in small factories. The most complete version is John Pelzel, "Social Stratification in Japanese Urban Economic Life." More accessible and equally well done is "Factory Life in Japan and China Today," in Craig, ed., *Japan*.

12. See *NRUS*, X, 168-169, for numbers employed by size of factory.

13. This may account for some of the difference in interpretation between this study and that of Professor Hyōdō Tsutomu, *Nihon ni okeru rōshi kankei no tenkai*.

14. Sumiya Mikio, *Nihon chin rōdō shi ron*, p. 215, has part of this quotation. The original is in Nihon kōgakukai, ed., *Meiji kōgyō shi: kikai hen*, pp. 82-83.

15. The summary of Ishikawajima is taken from: Arai Gensui, *Tokyo Ishikawajima 50 nen shi*, pp. 77-78; Nihon zōsen kyōkai, ed., *Nihon kinsei zōsen shi*, pp. 837-842; Nihon kōgakukai, ed., *Meiji kōgyō shi: zōsen hen*, pp. 360-363; Murayama Kōzō, ed., *Seiji keizai dai nempyō* (1971) Index, I, 43, 556-557.

16. The Shibaura summary is from: Komatsu Ryūji, *Kigyō betsu kumiai no seisei*, pp. 85-86; *Tokyo mainichi shimbun* 9/5/1985; Tokyo shibaura denki kabushiki gaisha, *Shibaura seisakujo 65 nen shi* (1940); Murayama, Index, I, 306.

17. Yokohama Dock summary from Nihon zōsen kyōkai, ed., *Nihon kinsei zōsen shi*, pp. 834-836, 939; Ueno Terumasa, "1920 nendai jūkōgyō rōdō undō no hatten: senzen Yokohama dokku rōdō kumiai kōshinkai no rekishi o chūshin ni," p. 29.

18. For Uraga, Nihon kogakukai, ed., *Meiji kōgyō: zōsen*, p. 356; *Nihon kinsei zōsen shi*, pp. 831-835; Yasuda Hiroshi, "Zōsengyō rōdō undō ni okeru shokuchō no rekishiteki ichi: Uraga dokku no bunseki o chūshin ni," pp. 37-38.

19. *Nippon kōkan kabushiki gaisha 40 nen shi* (1952), pp. 24-39; *Nihon kindai shi jiten* (1978), p. 520.

1. ORGANIZING INDUSTRIAL WORKERS

1. *NRUS*, X, 64-65, 74-75, 83, 126-127.

2. *Nihon kinsei zōsen*, pp. 279-280. Sumiya Mikio, ed., *Nihon shokugyō kunren hattatsu shi* I, 8, 12; Nakanishi Yō, "Nihon ni okeru jūkōgyō daikeiei no seisei katei," pp. 78-80.

3. Sumiya, *Kunren shi*, p. 12.

4. Nihon kōgakukai, ed., *Meiji kōgyō: kikai*, p. 84. Nihon zōsen kyōkai, ed., *Nihon kinsei zōsen*, pp. 935, 941-943.

5. Sumiya, *Kunren shi*, pp. 13-14.

6. *Tōyō keizai shimpō* 3/15/1910, p. 212.

7. Tetsuo Nakaoka, "Imitation or Self-reliance: A lesson from the early history of modern Japanese iron manufacturing technology."

8. *Oyakata* being the term for master, *wakate* or *watari shokunin* for journeymen, and *totei* or *deshi* for apprentices. Journeymen in modern occupations were later called *watari shokkō*.

9. Sumiya, *Kunren shi,* pp. 13–14.

10. *NRUS,* II, 257–258, 276.

11. Sumiya, *Chin rōdō shi ron,* p. 36.

12. Ibid., pp. 36, 47. Sumiya, *Kunren shi,* pp. 76–77.

13. Two recent works on British labor history (or prehistory) offer an illuminating analysis of the relationship between preindustrial craft organizations and practices and industrial unions and disputes. C. R. Dobson, *Masters and Journeymen: A Prehistory of Industrial Relations,* focuses on continuities in disputes and methods of dispute resolution. R. A. Leeson, *Travelling Brothers: The six centuries road from craft fellowship to trade unionism,* looks mainly at the evolution of tramp networks and craft societies into trade unions. The description here is based primarily upon his work.

14. Leeson, *Travelling Brothers,* Ch. 9, briefly discusses continental journeymen. It seems that control in their case was imposed from without, by the state, not from within by craft societies. The absence of effective controls of either sort is the distinguishing feature of the Japanese case.

15. Sumiya, *Chin rōdō shi ron,* pp. 45–47; Tokyo kōgyō gakkō, *Kōgyō kyōiku shisetsu shiryō,* pp. 32–33; Nakanishi, "Nihon ni okeru jūkōgyō," pp. 78, 83.

16. Yokoyama Gennosuke, *Naichi zakkyo go no Nihon* (1899), pp. 38–40; *Rōdō sekai,* 5/1/1898; Tsuda Masumi, *Nihon no toshi kasō shakai,* pp. 136–137.

17. *Tokyo mainichi shimbun,* 9/8/1895.

18. For example, Henry Rosovsky, *Capital Formation in Japan, 1868–1940,* p. 104, sees "the well-known willingness of the Japanese worker to be diligent and accurate," as a factor giving Meiji and twentieth-century Japan an "unusually good labor force," which contributed to economic growth.

19. Thomas Smith, *Agrarian Origins of Modern Japan,* pp. 122–123, 201, 211–213.

20. Nakanishi, "Nihon ni okeru jūkōgyō," pp. 45, 90.

21. Dore, *British Factory-Japanese Factory,* p. 38. Translation is Dore's. The original is found in Sumiya, *Chin rōdō shi ron,* pp. 234–235.

22. *Jiji shimpō,* 10/21/1897.

23. Nakanishi, "Nihon ni okeru jūkōgyō," p. 90.

24. Yokoyama Gennosuke, "Tokyo no kōjōchi oyobi kōjō seikatsu no panorama," reprinted in *NRUS*, III, 14–15.

25. Nōshōmushō shōkō kyoku, *Shokkō jijō*, II, 19–20. Volume and page numbers here refer to the 1976 Shin kigensha reprint.

26. *Shokkō jijō*, III, 172. *NRUS*, I, 599. *Rōdō sekai*, 12/15/1897, p. 8, and 1/1/1898, p. 5.

27. *Tōyō keizai shimpō*, 3/5/1910, p. 212.

28. *Yūai shimpō*, 8/1/1914, p. 4; 8/15/1914, p. 4.

29. *Ni roku shimpō*, 4/4, 4/5, 4/6/1901.

30. *NRUS*, I, 598.

31. Ibid., p. 597.

32. *Tokyo mainichi shimbun*, 11/13/1899, p. 2.

33. Katayama Sen, *Jiden*, p. 195 of the Iwanami reprint.

34. Tokyo daigaku shakai kagaku kenkyūjo, "Takayama Jiroichi shi to no mensetsu kiroku," pp. 41–44.

35. Nakanishi Yō, "Daiichiji taisen zengo no rōshi kankei," in Sumiya, ed. *Nihon rōshi kankei shi ron*, p. 86.

36. *Shokkō jijō*, II, 12.

37. Ibid.

38. *Shakai undō ōrai*, October 1935, pp. 110–113.

39. Yokoyama, *Nihon no kasō shakai*, p. 237; *Rōdō sekai*, 4/1/1898, p. 5.

40. For this quotation, see *Rōdō sekai*, 10/1/1898, pp. 4–5.

41. Ibid., 4/1/1898, p. 6.

42. Ikeda Makoto, *Nihon kikaikō kumiai seiritsu shi ron*, p. 25. Oyakata were referred to as *tōryō* in construction trades.

43. Nōshōmusho, *Shokkō jijō*, II, 36–38, III, 168–170.

44. Yokoyama, "Panorama," *NRUS*, III, 12.

45. Sumiya Mikio, *Nihon chin rōdō no shiteki kenkyū*, p. 8, quotes the 1904 Summary of Factory Reports (*Kōjō chōsa yōryō*).

46. *Tōyō keizai shimpō*, 5/25/1903, p. 9.

47. David Montgomery, "Workers Control of Machine Production in the Nineteenth Century," in Montgomery, *Workers Control in America*, p. 9.

48. These schools were actually meant to produce workers and foremen. However, teaching took place entirely in the classroom, not the workshop, and graduates invariably became staff technicians instead. Experienced skilled workers trained on the job filled foreman positions. Sumiya, *Chin rōdō shi ron*, pp. 223–227. Nihon zōsen kyōkai, ed. *Nihon kinsei zōsen*, p. 922.

49. Nōshōmusho, *Shokkō jijō*, III, 145. See Yokoyama *Naichi zakkyo go*, p. 45, for a less dramatic but similar scene.

50. Nōshōmusho, *Shokkō jijō,* III, 170.
51. *Tōyō keizai shimpō,* 3/15/1910, p. 212.
52. Hyōdō, *Rōshi kankei,* p. 80.
53. *Shokkō jijō,* III, 144.
54. Nakanishi, "Nihon ni okeru jūkōgyō," pp. 48–54.
55. Tokyo daigaku, "Takayama."
56. *Mainichi shimbun,* 12/14, 12/17, 12/18/1895. *Rōdō sekai,* 1/15/1898, p. 5. *Shokkō jijō,* III, 168.
57. *Tokyo Shibaura 65 nen shi,* pp. 38, 307.
58. Examples or descriptions of all these wage practices are found in *Yūai shimpō,* 6/1/1914; *Jiji shimpō,* 10/26/1897; *Shokkō jijō,* II, 19, III, 169, 178; Yokoyama, *Naichi zakkyo go,* pp. 41–42.
59. Sumiya, *Kunren shi,* pp. 22, 27.
60. For the Yokosuka story, Sumiya, *Chin rōdō shi ron,* p. 235, and Hyō-dō, *Rōshi kankei,* p. 76, note 6, and pp. 77–78. Emphasis is added. Also, Ikeda Makoto, "Nihon tetsudō kikaikō no tōsō," pp. 43–44, 53–54, shows that the Japan Railway Company, like Yokosuka, was unable to wrest authority from oyakata in the nineteenth century.
61. The Halsey system set a standard time for a particular individual or group job. If the job was completed exactly on time, the worker or work group received only the appropriate hourly pay. If completed in less than the standard time, the worker received the difference between actual work time and standard time, multiplied by his hourly wage and then divided by 2, as his premium. If a job rated at 10 hours was done in 6, the 4-hour difference, divided by 2 then multiplied by the hourly wage, was the premium, in this case 2 hours' extra pay.
62. Shōwa, *Chingin,* pp. 227–239.
63. *Tokyo Shibaura 65 nen shi,* p. 301.
64. Sumiya, *Kunren shi,* p. 20; *Shiteki kenkyū,* p. 73.
65. Sumiya, *Kunren shi,* p. 20.
66. Yokoyama, *Naichi zakkyo go,* pp. 41–42.
67. Sumiya, *Kunren shi,* p. 19; Hyōdō, *Rōshi kankei,* p. 198. The testing period was shortened over time, but the principle remained the same. Similar hierarchies and a similar "slotting in" process for recruits were found at railway factories.
68. Sumiya, *Chin rōdō shi ron,* p. 220. *Shokkō jijō,* II, 11–12 shows that only 19% of the Kure Naval Yard's 4,982 workers in 1901 had been employed for over 5 continuous years. Also, see Table 2.
69. Yokoyama, *Naichi zakkyo go,* pp. 41–42.
70. *Shokkō jijō,* III, 142.
71. A situation labeled that of the late developer by Ronald Dore, *British Factory-Japanese Factory,* pp. 401–403.

72. Sumiya, *Chin rōdō shi ron,* p. 235.
73. Aoki Masahisa, "Nittetsu kikankata sōgi kenkyū," pp. 11–32, and Ikeda Makoto, "Nihon tetsudō kikaikō no tōsō," pp. 58–71.
74. See Earl Kinmoth, *The Self-Made Man in Meiji Japanese Thought,* Ch. 5, for more on this point.
75. Matsuzawa Hiroaki, *Nihon shakaishugi no shisō,* pp. 116–142, and especially pp. 126–128, makes some of these points in his discussion of "The Closing of the Meiji State System and Worker Society." Although he focuses on the 1910s, this appears to stem from the abundant Yūaikai documents for that decade. He would probably agree that the Yūaikai view had roots going back to these late Meiji workers.
76. Andrew Gordon, "Workers, Managers, and Bureaucrats in Japan: Labor Relations in Heavy Industry, 1853–1945," Ch. 3, for details.
77. Nimura Kazuo first suggested to me that a very different tradition of craft organization pointed Japanese labor history in a direction distinct from that in Europe. Leeson, *Travelling Brothers,* makes a persuasive case that trade unions developed out of preindustrial craft organizations in England. See also Koike, *Shokuba no rōdō kumiai,* pp. 239–240.
78. Smith, *Agrarian Origins,* p. 212, concludes that labor "posed no major problem" for industrialization in Japan and that "for upward of two hundred years the agricultural labor force had been unwittingly preparing for the transition to factory employment." While he and others have demonstrated conclusively that rural industries and day-wage labor spread in the late Tokugawa years, the Meiji record suggests that such developments did little to prepare the workers for ready acceptance of factory life. The pace and intensity of work demanded of a day laborer in a rural town, or even in Edo, or of a cotton weaver taking in work from a broker in the Kinai area, was very likely a far cry from the pace demanded by new mechanized factories. A pool of laborers ready, willing, and soon able to enter the factory and work efficiently was not one of the preconditions the Tokugawa era offered Japan in its drive to industrialize.

2. PATERNALISM AND DIRECT MANAGEMENT

1. Hyōdō, *Rōshi kankei,* pp. 215–225; Miyake Akimasa, "Nichiro sensō zengo no rōdōsha undō," pp. 25–28.
2. Hyōdō, *Rōshi kankei,* pp. 65–67, 91, 225.
3. Tōdai, "Takayama," pp. 11, 12, 17, 14–15.
4. *Tokyo Shibaura 65 nen shi,* p. 47.
5. Yamamoto Kiyoshi, *Nihon rōdō shijō no kōzō,* pp. 33–35.
6. Hyōdō, *Rōshi kankei,* pp. 91, 93, 212–213, 224. Miyake, "Nichiro

sensō zengo," pp. 25–28, summarizes this process in shipbuilding, the arsenals, and the machine industry.

7. Tōdai, "Takayama," pp. 56–57; Hyōdō, *Rōshi kankei*, p. 224.

8. Tōdai, "Takayama," pp. 61–66.

9. Ikeda Makoto and Ōmae Sakuro, *Nihon rōdō undō shi ron*, pp. 48–50. Ikeda, *Kikaikō kumiai*, p. 88. Tōdai, "Takayama," confirms that conditions at Ishikawajima were similar. By the war years, the *tōmoku*, a term roughly equivalent to oyakata, who formerly controlled up to 100 workers, no longer did so. Foremen (*kumichō*) had appeared and ran groups of 8 to 20 workers in a single craft, such as riveting, caulking, or machine finishing. The foremen were workers who had risen from the ranks, and the groups were more stable than previously. The *tōmoku* now acted as general supervisors, coordinating jobs handed out to various foremen. See pp. 71–98.

10. Hyōdō, *Rōshi kankei*, p. 219, 259–260. See Ikeda and Ōmae, *Nihon rōdō undō shi ron*, pp. 85–100, for details on similar policies of Kansai-area factories. Also, Nimura Kazuo, "Rōdosha kaikyū no jōtai to rōdō undō."

11. The Shibaura summary is from Komatsu Ryūji, *Kigyō betsu kumiai no seisei*, pp. 85–86; *Tokyo mainichi shimbun* 9/5/1895; *Tokyo Shibaura seisakujo 65 nen shi* (1940); Murayama, *Seiji keizai dai nempyō* Index, I, 306.

12. Onō had impressive credentials. He was a major stockholder in and director of Ōji Paper Company and had been Director of the Mitsui Bank's Kobe branch previous to this difficult assignment; *Tokyo Shibaura 65 nen shi*, pp. 29–30.

13. From a memo to the director of Mitsui industrial operations, Mitsui Takenosuke; *Tokyo Shibaura 65 nen shi*, pp. 33–34.

14. Ibid., p. 37.

15. Ibid., pp. 38, 170.

16. Ibid., p. 39.

17. Ibid., pp. 162–163, 303, 306.

18. Ibid., p. 213; Tokyo kōtō shōgakkō, ed., *Shokkō toriatsukaikata ni kan suru chōsa*, p. 77.

19. *Tokyo Shibaura 65 nen shi*, pp. 195, 214.

20. *Taiheiyō shōkō sekai*, 8/1/1909, pp. 26–27.

21. Ibid., 8/1/1909, p. 26.

22. Tokyo, *Shokkō toriatsukai*, pp. 68–69.

23. *Taiheiyō shōkō sekai*, 8/1/1909, p. 27; *Tokyo Shibaura 65 nen shi*, p. 304.

24. *Tokyo Shibaura 65 nen shi*, p. 304; *Taiheiyō shōkō sekai*, 8/1/1909, p. 28.

25. *Tokyo Shibaura 65 nen shi*, pp. 193–194.

26. *Shibaura seisakujo eigyō hōkoku shō,* 1904-1943. *Tokyo Shibaura 65 nen shi,* pp. 35, 39, 456.

27. Nishinarita Yutaka, "Nichiro sensōgo ni okeru zaibatsu zōsen kigyō no keiei kikō to rōshi kankei: Mitsubishi zōsenjo no bunseki," pp. 54–66. Mitsubishi sources describe these changes as a response to a perceived new-worker concern with "rights."

28. *Ishikawajima 108 nen shi,* p. 321; *Hikari,* 2/20/1096. Komatsu, *Kigyō betsu kumiai no seisei,* p. 176, for more on Ishikawajima attempts to tighten control in this era. *Asahi shimbun,* 2/8/1906, 2/9/1906.

29. The aid society is described in *Uraga kangyō ni kan suru shorui* held at the Uraga gyōsei sentā in Yokosuka. Ikeda, *Kikaikō kumiai,* pp. 81–82, also stresses the importance of company efforts to strengthen direct control by drawing foremen into the company or absorbing foreman powers at the staff level, in an analysis of the Japanese machine industry from 1905-1919. See Table 6, for figures on seniority of foremen.

30. Mitsubishi Nagasaki zōsenjo, shokkō ka, ed., *Nagasaki zōsenjo rōmu shi,* pp. 53–57. Also see Hyōdō, *Rōshi kankei,* p. 227, for a list of other enterprises that attempted similar programs.

31. The fledgling Hitachi Engineering Works established a company school in 1910; Hitachi seisakujo shashi henshū bu, ed., *Hitachi seisakujo shi,* I, 28–29. For Yahata, see Shimada Haruo, "Nenkō sei no shiteki keisei ni tsuite," pp. 54–56.

32. *Uraga Dokku 60 nen shi,* pp. 137–138. Report on Uraga Dock Education Program in *Uraga kangyō ni kan suru shorui* (1911).

33. *Ishikawajima 108 nen shi,* p. 321.

34. *Tokyo Shibaura 65 nen shi,* pp. 47–48.

35. The law passed the Diet in 1911 but did not take effect until 1916.

36. Sumiya, "Kōjōhō taisei to rōshi kankei," p. 7, cites *Kōjōhō an no setsumei* (1910).

37. Obama Ritoku, ed., *Meiji bunka shiryō sōsho,* I, 38, 55; Kishimoto Eitarō, *Nihon zettaishugi shakai seisaku shi,* p. 83.

38. *Meiji bunka,* pp. 55–56.

39. Ibid., p. 119.

40. Sumiya, "Kōjōhō," p. 26, cites *Tōyō keizai shimpō,* 3/5/1910.

41. Sumiya, "Kōjōhō," pp. 24–25, emphasis added.

42. The account offered in this paragraph is based on Sumiya, "Kōjōhō," pp. 12–17.

43. Hazama, *Rōmu kanri,* pp. 52–53, cites *Kōjōhō to rōdō mondai* (1909).

44. Hazama, *Rōmu kanri,* p. 303, presents a representative statement of a textile-industry executive in 1910 who opposed the Factory Law because the warm master-servant relationship made it unnecessary.

45. Although the ideology claiming paternalistic management to be a special

Japanese social practice had won the day, bureaucrats in later years continued to be skeptical of business intentions and realistic in their appraisal of the true situation behind the talk of beautiful customs. They sought a health-insurance and a labor-union law in the 1920s, although the Diet approved only the former. Businessmen, for their part, continued to distrust bureaucrats and liberal politicians who assured them that social legislation was in the long-run interests of a stable industrial society. By holding back the operating funds from the national budget, Seiyūkai allies of textile interests resisted actual implementation of the Factory Law for 5 years after its passage, repeating the same praise of beautiful customs continuously. Sumiya, "Kōjōhō," pp. 36–37.

46. Tokyo shibaura denki kabushiki gaisha, ed., *Kobayashi Sakutarō den,* p. 77.
47. *Tokyo Shibaura 65 nen shi,* p. 48.
48. Nimura, "Rōdōsha kaikyū," pp. 94, 96, and Appendix, Table C(1). Sixty strikes involving over 11,000 workers took place in 1907. Ikeda, *Kikaikō kumiai,* p. 87, and Miyake, "Nichiro sensō zengo," pp. 32–37, both make this assertion. Miyake describes 6 disputes between 1902 and 1907 at Kure Naval Yard, Tokyo's Koishikawa Army Arsenal (2), Mitsubishi Nagasaki Shipyard (2), and Ishikawajima, in which workers resisted management efforts toward tighter control with mixed results. Nakanishi, "Daiichiji taisen zengo no rōshi kankei," pp. 64–73, also describes 3 strikes at the Mitsubishi Kobe Shipyard between 1906 and 1916 where workers attempted to preserve customary practices against management efforts to assert greater control.
49. Nishinarita, "Zaibatsu zōsen," 18.4:76.
50. Ibid., 18.2:60–61.
51. Stephen Large, *The Rise of Labor in Japan: The Yūaikai,* pp. x, 11, 22, 34–36, 41, 43.
52. *Rōdō oyobi sangyō,* IV, 237, V, 380; Komatsu, *Kigyō betsu kumiai,* p. 93.
53. Komatsu, *Kigyō betsu kumiai,* pp. 93–94; Large, *Yūaikai,* p. 51. The quantitative historian would like to see some numerical data to confirm the picture drawn through these cases. Unfortunately, detailed lists of union members are not available, and the accumulation of scattered individual cases must stand as support for this conclusion. Hyōdō, *Rōshi kankei,* p. 352, offers the only numerical data I have seen, for Yahata Steel in 1919. They show foremen directing the older Yūaikai branch and younger workers leading the newer Rōyūkai. The entry of the new group of younger workers into the new union reflects an important change in the labor movement.

54. *Shibaura seisakujo eigyō hōkoku sho,* 1913–1915.
55. *Tokyo Shibaura 65 nen shi,* p. 302. See also Ikeda and Ōmae, *Rōdō undō shi ron,* p. 56, on the importance of work rules in tightening factory discipline or asserting direct control over workers at the Kawasaki and Mitsubishi Shipyards in Kobe.
56. *Tokyo Shibaura 65 nen shi,* pp. 194, 203, 197. Many government and private enterprises introduced similar mutual-aid programs in these years. Typically, as at Shibaura, both workers and the company contributed.
57. *Tokyo Shibaura 65 nen shi,* pp. 189–190, and *Shibaura eigyō hōkoku sho,* 1916–1920.
58. *Tokyo Shibaura 65 nen shi,* pp. 175–176.
59. Ibid., pp. 63, 205.
60. Ibid., pp. 173–174. Twenty entrants were taken each year from 1905 to 1914, 30 a year from 1915 to 1935, and 40 a year from 1936 to 1938.
61. Ibid.
62. *Taiheiyō shōkō sekai,* 11/15/1908, p. 43.
63. *Hitachi seisakujo shi,* I, 169. Hyōdō, *Rōshi kankei,* p. 99, note 19, cites Mitsubishi personnel records published in 1914. Shimada, "Nenkō sei ni tsuite," pp. 61–62.
64. Nishinarita Yutaka, "Nichiro sensōgo ni okeru zaibatsu zōsen kigyō no keiei kōzō to rōshi kankei," 18.2:54–66.
65. See Chapter 3 for more on these Uraga policies. Nakanishi, "Taisen zengo no rōshi kankei," p. 59. Nimura, "Rōdōsha kaikyū," p. 139, note 24, describes the defense by labor of its rights under the Factory Law in the 1910s.
66. *Rōdō oyobi sangyō,* IV, 237, V, 380; *KRUS,* p. 288.
67. *Rōdō oyobi sangyō,* IV, 217 (September 1916).
68. Ibid.
69. Ibid., p. 218.
70. Ibid., pp. 218–219. This is a demand for a sort of *nenkō* or seniority wage.

3. *FAILURE OF THE FIRST ATTEMPT: 1917–1921*

1. Kamii Yoshihiko, "Daiichiji taisen chokugo no rōdō seisaku: chikeihō 17 jō no kaishaku, tekiyō mondai o chūshin to shite," p. 162, and Hyōdō, *Rōshi kankei,* p. 369, both describe the formation of the Kyōchōkai.
2. Unless noted otherwise, all information below concerning the Uraga Dock Company is taken from the handwritten, unpaginated Kyū kyōchōkai, "Uraga dokku kabushiki gaisha shiryō," held at the Ohara Institute for Social Research.

3. *Taiheiyō shōkō sekai,* 11/15/1908, p. 42. *Jitsugyō shōnen,* 2. 3 (9/1/ 1980), pp. 7–8, for first quotation, p. 9 for second.

4. Work Rules from Kyōchōkai report and Uraga Archives.

5. *Jitsugyō shōnen,* 2. 3 (9/1/1908), p. 9.

6. Uchida, *Jinsei,* p. 47, and Shiota Shōhei, ed., *Nihon shakai undō jinmei jiten,* p. 92 for Uchida, p. 263 for Saito Tadatoshi.

7. For factory inspection reports, see Nōshōmushō, *Kōjō kantoku nempō* (1919), pp. 51–52. The total number (N) of machine workers surveyed in 1919 is not available, but in *Kōjō kantoku nempō* (1921), pp. 15–16, machine-industry employment stood at 67,729. All surveys cover men and women unless noted otherwise.

8. David M. Gordon, Richard Edwards, Michael Reich, *Segmented Work, Divided Workers,* p. 148.

9. This involves a conservative assumption that school grads were 15 years old. They were probably often younger. For the data on the married proportion of the work force, see Naikaku tōkei kyoku, *Rōdō tōkei jitchi chōsa hōkoku* (1924) pp. 230–234, (1927) pp. 328–329, (1930) pp. 74–75.

10. The retirement estimate is probably a bit high. Despite the prevalence of travelers, I suspect that a group of those *newly hired* between 1904 and 1913 would be slightly younger on the whole than those *already present* at Uraga in 1921, simply because traveling appears most common among younger workers. If the bias is in this direction, however, it means fewer than 42% actually reached retirement age and thus strengthens our assertion that even adjusted retention was low in the prewar era. The mortality estimates are the mean between two sets of estimates, a low estimate using the age of workers when hired together with 1913 life tables found in Naikaku tōkei kyoku, *Dai Nihon teikoku tōkei nenkan,* (1921) No. 39, p. 56, and a high estimate using their age at retirement with 1936 life tables from the 1939 *Nenkan,* No. 58, p. 56. The former produces 11% attrition, the latter 22%. To see why these produce low and high estimates, consider the case of 16-year-olds hired in 1913. Their mortality in 1913 will be 5.88 per 1,000. We can calculate 25-year mortality rates simply by multiplying this by 25 (147 deaths per 1,000). But the mortality rate for these youths will rise as they approach retirement age, so this figure is too low. We can get a similarly high estimate by calculating their mortality rate 25 years later at age 41 in 1938. This is 9.33 per 1,000, for a 25-year rate of 233 deaths per 1,000. The estimates used here are therefore the means of such high and low figures.

11. *Tsukishima chōsa,* p. 219.

12. Ibid., pp. 219–220.

13. *Kōjō kantoku nempō* (1919) cited in Fujibayashi Keizō, "Waga kuni ni okeru rōdō idō no kenkyū," *Mita gakkai zasshi,* p. 86.
14. Uchida, *Jinsei,* pp. 45–47.
15. Ibid., p. 40.
16. Saitō interview, 6/3/1979.
17. Shōwa, *Chingin,* p. 267, quotes a labor manager in 1919 as saying that periodic raises must depend on skill and diligence to be useful.
18. Hyōdō, *Rōshi kankei,* pp. 327–328.
19. Ibid., pp. 328–329.
20. Ibid.
21. Saitō interview, 6/3/1979.
22. Nippon kōkan, "Jūyaku kai kiroku," 6/12/1919, 12/13/1919, 6/16/1920. Unfortunately, no breakdown on the relative size of these components is available.
23. Ikeda, *Kikaikō kumiai,* pp. 83–84, 102.
24. This estimate of 4 months is derived as follows. Average trainee day wage is estimated as 0.9 yen, the mean of the lowest entering trainee wage of 0.45 and the average graduating trainee wage of 1.4 yen. The company kept 3 days' pay per month for 60 months, a total of 180 days' pay, or 166 yen. This represents roughly 100 days' pay for an average skilled worker earning 1.6 yen a day, or 4 months if one assumes 25 working days in a month.
25. Large, *Yūaikai,* pp. 74–75, 90–95.
26. Watanabe Tōru, "Daiichiji taisen chokugo no rōdō dantai ni tsuite," offers a thorough, useful survey of the entire range of worker organizations of this era.
27. Matsuo Takayoshi, *Taishō demokurashii no kenkyū,* p. 194.
28. Shōwa, *Chingin,* pp. 269–270.
29. Ibid., p. 273.
30. Ibid., p. 274, for zaibatsu personnel office dates. Chapter 2 on Shibaura. *Rōdō oyobi sangyō,* November 1917, IV, 281 on Uraga.
31. *Rōdō oyobi sangyō,* November 1917, IV, 281.
32. The decision to allow the Kyōchōkai to compile the report in 1921 also indicates his concern with labor problems.
33. *Kanagawa-ken shi shiryō,* XVII, 877–880.
34. Kanagawa-ken Archives, Uraga File, "6/10/1919 Notice to All Employees."
35. See *Rōdō oyobi sangyō,* November 1917, IV, 281, for a discussion of the relation of these measures to labor disputes at Uraga.
36. *Uraga dokku eigyō kabushiki gaisha eigyō hōkokusho,* 1920, 1921.
37. Ibid., 1916, 1921.

38. *Rōdō oyobi sangyō,* November 1917, IV, 281.
39. Kamii, "Taisengo no rōdō seisaku: chikeihō," pp. 160–164; Hyōdō, *Rōshi kankei,* pp. 372–374.
40. Hyōdō, *Rōshi kankei,* pp. 372–374.
41. According to the company's semiannual shareholders' report, *Yokohama dokku eigyō hōkokusho* (1921), the Dock Company in fact recorded a profit of 1,010,636 yen between May and November 1921. Of this, 49% was distributed to shareholders as dividends.
42. Kyū Kyōchōkai, *Yokohama, Asano, Uraga chōsa,* reprinted in *KRUS,* pp. 283–285.
43. Masumoto Uhei, *Kokka no shōrai to kōjō kanri no hyōjun,* p. 47.
44. Nakanishi, "Taisen zengo no rōshi kankei," pp. 78, 110–119.
45. *Tokyo asahi shimbun,* 3/25/1920, p. 9.
46. This was a Mr. Ōtsuka, owner of the Ōtsuka Ironworks.

4. *Travelers' End? Hiring and Long-Term Employment*

1. *Kikai kōgyō,* pp. 43–44. Naimushō shakai kyoku shakai bu, *Jukuren rōdōsha kankei shiryō: idō.*
2. *Nippon kōkan 40 nen shi,* pp. 502–514, lists all workers with over 20 years' tenure as of 1952 and gives the exact dates of hiring, so we can easily calculate the proportion hired in each month. The sample is not random, but its bias strengthens our case. Only the relatively permanent employees are included, so that, if people hired immediately out of school tended to become permanent employees, an especially high percentage of this sample should have been hired in the spring each year. This is not the case. Even employees who stayed for most of their career were not hired regularly each spring in the 1920s.
3. Yoshida Atsushi, "Honpō zōsengyō rōdō jijō, 1," *Shakai seisaku jihō,* December 1926, pp. 128–129.
4. Yoshida, "Zōsengyō, 1," p. 128.
5. Ibid., p. 129. Interview with former Ishikawajima personnel managers Anzai Mitsuru and Kanai Tatsuo, 5/23/1979.
6. Yoshida, "Zōsengyō, 1," p. 130.
7. Ibid., p. 130; *Kikai kōgyō,* pp. 38, 89–90, 137–138; Uraga Archives, File A-20, 1921 and 1926 Work Rules.
8. Yoshida, "Zōsengyō, 1," p. 131.
9. *Shibaura rōdō,* April 1925, p. 23.
10. Mariko Kōsaburō interview, 5/23/1979; Hazama, *Rōmu kanri,* pp. 500–501.
11. Uraga Archives, A-20 file; *Uraga 60 nen shi,* Appendix, p. 9.
12. Hyōdō, *Rōshi kankei,* p. 427, offers evidence from Mitsubishi. Fukuda

Kōichirō, "Nihon ni okeru dokusen shihonshugi dankai no rōdōsha tōkatsu kikō," pp. 64–66. Even at Mitsubishi, fewer than 50% of company-school grads in the 1920s stayed the following 7 to 8 years.

13. Uraga Archives, A-20 File. Kanagawa-ken archives, Uraga File, "Revision of Trainee Regulations," 3/1/1924.

14. Yoshida, "Zōsengyō, 1," p. 132.

15. Ibid. *Kikai kōgyō*, p. 101, reports similar low completion rates for trainees in the machine industry.

16. Dore, *British Factory-Japanese Factory*, pp. 396, 399. Nor does it mean that a "swift transformation of Japan's industrial structure" to one of lifetime employment took place in this decade, as Hazama claims; Hazama, "Japanese Labor-Management Relations," p. 72.

17. Hyōdō, *Rōshi kankei*, p. 407.

18. *NRN* (1921), p. 1, Mitsubishi Yokohama zōsenjo, ed., *Yokosen no omoide* (1973), I, 100, *NRUS*, X, 32; Chūō shokugyō shōkai jimukyoku, ed., *Shokugyō betsu rōdō jijō, 3: kikai kōgyō*.

19. *NRN*, relevant years, and *NRUS*, X, 32, 154, for the figures in these two paragraphs.

20. Anzai Mitsuru interview, 5/23/1979.

21. Figures on profits are from *eigyō hōkokusho* of relevant years published by each company. Shibaura records indicate two types of profit: profits produced in the current semiannum; and the "accumulated" profit carried over from the previous period.

22. *NRUS*, X, 158–159.

23. Odaka Kōnosuke, "Dainiji taisen zengo no kyū Mitsubishi jūkō rōdō tōkei ni tsuite," p. 565.

24. Hyōdō, *Rōshi kankei*, p. 329; Nōshōmushō, *Kōjō kantoku nempō* (1919), p. 52, and (1920), pp. 15–16; Fujibayashi, "Rōdō idō no kenkyū," p. 86.

25. Hyōdō, *Rōshi kankei*, p. 405.

26. Fujibayashi, p. 111 for 1919; *Kikai kōgyō*, p. 45, for 1926; Kyōchōkai, Uraga, 1921, 1925 for Uraga data.

27. *Kikai kōgyō*, pp. 47–48, 94–96, 141–146.

28. Yoshida, "Honpō zōsengyō rōdō jijō, 2"; *Shakai seisaku jihō*, January 1927, p. 172.

29. Hyōdō, *Rōshi kankei*, p. 405, offers a chart of separation rates at 4 major firms where separations begin to drop sharply in 1920. Shibaura statistics in Table 3 indicate two major declines, between 1918 and 1919 and between 1920 and 1921. NKK figures in Table 13 show the largest drop between 1920 and 1921.

30. Hyōdō, *Rōshi kankei*, pp. 408–428; Hazama, "Japanese Labor-Management Relations," p. 72. Original in *Rōshi kyōchō no teiryū*, pp. 4–5.

Hazama, *Rōmu kanri,* p. 107. Hyōdō emphasizes specialization by firm in technology and skills as retarding mobility, while Hazama finds a wide range of policies all relevant. See Gordon, "Workers, Managers, and Bureaucrats," pp. 278–280, for fuller description and critique of their positions.

31. Yoshida, "Zōsengyō, 2," p. 125.

32. Hyōdō, *Rōshi kankei,* p. 310, cites Yahata Steel and Mitsubishi Nagasaki Yard figures that show 1924 retention rates ranging between 28 and 35% for Yahata cohorts of 1909 to 1913 and between 15 and 21% for Mitsubishi over the same period. I suspect that Yahata's isolated location made job-switching difficult for skilled men and accounts for the relatively high retention rates there.

33. On the other hand, from two-thirds to 90% of cohorts employed for 10 years or more by 1933 stayed the next 8 years, despite high demand for labor in these years. Management policy appears to have been effective in retaining workers who already had long tenure (and more to gain by staying) in the 1930s. I doubt this is a peculiarly Japanese phenomenon. Koike, *Shokuba no rōdō kumiai,* pp. 10 and passim, notes that the benefits of seniority have historically been a major factor keeping American workers from switching jobs.

34. The figures appear to be biased in favor of a high rate of persistency, especially in the 1930s, for, in one case (the 1921 entrants), the number remaining in 1941 *exceeds* by 1 the number present in 1933! Tomiyasu Nagateru, an NKK personnel manager at the time, speculates that, as NKK expanded and acquired other steel or shipbuilding concerns in the 1930s, some workers from Tsurumi Steel or elsewhere were transferred to the Kawasaki works after 1933, thus inflating the proportion of senior workers at Kawasaki in 1941. Tomiyasu interview, 8/21/1979.

35. Hazama, *Rōmu kanri,* pp. 509–510, offers an example of one reluctant major firm.

36. *Kikai kōgyō,* p. 48.

37. Miyake, "Jūkōgyō dai keiei," p. 39.

38. *KRUS,* p. 292.

39. Ibid.

40. *Kōshinkai hō,* 6/1/1925, p. 1.

41. Kyū kyōchōkai, *Rōdō sōgi, zōsen,* (1925), contains reports on Yokohama Dock Company, 11/10/1925 and 11/29/1925.

42. Ibid.

43. *Busō renmei,* August 1927, p. 27.

44. *Kōshinkai hō,* 1/1/1926, p. 3; 2/15/1927, pp. 8–10. Similar letters are found in 8/1/1926, pp. 1–2; 4/18/1927, pp. 21–22; 5/23/1927, p. 34; and *Rōdō jidai,* February 1930, pp. 15–16.

45. *Rōdō jidai,* March 1930, pp. 17–19.

46. *Busō renmei,* September 1937, p. 24.

47. Kanagawa-ken Archives, Uraga File, 1929 Report titled "Hanshin chihō rōmu jōkyō hōkoku," which includes a section on Yokohama Dock.

48. *Rōdō jidai,* August 1930, p. 28. The efforts of this union to protect temporary employees and admit them as union members stands in contrast to behavior of most present-day unions. It is no coincidence that these Yokohama Dock temporary workers attained some small measure of protection.

49. *Asahi shimbun,* evening, 7/22/1930, p. 2; 9/2/1930, p. 7. *Rōdō jidai,* August 1930, p. 29.

50. *Nihon zōsen rōdō renmei,* December 1930, p. 26.

51. *Yokosen no omoide,* I, 30.

52. Naimushō shakai kyoku rōdō bu, *Rōdō undō nempō* (1926), p. 331.

53. *Kōshinkai hō,* 5/1/1925, p. 3, and *Busō renmei,* August 1927, pp. 4, 7–8, 23, provide examples. Even this is more than many unions offered regular workers who were pressured into "voluntary" retirement in the 1970s.

54. *Musansha shimbun,* 12/25/1927, p. 2.

55. *Kōshinkai hō,* 1/1/1927, pp. 16–18.

56. Kyū kyōchōkai, *Rōdō sōgi, kikai, 4,* (1925), contains 8 police reports on the Shibaura strike, dated 7/9/1925 through 7/22/1925.

57. Kyū kyōchōkai, *Rōdō sōgi, kikai,* (1930), Police reports 1–6, 3/5 through 4/1/1930. *Jiyū rengō shimbun,* 3/1, 4/1, 5/1, 7/1, 10/1/1930.

58. Yoshida, "Zosengyō, 2," p. 124.

59. *Busō renmei,* October 1928, pp. 14–15. Yasue Masao interview, 5/19/1980. Yasue was employed at Yokohama Dock in the personnel section beginning in 1937. He recalls that, even in that era, the typical worker did not plan to spend a career with the company. He feels that white-collar attitudes were very different.

60. Interview with Mariko Kōsaburō, 5/23/1979.

61. Shōwa, *Chingin,* pp. 329–330. Hara Akira, "Senji tōsei keizai no kaishi," p. 219.

62. Kawasaki City Hall Archives, *Dai rokkai rōdō tōkei jitchi chōsa tōkei shorui,* (1939).

63. Kanagawa-ken shi Archives, Uraga File, 2/4/1939 memorandum and undated "Special Trainee Rules" accompanying it. Yokohama Dock Company also began to seek young adults as well as adolescents for its trainee program in the mid-1930s, sending recruiters to rural areas, according to Yasue Masao interview, 5/19/1980.

64. Kawasaki City Hall Archives, 8/7/1937 minutes of a discussion (*zadankai*) on labor recruiting problems.

65. Ujihara Shōjirō, "Sangyō hōkokukai undō no haikei," 212, quotes

Ōuchi Tsuneo, "Senjika no jukurenkō mondai." Ōuchi worked for the Bank of Japan, Yahata Steel, and, later, Sanpō. Yasue Masao recalls movement from Yokohama Dock to smaller places, as well as into the company from smaller factories, between 1937 and 1939; interview, 5/19/1980.

66. These statistics cover all enterprises, large and small. However, I have offered data only from industries in which most workers were in large companies. In metal refining, 96% were in factories of 100 or more; in rolling mills, 70%; in electric-wire makers, 80%. Seventy-four percent of gas- and steam-engine workers were in factories of 50 or more; 70% of electric-machine industry workers in factories of 100 or more. In shipbuilding, with the fewest career company workers, 86% were in factories of 300 or more; 84% of rolling-stock workers in places with 100 or more workers.

67. Naikaku tōkei kyoku, *Rōdō tōkei jitchi chōsa* (1938) pp. 100-101, 138-139, 200-201. These figures are for work experience in industry, not tenure at a single place.

68. Uraga Archives, A-66 File, Charts IIa, b, III, IV.

69. Uraga Archives, A-22 File, 2/9/1937 and 5/20/1938 memoranda.

5. THE WAGE TANGLE

1. *Tokyo Shibaura 65 nen shi,* pp. 125, 307-308; *Shibaura rōdō,* 2/15/1926, p. 4; Tokyo shibaura denki, ed., *85 nen shi,* p. 210.

2. *Shibaura rōdō,* January 1923, p. 14.

3. *Shibaura rōdō,* 6/7/1923, p. 22.

4. *Nippon kōkan 40 nen shi,* p. 588.

5. Interviews with Tomiyasu Nagateru, 8/21/1979 and 8/28/1979. His testimony is verified by documentary evidence in *Nippon kōkan 40 nen shi* and *NRUS,* VII, 159-169, but Tomiyasu's account is more thorough.

6. Yoshida, "Zōsengyō, 2," pp. 141-145; Ishikawajima interviews, 5/23/1979.

7. *Nippon kōkan 40 nen shi,* pp. 560-561; Tomiyasu interviews; Minami manshū tetsudō, ed., *Naichi ni okeru kōjō chingin seido no chōsa kenkyū,* charts between pp. 206 and 207 for Yahata, p. 138 for Mitsubishi.

8. *KRUS,* p. 522.

9. Yoshida, "Zōsengyō, 2," p. 136.

10. Mitsubishi, *Yokosen no omoide,* I, 454-455; II, 442. Yokohama Dock Company Work Rules, 1933. Shōwa, *Chingin,* pp. 445-449. Rules at Mitsubishi's Nagasaki Shipyard in this era were almost identical.

11. *Kōshinkai hō,* 6/1/1925, p. 3.

12. Ibid., 6/1/1926, p. 2.
13. Uraga Archives, A-21 File, 1921 and 1926 Work Rules.
14. Anonymous letter to *Busō renmei*, February 1929, pp. 24–25. "Kōaikai jūnen shi," *Shakai undō ōrai*, January 1933, p. 54; May 1933, p. 80.
15. Mariko interview, 5/23/1979.
16. Kyū kyōchōkai, *Rōdō sōgi, kikai 2, (1927)*, Police report 2, 1/17/1927.
17. Ibid., Police report 1, 12/26/1926.
18. *Shibaura rōdō*, 11/15/1929, p. 3, anonymous letter.
19. Ibid., January 1923, p. 22.
20. Ibid.
21. Ibid., January 1923, p. 10, by "Ningen no ko," a pen name meaning "Human child."
22. *Kikai kōgyō*, p. 48. Of the figures in Table 18, those from shipbuilding are of greatest interest, since they are limited to Ishikawajima workers; we can be sure the result is not affected by workers from tiny firms with different wage practices.
23. Shōwa, *Chingin*, pp. 267–269.
24. *Tetsuben*, December 1921, p. 21.
25. *Nippon kōkan 50 nen shi*, pp. 144–146; Fujiwara Kenzō interview, 8/23/1979.
26. *KRUS*, pp. 377–378.
27. Ibid., pp. 460, 623.
28. *Shibaura rōdō*, March 1924, p. 12.
29. Ibid., November 1924, pp. 15–16.
30. For the 1927 Tsurumi dispute: *Kanagawa-ken shi*, XIII, 521–532; Kyū kyōchōkai, *Rōdō sōgi, kikai kinzoku, 2, (1927)*, Police Reports; *Rōdō shimbun*, 1927, nos. 44, 45, 46, 47; *Musansha shimbun*, nos. 97, 98. *Rōdōsha*, no. 14, pp. 52–60.
31. See Chapter 6 for more on the group attacks.
32. Kyū kyōchōkai, *Rōdō sōgi, kikai, 2, (1927)*, Police report, 5/9/1927.
33. *Shibaura rōdō*, 10/26/1929.
34. *Shibaura dōshi renmei*, (Winter 1930), pp. 15–18.
35. Emphasis added.
36. Details of this strike from Kyū kyōchōkai, *Rōdō sōgi, kikai, (1930)*, Police reports 1–6, 3/5/1930 through 4/1/1930; *Jiyū rengō shimbun*, 3/1, 4/1, 5/1, 7/1, 10/1/1930.
37. Kyū kyōchōkai, *Rōdō sōgi, kikai, (1931)*, Police reports 1–9, 2/13 through 3/3/1931; *Jiyū rengō shimbun*, 2/10/1931, 4/19/1931.
38. See Chapter 6 for more on the struggle between Kōrō and the Nogi Society.
39. The account of the August-September dispute is from Kyū kyōchōkai,

Rōdō sōgi, zōsen 3, (1926), Police Reports of 8/4/1926 through 9/19/1926, and *Rōdō shimbun*, 8/20, 9/5, 9/20 and 10/5/1926.

40. *Hantō jichi*, 1/5/1929, p. 7; 6/25/1928, p. 3; 12/28/1928, p. 3.

41. Pay issue is covered in *Busō renmei*, July 1928, pp. 17–18, 28–30, for the union view; *Hantō jichi*, 8/5/1928, p. 6; 8/25/1928, p. 1; 10/15/1928, p. 4; 10/25/1928, p. 2; and 11/15/1928, p. 6 for the rank-and-file view.

42. *Rōdō jidai*, June 1930, pp. 15–16.

43. Ibid., October 1930, pp. 13–14.

44. Ibid., June 1929, p. 29. Emphasis added.

45. *Kanagawa-ken shi*, XIII, 536.

46. *Busō renmei*, July 1928, pp. 6–7, 27–32; August 1928, pp. 11–12; Mitsubishi, *Yokosen no omoide*, I, 22–23.

47. *KRUS*, p. 517.

48. *KRUS*, pp. 518–519.

49. *KRUS*, pp. 520–525.

50. *KRUS*, pp. 526–527.

51. *KRUS*, pp. 528–529.

52. *KRUS*, pp. 530–532.

53. Minami Manshū tetsudō, ed., *Chingin*, p. 164. *Busō renmei*, May 1929, pp. 10–14.

54. *Rōdō jidai*, June 1929, pp. 10–12, gives a feeling for the tense atmosphere of committee meetings.

55. The term *heikin* is used throughout these and other documents. It means "average" and does not make clear whether this was a mean, median, or mode.

56. *Busō renmei*, May 1929, pp. 13–14. Mantetsu, *Chingin*, p. 108.

57. Six years above age 34 and 6 years over the 5-year seniority average yields 12 sen above the average wage.

58. Mantetsu, *Chingin*, pp. 176, 180–181; *Rōdō jidai*, October 1929, p. 10; *KRUS*, pp. 530–532. Statistics held by the personnel office (*kinrō bu*) of the Mitsubishi Heavy Industries Yokohama factory.

59. Hazama, *Rōmu kanri*, p. 522. Hazama is the principal Japanese proponent of this view. Dore builds on his work to put forward a similar interpretation in *British Factory-Japanese Factory*.

60. *Shokkō jijō*, III, 142.

61. Shōwa, *Chingin*, pp. 262–264. Magota Ryōhei, ed., *Nenkō chingin no ayumi to mirai*, p. 28. The Japanese term literally means "the worsening of ideas."

62. The South Manchuria Railway surveyed wage practices at 4 "home-island" enterprises considered innovative and potential models for the

Railway. They were Yokohama Dock Company, Mitsubishi Electric, Japan National Railways, and Yahata Steel. Mantetsu, *Chingin.*

63. *NRUS,* VII, 159–169, for a part of this survey. The full text was published as Hōsei daigaku, *Keihin kōgyō chitai o chūshin to suru chingin chōsa hōkoku.*

64. *NRUS,* VII, 167.

65. Uraga Archives, A-22 File, 3/9/1937, 1/1/1939 memoranda.

66. Regression analysis of these 3 relationships yields R squared of 0.26 for age and day wage, 0.7 for experience and day wage, and 0.79 for years on the job and day wage. Raw data from Kanagawa-ken, ed., *Keihin kōgyō chitai chōsa hōkokusho,* pp. 96–97.

67. *NRUS,* VII, 162–163.

68. Records of the personnel office, Mitsubishi Heavy Industries Yokohama Factory.

69. As a basis for comparison, a university graduate's starting salary in the 1930s, including a bonus of several months' pay, was roughly 120 yen a month.

70. *Kanagawa-ken shi,* XIII, 856, cites *Keihin kōgyō jihō,* July 1939.

71. Dore, *British Factory-Japanese Factory,* pp. 100–101; Cole, *Japanese Blue Collar,* p. 103.

72. The sample is from a list of NKK workers responsible for carrying out the *Rōdō tōkei jitchi chōsa* survey at NKK. The list happens to give both rank and age of the workers, although not age at promotion. It is held at the Kawasaki City Hall Archives, in the Documents Section (Bunsho-ka) at the city hall. The 1935 survey of NKK is found in *NRUS,* VII, 160.

73. *NRUS,* VII, 160.

74. Mariko interview, 12/14/1979.

75. Miyake, "Jūkōgyō dai keiei," p. 32.

76. Ibid.

77. Dore, *British Factory-Japanese Factory,* p. 100. Cole, *Japanese Blue Collar,* p. 111, describes a rank ladder with a similar morale-boosting intent. Yoshida, "Zōsengyō, 1," p. 125. Yahata's "elongated" promotion ladder would seem exceptional. Solomon Levine and Hisashi Kawada, *Human Resources in Japanese Industrial Relations,* pp. 165–166.

78. Workers at Shibaura in 1920 and Mitsubishi's Nagasaki yard in 1917 were among those who demanded bonuses during labor disputes. Shōwa, *Chingin,* p. 269.

79. A different survey of 15 other companies in Kanagawa prefecture between 1929 and 1943 revealed a quite similar situation. *Kikai kōgyō,* pp. 107–108; Shōwa, *Chingin,* p. 283. Also. Yasue Masao of the

personnel section at Yokohama Dock recalls that worker bonuses in 1937, when he entered, were about 10 yen per worker, 20 for a foreman. Yasue interview, 5/19/1980.

80. Kyōchōkai, ed., *Saikin no shakai undō*, p. 136.

81. *Kikai kōgyō*, p. 107.

82. *Shibaura rōdō*, May 1923, p. 10.

83. *Kikai kōgyō*, p. 107.

84. Anzai Mitsuru and Kanai Tatsuo interview, 9/12/1979.

85. Worker fear of layoffs and of injury led to this emphasis. Hazama, *Rōmu kanri*, p. 526, mentions fear of injury but not layoffs, although both were important to workers in this sector, who had good reason to fear layoffs.

86. Yoshida, "Zōsengyō, 2," pp. 126–130, has details of the Mitsubishi policy and other less extensive programs. For Shibaura, see *Tokyo Shibaura 65 nen shi*, pp. 189–190.

87. See *Eigyō hōkoku sho* for all 3 companies, 1915 and 1916. Also *Tokyo Shibaura 65 nen shi*, p. 189. Shōwa, *Chingin*, p. 265, on demands for these benefits.

88. *Shibaura seisakujo eigyō hōkoku sho*, 1921–1931.

89. Shōwa, *Chingin*, p. 293.

90. *Shibaura eigyō hōkoku sho*, 1934–1938.

91. *Tokyo Shibaura 65 nen shi*, pp. 190–192.

92. Yoshida, "Zōsengyō, 2," p. 126.

93. *Tokyo asahi shimbun*, 6/5/1924, p. 4; Aoki Kōji, *Nihon rōdō undō shi nempyō*, p. 48. Also in the machine-engineering sector in Tokyo, a summer 1923 strike at Ikegai Ironworks centered on demands for severance and retirement pay. Kyū kyōchōkai, *Ikegai sōgi, (1923)*.

94. *KRUS*, p. 1056. *Yokohama bōeki shimpō*, 8/15/1926, p. 5; Yoshida, "Zōsengyō, 2," p. 130.

95. Kyū kyōchōkai, *Rōdō sōgi ippan, 2* (1929), pp. 164–165.

96. *Kikai kōgyō*, p. 163.

97. *Uraga dokku eigyō hōkoku sho*, 1916–1923; Kanagawa-ken Archives, Uraga File, 12/17/1920 memorandum.

98. *Hantō jichi*, 7/5/1928, p. 3.

99. *Busō renmei*, February 1929, pp. 17–18.

100. NKK, *Jūyaku kai*, 5/10/1938. *Nippon kōkan 40 nen shi*, p. 576.

101. *Shibaura rōdō*, 1/15/1926, p. 2.

102. Ibid., November 1924, pp. 9–10.

103. *Busō renmei*, May 1929, pp. 6–7. *Kōshinkai hō*, 1/1/1927, p. 5.

104. *KRUS*, pp. 526, 531.

105. *Tetsuben*, March 1922, pp. 14–16.

106. *Hantō jichi,* 10/15/1928, p. 2.
107. Shōwa, *Chingin,* p. 293. Mitsubishi, *Yokosen no omoide,* I, 320–330, 364. *Tokyo Shibaura 65 nen shi,* pp. 204, 208–230 and passim; *Nippon kōkan 30 nen shi,* pp. 385–393; *Nippon kōkan 40 nen shi,* pp. 568–575.
108. *Nippon kōkan 20 nen shi,* p. 271.

6. THE ENTERPRISE COMMUNITY: UNIONS, AND THE WORKING CLASS

1. Hazama, "Japanese Labor-Management Relations," pp. 72–73. Original in *Rōshi kyōchō no teiryū,* pp. 7–8. A more subdued statement of this same view is found in his earlier *Rōmu kanri,* pp. 39–42.
2. Dore, *British Factory–Japanese Factory,* p. 402, original emphasis. Cole, *Work, Mobility, and Participation,* pp. 222–223, also concludes that Japanese "management operates with a model of human nature which stresses the perfectability of human nature," but he limits this claim to post-World War II managers. "These benevolent views of human nature were hardly characteristic of much of pre-world War II industry."
3. Magota, "Senji rōdō."
4. Kamii, "Rōdō seisaku: chikeihō," pp. 154–155.
5. Kamii, "Rōdō seisaku: 1926 rōshi kankei hō," p. 132; Nimura, "Rōdōsha kaikyū," pp. 125–128.
6. The discussion of labor policy is based largely on Kamii, "Rōdō seisaku: chikeihō," and "Rōdō seisaku: 1926 rōshi kankei hō."
7. Rōdōshō, ed., *Rōdō gyōsei shi,* I, 209, 211, 216; *Kikai kōgyō,* pp. 113–117.
8. Kyōchōkai, *Saikin no shakai undō,* pp. 794–805, has a good discussion of the Health Insurance Law.
9. Tomiyasu Nagateru interview, 8/21/1979.
10. *Nippon kōkan 30 nen shi,* p. 379.
11. *KRUS,* pp. 593–594, 623. Tomiyasu interview, 8/21/1979, for recruiting.
12. Fujiwara interview, 8/23/1979.
13. Tomiyasu interview, 8/21/1979.
14. David Brody, *Steelworkers in America: The Non-union Era.*
15. Miura Tetsukichi, "Uraga dokku kōaikai 10 nen shi, 1," December 1932, pp. 57–59.
16. Ibid., p. 59.
17. Ibid., 2, January 1933, p. 57.
18. Ibid., 1, p. 61; 2, pp. 55, 59.

19. Miura, "Kōaikai 10 nen shi, 2," p. 56. Aoki Kōji, *Nempyō*, p. 403. *Kanagawa-ken shi*, XIII, p. 319.

20. Miura, "Kōaikai 10 nen shi, 3," February 1933, p. 59.

21. *Hantō jichi*, 7/5/1928, p. 3; 8/15/1928, p. 1; 9/15/1928, pp. 2, 6; 10/25/1928, p. 2; 11/5/1928, p. 7; 1/5/1929, p. 7.

22. *Hantō jichi*, 1/15/1929, p. 5.

23. Miura, "Kōaikai 10 nen shi, 2," p. 58.

24. Mitsubishi, *Yokosen no omoide*, I, 5, 75-76, 92-93. Strikes occurred in 1916, 1917, 1919, 1920, 1921, 1922.

25. *KRUS*, pp. 292-297. Kyū kyōchōkai, *1922 Kanagawa-ken ka no rōdō dantai*.

26. *KRUS*, pp. 297-298.

27. *KRUS*, pp. 298-310; Yasuda Hiroshi, "1921-1922 nen no Yokohama dokku sōgi no undō kōzō," has details on this fascinating strike.

28. Ueno, "Yokohama dokku rōdō kumiai," p. 31.

29. *Kōshinkai hō*, 7/1/1926, p. 2.

30. Ibid., 10/1/1925, pp. 1-3; 4/1/1926, pp. 1-3; 11/1/1926, p. 6; 7/1/1926, p. 2.

31. Ibid., 8/1/1926, p. 1.

32. Ibid., April 1926, p. 3; 8/1/1926, p. 4; 11/1/1926, p. 3; 1/1/1926, pp. 1-2.

33. Ueno, "Yokohama dokku rōdō kumiai," p. 39.

34. Kyū kyōchōkai, *Rōdō sōgi, zōsen*, (1925); *Busō renmei*, August 1927, p. 27; *Rōdō jidai*, March 1930, pp. 17-19.

35. *Rōdō jidai*, June 1929, pp. 8-9; May 1930, p. 3.

36. *Busō renmei*, May 1929, p. 20.

37. *Rōdō jidai*, February 1930, pp. 3-4. In most statements, the Jikyōkai did not oppose capitalism as a system but attacked the "bad capitalists" who did not understand the need to work together.

38. *Busō renmei*, May 1929, p. 30; *Rōdō jidai*, September 1929, pp. 8-9; Ueno, "Yokohama dokku rōdō kumiai," pp. 46-47.

39. Ueno, "Yokohama dokku rōdō kumiai," pp. 46-47, on arrests. Mitsubishi, *Yokosen no omoide*, I, 497-499, offers good detail on council elections and meetings and the formation of shop-level "friendship" groups. According to former personnel manager Yasue Masao, many council representatives had been active in the union. *Shakai undō ōrai*, December 1935, p. 93, has a brief article on the Mitsubishi takeover, union dissolution, and creation of the council.

40. Ishikawajima, ed., *108 nen shi*, pp. 205, 320-321. *Shakai undō ōrai*, April 1931, p. 3.

41. Kyōchōkai, *Kōjō kōzan ni okeru kyōiku shisetsu yōran* (1935), cited in Hazama, *Rōmu kanri*, p. 535.

42. *Tetsuben,* January 1922, pp. 23–24.

43. Ibid., March 1922, p. 13.

44. *Kōrō,* 11/25/1924, p. 1.

45. *Kōrō,* November 1925, p. 3; 1/28/1925, p. 3; *Rōdō kumiai,* 6/1/1923, p. 9.

46. *Kōrō,* 1/28/1925, p. 1, on the need for industrial organization.

47. *Rōdō shimbun,* 9/20/1925, p. 2.

48. *NRN,* (1923), p. 41.

49. Aoki Kōji, *Nempyō,* p. 492; Kyū kyōchōkai, *Rōdō sōgi, ippan, (1924),* Police Report 7/2/1924.

50. *Kōrō,* 1/28/1925, p. 3; *Rōdō shimbun,* 3/20/1926.

51. Ishikawajima, *108 nen shi,* p. 366, on Matsumura.

52. Biographical information is taken from Kakeya Saihei, "Rōdō undō ni okeru fashizumu no tanshoteki keisei," pp. 572–579.

53. Kakeya, "Fashizumu," pp. 585, 587; Ishikawajima, *108 nen shi,* pp. 373–374. *Kōrō,* 1/28/1925, p. 2, a worker comments that free meals were the major inducement for the members he knew.

54. Ishikawajima, *108 nen shi,* pp. 373–374. Kakeya, "Fashizumu," p. 385. "Nogi kō no genkyō," 9/1/1922 and 10/31/1924. Their role in the villages was perhaps akin to that of the Reservist Associations (*zaigo gunjinkai*) described by Richard Smethurst, *A Social Basis for Pre-war Japanese Militarism.*

55. Kakeya, "Fashizumu," pp. 589–590. *Kōrō,* 12/28/1924, 1/28/1925, on Kōrō resistance. Ishikawajima, *108 nen shi,* p. 375, on Jikyōkai.

56. Ishikawajima, *108 nen shi,* pp. 374–375; Kakeya, "Fashizumu," p. 591. An important factor behind Kamino's prestige was his reputation for great skill and expertise in turbine-engine assembly.

57. Mariko interview, 12/14/1979.

58. *Rōdō jidai,* July 1930, pp. 6–8; Kamino Shinichi, *Nihonshugi rōdō undō no shinzui,* p. 131.

59. Kamino, *Nihonshugi rōdō undō,* pp. 125–126.

60. Shiota, *Nihon shakai undō jinmei jiten,* p. 435, on Nishiyama, who in 1933 succeeded Kamino as the leader of the national Japanist union movement described below.

61. *Shakai undō ōrai,* December 1932, pp. 37–39; Ishikawajima, *108 nen shi,* pp. 402–406; Kakeya, "Fashizumu," pp. 594–598.

62. *Rōdō jidai,* November 1926, pp. 8–9.

63. *Shakai undō ōrai,* March 1931, p. 4.

64. Kakeya, "Fashizumu," p. 597.

65. *Shakai undō ōrai,* August 1932, pp. 34–39; March 1933, pp. 50–55; April 1932, pp. 60–63 on Jikyōkai activities.

66. Kamino, *Nihon shugi rōdō undō*, p. 123.

67. *Shakai undō ōrai*, July 1933, p. 94; June 1934, p. 71; July 1934, pp. 7–11; Kakeya, "Fashizumu," pp. 567–602.

68. Kakeya, "Fashizumu," pp. 567–569, 602.

69. *Rōdō jidai* (1929–1933) and *Shakai undō ōrai* (1931–1936) chronicle the challenge posed by rightist unions in numerous factories.

70. *Shibaura rōdō*, November 1924, pp. 15–16.

71. Hyōdō, *Rōshi kankei*, pp. 393–403.

72. Kyōchōkai, ed., *Kōjō iinkai seido*, pp. 4–5, for factory-council figures. *NRN (1925)*, pp. 354–368, for union figures.

73. Nishinarita Yutaka, "1920 nendai Nihon shihonshugi no rōshi kankei: jūkōgyō rōshi kankei o chūshin ni," p. 2.

74. Ibid., pp. 9–13.

75. The role played by rightist groups and Japanist unions at the factory level in chipping away first at the Hyōgikai and, after its dissolution, then at the Sōdōmei, seems to be an important, understudied aspect of the political history of this era. See Nishinarita, "1920 rōshi kankei," p. 8, on Sumitomo.

76. Nimura, "Rōdōsha kaikyū," pp. 118–119.

77. *Shibaura rōdō*, December 1922, p. 7; 9/30/1927, p. 4. Also, similar sentiments in March 1924, pp. 10–11. All anonymous.

78. Ibid., June–July 1923, p. 9, by "A tool-shop worker." Similar sentiments found in January 1923, p. 6, by Arakawa, a plate-metal worker.

79. Ibid., April 1923, pp. 6–7. Similar letter, June–July 1923, p. 14.

80. *Busō renmei*, October 1927, pp. 13–15. Other Uraga voices are found in *Hantō jichi*, 11/5/1928, p. 7. For a Kōrō worker with a similar message, see *Tetsuben*, July 1921, p. 13.

81. *Busō renmei*, November 1927, p. 12.

82. *Busō renmei*, May 1928, p. 17. The title of this short song is "A Dock-Worker's March" (or Song of the Poor), making a pun on the word for "march," *kōshin*, and a similar sounding term for "poor," *kōhin*.

83. Thomas Rohlen, *For Harmony and Strength*, writes sensitively of the importance of membership for white-collar workers, and in a perceptive footnote (p. 173) he argues that this was important to blue-collar workers also.

84. Kakeya, "Fashizumu," p. 587.

85. *Tetsuben*, October 1921, p. 29.

86. Ibid., February 1922, p. 24. Other Ishikawajima opinions of supervisors in January 1922, pp. 16–18; April 1922, pp. 11–12.

87. *Shibaura rōdō*, February–March 1923, p. 12; 6/7/1923, p. 18, expresses similar sentiments.

88. Ibid., 10/26/1929, p. 3.
89. Ibid., December 1922, p. 2.
90. Ibid., April 1923, pp. 7–8. For similar voices raised against superiors at Shibaura, see January 1923, passim; February-March 1923, p. 9; April 1923, p. 11.
91. *Rōdō jidai,* May 1930, p. 4. For a Yokohama Dock worker upset with foremen, see *Kōshinkai hō,* 5/1/1926.
92. *Shibaura rōdō,* December 1922, p. 5. The words of the company general manager, here quoted in a union magazine, were certainly susceptible to distortion. However, Sekiguchi is the same man referred to above as an advocate of a soft-line policy toward the union. His attitude as expressed here fits that evaluation. Also, the writer of this piece goes on to call for even bigger gatherings to "cause more trouble," a good indication that the incident here did take place. Another short piece, *Shibaura rōdō,* March 1924, p. 2, again extolls the virtues of group attacks as labor's best tactic, one which really had the company worried.
93. Ibid., April 1925, pp. 18–20.
94. Ibid., October 1926, p. 4; *Musansha shimbun,* 11/20/1927, p. 2.
95. *Shibaura rōdō,* 11/8/1926, p. 4; 10/22/1929 for a similar view in the form of a poem.
96. Ibid., February-March 1925, pp. 22–24.
97. Matsuzawa, *Nihon shakaishugi no shisō,* pp. 128–129, agrees that such a change occurred.
98. Yoshida, "Zōsengyō, 2," pp. 133–134.
99. Yasue Masao recalls that similar practices were common when he entered Yokohama Dock Company in 1937; interview, 5/19/1980.
100. *Busō renmei,* August 1927, p. 27.
101. Uraga data from Kyū kyōchōkai, "Uraga Dokku" (1921). Ishikawajima from Kyū kyōchōkai, *Rōdō sōgi: zōsen, 3,* (1925), Police reports of 9/15 through 9/17/1926. Shibaura from Kyū kyōchōkai, *Rōdō sōgi: kikai, 4* (1925), Police reports of July 1925 and *Kanagawa-ken shi,* XIII, p. 524. These police reports were compiled during labor disputes, or directly after. They offer attendance figures for days when workers were *not* on strike but were negotiating or engaging in on-the-job slowdowns. It was in the interest of the Ishikawajima and Shibaura unions to encourage attendance so as to muster forces within the factory at such times. If these figures are biased, it is likely in the direction of higher than average attendance. The 1927 Tsurumi report quoted in the *Ken shi* goes to great length to stress that a *mere* 15% were absent. This meant that operations were normal, since, according to the company, that number were generally absent on any given day.

102. Mitsubishi Heavy Industries, Yokohama Factory, Personnel Office Statistics.
103. *Kikai kōgyō,* p. 50.
104. Uraga Archives, A-21 File, Guard Regulations.
105. Uraga Archives, A-21 File, 1921, 1926 Work Rules.
106. Dore finds the fact that Hitachi's work rules in the 1970s placed the section on rewards ahead of that on punishments indicative of a positive view of the worker. Uraga also listed rewards first, but the evidence does not imply that managers used rewards more often or went to great lengths to avoid meting out punishment, as was true of Hitachi in the 1970s. Dore, *British Factory-Japanese Factory,* p. 242; *Busō renmei,* December 1927, pp. 11–12; January 1928, pp. 12–14; *Hantō jichi,* 9/15/1928, p. 2.
107. *Uraga 60 nen shi,* pp. 168–169, on his career. Imaoka speech, pp. 40–41, held in Kanagawa-ken archives, Uraga file.
108. One cannot accept the conclusion that prewar Japanese managers were "rather less predisposed than their Western counterparts to see their subordinates as donkeys responsive to sticks and carrots, and more disposed to see them as human beings responsive to moral appeals." Dore, *British Factory-Japanese Factory,* pp. 401–402.
109. *Kanagawa-ken shi,* XIII, 854–861.
110. Ibid., pp. 854–857.
111. Mitsubishi, *Yokosen no omoide,* I, 263–264.
112. *Kanagawa-ken shi,* XIII, 854–857.
113. Mitsubishi, *Yokosen no omoide,* I, 452–453.
114. Ibid., p. 319.
115. *Kanagawa-ken shi,* XIII, 854–857.
116. *Shakai undō ōrai,* September 1933, pp. 68–69.
117. *Nihon zōsen rōdō renmei,* December 1930, p. 33.
118. *Shakai undō ōrai,* October 1935, p. 113; March 1933, p. 88; *Busō renmei,* May 1929, p. 3.
119. *Kikai kōgyō,* p. 20.
120. Matsuzawa, *Nihon shakaishugi no shisō,* p. 168.
121. *Rōdō jidai,* September 1929, p. 2.
122. *Kōshinkai hō,* 11/1924, p. 4.
123. *NRUS,* X, 469; Nimura, "Rōdōsha kaikyū," pp. 112–113, 116.
124. Nimura, "Rōdōsha kaikyū," pp. 125–128.
125. *KRUS,* pp. 329, 360–361, for Kanagawa statistics.
126. Nimura, "Rōdōsha kaikyū," p. 116, for the argument about timing.
127. Large, "Perspectives on the Failure of the Labour Movement," pp. 23–24, also speaks of the worker "enterprise consciousness" hindering the

emergence of a labor movement, but for him this consciousness was fostered by management policy. I see it as an attitude which, while encouraged by management, was also one part of a general outlook among workers which stressed respect, social equality, and membership, and which predated these management policies. These attitudes were as responsible for some of the movement's successes as for its failures.

128. *Busō renmei,* September 1927, pp. 13–14; October 1927, pp. 15–16.

129. Kyū kyōchōkai, *Rōdō sōgi: kikai* (1930), Police Report 5, 3/15/1930.

130. *Busō renmei,* September 1927, pp. 8–9.

131. Kyū kyōchōkai, *Kantō, Hokkaidō chihō hyōgikai (1926)* Police report of 3/8/1926.

132. *Shibaura rōdō,* 11/8/1926.

133. Kyū kyōchōkai, *Nihon rōdō kumiai hyōgikai zenkoku kyōgikai,* 1929–1930.

134. Kyū kyōchōkai, "Shibaura sōgi," Police Report 9, 3/3/1931, in *Rōdō sōgi: kikai,* 1931.

135. Both the attitudes and the behavior of managers and workers of the 1920s force us to reject the ideas that managers in large firms "thought of themselves as looking after all aspects of their employees' lives," that the employees had the "deeply engrained attitude of committing themselves to the care of the managers of the firm," that the enterprise or the factory was a "quasi community" or an enterprise family; Hazama, "Japanese Labor-Management Relations," pp. 72–73.

7. PERMANENT JOBS AND REGULATED WAGES

1. *NRN* (1937), pp. 404–415; Terashima Shirō, "Kaiko teate seido no igi," pp. 110–119.

2. A personnel manager at Ishikawajima recalls that the company had been paying less than the new legal minimum and was forced to raise retirement pay levels. Ishikawajima Interview, 5/20/1979; Noda keizai kenkyūjo, ed., *Taishoku tsumitate kin hō no kaisetsu* (1936), pp. 99–102.

3. Terashima, "Kaiko teate," pp. 110–111.

4. *NRN* (1937), p. 415.

5. Uraga Archives, A-21 File, 1/22/1937 memorandum.

6. *NRN* (1937), pp. 404–422, analyzes the law and reprints the text. Rōdōshō, ed., *Rōdō gyōsei shi,* I, 310–324, also discusses this law. Relatively small companies were reportedly affected even more, since almost none of them had retirement funds, and few could easily afford them.

7. Uraga Archives, A-66 File, 10/31/1936 and 5/6/1937 memoranda.

8. Minami Iwao, "Rōmu kanri no mujunsei," *Shakai undō ōrai*, 8/4/1936, pp. 7–17.

9. *Kanagawa-ken shi*, XIII, 853–865, especially pp. 858, 859, 864.

10. Ujihara, "Sangyō hōkokukai undō," pp. 195–234, offers the best analysis of the 1936–1938 Sanpō movement. See also Ōkōchi Kazuo, "Sangyō hōkokukai no mae to ato to," *Kindai Nihon keizai shisō shi*, II, 73–107; Sakurabayashi Makoto, "Senji Nihon rōshi kyōgisei," (1972), pp. 37–85; Yoshii Yukiko, "Sangyō hōkoku undō," pp. 35–52.

11. The Welfare Ministry was founded in 1938. It was responsible for most regulations pertaining to labor, although the Navy, Army, and Munitions Ministries also issued some relevant ordinances. Magota, "Senji rōdō," succinctly presents the case for the impact of these regulations.

12. Magota, "Senji rōdō," p. 12.

13. Ibid., pp. 18–20; Magota, *Nenkō chingin*, pp. 141–152; Hara, "Senji tōsei keizai," p. 241.

14. Magota, "Senji rōdō," p. 12.

15. Ibid.

16. Ōnishi and Takimoto, *Chingin seido*, pp. 226–228.

17. Ōhara, *Rōdōsha jōtai*, p. 3.

18. Mitsubishi, *Yokosen no omoide*, I, 253–254; Yasue interview, 5/9/1980; Hongo Takanobu interview, 8/29/1980.

19. Uraga Archives, A-66 File, 8/16/1939.

20. Ōhara, *Rōdōsha jōtai*, pp. 60–61. Company X here refers to Ishikawajima.

21. United States Strategic Bombing Survey in Japan, "Report on The Shibaura Engineering Works," Item 38s(2) in *Index to Records of United States Strategic Bombing Survey in Japan* (USSBS). Hongo interview, 8/29/1980.

22. Uraga Archives, A-23 File, 3/17/1944 memorandum; Mitsubishi, *Yokosen no omoide*, I, 253–255; Hongo interview, 8/29/1980; *NKK 40 nen shi*, pp. 519–520.

23. Masuda Tomio, *Senji rōdō seisaku no shōmondai*, p. 13.

24. Ōhara, *Rōdōsha jōtai*, pp. 2–4.

25. Shōwa kenkyūkai, *Chōki kensetsuki ni okeru waga kuni rōdō seisaku*, pp. 3–32, 76–80, 87, 97–99.

26. Uraga Archives, A-20 File, *Zenkoku sangyō dantai rengōkai kaihō*, 4/18/1939, pp. 21–22. Special edition on wage and hiring controls.

27. Masuda, *Rōdō seisaku*, p. 100.

28. Jerome B. Cohen, *Japan's Economy in War and Reconstruction*, p. 317.

29. Ōhara, *Rōdōsha jōtai*, p. 3; Cohen, *Economy in War*, p. 296.

30. Ōhara, *Rōdōsha jōtai*, p. 4.

31. Ibid., p. 41.

32. *Keihin kōgyō jihō,* September 1939, pp. 21–23.
33. Kyōchōkai, "Zadankai," in *Shakai seisaku jihō,* November 1940, pp. 169–171, 172, 195.
34. Ibid., pp. 189, 190, 216.
35. Ibid., pp. 188, 193.
36. Ibid., p. 214.
37. Ibid., p. 192.
38. Ibid., p. 178.
39. Ibid., p. 199.
40. *Keihin kōgyō jihō,* 6/15/1941, pp. 17–19.
41. *Shakai seisaku jihō,* March 1942, pp. 336–346.
42. *Tokyo Shibaura 85 nen shi,* pp. 199, 203.
43. Yasue interview, 5/19/1980.
44. Shōwa kenkyūkai, *Rōdō shintaisei kenkyū,* p. 13; Ōhara, *Rōdōsha jōtai,* p. 9.
45. Yasue interview, 5/19/1980. Kanai Tatsuo and Anzai Mitsuru interviews, 5/23/1979.
46. Uraga Archives, A-66 File, Report of March 1943.
47. *Shakai seisaku jihō,* March 1942. Kanagawa-ken Archives, Uraga File, 6/9/1942 report, p. 43.
48. *Kanagawa kenshi,* XVII, 955–956. It is not clear whether this is monthly or yearly turnover. My hunch is that this is a yearly figure. It is hard to believe monthly turnover could be so high, but, considering the anti-turnover regulations then in force, this is still considerable turnover, even on a yearly basis.
49. After that, material shortages may have been the greater problem.
50. Masuda, *Senji rōdō seisaku no shōmondai,* p. 13.
51. Cohen, *Economy in War,* pp. 298, 203.
52. Ibid., pp. 298–299; Tomiyasu interview, 8/21/1979.
53. Yasue interview, 5/19/1980; Hongo interview, 8/29/1980.
54. Thomas Havens, *Valley of Darkness: The Japanese People and World War Two,* p. 93; Cohen, *Economy in War,* p. 354; Odaka Kōnosuke, "Kyū Mitsubishi rōdō tōkei," p. 575. One additional factor behind the dramatic Mitsubishi decline is the fall in the proportion of highly paid workers in the shipyard.
55. *Keihin kōgyō jihō,* 10/5/1938, p. 3; 9/5/1939, pp. 18–19; 5/5/1939, pp. 1, 14; 7/5/1939, p. 19.
56. Nihon gakujutsu shinkōkai, ed., *Bukka mondai,* p. 131, offers one example.
57. *Shakai saisaku jihō,* November 1940, pp. 196, 203–205.
58. Shōwa, *Chingin,* p. 302.
59. *Shakai seisaku jihō,* March 1942, pp. 469–470.

60. Fujibayashi Keizō, *Rōdōsha seisaku no kihon mondai*, pp. 47-48.
61. Ibid., pp. 50-57.
62. Ōnishi and Takimoto, *Chingin*, pp. 392-393.
63. Ōya Saburō, *Uketori chingin seido ron*, pp. 195-209, 219.
64. *Shakai seisaku jihō*, November 1940, p. 63. Kōno had been an early Shinjinkai student radical, a union supporter through the 1920s, and theoretician for the Japan Labor Farmer Party. Later he was active in the Shōwa kenkyūkai. Shiota, *Jinmei jiten*, pp. 239-240.
65. Shōwa kenkyūkai, *Rōdō shintaisei*, pp. 134-137. Hirotsu Kyōsuke became a leader in the new postwar police system (Kōan keisatsu).
66. Shōwa, *Chingin*, p. 304.
67. Ibid., pp. 304-305. Also Masuda, *Rōdō seisaku*, proposed a very similar wage structure.
68. Ōnishi and Takunoto, *Chingin seido*, pp. 397-401.
69. Ibid., p. 293.
70. Mori Kiichi, *Jūkōgyō no chingin to seikatsu*, pp. 139, 141-142, 146.
71. *Shakai seisaku jihō*, November 1940, pp. 237-239; Shōwa, *Chingin*, pp. 300-302. Of the machine factories, 61.1% used both day and output wages, 7.7% output alone. Of the metal plants, 48.2% used both and 8.2% used output pay exclusively. Mori, *Jūkōgyō chingin*, pp. 73, 84-94.
72. The portion derived from incentive wages ranged from almost zero in 10% of the cases to over half of total income in a handful of cases (9 workers). *Shakai seisaku jihō*, November 1940, pp. 157-158.
73. Ibid.; Mori, *Jūkōgyō chingin*, pp. 131-133; Cohen, *Economy in War*, p. 328. An employee for an engineering company participating in the Kyōchōkai survey confirms Cohen's conclusion, stating that output wages were roughly equal to the base portion for most.
74. *Shakai seisaku jihō*, March 1941, pp. 263-264.
75. Odaka, "Kyū Mitsubishi rōdō tōkei," pp. 571-573.
76. Mitsubishi Heavy Industries, Yokohama Factory, Personnel Office Records.
77. *Tōshiba 85 nen shi*, p. 212.
78. *NRUS*, VII, 162-163; *NKK 40 nen shi*, p. 560; Chūshō kigyō rōdō mondai shiryō, No. 14, *Nenkō chingin seido no kindaika to jitsumu*, p. 6; Tomiyasu interviews, 8/21/1979, 8/28/1979.
79. Tōshiba denki kabushiki gaisha, *Tokyo Shibaura 85 nen shi*, p. 203.
80. Cohen, *Economy in War*, pp. 346-351.
81. Ōhara, *Rōdōsha jōtai*, p. 73.
82. Kaneko Yoshio, "Chingin mondai no kakō, genzai, mirai," in Kaneko, ed., *Chingin: sono kakō, genzai, mirai*, p. 274.

83. Shōwa, *Chingin*, pp. 290–291; *Keihin kōgyō jihō*, 6/5/1938, pp. 14–15.

84. *Shakai seisaku jihō*, November 1940, p. 221.

85. Ibid., March 1940, p. 202.

86. Ōhara, *Rōdōsha jōtai*, pp. 6, 91–94.

87. Ibid.

88. *Shakai seisaku jihō*, November 1940, pp. 53–59; Ōhara, *Rōdōsha jōtai*, pp. 94–95.

89. Ōhara, *Rōdōsha jōtai*, p. 98.

90. *Rōdō jihō*, March 1942, pp. 72–79.

91. Ibid., p. 73.

92. Ibid., pp. 75–77. See Article 10 of the ordinance and Articles 5 and 8 of the Administrative Supplement to the ordinance.

93. Ōhara, *Rōdōsha jōtai*, p. 98.

94. Ibid., p. 73; Kaneko, *Chingin*, p. 275; Kōseishō rōdō kyoku, ed., *Jūyō jikgyōjo rōmu kanri rei unyō hōshin*, pp. 6, 45–46.

95. Shōwa, *Chingin*, pp. 286–289; Ōhara, *Rōdōsha jōtai*, pp. 73–74.

96. Mitsubishi, *Yokosen no omoide*, I, 454–455; Yasue interview, 5/19/1980.

97. Ōnishi and Takimoto, *Chingin*, p. 258.

98. The "large" of the 1932 survey was not defined. Twelve of 20 allowances studied in depth in 1940 were for staff only. All from Kyōchōkai, *Waga kuni ni okeru kazoku teate*, pp. 5–9, 16–36.

99. Cohen, *Economy in War*, p. 327.

100. Dore, *British Factory-Japanese Factory*, p. 103, approaches the issue differently, attributing the spread of family allowances "largely" to the "particular exigencies of the postwar period."

101. Ōhara, *Rōdōsha jōtai*, p. 88; Kyōchōkai, *Rōdō nenkan* (1941), p. 191.

102. Ōhara, *Rōdōsha jōtai*, p. 98.

103. Kyōchōkai, *Kazoku teate*, p. 53.

104. Ibid.

105. *Keihin kōgyō jihō*, 3/15/1941, p. 14; Mitsubishi Heavy Industries, Yokohama Factory, Personnel Office Records, 1/13/1941, 12/26/1942. Ishikawajima, *Jikyōkai hō*, 7/10/1941, pp. 2–3; 4/20/1942, p. 3; Uraga Archives, File A-22, 1/23/1941 directive; *Tōshiba 85 nen shi*, p. 211.

106. Uraga Archives, File A-23, 4/9/1944, 8/5/1944.

107. *Keihin kōgyō jihō*, 2/15/1941, p. 28.

108. Kōseishō, *Unyō hōshin*, pp. 65–72.

109. *Keihin kōgyō jihō*, December 1938, p. 21; June 1939, pp. 20–22. Loans of this amount would have allowed Shibaura workers to purchase homes. Kanagawa-ken Archives, Uraga File, 6/9/1942 report.

110. *Keihin kōgyō jihō*, 7/15/1941, pp. 7–12; 3/15/1941, pp. 10–12.

111. *Shakai seisaku jihō*, November 1940, pp. 209, 212; Ōya, *Uketori chingin*,

p. 97; Fujibayashi, *Rōdōsha seisaku,* p. 265. In this, of course, the Japanese are no different from workers elsewhere. "Rate-buster" is a pejorative in the United States, too.

112. *Shakai seisaku jihō,* November 1940, p. 213, 177.
113. Ōhara, *Rōdō undō,* p. 15, for Kawasaki incident; pp. 16–17; for Hitachi.
114. Ōhara, *Rōdōsha jōtai,* p. 98.
115. Naimushō keiho kyoku hoan ka, *Tokkō geppō,* October 1943, pp. 150–151.

8. *SANPŌ: LABOR ORGANIZATION WITHOUT UNIONS*

1. Magota, "Senji rōdō," makes a persuasive general case, of pleasing logic but devoid of specific examples, for a significant Sanpō impact: It drew workers closer to the company, extending welfare facilities and benefits and narrowing the gap between staff and laborers. Our examination of a variety of actual cases paints a rather different picture.
2. Magota, "Senji rōdō," p. 12.
3. Ibid., p. 14. Ōuchi Tsuneo, *Rōmu shidō no jissai,* pp. 84–94.
4. Sakurabayashi, "Senji Nihon no rōshi kyōgi sei," p. 50, quotes Wada writing in a Kyōchōkai publication.
5. Ōkochi Kazuo, "Sangyō hōkokukai no mae to ato to," pp. 94–95.
6. Shōwa kenkyūkai, *Chōki rōdō seisaku,* pp. 67, 48–51.
7. *Shakai seisaku jihō,* March 1941, p. 354.
8. Shōwa kenkyūkai, *Rōdō shintaisei,* p. 60.
9. Ibid., pp. 74, 92, 102–103, 40–41.
10. Naimushō keiho kyoku, *Shakai undō jōkyō* (1942), p. 400. This report may also be found in Awaya Kentarō, "Kokumin dōin to teikō," p. 187, and Ōhara, *Rōdō undō,* pp. 57–58.
11. Fujibayashi, *Rōdōsha seisaku,* pp. 198–207.
12. Ibid., pp. 225–229; Sakurabayashi, "Senji no rōshi kyōgi," p. 42; *Shakai seisaku jihō,* March 1942, p. 571; Masuda, *Rōdō seisaku,* p. 110.
13. Sakurabayashi, "Senji no rōshi kyōgi," pp. 63–67.
14. Cohen, *Economy in War,* p. 284; *Jikyōkai hō,* p. 8.
15. *Keihin kōgyō jihō,* 9/5/1938, p. 35.
16. Ishikawajima, *Jikyōkai hō,* 8/5/1941, p. 7; 2/10/1942, p. 4.
17. Ibid., 4/20/1942, p. 9.
18. Ibid., 6/1/1942, pp. 6–7.
19. Ibid., 6/1/1942, p. 7.
20. Ibid., 4/20/1942, pp. 8–9.
21. Ibid., 6/1/1942, p. 18. A manager in the Labor Section of the company's Fukagawa factory made this statement.

22. Yasue interview, 5/19/1980. Yasue was involved in council activities from his first year with the company, 1937. He was made a director of the factory council in 1939 and was responsible for drawing up meeting agendas.

23. *Keihin kōgyō jihō*, 6/5/1938, p. 2.

24. *KRUS*, p. 787; *Uraga 60 nen shi*, p. 288-289; *Keihin kōgyō jihō*, 11/15/ 1938, p. 10.

25. Kanagawa Archives, Uraga File, 6/9/1942 report, p. 44.

26. Uraga Archives, A-21 File, 1/19/1944 memorandum.

27. Uraga Archives, A-24 File, 11/1/1944 report.

28. Ōhara, *Rōdō undō*, p. 49.

29. Sakurabayashi, "Senji no rōshi kyōgi," pp. 63-67; *KRUS*, p. 790.

30. Ishikawajima, *Jikyōkai hō*, 6/1/1941, p. 4; 7/10/1941, pp. 6-7; 8/5/ 1941, p. 2.

31. The activities at Tōshiba reflect the presence of a large number of female employees in factories previously part of Tokyo Electric Company. *Uraga 60 nen shi*, pp. 289-296, 369-372; *Tokyo Shibaura 85 nen shi*, p. 219.

32. Ishikawajima, *Jikyōkai hō*, 7/10/1941, p. 5.

33. Magota, "Senji rōdō," pp. 16-17, and Sakurabayashi, "Senji no rōshi kyōgi," p. 73, discuss income and ideology, respectively.

34. *Shakai seisaku jihō*, November 1940, pp. 179-180.

35. Shōwa kenkyūkai, *Rōdō shintaisei*, pp. 180-182, 185-186, 193-195.

36. Naimushō, *Shakai undō no jōkyō* (1941), pp. 632-634, 639.

37. Minami Iwao, *Nihon kinrō kanri ron*, pp. 18-19, 41-50, 195; Fujibayashi, *Rōdōsha seisaku*, pp. 104-105, issues a similar call.

38. Kaneko, *Chingin*, p. 274, on the Welfare and Munitions Ministry plans; *Shakai seisaku jihō*, 11/1940, pp. 218-225, and Ōnishi and Takimoto, *Chingin*, pp. 128-134, on bonuses. "Office staff" does not include executives, whose bonuses were separate.

39. *Shakai seisaku jihō*, March 1942, pp. 353, 364-365.

40. Tomiyasu interview, 8/28/1979.

41. *Keihin kōgyō jihō*, 5/5/1938, p. 3.

42. Kanai interview, 9/12/1979.

43. Yasue also feels the postwar union movement changed most of this; Yasue interview, 5/19/1980.

44. Uraga Archives, A-21 File, 1/17/1944 Staff Rules; A-22 File, 12/27/1939, 9/27/1940, and 3/30/1942 Regulations; A-23 File, 1944 launching Allowance Lists, October 1944 Air Raid Regulations. Similar discrimination is found in the few Tōshiba allowances described in *Tokyo Shibaura 85 nen shi*, p. 204.

45. Magota, "Senji rōdō," p. 17.

46. Cohen, *Economy in War,* pp. 341, 343–345.
47. *KRUS,* p. 749, quotes *Kanagawa-ken kōjō kyōkai shimbun.*
48. *Shakai seisaku jihō,* March 1942, p. 321.
49. Mitsubishi, *Yokosen no omoide,* I, 158. Yasue interview, 5/19/1980.
50. Ishikawajima, *108 nen shi,* pp. 473–478.
51. *Keihin kōgyō jihō,* 8/1939, p. 8.
52. *Shakai seisaku jihō,* March 1940, p. 298. These were disputes that did not become strikes.
53. Kyōchōkai, *Rōdō nenkan,* 1940, p. 286.
54. Naimushō, *Shakai undō jōkyō* (1941), p. 624.
55. Ibid., p. 635.
56. *Keihin kōgyō jihō,* 6/15/1941, p. 18.
57. Naimushō, *Shakai undō jōkyō* (1942), pp. 437–443.
58. Ibid.
59. Cohen, *Economy in War,* p. 345.
60. *Shakai seisaku jihō,* March 1940, p. 295; Ōhara, *Rōdōsha jōtai,* p. 7; Shōwa kenkyūkai, *Rōdō shintaisei,* pp. 139–140.
61. Kyōchōkai, *Rōdō nenkan* (1942), p. 261; Naimushō, *Shakai undō jōkyō* (1942), p. 529.
62. Ōhara, *Rōdō undō,* pp. 20–22. Awaya, "Dōin to teikō," p. 187.
63. *Tokkō geppō,* February 1943, p. 37.
64. Ibid., January 1943, p. 41; July 1943, p. 62; September 1943, pp. 63–64; October 1943, pp. 142–146; April 1944, p. 44.
65. Cohen, *Economy in War,* pp. 341–342.
66. Magota, "Senji rōdō," p. 22. Naimushō, *Shakai undō jōkyō* (1941), p. 714.
67. Dispute statistics are found in: Naimushō, *Shakai undō jōkyō* (1940), pp. 930–932; (1941), p. 735; and (1942) pp. 544–545, 548, 553; *Shakai seisaku jihō,* March 1940, p. 293; March 1941, pp. 331–340; Kyōchōkai, *Rōdō nenkan* (1941), pp. 277, 284; (1942), pp. 257–258; *Tokkō geppō,* December 1943, p. 71; November 1944, p. 45.
68. Ōhara, *Rōdō undō,* pp. 23–27.
69. *Shakai seisaku jihō,* March 1941, pp. 348, 352.
70. *KRUS,* pp. 770–771. Another 1940 dispute over misbehavior by a supervisor took place at NKK's Tsurumi Shipyard that February; *Shakai seisaku jihō,* March 1941, p. 339.
71. *Tokkō geppō,* September 1943, p. 62.
72. These reports are held at the Ōhara Institute for Social Research. They were donated by the new Labor Ministry soon after World War II. They are titled variously *Rōdō sōgi mizen bōshi shirabe, Rōdō sōgi mizen bōshi geppō, Rōdō sōgi hōkoku hyō,* and *Rōdō sōgi hassei ni kan suru*

ken. Ōhara, *Rōdō undō,* pp. 22–23, describes these reports in greater detail.

73. *Rōdō sōgi mizen bōshi shirabe,* Aichi prefecture, August 1944.
74. Ibid.
75. Ibid., Aichi prefecture, September 1944.
76. Ibid., Aichi prefecture, October 1944. Also found in Ōhara, *Rōdō undō,* pp. 24–25.

9. JAPANESE LABOR RELATIONS: THE WORKER VERSION

1. Charles Maier, "The Two Postwars and the Conditions for Stability in Europe," p. 327.
2. Joe Moore, "The Fight Over Labor's Place in the Postwar Reconstruction of Japan: Industrial Unionism and Plans for Capitalist Revival During the First Yoshida Cabinet," p. 2.
3. Kuriki Yasunobu, "Keizai kiki to rōdō undō," pp. 240–241. Joe Moore, *Japanese Workers and the Struggle for Power, 1945–1947* is an important study of the production-control tactic and the early postwar union movement.
4. K. Ōkōchi, B. Karsh, and S. B. Levine, eds., *Workers and Employers in Japan,* Ch. 4, "The Legal Framework,"; Solomon Levine, *Industrial Relations in Postwar Japan,* pp. 21–30.
5. Zen Nihon zōsen rōdō kumiai Mitsubishi jūkōgyō Yokohama zōsen bunkai, ed., *Jūnen no ayumi,* p. 12, has this price and wage information.
6. Moore, "Industrial Unionism," and Chalmers Johnson, *MITI and the Japanese Miracle: The Growth of Industrial Policy,* pp. 173–195, for economic policy in this period.
7. A partial list of reparations designations in the Tokyo area is found in *Asahi shimbun,* 8/25/1946 and 8/26/1946.
8. *Nihon keizai shimbun,* 11/23/1946.
9. Ōhara, *Rōdō undō,* pp. 60–61; Yasue interview, 5/17/1980; Zen Nihon Yokohama zōsen, *Ayumi.*
10. *KRUS,* II, 21. See also Ishikawa Tadanobu, "Shūsen chokugo no Tōshiba rōren tōsōki," pp. 182–188. And Tōshiba, *Kumiaishi,* pp. 4–20.
11. Kanai interview, 9/12/1979. Ishikawajima, *Ayumi,* p. 8.
12. *KRUS,* II, 22.
13. Zenzōsen jūgo nen shi henshūiinkai, ed., *Zenzōsen jūgo nen shi,* pp. 97–107.
14. Tekkō rōren Nippon kōkan Kawasaki rōdō kumiai, ed., *Arasoi no ayumi: Nippon kōkan Kawasaki rōdō kumiai undō shi,* pp. 40–47; *KRUS,* p. 262.

15. Tōshiba, *Kumiaishi,* p. 30; Hongō interview, 8/29/1980.
16. Nippon kōkan Kawasaki seitetsujo rōdō kumiai, *Jū nen no ayumi* (1956), p. 6.
17. *KRUS,* II, 30–32, 240–245.
18. Satō Kōichi, *Sengo Nihon rōdō undō shi,* pp. 67–68. Moore, *Japanese Workers,* Ch. 6, especially pp. 156–160, documents one fascinating and important case in the late winter of 1946 where farmers, workers, and miners, in Niigata, Tokyo, and Hokkaidō did establish such links. He argues that the mass movement was at this point on the verge of a "breakthrough to revolutionary workers' control." It would be interesting to see a few other similar cases documented. I suspect that the distance yet to be traveled from March 1946 to a revolutionary transfortion of the capitalist system in Japan was great. Due to SCAP response, in any case, we shall never know how close the Japanese popular movement was in fact to such a breakthrough. It was not close enough to stand up to SCAP.
19. *KRUS,* pp. 34–36, 42–43.
20. Tekkō rōren, *Arasoi,* pp. 43–44; Satō, *Rōdō undō,* p. 125; Tōshiba, *Kumiaishi,* pp. 29–32.
21. Keieishi henshūshitsu, ed., *Nihon keieishi: sengo keieishi,* p. 220.
22. Tōshiba, *Kumiaishi,* p. 28.
23. Tokyo daigaku shakai kagaku kenkyūjo, ed., *Densan jūgatsu tōsō 1946: Sengo shoki rōdō sōgi shiryō,* contains a fascinating set of transcripts of collective bargaining sessions in 1946.
24. NKK Kawasaki, *Ayumi,* p. 6.
25. Ibid., pp. 6, 48, 71; *Keieishi,* pp. 222–223.
26. Zenzōsen, *Jūgo nen shi,* p. 99.
27. Kuriki, "Keizai kiki," p. 229; Uraga Archives, A-23 file, Memoranda of 4/2/1947, 5/14/1947.
28. Kaneko, *Chingin,* pp. 278–282; *Keieishi,* p. 223.
29. *Keieishi,* p. 446.
30. Uraga Archives, A-26 files; Uraga dokku, *Ayumi,* pp. 29–31.
31. Ariizumi Ryō et al., "Densan jūgatsu tōsō," pp. 33–40.
32. Ibid., pp. 41–48.
33. Kaneko, *Chingin,* p. 311.
34. Kawanishi Kōyū, "Densan jūgatsu tōsō to densan gata chingin no keisei," pp. 114–117; Ariizumi, "Densan," pp. 48–55.
35. Kawanishi, "Densan," p. 111.
36. *KRUS,* pp. 78, 253.
37. Tekkō rōren, *Arasoi,* pp. 60–61.
38. Zenzōsen, *Jūgo nen shi,* pp. 115–119, 121–123, 130–133.

39. *Keieishi,* p. 446.
40. Tōshiba, *Kumiaishi,* pp. 8, 33–37, 206.
41. Tekkō rōren, *Arasoi,* pp. 60–61.
42. Kaneko, *Chingin,* p. 277.
43. Ishikawajima, *Ayumi,* passim; Uraga dokku, *Ayumi,* passim; Yokohama zōsen, *Ayumi,* passim.
44. Tōshiba, *Kumiaishi,* pp. 93, 201–207. Yokohama Dock records held in the personnel division of Mitsubishi Heavy Industries Yokohama Factory; hereafter, Yokohama Dock Archives. Ishikawajima, *Ayumi,* p. 78.
45. *Nihon keizai shimbun,* 8/6/1946.
46. Zenzōsen, *Jūgo nen shi,* pp. 144–147.
47. Tōshiba, *Kumiaishi,* pp. 199–208.
48. Yokohama Dock Archives.
49. Uraga Archives, A-23 file. Tekkō rōren, *Arasoi,* pp. 71–72.
50. *KRUS,* pp. 250–253.
51. *KRUS,* pp. 20–21.
52. Kuriki, "Keizai kiki," p. 226.
53. *KRUS,* pp. 49–51, 250–253; Tōshiba, *Kumiaishi,* pp. 45–86.
54. *KRUS,* pp. 54–55.

10. THE MANAGEMENT REVISION

1. *Keieishi,* pp. 242–246, 462–464.
2. Ibid., pp. 335–358, 437–441.
3. Satō, *Rōdō undō,* pp. 123–124.
4. Hyōdō Tsutomu, "Rōdō kumiai undō no hatten," p. 102.
5. *Keieishi,* pp. 337–338, for general description of this issue. For company specifics, Tsurumi is covered in Satō, *Rōdō undō,* p. 125, and Nippon kōkan, *Tsurutetsu rōdō,* pp. 59–60, 84–89. Shipbuilding, in Zenzōsen, *Jūgo nen shi,* p. 163. Kawasaki steel, in Tekkō rōren, *Arasoi,* pp. 119–120.
6. Tōshiba, *Kumiaishi,* pp. 148–198, 230–255.
7. Tekkō rōren, *Arasoi,* pp. 84–85.
8. See Zenzōsen, *Jūgo nen shi,* p. 204, for the Yokosen example.
9. Zenzōsen, *Jūgo nen shi,* pp. 215–216.
10. *Keieishi,* pp. 441–447. Kaneko, *Chingin,* p. 287.
11. For Zenzōsen examples see, Zenzōsen, *Jūgo nen shi,* p. 157.
12. *Keieishi,* p. 445.
13. Tōshiba, *Kumiaishi,* p. 222; Tekkō rōren, *Arasoi,* pp. 87–89.
14. Zenzōsen, *Jūgo nen shi,* pp. 215–216.
15. *Keieishi,* pp. 745–750, 664.

16. Tekkō rōren, *Arasoi*, pp. 107–111, 114–118, 122–125.
17. Tōshiba, *Kumiaishi*, pp. 269–272, 280–284, 315–318.
18. Zenzōsen, *Jūgo nen shi*, pp. 219–224.
19. Ishikawajima, *Ayumi*, pp. 30–37, 82–88; Yokohama zōsen, *Ayumi*, pp. 66–73.
20. Tekkō rōren, *Arasoi*, pp. 110–111.
21. Zenzōsen, *Jūgo nen shi*, pp. 219–224; Tekkō rōren, *Arasoi*, pp. 122–125; Tōshiba, *Kumiaishi*, p. 355.
22. Yasue interview, 5/17/1980.
23. Rōdōshō, *Hakusho* (1956), p. 218.
24. *Keieishi*, pp. 665–666.
25. Rōdōshō, *Hakusho* (1957), p. 204.
26. See Ishikawajima, *Ayumi*, pp. 82–88, for examples.
27. Rōdōshō, *Hakusho* (1955), p. 170; Naomichi Funahashi, "The Industrial Reward System: Wages and Benefits," p. 364.
28. *Tokyo Shibaura 85 nen shi*, pp. 908–911. For other similar examples, Tekkō rōren, *Arasoi*, pp. 114–118, and Zenzōsen, *Jūgo nen shi*, pp. 189–193.
29. *Keieishi*, pp. 742–744.
30. Tekkō rōren, *Arasoi*, pp. 144–145.
31. *Keieishi*, pp. 547–550, 742–744.
32. Nihon kōkan, *Tsurutetsu rōdō*, p. 87.
33. Dore, *British Factory-Japanese Factory*, pp. 98–101.
34. See Cole, *Japanese Blue Collar*, pp. 75–78, for an example.
35. Ibid., p. 86.
36. Takafusa Nakamura, *The Postwar Japanese Economy* (1981), chart on p. 165.
37. Funahashi, "Industrial Reward System," pp. 373–374.
38. Zenzōsen, *Jūgo nen shi*, pp. 158–159, 212–214. Ishikawajima, *Ayumi*, pp. 28–31.
39. Tokyo daigaku shakai kagaku kenkyūjo, *Tōshiba sōgi chōsa shiryō*, VIII, 7–10.
40. Tōshiba, *Kumiaishi*, pp. 147–198, for the union's version; KRUS, pp. 318–322, for a third-party account.
41. *KRUS*, pp. 145–148, 163, 343.
42. Zenzōsen, *Jūgo nen shi*, p. 59; Tekkō rōren, *Arasoi*, pp. 144–145.
43. NKK Kawasaki, *Ayumi*, p. 121.
44. Zenzōsen, *Jūgo nen shi*, pp. 213–217.
45. Cole, *Japanese Blue Collar*, pp. 256–258, has a good example of similar transfers essentially forced on workers by the union and company.
46. Tōshiba, *Kumiaishi*, pp. 327–330.
47. Koike, *Shokuba no rōdo kumiai*, offers an interesting elaboration of this point.

48. Yamamoto, *Rōdō shijō no kōzō*, pp. 266–270, for this case.
49. Koike, *Shokuba no rōdō kumiai*, p. 232. The same data, with a simila discussion, are presented by the same author in English in Kazuo Koike, "Internal Labor Markets: Workers in Large Firms," in Shirai, ed., *Contemporary Industrial Relations in Japan*, p. 36.
50. Yamamoto, *Rōdō shijō*, pp. 266–270.
51. Cole, *Japanese Blue Collar*, p. 126, makes similar points regarding this implicit agreement.
52. Nakamura, *Postwar Economy*, pp. 165–167.
53. For annual statistics nationwide and by industry, consult two series produced by the Labor Ministry (Rōdōshō): *Rōdō idō chōsa kekka hōkoku* (1956–1963) and *Koyō dōkō chōsa hōkoku* (1964–1978). For specific data in this paragraph, also see Rōdōshō, *Hakusho* (1957), pp. 62–64, (1969) pp. 79–80, and other volumes of the series, passim. Tōshiba, *Kumiaishi*, p. 383. *Tokyo Shibaura 85 nen shi*, p. 401.
54. Tōshiba, *Kumiaishi*, pp. 375, 380, 383, for numbers of temporaries and pay. The wage calculation assumes an average temporary worker received 372 yen per hour, midway between the low and high hourly rates for temporaries of 200 and 545 yen. It also assumes 29 days worked per month. The resulting total of 10,788 yen is 6,417 yen less than the average regular wage of 17,205 yen. I suspect this is a slightly conservative estimate. Probably the average hourly rate was closer to the bottom end of the scale. For figures on profits, *Tokyo Shibaura 85 nen shi*, p. 387.
55. *Shiryō: rōdō undō*, 1959), p. 957 notes two major successful struggles to end reliance on temporaries, at Sumitomo Chemical Company and the Tokyo Waterworks.
56. NKK Kawasaki, *Arasoi*, pp. 126–129; NKK Kawasaki, *Ayumi*, p. 211; Tōshiba, *Kumiaishi*, pp. 380–382, 400, 439–440, 481, 509, 522; Rōdōshō, *Hakusho* (1963), p. 79; (1964) p. 77; (1965) p. 91.
57. Rōdōshō, *Hakusho* (1962), p. 106; Rōdōshō, *Koyō dōkō*, 1964–1978 on long-run trends.
58. Rōdōshō, *Hakusho* (1962), p. 106; Rōdōshō, *Koyō dōkō*, 1964–1978.
59. Nakamura, *Postwar Economy*, p. 169.
60. Ibid., p. 170. Rōdōshō, *Hakusho* (1967) p. 86, notes that 38% of manufacturing firms who hired part-timers gave them "regular" not "temporary" contracts.
61. Rōdōshō, *Hakusho* (1981) has a special section on part-time labor which supplied these data; pp. 140, 184–188, 192 and passim.
62. Ibid. (1981), pp. 187–189.
63. Ibid. (1981), pp. 179, 198, 200–201.
64. Tōshiba figures from company personnel-office records.

65. Rōdōshō, *Hakusho* (1972), p. 73; (1975), p. 69.
66. Rōdōshō, *Hakusho* (1981), p. 204.
67. Dore, *British Factory–Japanese Factory,* pp. 384 and passim. I would take issue only with the period to which Dore applies the term. It is excellent for the 1950s and beyond, but I find it misleading for earlier periods.
68. John Dower, *Empire and Aftermath: Yoshida Shigeru and the Japanese Experience,* pp. 260–264 and passim.

CONCLUSION

1. See Pelzel, "Social Stratification" and "Factory Life." Many of the labor activists blacklisted by zaibatsu firms in the 1920s eventually settled down to run small machine or metalworking shops in the 1930s and 1940s. Three of the men whose careers are detailed in this book followed this pattern: Saitō Tadatoshi, Takayama Jiroichi, and Uchida Tōshichi. See entries for each in Shiota, *Shakai undō jinmei jiten.*
2. Craig, "Introduction" in *Japan: A Comparative View,* p. 9, makes a general point relevant to the comparison between artisan organization and unionism in Japan and the West. In terms of our concerns, his argument suggests that we not consider the factory union of Japan distorted because it does not follow the European pattern in which trade unions evolved first, followed by industrial federations. We should rather reconsider the extent to which *trade* unionism is a natural or necessary starting point in the development of a labor movement.
3. Alexander Gerschenkron, *Economic Backwardness in Historical Perspective,* and Dore, *British Factory-Japanese Factory,* Ch. 15, and "Industrial Relations," discuss labor and the late-development issue. Major early studies that viewed turnover as a problem came after World War I in the United States: Sumner Slichter, *The Turnover of Factory Labor* (1919); Paul Brissenden and Emil Frankel, *Labor Turnover in Industry: A Statistical Analysis* (1922).
4. In an incisive and suggestive footnote, Rohlen, *For Harmony and Strength,* p. 173, briefly elaborates the distinction between treatment of white and blue collar and the historical spread of a white-collar model to workers. More historical study is needed on the origins of white-collar employment patterns and the actual work conditions and benefits offered to white-collar people. The term *white collar* embraces a wide range of employees, some of whom were probably more "equal" than others, especially in the nineteenth and early twentieth century. If conclusions reached in this study can be applied to other groups in society, it may

turn out that a similar dialectic led to the spread of "Japanese employment practices" from a fairly select group of high-ranking white-collar bureaucrats and managers to other staff members, before or to some extent overlapping the long period in which such policies began to include workers.

5. As I have suggested in several places, the greatest problem with Dore's approach to prewar labor relations lies in his belief that managers were motivated by faith in the "efficiency of benevolence in evoking loyalty, and of trust in evoking responsibility." See *British Factory-Japanese Factory,* pp. 401–402.

6. Naimushō, *Shakai undō no jōkyō* (1941), p. 639.

Bibliography

INTERVIEWS

Anzai Mitsuru (Ishikawajima; labor manager)	5/23/1979, 9/12/1979
Fujiwara Kenzō (NKK; labor manager)	8/23/1979
Hongo Takanobu (Tōshiba; labor manager)	8/29/1980
Kaneko Yoshio (Welfare Ministry; wage section)	10/23/1979
Kanai Tatsuo (Ishikawajima; labor manager)	5/23/1979, 9/12/1979
Mariko Kōsaburō (Ishikawajima; boilermaker, foreman)	5/23/1979, 12/4/1979
Moji Ryō (Asano Dock; shipbuilder, union leader)	11/2/1979
Ōhashi Takeo (Welfare Ministry; wage section)	10/23/1980
Saitō Tadatoshi (Ishikawajima; lathe worker, union leader)	6/3/1979, 8/28/1979
Tomiyasu Nagateru (NKK; labor manager, wage section)	8/21/1979, 8/28/1979
Yasuda Tatsuma (Welfare Ministry)	10/14/1980
Yasue Masao (Yokohama Dock; labor manager)	5/19/1980

ARCHIVAL COLLECTIONS

Kanagawa-ken shi shiryō shitsu (Kanagawa Prefectural Archives), part of Kanagawa-ken, kikaku chōsa-bu, in Yokohama.

Kawasaki shiyakusho, bunshoka (Kawasaki City Hall Archives).

Uraga Dock Archives now held at Zōsen shiryō shitsu at the Oppama Shipyard of Sumitomo Heavy Industries.

PERIODICALS, NEWSPAPERS, UNION PUBLICATIONS

Asahi shimbun
Busō renmei (1927–1929)
Hantō jichi (1928–1929)

Hikari (1906)
Jiji shimpō
Jikyōkai hō (1941-1943)
Jitsugyō shōnen (1908)
Jiyū rengō shimbun (1929-1939)
Keihin kōgyō jihō (1937-1941)
Kōrō (1924-1925)
Kōshinkai hō (1924-1927)
Mainichi shimbun
Musansha shimbun (1927)
Ni roku shimpō (1901)
Nihon zōsen rōdō renmei (1930)
Rōdō dōmei (1922)
Rōdō jidai (1929-1930)
Rōdō jihō (1939-1945)
Rōdō kumiai (1928)
Rōdō oyobi sangyō (1914-1919)
Rōdō sekai (1897-1901)
Rōdō shimbun (1925-1926)
Rōdō undō (1921)
Rōdōsha (1928)
Shakai seisaku jihō
Shakai undō ōrai (1929-1936)
Shibaura dōshi renmei (1930)
Shibaura rōdō (1922-1929)
Taiheiyō shōkō sekai (1908-1909)
Tetsuben (1921-1922)
Tokyo asahi shimbun
Tokyo mainichi shimbun
Tokyo nichi nichi shimbun
Tōyō keizai shimpō
Yokohama bōeki shimpō
Yūai shimpō (1912-1914)

ALL OTHER SOURCES

Abe Goichi. "Yokohama dokku kaisha ni jisshi sareru gōriteki chingin seido" (The rational wage system implemented at Yokohama Dock Company), *Shakai seisaku jihō* (October 1929).

Abegglen, James. *The Japanese Factory: Aspects of its Social Organization.* Glencoe, The Free Press, 1958.

————. *Management and Worker: The Japanese Solution.* Tokyo, Sophia University Press, 1973.

An Rui Sei. "Shokkō seikatsu 20 nen no kokuhaku" (Confessions of twenty years of a worker's life), *Yūai shimpō* Nos. 26–34 (1914).

Aoki Kōji. *Nihon rōdō undō shi nempyō* (Chronology of Japanese labor-movement history). Shinseisha, 1968.

Aoki Masahisa. "Nittetsu kikankata sōgi kenkyū" (A study of the locomotive engineers' strike at Japan Railway Company), *Rōdō undō shi kenkyū* No. 62 (1979).

Arai Gensui. *Tokyo Ishikawajima 50 nen shi* (50-year history of Tokyo Ishikawajima). Tokyo, 1930.

Ariizumi Ryō et al. "Densan jūgatsu tōsō (1946)" (The electric power October struggle), in Tokyo daigaku shakai kagaku kenkyūjo chōsa hōkoku, 13: *Sengo shoki rōdō sōgi chōsa* (Survey of early postwar labor disputes). March 1971.

Awaya Kentarō. "Kokumin dōin to teikō" (National civilian mobilization and resistance), *Iwanami kōza: Nihon rekishi,* 21 (Iwanami symposium: Japanese history, 21). Iwanami shoten, 1977.

Brody, David. *Steelworkers in America: The Non-union Era.* Cambridge, Harvard University Press, 1960.

Chūō shokugyō shōkai jimukyoku, ed. *Shokugyō betsu rōdō jijō, 3: kikai kōgyō* (Labor conditions in industry, 3: Machine industry). Tokyo, 1927.

Chūshō kigyō rōdō mondai shiryō, No. 14, *Nenkō chingin seido no kindaikai to jitsumu* (The modernization of the seniority wage system). 1964.

Cohen, Jerome B. *Japan's Economy in War and Reconstruction.* Minneapolis, University of Minnesota Press, 1949. Reprinted Westport, Greenwood Press, 1973.

Cole, Robert E. *Japanese Blue Collar: The Changing Tradition.* Berkeley, University of California Press, 1971.

————. "The Theory of Institutionalization: Permanent Employment and Tradition in Japan," *Economic Development and Cultural Change* 20.1 (October 1971).

————. "The Late Developer Hypothesis: An Evaluation of its Relevance for Japanese Employment Practices," *Journal of Japanese Studies* 4.2 (Summer 1978).

————. *Work, Mobility, and Participation: A Comparative Study of American and Japanese Industry.* Berkeley, University of California Press, 1979.

Craig, Albert M., ed. *Japan: A Comparative View.* Princeton, Princeton University Press, 1979.

Crawcour, Sydney. "The Japanese Employment System," *Journal of Japanese Studies* 4.2 (Summer 1978).

Dobson, C. R. *Masters and Journeymen: A Prehistory of Industrial Relations, 1718-1800.* London, Croon Helm, 1980.

Dore, R. P. "The Modernizer as a Special Case: Japanese Factory Legislation, 1882-1922," *Comparative Studies in Society and History* 11.4 (October 1969).

———. *British Factory-Japanese Factory.* Berkeley, University of California Press, 1973.

———. "More about Late Development," *Journal of Japanese Studies* 5.1 (Winter 1979).

———. "Industrial Relations in Japan and Elsewhere," in Albert M. Craig, ed. *Japan: A Comparative View.* Princeton, Princeton University Press, 1979.

Dower, John. *Empire and Aftermath: Yoshida Shigeru and the Japanese Experience.* Cambridge, Council on East Asian Studies, Harvard University, 1980.

Fruin, W. Mark. "The Japanese Company Controversy," *Journal of Japanese Studies* 4.2 (Summer 1978).

Fujibayashi Keizō. "Waga kuni ni okeru rōdō idō no kenkyū" (The study of labor mobility in Japan), *Mita gakkai zasshi* 35.3 (March 1941).

———. *Rōdōsha seisaku no kihon mondai* (Basic issues in policy toward workers). Keiō shuppankai, 1943.

Fukuda Kōichirō. "Nihon ni okeru dokusen shihonshugi dankai no rōdōsha tōkatsu kikō: shokuchō seido to kōgyō kyōiku" (Structures for the control of laborers in the monopoly capital stage in Japan: The foreman system and industrial education), *Nihon shi kenkyū* No. 131 (January 1973).

Funahashi Naomichi, "The Industrial Reward System: Wages and Benefits," in Ōkōchi Kazuo, ed., *Workers, Managers, and Employers in Japan.* Tokyo University Press, 1974.

Gerschenkron, Alexander. *Economic Backwardness in Historical Perspective.* Cambridge, The Belknap Press of Harvard University Press, 1966.

Gordon, Andrew D. "Workers, Managers, and Bureaucrats in Japan: Labor Relations in Heavy Industry, 1853-1945." PhD dissertation, Harvard University, 1981.

Gordon, David M., Richard Edwards, and Michael Reich. *Segmented Work, Divided Workers.* Cambridge, Cambridge University Press, 1982.

Hara Akira. "Senji tōsei keizai no kaishi" (Inaugurating the wartime controlled economy), *Iwanami kōza: Nihon rekishi,* XX. (Iwanami symposium: Japanese history, XX). Iwanami shoten, 1976.

Havens, Thomas. *Valley of Darkness: The Japanese People and World War Two.* New York, Norton, 1978.

Hazama Hiroshi. *Nihon rōmu kanri shi kenkyū* (Studies in the history of Japanese labor management). Dayamondo sha, 1969.

————. *Rōshi kyōchō no teiryū* (The undercurrent of labor-management cooperation). Waseda daigaku shuppankai, 1978. Portions translated as "Japanese Labor-Management Relations and Uno Riemon," *Journal of Japanese Studies* 5.1 (Winter 1979).

Hirokawa Sadahide. "1920 nendai ni okeru rōdō undō hatten: Shibaura seisakujo ni okeru 'gōrika' hantai tōsō o chūshin ni" (The development of the labor movement in the 1920s: On the anti-rationalization struggle at Shibaura Engineering Works), *Nihon shi kenkyū* No. 118 (April 1971).

Hitachi seisakujo shashi henshū bu, ed. *Hitachi seisakujo shi* (A history of Hitachi Engineering Works). 1949.

Hōsei daigaku keizaigakubu kenkyū bu, ed. *Keihin kōgyō chitai o chūshin to suru chingin chōsa hōkoku* (Report on a wage survey of the Keihin industrial region). 1936.

Hyōdō Tsutomu. *Nihon ni okeru rōshi kankei no tenkai* (The evolution of labor-capital relations in Japan). Tokyo daigaku shuppankai, 1971.

————. "Rōdō kumiai undō no hatten (The development of the labor-union movement), *Iwanami kōza Nihon rekishi* 23: *gendai* 2 (Iwanami symposium: Japanese history, 23: Contemporary, 2). Iwanami shoten, 1977.

Hyōgikai nempyō henshū sewajinkai. *Ishikawajima zōsenjo kōjō bunkai shiryō* (Documents on the Hyōgikai Chapter at Ishikawajima Shipyard). 1964.

Hyōgo-ken, keisatsu bu, kōjō ka, ed. *Shokkō idō jōkyō chōsa hyō* (Report on a survey of labor mobility). 1925.

Ikeda Makoto. *Nihon kikaikō kumiai seiritsu shi ron* (On the history of the formation of Japanese machine-worker unions). Nihon hyōronsha, 1970.

————. "Nihon tetsudō kikaikō no tōsō" (The disputes of machine workers at Japan Railway Company), *Rōdō undō shi kenkyū* No. 62 (1979).

———— and Ōmae Sakuro. *Nihon rōdō undō shi ron* (On the history of the Japanese labor movement). Nihon hyōronsha, 1966.

Ikegai tekkōjo, ed. *Ikegai tekkōjo 50 nen shi* (50-year history of Ikegai Iron Works). 1941.

Ishikawa Tadanobu. "Shūsen chokugo no Tōshiba rōren tosōki" (Record of the immediate postwar dispute of the Tōshiba Labor Federation), *Rōdō undō shi kenkyū* No. 62 (1979).

Ishikawajima jūkōgyō kabushiki gaisha shashi henshū iinkai, ed. *Ishikawajima jūkōgyō kabushiki gaisha 108 nen shi* (108-year history of Ishikawajima Heavy Industries Incorporated). 1961.

Ishikawajima zōsenjo eigyō hōkoku sho, 1903-1944 (Semiannual business reports of Ishikawajima Shipyard, 1903-1944).

Ishikawajima zōsenjo sanpō nyūzu, ed. (The Ishikawajima Sanpō News, ed.). *Jikyōkai hō* (Jikyōkai bulletin). 1941-1943.

Johnson, Chalmers. *MITI and the Japanese Miracle: The Growth of Industrial Policy.* Stanford, Stanford University Press, 1982.

Kakeya Saihei. "Rōdō undō ni okeru fashizumu no tanshoteki keisei" (The preliminary formation of fascism in the labor movement), *Ritsumeikan bungaku* No. 277 (1968).

Kamii Yoshihiko. "Daiichiji taisen chokugo no rōdō seisaku: chikeihō 17 jō no kaishaku, tekiyō mondai o chūshin to shite" (Labor policy immediately after World War I: On the problem of interpreting and applying Article 17 of the Public Order Police Law), *Rōdō undō shi kenkyū* No. 62 (1979).

———. "Daiichiji taisengo no rōdō seisaku: 1926 rōshi kankei hō o megutte" (Post-World War I labor policy: Concerning the 1926 Labor Relations Law), *Shakai seisaku nempō* No. 23 (1979).

Kamino Shinichi. *Kamino Shinichi kōen shū* (Collected lectures of Kamino Shinichi). 1932.

———. *Nihonshugi rōdō undō no shinzui* (The spirit of the Japanist labor movement). Ajia kyōkai shuppan bu, 1933.

Kanagawa-ken, ed. *Keihin kōgyō chitai chōsa hōkokusho* (Survey report on the Keihin industrial region). March 1954.

Kanagawa-ken keisatsu shi hensan iinkai, ed. *Kanagawa-ken keisatsu shi* (The history of the Kanagawa prefecture police). Taiyōsha, 1970.

Kanagawa-ken, kenshi henshūshitsu, ed. *Kanagawa-ken shi shiryō* (Documents on the history of Kanagawa prefecture) Vols. XIII, XVII. 1977, 1976.

Kanagawa-ken, Miura-gun kyōiku iinkai, ed. *Miura-gun shi* (Miura county gazetteer). 1918.

Kanagawa-ken, rōdō-bu, rōsei-ka, ed. *Kanagawa-ken rōdō undō shi: senzen hen* (History of the labor movement in Kanagawa precture: Prewar era). Yokohama, 1966.

Kaneko Yoshio, ed. *Chingin: sono kakō, genzai, mirai* (Wages: Past, present, future). Nihon rōdō kyōkai, 1972.

Katayama Sen. "Nihon ni okeru rōdō" (Labor in Japan) *Shakai* 1.4 (July 1899). Reprinted in *Nihon rōdō undō shiryō*, I, 597-598.

———. *Jiden* (Autobiography). 1922. Reprinted, Iwanami shoten, 1954.

————. *Waga kaisō* (Memoirs). 1929. Reprinted, Tokuma shoten, 1967.

Katayama Sen and Nishikawa Kōjirō. *Nihon no rōdō undō* (The Japanese labor movement). 1901. Reprinted, Iwanami shoten, 1952.

Kawanishi Kōyū. "Densan jūgatsu tōsō to densan gata chingin no keisei" (The electric-power workers' October struggle and the formation of the electric-power industry wage structure), *Rōdō mondai* (December 1979).

Kawasaki shiyakusho, bunsho ka. *Daiikkai rōdō tōkei jitchi chōsa shorui* (Documents on the First Labor Statistics Field Survey). 1924.

————. *Daisankai rōdō tōkei jitchi chōsa shorui* (Documents on the Third Labor Statistics Field Survey). 1930.

————. *Dai rokkai rōdō tōkei jitchi chōsa shorui* (Documents on the Sixth Labor Statistics Field Survey). 1939.

Keieishi henshūshitsu, ed. *Nihon keieishi: sengo keieishi* (The history of Japanese business management: Postwar management history). Nihon seisansei honbu, 1965.

Kikuda Zengorō. "Shibaura seisakujo sōgi hihan" (A critique of the Shibaura Engineering Works dispute), *Rōdōsha* (March 1928).

Kinmoth, Earl. *The Self-Made Man in Meiji Japanese Thought.* Berkeley, University of California Press, 1981.

Kishimoto Eitarō. *Nihon zettaishugi shakai seisaku shi* (The history of social policy under Japanese absolutism). Yūhikaku, 1955.

Koike Kazuo. *Shokuba no rōdō kumiai to sanka* (Labor unions and work place participation). Tōyō keizai shimpōsha, 1977.

Kokuseiin, ed. *Nihon teikoku jinkō dōtai tōkei* (Statistics on population trends in imperial Japan). 1913.

Komatsu Ryūji. *Kigyō betsu kumiai no seisei* (The founding of enterprise-level unions). Ochanomizu shobō, 1971.

Kōseishō, rōdō kyoku, ed. *Jūyō jigyōjo rōmu kanri rei unyō hōshin* (Procedures for the implementation of the Ordinance on Labor Management in Important Enterprises). 1942.

Kuriki Yasunobu, "Keizai kiki to rōdō undō" (The economic crisis and the labor movement), *Iwanami Kōza Nihon rekishi,* 22: *gendai 2.* Iwanami shoten, 1977.

Kyōchōkai, ed. *Kōjō iinkai seido* (The factory-council system). 1926.

————. *Saikin no shakai undō* (Recent social movements). 1929.

————. *Rōdō nenkan* (Labor yearbook). 1938–1942.

————. *Waga kuni ni okeru kazoku teate* (Family allowances in Japan). 1940.

Kyū kyōchōkai monjo. *Ishikawajima zōsenjo sōgi* (The Ishikawajima Shipyard dispute). 1921.

————. *Yokohama dokku, Asano dokku, Uraga dokku sōgi chōsa* (Survey of the disputes at the Yokohama, Asano, and Uraga Dock Companies). 1921.

——. *Kanagawa-ken ka no sōgi* (Labor disputes in Kanagawa prefecture). 1921, 1922.

——. "Uraga dokku kabushiki gaisha shiryō" (Documents on the Uraga Dock Company). 1921, 1925.

——. *Kanagawa-ken ka no rōdō dantai* (Labor organizations in Kanagawa prefecture). 1922.

——. *Rōdō sōgi: ippan* (Labor disputes: general). 1924.

——. *Ikegai sōgi* (The Ikegai dispute). 1923.

——. *Rōdō sōgi: zōsen, sharyō, 4* (Labor disputes: Shipbuilding, rolling stock). 1925.

——. *Rōdō sōgi: kikai, 4* (Labor disputes: Machine industry). 1925.

——. *Kantō, Hokkaidō chihō hyōgikai* (The Hyōgikai Federation in the Kantō and Hokkaidō regions). 1926.

——. *Rōdō sōgi: zōsen, 3* (Labor disputes: Shipbuilding). 1926.

——. *Rōdō sōgi: kikai, 2.* (Labor disputes: Machine industry). 1927.

——. *Rōdō sōgi: kikai, kinzoku, 2* (Labor disputes: Machine and metal industries). 1927.

——. *Nihon rōdō kumiai hyōgikai zenkoku kyōgikai* (The National Council of the Japan Labor Union Council). 1927, 1929–1930.

——. *Rōdō sōgi: ippan, 2* (Labor disputes: General). 1929.

——. *Rōdō sōgi: kikai* (Labor disputes: Machine industry). 1930.

——. *Rōdō sōgi: zōsen, 4* (Labor disputes: Shipbuilding). 1930.

——. *Rōdō sōgi: kikai* (Labor disputes: Machine industry). 1931.

Large, Stephen. *The Rise of Labor in Japan: The Yūaikai, 1912-1919.* Tokyo, Sophia University Press, 1972.

——. "Perspectives on the Failure of the Labour Movement in Prewar Japan," *Labour History* (Australia) No. 37 (November 1979).

Leeson, R. A. *Travelling Brothers: The six centuries road from craft fellowship to trade unionism.* London, Allen and Unwin, 1979.

Levine, Solomon, *Industrial Relations in Postwar Japan,* Urbana, University of Illinois Press, 1958.

—— and Hisashi Kawada. *Human Resources in Japanese Industrial Development.* Princeton, Princeton University Press, 1980.

Magota Ryōhei. "Senji rōdō ron e no gimon" (Some doubts on the debate about wartime labor), *Nihon rōdō kyōkai zasshi* No. 75 (July 1965).

——, ed. *Nenkō chingin no ayumi to mirai: chingin taikei hyaku nen shi* (The history and future of seniority wages: A 100-year history of the wage structure). Sangyō rōdō chōsajo, 1970.

Maier, Charles. "The Two Postwars and the Conditions for Stability in Twentieth Century Europe," *American Historical Review* (April 1981).

Marshall, Byron K. *Capitalism and Nationalism in Prewar Japan.* Stanford, Stanford University Press, 1967.

Masuda Tomio. *Senji rōdō seisaku no shōmondai* (Some problems in wartime labor policy). 1943.

Masumoto Uhei. *Kōjō yori mitaru Nihon no rōdō seikatsu* (Japanese working life viewed from the factory). Dobunkan, 1919.

————. *Kokka no shōrai to kōjō kanri no hyōjun* (The future of the nation and standards for factory management). Waseda daigaku shuppankai, 1923.

Matsuo Takayoshi. *Taishō demokurashii no kenkyū* (Studies on Taishō democracy). Aoki shoten, 1966.

Matsuzawa Hiroaki. *Nihon shakaishugi no shisō* (Socialist thought in Japan). Chikuma shobō, 1973.

Minami Iwao. *Nihon kinrō kanri ron* (On Japanese labor management). Yaegumo shoten, 1944.

Minami Manshū tetsudō, ed. *Naichi ni okeru kōjō chingin seido no chōsa kenkyū* (Research report on the wage system in the Home Islands). 1930.

Minoguchi Tokijirō. *Nihon kōgyō rōdō ryoku ron* (On the Japanese industrial labor force). Kōbundō shoten, 1943.

Mitsubishi Nagasaki zōsenjo shokkō ka, ed. *Nagasaki zōsenjo rōmu shi* (Labor management history of the Nagasaki Shipyard). 1930.

Mitsubishi Yokohama zōsenjo, ed. *Yokosen no omoide* (Memories of Yokosen). 2 vols. 1973.

Miura Tetsukichi. "Uraga dokku kōaikai jū nen shi" (A 10-year history of the Uraga Dock Kōaikai), *Shakai undō ōrai* (December 1932, January, February, May, August 1933).

Miyake Akimasa. "Kindai Nihon ni okeru tekkō kumiai no kōseiin" (The composition of the ironworkers' union in modern Japan). *Rekishigaku kenkyū* (March 1978).

————. "Daiichiji taisengo no jūkōgyō daikeiei rōdō undō" (The labor movement in large heavy industrial enterprises after World War I), *Nihon shi kenkyū* (January 1979).

————. "Nichiro sensō zengo no rōdōsha undō" (The workers' movement before and after the Russo-Japanese War), *Shakai keizai shigaku* 44.5 (March 1979).

Moji Ryō. *Waga jinsei* (My life). Yokohama, Kanagawa shimbunsha, 1980.

Montgomery, David. *Workers Control in America.* Cambridge, Cambridge University Press, 1979.

Moore, Joe. "The Fight Over Labor's Place in the Postwar Reconstruction of Japan: Industrial Unionism and Plans for Capitalist Revival During the First Yoshida Cabinet." Unpublished paper prepared for the Amherst College Conference on the Allied Occupation of Japan, 8/20-23/1980.

————. *Japanese Workers and the Struggle for Power.* Madison, University of Wisconsin Press, 1983.

Mori Kiichi. *Jūkōgyō no chingin to seikatsu* (Wages and livelihoods in heavy industry). Minzoku kagakusha, 1944.

———. *Nihon rōdōsha kaikyū jōtai shi* (A history of the condition of the Japanese working class). Sanichi shobō, 1961.

Muramatsu Mintarō. "Shokkō no gijutsu to kikai kōgyō no hattatsu" (The skills of laborers and the development of the machine industry), *Tōyō keizai shimpō* (3/15/1910, p. 21).

Murayama Kōzō, ed. *Seiji keizai dai nempyō* (Chronology of politics and economics). Tōyō keizai shimpōsha, 1971.

Naikaku tōkei kyoku. *Dai Nihon teikoku tōkei nenkan* (Statistical yearbook of imperial Japan). No. 39 (1921); No. 58 (1939).

———. *Rōdō tōkei jitchi chōsa hōkoku* (Report on the Labor Statistics Field Survey). 1924, 1927, 1930, 1933, 1936, 1938.

Naimushō eisei kyoku. *Tokyo shi, kyōbashi-ku, tsukishima ni okeru jitchi chōsa hōkoku* (Report on the field survey in Tsukishima, Kyōbashi ward, Tokyo). 1921. Reprinted as *Tsukishima chōsa* (Tsukishima report). Kōseikan, 1970.

Naimushō keiho kyoku. *Rōdō sōgi gaikyō* (Survey of labor disputes). 1917, 1919.

———. *Shakai undō jōkyō* (The state of the social movement). 1927–1942.

Naimushō keiho kyoku hoan ka. *Tokkō geppō* (Special higher police monthly bulletin). 1943–1945.

Naimushō shakai kyoku rōdō bu. *Rōdō undō nempō* (Labor movement yearly report). 1925–1937.

Naimushō shakai kyoku shakai bu. *Jukuren rōdōsha kankei shiryō: idō* (Documents concerning skilled workers: Turnover). 1930.

Nakamura Takafusa. *The Postwar Japanese Economy*. University of Tokyo Press, 1981.

Nakanishi Yō. "Nihon ni okeru jūkōgyō daikeiei no seisei katei" (The formative process of large-scale heavy industrial management in Japan), *Keizaigaku ronshū* 35.1–3 (1969).

———. "Daiichiji taisen zengo no rōshi kankei" (Labor relations before and after World War I), in Sumiya Mikio, ed., *Nihon rōshi kankei shi ron*. Tokyo daigaku shuppankai, 1977.

Nakaoka Tetsuo. "Imitation or Self Reliance: A lesson from the early history of modern Japanese iron manufacturing technology," *Japan Foundation Newsletter* 7.4 (October 1979, November 1979).

Nihon gakujutsu shinkōkai, ed. *Bukka mondai no ōkyūsaku* (Emergency inflation policy). 1939.

Nihon ginkō. *Rōdō tōkei* (Labor statistics). 1922–1925.

Nihon kōgakukai, ed. *Meiji kōgyō shi: kikai hen* (Meiji industrial history: Machine industry). 1930.

———. *Meiji kōgyō shi: zōsen hen* (Meiji industrial history: Shipbuilding). 1930.

Nihon zōsen kyōkai, ed. *Nihon kinsei zōsen shi* (The history of modern Japanese shipbuilding). 1911.

Nimura Kazuo. "Ashio bōdō no kiso katei" (The basic issues in the Ashio disturbance), *Hōgaku shirin* 52.1 (1959).

———. "Rōdō undō shi: senzen ki" (The history of the labor movement: Prewar era), in Ujihara Shōjiro, *Bunken kenkyū: Nihon no rōdō mondai* (Bibliographic studies: Japanese labor problems). Expanded edition, Sōgō rōdō kenkyūjo, 1971.

———. "Rōdōsha kaikyū no jōtai to rōdō undō" (The condition of the working class and the labor movement), *Iwanami kōza: Nihon rekishi, 18* (Iwanami symposium: Japanese history, 18). Iwanami shoten, 1975.

Nippon kōkan eigyō hōkokusho (Nippon Kōkan business reports). 1912–1944.

Nippon kōkan. "Jūyaku kai kiroku" (Executive board meeting records). Held at Kanagawa-ken archives.

Nippon kōkan Kawasaki seitetsujo rōdō kumiai. *Jū nen no ayumi* (Our 10-year journey). 1956.

Nippon kōkan Tsurumi rōdō kumiai ed. *Tsurutetsu rōdō undō shi* (History of the labor movement at Tsurumi Steel). 1970.

Nippon kōkan sōgyō 20 nen kaikoroku (Recollections of the 20 years since the founding of Nippon Kōkan). 1933.

Nippon kōkan kabushiki gaisha 30 nen shi (30-year history of Nippon Kōkan). 1942.

Nippon kōkan kabushiki gaisha 40 nen shi (40-year history of Nippon Kōkan). 1952.

Nippon kōkan kabushiki gaisha 50 nen shi (50-year history of Nippon Kōkan). 1962.

Nishinarita Yutaka. "Nichiro sensōgo ni okeru zaibatsu zōsen kigyō no keiei kikō to rōshi kankei: Mitsubishi zōsenjo no bunseki" (Labor relations and management structure in zaibatsu shipbuilding firms after the Russo-Japanese War: Analysis of the Mitsubishi Shipyard), *Ryūgoku daigaku keizai keiei ronshū* 18.1–4 (June 1978–March 1979).

———. "1920 nendai Nihon shihonshugi no rōshi kankei: jūkōgyō rōshi kankei o chūshin ni" (Labor relations in Japanese capitalism of the 1920s: Heavy industry), *Rekishigaku kenkyū,* No. 512 (January 1983).

Noda keizai kenkyūjo, ed. *Taishoku tsumitate kin hō no kaisetsu* (An explanation of the Retirement Fund Law). 1936.

"Nogi kō no genkyō" (The present status of the Nogi Society). 1922, 1924, pamphlets.

Nōshōmushō. *Kōjō chōsa yōryō* (A summary of the Factory Survey) No. 2. 1904.

Nōshōmushō shoko kyoku, ed. *Shokkō jijō* (The condition of the workers). 1903. Reprint, 3 vols. Shinkigensha, 1976.

———. *Kōjō tōkei hyō* (Tables of factory statistics). 1914, 1919.

———. *Kōjō kantoku nempō* (The Factory Inspection Yearly Report). 1917, 1919, 1920, 1921.

Obama Ritoku, ed. *Meiji bunka shiryō sōsho* (A library of documents on Meiji culture), Vol. I. Kazama shobō, 1961.

Odaka Kōnosuke. "Dainiji taisen zengo no kyū Mitsubishi jūkō rōdō tōkei ni tsuite" (On prewar labor statistics of the former Mitsubishi Heavy Industries), *Hitotsubashi ronsō* (December 1975).

Odaka Kunio. *Toward Industrial Democracy: Management and Workers in Modern Japan.* Cambridge, Harvard University Press, 1975.

Ōhara shakai mondai kenkyū jo. *Nihon rōdō nenkan* (Japan labor yearbook). 1920–1940.

———. *Taiheiyō sensō ka no rōdōsha jōtai* (The condition of workers during the Pacific War). Tōyō keizai shimpōsha, 1964.

———. *Taiheiyō sensō ka no rōdō undō* (The labor movement during the Pacific War). Rōdō jumposha, 1965.

Ōkōchi Kazuo. *Nihon no rōdō kumiai* (Japanese labor unions). Tōyō keizai shimpōsha, 1954.

———. "Sangyō hōkokukai no mae to ato to" (Before and after the Sanpo Association), in Chō Yukio and Sumiya Kazuhiko, eds., *Kindai Nihon keizai shisō shi* (A history of modern Japanese economic thought), Vol. II. Yūhikaku, 1971.

Ōkōchi Kazuo, Bernard Karsh, and Solomon Levine, eds. *Workers and Employers in Japan.* University of Tokyo Press and Princeton University Press, 1974.

Okuda Kenji. "Managerial Evolution in Japan," *Management Japan* 5.3,4 and 6.1 (1972).

Ōnishi Seiji and Takimoto Tadao. *Chingin seido* (The wage system). Tōyō shokan, 1944.

Ōtaguro Jūgorō. "Honpo no gishi to sono kyūsai hō" (How to improve the quality of technicians in our country), *Tōyō keizai shimpō,* (5/25/1903, p. 9).

Ōuchi Tsuneo. *Rōmu shidō no jissai* (The real story of labor management). 1941.

————. "Senjika no jukurenkō mondai" (The problem of skilled labor in wartime). Shakai kyōiku kyōkai pamphlet, 1938.

Ōya Saburō. *Uketori chingin seido ron* (On the contract-wage system). Dayamondo sha, 1944.

Pelzel, John C. "Social Stratification in Japanese Urban Economic Life." PhD dissertation, Harvard University, 1950.

————. "Factory Life in Japan and China Today," in Albert Craig, ed. *Japan: A Comparative View*. Princeton, Princeton University Press, 1979.

Rōdō sōgi hassei ni kan suru ken (Items concerning the oubreak of labor disputes). 1943–1945.

Rōdō sōgi hōkoku hyō (Table of reports on labor disputes). 1943–1945.

Rōdō sōgi mizen bōshi geppō (Monthly report on the prevention of labor disputes), 1943–1945.

Rōdō sōgi mizen bōshi shirabe (Reports on the prevention of labor disputes). 1943–1945.

Rōdō undō shiryō iinkai, ed. *Nihon rōdō undō shiryō* (Documents on the labor movement in Japan) Vols. I–III, VII–X. Tokyo daigaku shuppankai, 1959–1975.

Rōdōshō, ed. *Koyō dōkō chōsa hōkoku* (Survey report on employment trends). 1964–1978.

————. *Rōdō gyōsei shi* (A history of labor administration) Vol. I. Rōdō hōrei kyōkai, 1961.

————. *Rōdō hakusho* (Labor yearbook). 1953–1978.

————. *Rōdō idō chōsa kekka hōkoku* (Report on results of the Labor Mobility Survey). 1956–1967.

Rohlen, Thomas. *For Harmony and Strength: Japanese White-Collar Organization in Anthropological Perspective*. Berkeley, University of California Press, 1974.

Rosovsky, Henry. *Capital Formation in Japan, 1868–1940*. New York, Free Press of Glencoe, 1961.

Sakurabayashi Makoto. "Senji Nihon rōshi kyōgisei: sangyō hōkokukai no konwakai o chūshin to shite" (Labor-management consultation systems in wartime Japan: The Sanpō Discussion Councils), *Jōchi daigaku keizai ronshū* 9.2 (December 1972).

————. "Senji Nihon rōshi kyōgisei: sangyō hōkokukai no konwakai o chūshin to shite" (Labor-management consultation systems in wartime Japan: The Sanpō Discussion Councils). *Jōchi daigaku keizai ronshū* 18.3 (March 1972).

Satō Kōichi, *Sengo Nihon rōdō undō shi* (A history of the postwar Japanese labor movement). Shakai hyōronsha, 1976.

Shibaura seisakujo eigyō hōkoku sho (Shibaura Engineering Works business reports). 1904–1943.

Shimada Haruo. "Nenkō sei no shiteki keisei ni tsuite" (On the historical formation of the seniority system), *Mita gakkai zasshi* Vol. LXI (April 1968).

Shiota Shōhei, ed. *Nihon shakai undō jinmei jiten* (Biographical dictionary of the Japanese social movement). Aoki shoten, 1979.

Shirai Taishirō, ed. *Contemporary Industrial Relations in Japan.* Madison, University of Wisconsin Press, 1983.

Shōwa dōjinkai, ed. *Waga kuni chingin kōzō no shiteki kōsatsu* (Historical reflections on the Japanese wage structure). Tōseidō, 1960.

Shōwa kenkyūkai. *Chōki kensetsuki ni okeru waga kuni rōdō seisaku* (Japanese labor policy in the period of long-term construction). 1939.

———. *Rōdō shintaisei kenkyū* (Studies on the new labor order). 1941.

Smethurst, Richard. *A Social Basis for Prewar Japanese Militarism.* Berkeley, University of California Press, 1974.

Smith, Thomas C. *Agrarian Origins of Modern Japan.* Stanford, Stanford University Press, 1970.

Sōdōmei 50 nen shi iinkai, ed. *Sōdōmei 50 nen shi* (A 50-year history of Sōdōmei). Taiyō, 1964.

Sōri fu tōkei kyoku. *Nihon teikoku tōkei nenkan* (Statistical annual of imperial Japan). 1900–1945.

———. *Rōdō tōkei yōran* (Survey of labor statistics). 1927–1937.

Sumiya Mikio. *Nihon chin rōdō shi ron* (On the history of wage labor in Japan). Tokyo daigaku shuppan kai, 1955.

———, ed. *Nihon shokugyō kunren hattatsu shi* (The history of the development of industrial training) Vol. I. Nihon rōdō kyōkai, 1970.

———. *Nihon chin rōdō no shiteki kenkyū* (Historical study of Japanese wage labor). Ochanomizu shobō, 1976.

———. "Kōjōhō taisei to rōshi kankei" (The Factory Law system and labor relations), in Sumiya, ed. *Nihon rōshi kankei shi ron* (On the history of labor relations in Japan). Tokyo daigaku shuppan kai, 1977.

Suzuki Bunji. *Rōdō undō nijū nen* (20 years in the labor movement). Ichigensha, 1931.

Taira, Kōji. *Economic Development and the Labor Market in Japan.* New York, Columbia University Press, 1970.

Takeuchi Shizuko. *1930 nendai no kōzō* (The structure of the 1930s). Tabata shoten, 1975.

Tekkō rōren Nippon kōkan Kawasaki rōdō kumiai, ed. *Arasoi no ayumi: Nippon kōkan Kawasaki rōdō kumiai undō shi* (Our path of struggle: A history of the Nippon Kōkan Kawasaki Labor Union). Kawasaki, 1970.

Terashima Shirō. "Kaiko teate seido no igi" (The significance of the retirement-allowance system), *Shakai seisaku jihō* (January 1936).

Terashima Kōichi. "Totei kyōiku shisetsu ni kan suru ikensho" (An opinion on facilities for apprentice education), *Kyōiku jiron* 1/15/1892.

Thompson, E. P. *The Making of the English Working Class.* New York, Vintage Books, 1963.

Tokyo daigaku shakai kagaku kenkyūjo, ed. "Takayama Jiroichi shi to no mensetsu kiroku" (Record of an interview with Takayama Jiroichi). Unpublished manuscript, 1961.

———. *Tōshiba sōgi chōsa shiryō* (Documents on the Tōshiba dispute). 2 Vols. (VIII and X) of a larger series. 1977, 1978.

———. *Densan jūgatsu tōsō 1946: Sengo shoki rōdō sōgi shiryō* (The October 1946 struggle of the electric-power workers: Documents on early postwar labor disputes). 1979.

Tokyo daigaku shūkyō gaku kenkyū shitsu. *Rōdōsha no shisō ni kan suru chōsa* (A survey of worker attitudes). 1923.

Tokyo kōgyō gakkō. *Kōgyō kyōiku shisetsu shiryō* (Materials on industrial education facilities). 1896.

Tokyo kōtō shogakkō, ed. *Shokkō toriatsukaikata ni kan suru chōsa* (Survey of the treatment of labor). Report No. 3, 1912.

Tokyo shibaura denki kabushiki gaisha, ed. *Kobayashi Sakutarō den* (Biography of Kobayashi Sakutarō). 1939.

———. *Shibaura seisakujo 65 nen shi* (A 65-year history of the Shibaura Engineering Works). 1940.

———. *Tokyo shibaura 85 nen shi* (An 85-year history of Tokyo Shibaura). 1963.

Tokyo shi shakai kyoku. *Tokyo shinai no saimin ni kan suru chōsa* (A report on the poor in the city of Tokyo). 1921.

Tōshiba rōren jūnen shi henshū iinkai. *Kumiai undōshi: Tōshiba rōren soritsu jūnen kinen* (History of the union movement: Commemorating the 10th anniversary of the Toshiba Labor Federation). 1963.

Totten, George. "Collective Bargaining and Work Councils as Innovations in Industrial Relations in Japan During the 1920's," in R. P. Dore, ed. *Aspects of of Social Change in Modern Japan.* Princeton, Princeton University Press, 1967.

Tsuda, Masumi. *Nihon no toshi kasō shakai* (Urban lower-class society in Japan). Minerva shobō, 1972.

Uchida Tōshichi. *Jinsei gojū yo nen* (The story of my 50-odd years). Kawasaki, 1961.

———. "Tekkō rōdōsha to shite" (As a metalworker), *Rōdō undō shi kenkyū* No. 31 (May 1962).

Ueno Terumasa. "1920 nendai jūkōgyō rōdō undō no hatten: senzen Yokohama dokku rōdō kumiai kōshinkai no rekishi o chūshin ni" (The development of the heavy-industrial labor movement in the 1920s: The history of the Kōshinkai Union at the prewar Yokohama Dock Company), *Nihon shi kenkyū* No. 154 (June 1975).

———. "Daiichiji sekai taisengo no Nihon rōdō undō no tenkai: kaigun kōshō ni okeru rōdō undō to rōdō seisaku" (The evolution of the Japanese labor movement after World War I: The labor movement and labor policy at the Naval Arsenal), *Nihon shi kenkyū* No. 163 (March 1976).

Ujihara Shōjirō. *Nihon rōdō mondai kenkyū* (Studies on labor problems in Japan). Tokyo daigaku shuppankai, 1966.

———. "Sangyō hōkokukai undō no haikei" (The background of the Sanpō Movement), in Tokyo daigaku shakai kagaku kenkyū jo, ed. *Undō to teikō* (The movement and resistance) Vol. I. Tokyo daigaku shuppankai, 1979.

United States Strategic Bombing Survey. *Records of the United States Strategic Bombing Survey in Japan.* 1947.

Uraga dokku kabushiki gaisha eigyō hōkoku sho (Uraga Dock Company business reports). 1903–1944.

Uraga dokku gaisha, ed. *Uraga dokku 60 nen shi* (A 60-year history of the Uraga Dock Company). 1957.

Uraga kangyō ni kan suru shorui (Documents concerning the promotion of industry in Uraga). 1911. Held at Yokosuka-shi, Uraga gyōsei sentā.

Uraga shōgakkō shokuin konwakai, ed. *Uraga annai ki* (A guide to Uraga). 1915.

Ushiyama Saijirō. "Kōjō junshi ki" (Touring the factories: A record), *Jiji shimpō,* September–October 1897.

Watanabe Tōru. "Daiichiji taisen chokugo no rōdō dantai ni tsuite" (On labor organizations immediately after World War I), *Jimbun gakuhō* No. 26 March 1968).

Yamamoto Kiyoshi. *Nihon rōdō shijō no kōzō* (The structure of the Japanese labor market). Tokyo daigaku shuppankai, 1967.

Yasuda Hiroshi. "Zōsengyō rōdō undō ni okeru shokuchō no rekishiteki ichi: Uraga dokku no bunseki o chūshin ni" (The historical position of the foreman in the shipbuilding labor movement: Analysis of Uraga Dock), *Nihon shi kenkyū* (July 1977).

———. "1921-1922 nen no Yokohama dokku sōgi no undō kōzō: rōdōsha soshiki keisei no Nihonteki tokushitsu e no hito kōsatsu" (The structure of the movement in the Yokohama Dock dispute of 1921–1922: An observation on special Japanese characteristics in the formation of worker organizations), *Saitama daigaku kiyō* No. 28 (1979).

Yokohama dokku eigyō hōkokusho (Yokohama Dock Company business reports). 1914–1935.

"Yokohama dokku kabushiki gaisha shi" (The history of the Yokohama Dock Company). Unpublished manuscript. 1964. Mimeograph copy held by Mitsubishi jūkōgyō Yokohama zōsenjo.

Yokohama shi, ed. *Yokohama shi shi* (The history of the city of Yokohama) Vol. IV. 1968.

Yokoyama Gennosuke. *Nihon no kasō shakai* (Japanese lower-class society). 1898. Reprinted by Iwanami shoten, 1949.

———. *Naichi zakkyo go no Nihon* (Japan after the start of foreign residence in the interior). 1899.

———. "Hinkon jōtai no kenkyū" (Studies of the condition of poverty), *Chūō kōron* (June 1903).

———. "Tokyo no kōjōchi oyobi kōjō seikatsu no panorama" (A panorama of the Tokyo industrial area and factory life), *Shin kōron*, 9/1/1910. Reprinted in *NRUS*, Vol. III.

Yoshida Atsushi. "Honpo zōsengyō rōdō jijō" (Labor conditions in the Japanese shipbuilding industry), *Shakai seisaku jihō* (December 1926 and January 1927).

Yoshii Yukiko. "Sangyō hōkoku undō: sono seiritsu o megutte" (The Sanpo movement: Concerning its founding), *Hitotsubashi ronsō* 73.2 (February 1975).

Yoshino, Michael. *Japan's Managerial System*. Cambridge, MIT Press, 1968.

Yūaikai shibaura shibu. *Nazo no rōdō sōgi* (The Riddle labor dispute). 1920.

Zen Nihon zōsen rōdō kumiai Ishikawajima bunkai, ed. *Jūnen no ayumi* (Our 10-year path). 1956.

Zen Nihon zōsen rōdō kumiai Uraga Dokku bunkai, ed. *Jūnen no ayumi* (Our 10-year path). Uraga, 1957.

Zen Nihon zōsen rōdō kumiai Mitsubishi jūkōgyō Yokohama zōsen bunkai, ed. *Jūnen no ayumi* (Our 10-year path). Yokohama, 1956.

Zenzōsen jūgo nen shi henshūiinkai, ed. *Zenzōsen jūgo nen shi* (A 15-year history of Zenzōsen). 1965.

Index

Harvard East Asian Monographs

21. Kwang-Ching Liu, ed., *American Missionaries in China: Papers from Harvard Seminars*

22. George Moseley, *A Sino-Soviet Cultural Frontier: The Ili Kazakh Autonomous Chou*

23. Carl F. Nathan, *Plague Prevention and Politics in Manchuria, 1910–1931*

24. Adrian Arthur Bennett, *John Fryer: The Introduction of Western Science and Technology into Nineteenth-Century China*

25. Donald J. Friedman, *The Road from Isolation: The Campaign of the American Committee for Non-Participation in Japanese Aggression, 1938–1941*

26. Edward Le Fevour, *Western Enterprise in Late Ch'ing China: A Selective Survey of Jardine, Matheson and Company's Operations, 1842–1895*

27. Charles Neuhauser, *Third World Politics: China and the Afro-Asian People's Solidarity Organization, 1957–1967*

28. Kungtu C. Sun, assisted by Ralph W. Huenemann, *The Economic Development of Manchuria in the First Half of the Twentieth Century*

29. Shahid Javed Burki, *A Study of Chinese Communes, 1965*

30. John Carter Vincent, *The Extraterritorial System in China: Final Phase*

31. Madeleine Chi, *China Diplomacy, 1914–1918*

32. Clifton Jackson Phillips, *Protestant America and the Pagan World: The First Half Century of the American Board of Commissioners for Foreign Missions, 1810–1860*

33. James Pusey, *Wu Han: Attacking the Present through the Past*

34. Ying-wan Cheng, *Postal Communication in China and Its Modernization, 1860–1896*

35. Tuvia Blumenthal, *Saving in Postwar Japan*

36. Peter Frost, *The Bakumatsu Currency Crisis*

37. Stephen C. Lockwood, *Augustine Heard and Company, 1858–1862*

38. Robert R. Campbell, *James Duncan Campbell: A Memoir by His Son*

39. Jerome Alan Cohen, ed., *The Dynamics of China's Foreign Relations*

40. V. V. Vishnyakova-Akimova, *Two Years in Revolutionary China, 1925–1927*, tr. Steven I. Levine

41. Meron Medzini, *French Policy in Japan during the Closing Years of the Tokugawa Regime*

42. *The Cultural Revolution in the Provinces*

43. Sidney A. Forsythe, *An American Missionary Community in China, 1895–1905*

44. Benjamin I. Schwartz, ed., *Reflections on the May Fourth Movement: A Symposium*

45. Ching Young Choe, *The Rule of the Taewŏn'gun, 1864–1873: Restoration in Yi Korea*

STUDIES IN THE MODERNIZATION OF THE REPUBLIC OF KOREA: 1945-1975